MW01193335

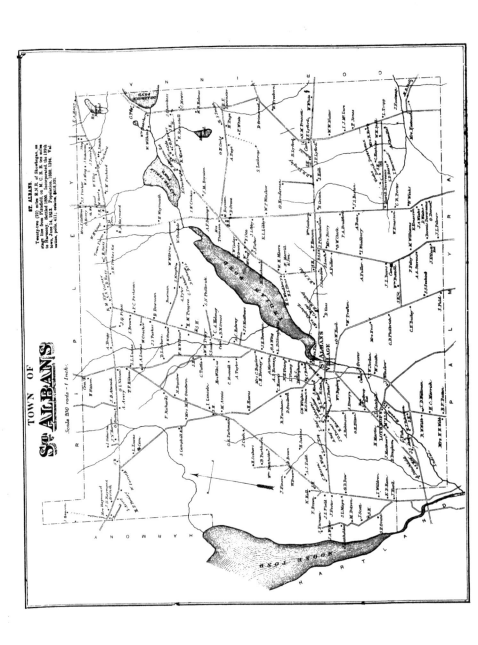

# TOWN OF
# ST. ALBANS

Scale 200 rods = 1 inch.

### ST. ALBANS

Twenty-two (22) miles N.N.E. of Skowhegan, on stage line from Pittsfield, on C. R. R., ten miles to Harmony. Settled 1800. Incorporated the 196th town, June 14, 1813. Population, 1890, 1294. Valuation, poll, 411; estate, $413,231.

# History *of* St. Albans Maine

*2003 Revised Edition*

Gladys M. Bigelow and
Ruth McGowan Knowles

HERITAGE BOOKS
2008

# HERITAGE BOOKS
*AN IMPRINT OF HERITAGE BOOKS, INC.*

## Books, CDs, and more—Worldwide

For our listing of thousands of titles see our website
at
www.HeritageBooks.com

Published 2008 by
HERITAGE BOOKS, INC.
Publishing Division
100 Railroad Ave. #104
Westminster, Maryland 21157

Copyright © 1982 Gladys M. Bigelow
and Ruth McGowan Knowles

Copyright © 1995, 2003 Ruth McGowan Knowles

Other books by the authors:

*History of St. Albans, Maine*

All rights reserved. No part of this book may be reproduced or
transmitted in any form or by any means, electronic or mechanical,
including photocopying, recording or by any information storage
and retrieval system without written permission from the author,
except for the inclusion of brief quotations in a review.

International Standard Book Numbers
Paperbound: 978-0-7884-2462-5
Clothbound: 978-0-7884-7560-3

# CONTENTS

# DEDICATION

Ruth Knowles dedicates the addendum to the people that I love the most; my family, including Joshua Dale Dunlap and Nathaniel Harrison Gordon Dunlap. Also in memory of my husband, Lowell "Kip" Elwin Knowles, who died December 23, 1985. In believing in me he added strength to my life.

# ACKNOWLEDGEMENTS

Our special thanks to the following who contributed significant materials.

Peter S. Mallet, Milton, Vt.
Frank A. Beard, Augusta, Me.
    Historic Preservation Commission
Mary K. Murphy, Portland, Me.
Maine Historical Society
Homer and Helen Ray
Helen Finson
Newton Smith
Carroll Patten
Charles Boyd
Norman Bailey
Glenna Bartlett
Vera Hanson
Meredith Fisher
Curtis and Marie Lombard
Glenice Avery Lord
Joyce Frost Sally
Irene Mower
Elwood Osborne
and to the many others in the community who have so graciously contributed information.
    Thanks to our typist Darlene Hall of St. Albans, Maine.
    Thanks to Jennifer Dunlap of Vassalboro, Maine, who typed the 1994 addendum.
    Thanks to Frank and Colleen Dunlap for their helpful suggestions.

DEDICATED TO MY GRANDCHILDREN

Ruth M. Knowles

Matthew Lowell Dunlap
Jennifer Margaret Dunlap
Children of Frank and Colleen Dunlap
Grandparents
Mr. and Mrs. Lowell Knowles
Mr. and Mrs. George Dunlap

DEDICATED TO ALL THE CHILDREN OF THE
TOWN OF ST. ALBANS, MAINE

Gladys M. Bigelow

# ACKNOWLEDGEMENTS

Our special thanks to the following who contributed significant materials.

Peter S. Mallet, Milton, Vt.

Frank A. Beard, Augusta, Me.
    Historic Preservation, Historic Commission

Mary K. Murphy, Portland, Me.

Maine Historical Society

Homer and Helen Ray

Helen Finson

Newton Smith

Carroll Patten

Charles Boyd

Norman Bailey

Glenna Bartlett

Vera Hanson

Meredith Fisher

Curtis and Marie Lombard

Glenice Avery Lord

Joyce Frost Sally

Irene Mower

Elwood Osborne

and to the many others in the community who have so graciously contributed information.

Thanks to our typist Darlene Hall of St. Albans, Maine.

Thanks to Frank and Colleen Dunlap for their helpful suggestions.

# REFERENCES

Pertinent information has been gleaned from the following sources:

East Somerset Register, 1911-1912, Chatto & Turner
Hartland and St. Albans Register, 1904, Mitchell, Remick & Bean
Hartland and St. Albans Register, 1913-1914, Mitchell, Remick & Bean
St. Albans Town Records
Town Reports
Maine State Archives, micro film census record.
The Old Families of Salisbury & Amesbury, Mass., David W. Hoyt
New England Historical & Genealogical Register
Genealogical & Family History of Maine, Little, Ed.
Savages Genealogical Dictionary
Soco Valley, Ridlon
Genealogical Dictionary of Maine & New Hampshire, Sybil Noyes, Charlene Thornton Libby, Walter Goodman Davis
History of Kennebec Co., Kingsbury & Deego
History of Greene, Me., Walter Mower
History of Maine, Williamson
Somerset Co. World War I, Florence Atwood
Skowhegan on the Kennebec, Coburn
The Essex Institute Historical Collections
      Vol. XXXVII — 1901 — Salem, Mass., Printed by the Essex Institute
Passenger Ship Lists
History of Wayne, Me., George Walton
The Libby Family in America, Libby
Thomas Philbrick & Family, 1583-1883, Rev. Jacob Chapman, Exeter, N.H.
Descendants of the Sons of Daniel and Hannah (House) Parkman, Horace A. Pratt
Old Families of St. Albans, Vertine Ellis
History of St. Albans, Pauline Lombard
Newspaper Clippings, Helen Moore Smith
Frost Genealogy, by Norman Seane Frost
Avery Genealogy, by Samuel Putnam Avery
Anthony Emery And His Descendents by Rev. Rufus Emery
Genealogical Notes of Barnstable Families
The Heyday of Their Strength, by M. E. Lonsdale

# ERRATA

Page 25: The following names were accidentally omitted: Hanson, Winston E. and Hughes, Harold F.

Page 263: The name "Webb, Christoper" should read "Webb, Christopher."

Page 279: The name "Yarney, Treasa" should read "Varney, Treasa."

Page 282: The name "Safford, Margaret" should read "Stafford, Margaret."

Page 313: The name "Footmand, Mary" should read "Footman, Mary."

Page 317: The name "Footman, Arrin" should read "Footman, Orrin."

Page 407: The name "O. S. Hoskell" should read "O. S. Haskell."

# CHAPTER I
## FORMATIVE YEARS

The year 1789 begins the United States as we know it. George Washington is elected President and John Adams Vice President. Alexander Hamilton is appointed Secretary of the Treasury. The nation is open for business. It is a small nation in terms of population-4,000,000 in the first census, 1790. There are only twelve states, Maine being a part of Massachusetts.

St. Albans, or Township No. 5, was first surveyed as a part of this section of Maine in 1794. It is in the first range north of the Plymouth Patent, granted by King James of England to the Plymouth Colony in 1606. (History of Maine, Williamson's)

In New England a township is known as a town where it exists in its primative form except as modified and partly subordinated by the last formed units, the County and State.

Tradition states Township No. 5 was first called Berlin, then Fairhaven, and finally St. Albans, but only the name Fairhaven has been documented. In the early census, records, and maps it is called Fairhaven.

The history of St. Albans is so interwoven with that of Hartland, Palmyra, and even Corinna in Penobscot County that they have to be considered as a unit.

Some time after the Revolutionary War, Dr. John Warren purchased the towns of Corinna and Palmyra and appointed Shepherd from Bloomfield, now Skowhegan, as his agent. Hartland was purchased of the Commonwealth of Mass. Feb. 26, 1796 by Dr. Warren. He is believed to have purchased St. Albans in 1799.

It was not unusual in those days for rich Massachusetts men to own several townships in Maine. Many of the debts of the Revolution were paid in that manner, and to deed over an entire township of Maine wilderness in order to cancel an obligation involving only a few hundred dollars was an incident of common occurrance.

Some feel that Dr. Warren never visited his purchase. Others say the doctor was not a frequent visitor, but when he came dressed in the fashion of the Boston aristocracy of the day, he created quite an impression. Dr. Warren's death date is given as April 4, 1815. It was his son Henry who settled on what is now the Perry Furbush estate in Palmyra. Henry never married, but it is thought he loved the young wife of a Mr. Vance. He practiced law in Penobscot and Somerset counties. His death took place in New York at the home of

1

the widow of Mr. Vance. Information on the Warren family is incomplete.

The name St. Albans had both a religious and political significance in English history. The religious significance - goes back as it does to Alban, a Roman soldier stationed in Britain, who was converted to Christianity in the fourth century and martyred for his faith. In his honor, King Offa of Mercia founded a Benedictine abbey in 793 at the site of the Roman town Verulamium, just outside present day London. Of this original structure, only a gateway remains today. The church was rebuilt in 1077 and is regarded as a fine example of Norman (Romanesque) architecture, second only to Winchester in size. Perhaps the most notable event associated with St. Albans' monastery is the printing of Tyndale's New Testament (1525), the first English translation to be printed.

Cathedral and Abbey Church of St. Alban, St. Albans, England, Herts, from the S.W. showing unique Norman tower made of bricks from Roman Verulamium.

Contributed by - George Dunlap
Annapolis, Md.

The political significance found in English history goes back to 1213. Here the assembly of St. Albans was convened by King John as a jury from all England to assess the damages of the clergy. This meeting was the germ of the future House of Commons. It furnished a precedent for producing the Charta of Henry the First, and was once welcomed as a base for needed reform. This finally resulted in the securing of the Magna Charta in 1217 to which, from age to age, patriots have looked back as a basis of English liberty.

We would like to think that the founding fathers of this small village here in Maine in 1813, when they adopted the name of the English town, knew that St. Albans, England was the birthplace of the rights of the common people.

St. Albans and what it stands for must have made quite an impression on people in years gone by. They sailed across the world, settled in distant parts, struggled to make a new home and called it St. Albans.

There are nine places called St. Albans in four countries apart from England. (Review & Express - June 23, 1977 Historian, Geoff Duvak, St. Albans, England.)

The act of the Incorporation of St. Albans was passed by the House of Representatives on June 14, 1813, signed by Timothy Bigelow, Speaker, and John Philip, President of the Senate, and appointed the same day by Caleb Strong, Governor of Massachusetts. St. Albans was incorporated the 199 town in Massachusetts.

The following is a copy of the Incorporation:

Laws of Mass. - Vol. C 1812-1815 p. 259

June 14, 1813 Chapter XXXII

An act to incorporate the township numbered five, in the 4th range of townships, north of the Waldo patent in the county of Somerset, as a town by the name of St. Albans.

SEC 1 - Be it enacted by the Senate and House of Representatives in the General Court asembled, and by the authority of the same, That the township numbered five, in the fourth range of townships north of Waldo patent, in the county of Somerset, as contained within the following described boundaries, be and the same is hereby incorporated as a town, by the name of St. Albans, viz. - North, by the township numbered five, in the fifth range; east, by the township numbered four, in the fourth range; south, by the township numbered five, in the third range; and west, partly by the town of Harmony, and partly by the township numbered three, in the first range of townships east of the Kennebec River. And the said town of St. Albans is hereby vested with all the corporate powers and privileges, and shall be also subject to the duties and requisitions of other corporate towns; according to the Constitution and laws of this Commonwealth.

SEC B

Be it further enacted, that any Justice of the Peace for the county of Somerset, upon application therefore, is hereby authorized to issue a warrant, directed to a freeholder and inhabitant of the said town of St. Albans, requiring him to notify and warn the first meeting of the qualified freeholders and voters thereof, to meet at such convenient time and place as shall be appointed in the said warrant, for the choice of such officers as towns are by law required to choose at their annual town meetings.

Approved by the Governor, June 14, 1813

3

The warrant for the first town meeting was issued by Benjamin French, Justice of the Peace, to Joseph Dearborn, a freeholder and inhabitant of the town of St. Albans. The meeting was held at the dwelling house of Mr. Abraham Moor on Monday August 9 at one o'clock in the afternoon.

The following is a copy of the first warrant of the town of St. Albans:

## Warrant

July 3, A.D. 1813

To Joseph Dearborn, a free holder and inhabitant of this town of St. Albans,

GREETINGS:

You are hereby required in the name of the Commonwealth of Mass. to summon and notify the free holders and other inhabitants of said town, qualified by law to vote in town meetings, to assemble at the dwelling house of Mr. Abraham Moor on Monday the 9th day of August next, at one o'clock in the afternoon of said day, to act on the following articles:

1. To choose a moderator to regulate said meeting.
2. To choose a town clerk for the ensuing part of the year.
3. To choose all other officers towns are by law required to choose at their annual town meetings at the time and place of this meeting; you are to make return of this warrant to me, with your doings there on.

Given under my hand and seal this 19th day of July, A.D. 1813

Benjamin French
Justice of the Peace

Pursuant to the within warrant, I have summoned and notified the inhabitants of said town qualified as therein expressed to assemble at the time and place, and for the purposes within mentioned.

Joseph Dearborn

A vote for the separation of Maine from Massachusetts, and the establishment of statehood was passed unanimously on May 20, 1816, but it was not until March 3, 1820 did Congress admit Maine into the Union as the 23rd state.

The town of St. Albans voted on the question of separating from Massachusetts, twenty for the measure and three against it.

On the vote the first Governor, William King received 38 votes.

Many of our first settlers followed Indian trails coming from southern portions of New Hampshire. Many of these were originally from Massachusetts, and removed to Maine after a residence of a few years in New Hampshire. As we record the trails and trials of our forebears, we find many exciting tales of successes, failures, loves, and sorrows.

The first settler was Judah Hackett and family of Epping, N.H.

4

who came here to settle in 1800 and built a log house on what has been called Hackett's Hill, about two miles northwest of St. Albans village. His daughter, Susanne Hackett, married Isachar Cook from Wakefield, N.H.

She spun her yarn at home, carried it on horseback through the woods, wading across Mainstream to Cornville, to find a loom to weave it, then back through the wilderness.

To add to the settlement on Hackett's Hill came Joseph Watson in 1804 with his family. Here another log cabin was built and goodly sons and daughters grew up by his side.

In 1810 according to the census records, there were 22 families living in Fairhaven so called. Total population - 116. Heads of families were: William Moor, Isachar Cook, Sam Grant, John Lyford, Asa Russell, Abraham Moor, Isaac Rowell, Samuel Moor, James Martin, Abel Hackett, Judah Hackett, John Smart, Paul Felker, Asa Wiggin, Joseph Watson, Willowby Cook, Luke Grover, Joseph Dearborn, James Palmer, Benjamin French, David Rowe, and John Johnson. These constituted the pioneers of the town.

Other early settlers were Thomas Skinner, Thomas Smith, Benjamin Richards, and Jonathan Hilton.

Below is a list of the voters in the Town of St. Albans in 1816: John Butterfield, Willowby Cook, Noah Cook, Amaziah Cook, Jonathan Church, William Cook, George Church, Joseph Dearborn, Samuel Dearborn, Benjamin French, Paul Felker, Luke Grover, Ephraim Goodwin, Abel E. Haskell, Judah Hackett, John Johnson, John Lyford, Levi Lyford, Joseph Magoon, Abraham Moor, Samuel Moor, William Moor, Daniel Moor, Joseph Moor, Bartlett Nye, Joseph Prescott, Abraham Prescott, David Rowe, Benjamin Richards, John Stinchfield, Benjamin Stinchfield, Judah Stinchfield, John Smart, Thomas Tenney, Asa Wiggin, Joseph Watson, Jonathan Watson, Christopher Webb, Jonathan Hilton, Daniel Lucas.

St. Albans Mountain and the surrounding area was settled first. The village of St. Albans as we know it is of much later growth, having been built up by water power and lumber for its mills.

It has been recorded that Jeremiah Skinner felled the first tree where St. Albans village is now located.

St. Albans Oldest Framed House (1829)
Photo by Richard Jones

The first house in the village was erected by Stephen Hartwell in 1823. It was a log house built of cedar logs hewn on two sides and put together after the fashion of a boys' cobhouse. In 1829 he erected the first framed house in the village. This is presently the home of Jennie Springer.

An act to set off a part of the town of Hartland and annex the same to the town of St. Albans is as follows: (Chapter LXXI)

> Be it enacted by the Senate and House of Representatives in Legislature assembled, that all that part of the town of Hartland lying east of Moose Pond, and the centre of the stream issuing therefrom, and a line running a due north course from the head of said stream, through said pond to the south line of the town of Harmony, together with the inhabitants thereon, be, and hereby is set off from the said town of Hartland, and annexed to the Town of St. Albans; and said inhabitants shall enjoy the same rights as other inhabitants of the said town of St. Albans: Provided however, the inhabitants thus set off, shall be held to pay their assessments of all taxes and expenses, assessed upon them and remaining unpaid prior to the passing of this act. (This act passed March 15, 1821.)

Up until 1846, a large part of Hartland village was St. Albans. The west boundry line ran in a northerly direction from the so-called horseback, through the middle of the house which is the property where Michael Wiers Esq. law office is today across the river and ran between the property line of Ray Spaulding on North Street to touch the corner of the former Withee farm and contining north until it struck the present St. Albans line near the junction of the Pond and Mountain roads.

Years ago the Bullens ate in two different towns while sitting at the same table. The present west line of St. Albans lies a short distance east of Hartland Junior High just east of Wayne Libby's homestead.

In Chapter 384 an act to set off a part of the town of St. Albans and annex the same to the town of Hartland.

Be it enacted by the Senate and House of Representatives in Legislature assembled, as follows:

SEC 1. From and after the passage of this act all that part of the town of St. Albans, in the county of Somerset, which lies west of Lot numbered sixteen, in the first range of lots in said town of St. Albans, be, and is hereby set off from said town of St. Albans and annexed to the town of Hartland in said county.

SEC 2. The treasurer of the State is hereby authorized and directed to deduct 26 polls and the sum of $15,500 from the valuation of St. Albans and annex the same to the valuation of Hartland.

SEC 3. The inhabitants on the territory aforesaid shall pay all taxes legally assessed on their polls or estates that remain due and unpaid, to the collector of St. Albans; and Elizabeth E. Shean, together with all paupers having their legal settlement on the territory aforesaid shall hereafter be supported by the Town of Hartland.

SEC 4. The inhabitants of the territory aforesaid shall have their proportion of the school money belonging to the town of St. Albans, to be divided according to the number of scholars.

(Approved August 7, 1846)

Big Indian Lake is the approximate center of the town with its length northeast and southwest; in the same line, Big Indian is between three and four miles long and a mile wide at the widest point.

Northeastward is Little Indian connected by a narrow strait of water, which is crossed by a bridge about a mile from Five Corners on the Ripley road. The lake is on the righthand side and about one mile long. It receives water from Ripley stream and from Dearborn Pond in the eastern part of the town.

The origin of the name is not actually known except that many years ago, the Indians had an encampment between Big - Little Indian Ponds. There used to be many oak trees in this section, which were said to have been planted by the Indians for the acorns which they used. Another encampment was located on the Little Indian Lake across from Blaine Mower's homestead.

This section of the state is rich in associations which recall the tribes which once hunted through our forests and traveled in birch canoes up and down the lakes and streams.

The Indians of the whole state of Maine were divided at the time of the first explorations into two main tribes, the Abnakis, and the Etchemins, the former of which held the lands between the Piscataqua and Penobscot Rivers and is estimated at the time of the first coming of the English to have numbered about 20,000.

Probably in this area lived the powerful nation of the Etchemins, which occupied the whole eastern part of the state from the Penobscot to the St. Croix. The most important tribe of this nation in relation to the territory in Eastern Somerset County, was the Sarratines which held all the lands about the Penobscot River. It is the remnant of this tribe which make their home on Indian Island. By 1800, practically nothing was left of this once powerful tribe.

Whatever deeds of war or love might have been witnessed here in the long ago have now faded. yet the arrowheads brought up by the plowshare and the knowledge of their encampment between our lakes remind us that Indian lore is prehistoric.

Today one hundred eighty six camps are located on Big & Little Indian. This also includes camps on Birch Island - Photo taken in the 1920's.

### Big Indian Lake

An artist came in the evening and
   Worked through the chilly night
Painting a wonderful picture to
   be seen in the autumn light.
The view that he worked on special
   was the shore of Big Indian Lake
A beautiful sheet of water
   None prettier found in the state.

The maples be painted in colors
   of scarlet, crimson, and gold,

8

The beeches and willows in yellow,
in shades that cannot be told.
The sumac berries are crimson
but the leaves he painted red,
And the oak trees of many seasons
In new bronze dresses dressed.

And with the green of the pine trees
Also the hemlock and spruce,
And the light green of the cedars
Noted by elders and youths
Were left to tone down the colors
untouched by the artist's wand;
And admired in summer and winter
More than ever before.

By Vertine Ellis

## STREETS OF ST. ALBANS

Streets of St. Albans were named as follows: Main Street, running north and south by the former post office; Friends Street, leading up by the Friends Church, now the Chatterbox Club; Bridge Street, going east from Main Street across the bridge; Water Street, leading from Bridge Street to Mill Street on which is located the St. Albans Town Hall and Grange Hall; Mill Street, leading east from the southern part of Main Street toward Mill Hill; High Street, connecting Mill Street with Bridge Street past the residence of Sherburn Lary and the Mountain Road from Main Street left to the mountain.

St. Albans Village in 1895. The A. P. Bigelow store on left, burned in 1899.

Buker House 1907 (Melvin Bigelow's home)

St. Albans, Maine (1909)

10

## The Borough
### (A Deserted Village in St. Albans)

Some years previous to 1872, eight or ten families were living in the Borough, now a deserted village in St. Albans where probably a few cellars may remain. The road leading to the Borough from the west side of Lyfords Corner Road was just a little way east of the home of Chester Cooley. It was about 1½ miles to the Borough and about one half mile from there to the Dixie Road.

Early families living in this section included Shaker Nickerson, Joseph Booker, and Benjamin Hutchins.

But as time went on, all of the families left the Borough. The last family to reside there previous to 1890 was Charles Clark and his three sons, Walter, Clarence, and Verno.

## Dixie Road

The fifth road between the Palmyra and Dexter Road was given the name Dixie Road, owing to people living near the Corinna line in Civil War days expressing sympathy for the South.

This road was used by early settlers in going to Corinna and Bangor. The old road can be seen near the home of Bernard Weymouth.

## Five Corners Road

Five Corners Road was given the name by five roads meeting in East St. Albans. The north road to Ripley, the south road to Palmyra, Corinna east to Dexter, leading over Ramsdell Hill. Ramsdell Hill was first called Mt. Nebo.

## Shakerag

Years ago the settlement known as Shakerag was a busy place. It was located between St. Albans village and Hartland. The name "Shakerag" was given this area as the poorer families used rags in their windows to keep out the cold. The rags were often seen blowing in the wind.

## Cross Roads Place

(Road between Nye's Corner and Nelson's Corner - discontinued; once the home of Skinners and Braggs)

> Gone are the people of the Cross Roads Place
> And the buildings are things of the past
> But the bubbling brook still wanders on
> And will through ages last.

But the work on homes done years ago
Through ages is not now seen
And the only time we see what we've lost
Is only in our dreams.
Some are buried under Sleepers mounds
But the graves are hard to find.
Bushes cover our neighbor's graves
But the silence seems sublime.
Now they are resting beneath the shade
And we hope that they do not know
Of the many changes that have taken place
Since the years of long ago.

                                        Vertine Ellis

*Sleeper cemetery is located on St. Albans Mt.

## Webb Ridge

Early settlers on Webb Ridge were the Hansons, Converse, Chandlers and Ruel Webb.

## Devil's Head

DEVILS HEAD - (A picnic area for many years). Milton Hill, Dorian Hill. (1962)

12

# CHAPTER II
## TOWN OFFICIALS

| YEAR | SELECTMEN OF ST. ALBANS |
|------|-------------------------|
| 1813 | Ephraim Goodwin, Wm. Moor, Abraham Moor |
| 1814 | Jonathan Hilton, John Johnson, Jos. Dearborn |
| 1815 | Jonathan Hilton, Ephraim Goodwin, Bartlett Nye |
| 1816 | Sam'l Dearborn, Benj. French, John Stinchfield |
| 1817 | Wm. Moor, Sam'l Moor, Benj Stinchfield |
| 1818 | Sam'l Moor, John Lyford, Jos. Dearborn |
| 1819 | Sam'l Moor, John Lyford, Sam'l Dearborn |
| 1820-21 | Thos. Smith, Jonathan Hilton, David Maloon |
| 1822 | Thos. Smith, Jonathan Hilton, David Brown |
| 1823 | Thos. Smith, Wentworth Libby, Lewis Rowe |
| 1824 | John Lyford, Sam'l Moor, Thos. Skinner |
| 1825-26 | Thos. Skinner, Thos. Smith, Sam'l Sanborn |
| 1827 | Thos. Skinner, Joseph Jewett, James Footman |
| 1828-30 | Thos. Skinner, Thos. Smith, Jonathan Hilton |
| 1831 | Thos. Smith, David Given, Jonathan Hilton |
| 1832 | Thos. Skinner, Peleg Haskell, Sam'l Hartwell |
| 1833 | Thos. Smith, Jonathan Hilton, Randall Steward |
| 1834 | Thos. Skinner, Thos. Smith, Jonathan Hilton |
| 1835 | Thos. Smith, Jonathan Hilton, Merrill Prescott |
| 1836 | Merrill Prescott, Thos. B. Tenney, Harris Garcelon |
| 1837 | Sam'l Sanborn, Peleg Haskell, S. Lothrop |
| 1838 | S. Lothrop, Peleg Haskell, Merrill Prescott |
| 1839 | Thos. Smith, Sullivan Lothrop, Thos. Skinner |
| 1840-41 | Thos. Smith, Thos. Skinner, Eleazer Crocker |
| 1842-43 | S. Lothrop, Eleazer Crocker, Randall Steward |
| 1844 | Eleazer Crocker, Thos. Smith, Thos. Tenney |
| 1845 | S. Lothrop, Joshua Parker, Thos. B. Tenney |
| 1846 | S. Lothrop, Thos. B. Tenney, Eleazer Crocker |
| 1847 | S. Lothrop, Eleazer Crocker, Thos. Tenney |
| 1848-49 | Thos. Skinner, Jessie S. Boston, Randall Steward |
| 1850 | Thos. Skinner, Eleazer Crocker, Stephen L. Hilton |
| 1851 | S. Lothrop, Jas. L. Merrill, Stephen L. Hilton |
| 1852-53 | S. Lothrop, Jas. L. Merrill, Thos. Skinner |
| 1854 | S. Lothrop, S. C. Glidden, John Robinson |
| 1855 | Jas. L. Merrill, John Robinson, Randall Steward |
| 1856 | Sullivan Lothrop, Albert Smith, Chas. Moor |
| 1857 | Sullivan Lothrop, Albert Smith, Herman Gage |
| 1858 | S. Lothrop, Levi Lucus, Ebenezer Merrill |

| | |
|---|---|
| 1859-60 | Levi Lucus, Ebenezer Merrill, W. G. Foss |
| 1861 | S. Lothrop, N. C. McGray, Ebenezer Merrill |
| 1862 | E. Merrill, W. G. Foss, N. B. Turner |
| 1863 | S. Lothrop, Thos. Tenney, Daniel Bowman |
| 1864-65 | S. Lothrop, F. R. Webber, Henry Fairbrother |
| 1866-67 | S. Lothrop, F. R. Webber, John Lyford |
| 1868-69 | S. Lothrop, F. R. Webber, John L. Field |
| 1870 | S. Lothrop, John L. Field, James Cyphers |
| 1871 | S. Lothrop, Levi Lucus, Geo. Jones |
| 1872 | S. Lothrop, Jas. Cyphers, J. F. Hilton |
| 1873 | S. Lothrop, J. F. Lyford, J. F. Hilton |
| 1874 | S. Lothrop, Wm. Winslow, J. M. Skinner |
| 1875 | S. Lothrop, J. M. Skinner, J. F. Hilton |
| 1876 | J. M. Skinner, Wm. Winslow, J. F. Hilton |
| 1877 | J. M. Skinner, Wm. Winslow, L. D. Cole |
| 1878-79 | S. Lothrop, Lewis Fish, A. J. Bonney |
| 1880-81 | J. M. Skinner, A. J. Bonney, J. C. Moor |
| 1882-83 | J. M. Skinner, N. H. Vining, S. L. Mayr |
| 1885 | M. L. Merrill, Ruel W. Webb, Solomon Crocker |
| 1886 | M. L. Merrill, Isaac Winslow, S. S. Parker |
| 1887 | M. L. Merrill, J. C. Winslow, J. F. Hilton |
| 1888 | M. L. Merrill, I. O. Winslow, S. S. Parker |
| 1889 | M. L. Merrill, D. N. Grant, Melvin Bigelow |
| 1890-1-2 | I. O. Winslow, Fred Lucus, N. B. Turner |
| 1893 | H. A. Hurd, J. L. Field |
| 1894 | H. A. Hurd, N. H. Vining, J. B. Atwood |
| 1895 | M. L. Merrill, J. F. Boynton, P. F. Emery |
| 1896 | M. L. Merrill, J. F. Boynton, W. O. Hilton |
| 1897 | N. H. Vining, W. O. Hilton, D. N. Grant |
| 1898 | W. O. Hilton, D. N. Grant |
| 1899 | W. P. Winslow, P. W. Libby, D. N. Grant |
| 1900-1-2 | P. W. Libby, W. O. Hilton, P. F. Emery |
| 1903 | S. B. Prescott, Fred Lucus |
| 1904 | S. B. Prescott, W. O. Hilton, A. F. Hurd |
| 1905 | S. B. Prescott, P. W. Libby, M. H. Martin |
| 1906 | S. B. Prescott, M. H. Martin, Fred Lucus |
| 1907 | Fred Lucus, W. O. Hilton, F. N. Vining |
| 1908-09 | W. O. Hilton, F. N. Vining, C. W. Worthen |
| 1910 | J. F. Libby, C. H. Ross, S. W. Seekins |
| 1911-12 | W. O. Hilton, Fred Lucus, D. L.Frost |
| 1913 | Fred Lucus, D. L. Frost, L. B. Johnson |
| 1914 | P. W. Libby, L. B. Johnson, C. M. Lancaster |
| 1915 | Fred Lucus, W. O. Hilton, Hugh F. Goodwin |
| 1916 | W. O. Hilton, Edgar Crocker |

| | |
|---|---|
| 1917 | W. O. Hilton, E. J. Crocker, Freeman Mills |
| 1918-19-20 | Freeman Mills, Albert Ward, D. S. Emerson |
| 1921 | Freeman Mills, Albert Ward, A. P. Bigelow |
| 1922 | Freeman Mills, A. P. Bigelow, R. W. Hanson |
| 1923 | Freeman Mills, A. P. Bigelow, M. H. Martin |
| 1924 | Freeman Mills, W. O. Hilton, M. H. Martin |
| 1925 | Freeman Mills, W. O. Hilton, F. W. Seekins |
| 1926 | W. O. Hilton, P. E. Cole |
| 1927-28 | A. P. Bigelow, P. E. Cole, E. M. Thorne |
| 1929 | G. A. Libby, E. N. Grant, E. M. Thorne |
| 1930-31-32 | A. P. Bigelow, P. E. Cole, F. J. Hersey |
| 1933 | P. E. Cole, M. H. Martin, A. C. Smith |
| 1934 | M. H. Martin, Chester Carson |
| 1935-36-37 | Chester Carson, V. S. Patterson, H. E. Wing |
| 1938 | Thomas Mills, Robert E. Martin, Elmer Chambers |
| 1939 | Thomas Mills, Chester Carson, Elmer Chambers |
| 1940 | Thomas Mills, Chester Carson, Melvin H. Martin |
| 1941 | Thomas Mills, Chester Carson, Harold E. Wing |
| 1942 | Thomas Mills, Chester Carson, V. S. Patterson |
| 1943 | Chester Carson, Harold E. Wing, V. S. Patterson |
| 1944 | Chester Carson, M. H. Martin, V. S. Patterson |
| 1945 | G. R. Smith, R. E. Martin, Gerald Clark |
| 1946 | B. F. Nelson, R. E. Martin, G. W. Webber |
| 1947 | Chester Carson, Kenneth Hughes, John Webber |
| 1948 | George Crocker, Burnes Nelson |
| 1949 | Thomas Mills, Kenneth Hughes, Harold Wing |
| 1950 | Burnes Nelson, Kenneth Hughes, George Webber |
| 1951 | Burnes Nelson, Guy R. Smith, George Webber |
| 1952 | Burnes Nelson, George Webber, Wendall Bubar |
| 1953 | Wendall Bubar, Harold E. Wing, Kenneth E. Chambers |
| 1954 | Elmer Fisher, George Crocker, Victor Springer |
| 1955 | Elmer Fisher, P. W. Webber, Joseph F. Seekins |
| 1956 | Allen Thorne, Kenneth Chambers, Hugh P. Cooney |
| 1957 | R. E. Martin, Charles Boyd, R. D. McLean |
| 1958 | Charles Boyd, R. D. McLean, Byron Wiers |
| 1959 | R. D. McLean, Byron Wiers, Everett Graham |
| 1960 | Byron Wiers, Charles Boyd, Thomas Mills |
| 1961 | Thomas Mills, Charles Boyd, Byron Wiers |
| 1962 | Thomas Mills, Charles Boyd, Ivan Crocker |
| 1963 | Ivan Crocker, Charles Boyd, Brian Hanson |
| 1964 | Ivan Crocker, Thomas Mills, Charles Boyd |
| 1965 | Ivan Crocker, Charles Boyd, Dana Leavitt |
| 1966 | Charles Boyd, Dana Leavitt, Irving Wentworth |

| Year | Officials |
|---|---|
| 1967-68 | Charles Boyd, Irving Wentworth, Bruce Ballard |
| 1969 | E. Clair Russell, Irving Wentworth, John Gee |
| 1970 | Irving Wentworth, John Gee, Bruce Ballard |
| 1971 | Irving Wentworth, Dana Leavitt, Larry Wintle |
| 1972 | Dana Leavitt, Larry Wintle, Lowell Knowles |
| 1973 | Dana Leavitt, Lowell Knowles, Bernard Charrier |
| 1974-75 | Bernard Charrier, Garnett Bubar, John Michaud |
| 1976 | Walter Butler, John Webber, John Michaud |
| 1977-78-79 | John Webber, John Michaud, Oren Neal |
| 1980 | Edward Walker, John Michaud, Brian Hanson |

## TOWN CLERKS AND TREASURERS

| Years | Clerk | Treasurer |
|---|---|---|
| 1813-1814 | Benjamin French | John Lyford |
| 1814-1815 | Benjamin French | Samuel Moor |
| 1815-1817 | Benjamin French | John Atwood |
| 1817-1818 | William Moor | |
| 1818-1819 | Benjamin French | |
| 1819-1820 | Samuel Moor | |
| 1820-1822 | Benjamin French | |
| 1822-1824 | Thomas Smith | |
| 1824-1831 | Thomas Skinner | |
| 1832-1833 | Nathan Douglas | Thomas Smith |
| 1834 | Nathan Douglas | Sullivan Lothrop |
| 1835 | Nathan Douglas | Harris Garcelon |
| 1836 | Nathan Douglas | Sullivan Lothrop |
| 1837-1838 | Nathan Douglas | Harris Garcelon |
| 1839-1840 | Nathan Douglas | Thomas Skinner |
| 1841 | Nathan Douglas | Sullivan Lothrop |
| 1842-1843 | Thomas Skinner | Sullivan Lothrop |
| 1844-1847 | Thomas Skinner | Thomas Skinner |
| 1848-1849 | Thomas Skinner | Moses Foss |
| 1850-1854 | Albert Smith | Moses Foss |
| 1855 | Albert Smith | Benjamin Steward |
| 1856-1857 | William Foss | Albert Smith |
| 1858-1860 | William Foss | Israel Vining |
| 1861 | William Foss | F. R. Webber |
| 1862 | William Foss | William Foss |
| 1863-1865 | F. R. Webber | Henry Fairbrother |
| 1866 | F. R. Webber | Nathaniel Vining |
| 1867-1868 | F. R. Webber | Sullivan Lothrop |
| 1869 | S. Lothrop | S. Lothrop |
| 1870 | G. A. Lovejoy | S. Lothrop |

| 1871-1873 | G. A. Lovejoy | John Skinner |
|---|---|---|
| 1874 | G. A. Lovejoy | M. C. Foss |
| 1875 | S. A. Maxim | C. H. Skinner |
| 1876 | S. A. Maxim | T. B. Seekins |
| 1877 | R. L. Parker | N. B. Turner |
| 1878-1880 | S. A. Maxim | N. H. Vining |
| 1881 | F. A. Morse | N. H. Vining |
| 1882-1883 | S. B. Prescott | A. J. Bonney |
| 1884-1886 | C. R. Gray | |
| 1886-1887 | Millard Metcalf | |
| 1887-1891 | S. A. Maxim | |
| 1891-1893 | C. A. Southard | |
| 1893-1896 | E. P. Dyer | |
| 1896-1911 | D. L. Frost | |
| 1911-1912 | H. E. Cyphers | H. E. Cyphers |
| 1912-1913 | H. E. Cyphers | H. E. Cyphers |
| 1913-1914 | C. C. Hanson | C. C. Hanson |
| 1914-1915 | George Libby | George Libby |
| 1915-1919 | George Libby | George Libby |
| 1919-1920 | Henry C. Prescott | George Libby |
| 1920-1929 | George Libby | George Libby |
| 1929-1930 | George Libby | G. H. Hanson |
| 1930-1935 | George Libby | G. H. Hanson |
| 1935-1937 | George Libby | Ruth Mills |
| 1937-1938 | Ethel Libby | Ruth Mills |
| 1935-1947 | Ethel Libby | |
| 1948-1952 | Mary Pease | |
| 1953-1973 | Barbara Patten | |
| 1974-1975 | Patricia Chambers | |
| 1975-1976 | Joan Trembley | |
| 1976-1982 | Angilee Seekins, Certified Town Clerk | |

## STATE AND LOCAL GOVERNMENT

D. D. Stewart 1851-1865 — Legislature — Senator

Eleazor Crocker — Legislature — Senator

Luther Webb 1869-1870 — Senator

Stuart H. Goodwin 1883-1884 — Senator — Legislature — Probate Court

William Seekins — Clerk of Courts

Milton Merrill 1891-1908 — County Commissioner — Senator

Kenneth A. Hughes 1957-1961 — Legislature; 1963-1969 — County Commissioner

17

## ST. ALBANS TOWN OFFICIALS
## FOR 1981

TOWN MANAGER - Larry Post

SELECTMEN - 1st, Edward Walker, 2nd, John Michaud, 3rd, Oren Neal

TOWN CLERK - Angilee Seekins

ROAD COMMISSIONER - Lewis McLeod

PLANNING BOARD - Hobart Kemp, Richard LaChance, Kenneth Hughes, Michael Wiers, Lowell Knowles, Frank Sargent.

BUDGET COMMITTEE - Bruce Ballard, Lowell Knowles, Helen Snowman, Philip Bowman, Fred Cooper, Bernard Charrier, Frank Sargent, Michael Wiers and Byron Wiers.

SCHOOL COMMITTEE - Peter Duncombe, Ruth Knowles.

# CHAPTER III
## ST. ALBANS IN THE WARS

### MILITARY HISTORY

The military history of the town of St. Albans should be a source of just pride. As time rolls on, we are likely to forget the value of the service rendered by the soldiers in war.

It has been one of our more difficult tasks obtaining lists of St. Albans service men. We have done our best but don't submit it as a complete list.

### St. Albans, Maine

St. Albans, you are just a little town
In this dear old State of ours.
We cannot boast of greatness
Not of palaces and towers.

We love you for your noble past
In times of war and peace.
Your loyalty in all great works
And your help will never cease.

We love you at present
For your citizens and homes,
Your hills and valleys, ponds and brooks,
Beneath bright heaven's dome.

We shall love you in the future
Because if we chance to roam
You will always be our St. Albans
The place that we call home.

Composed during World War I
Irene Libby (Mayo)
1918

### REVOLUTIONARY WAR (1775-1783)

St. Albans has listed Benjamin Collins as their only Revolutionary soldier. The Kennebec Journal, May 3, 1844 also lists the following:

Hartwell, Edward - d. about age 97

Revolutionary Soldier
St. Albans

Hartwell, Mrs. Lydia - d. age 82

St. Albans, Kennebec Journal May 3, 1837

## WAR OF 1812 (1812-1814)

Nicholas Brown
Mark Buzzell
Jonathan Carr
Samuel Emery, II

Many of the citizens of St. Albans served in the "Second Maine" during the Civil War. This regiment was the first to reach Virginia and was presented with a beautiful silk flag by the citizens of Sacramento through Congressman Rice of California.

When the flag was presented, the regiment formed in a hollow square and swore to protect it with their lives through thick and thin. This they did. It had many narrow escapes from capture, notably at Bull Run, where the color bearer Sargent Dean was shot. A second man seized it, and he, too, fell. Lt. Farnam then grasped the staff and carried the flag on the victorious charge. The regiment carried the flag through the war, and now it is placed in the State House with other Maine flags.

## CIVIL WAR (1861-1865)

The following list, is compiled from the following sources:

Adjutant General's Reports, Vols. 1 & 2
Somerset Registers, 1904, 1911-1912
List of Civil War Soldiers buried in St. Albans
Cemetery Records

Total men called from Maine - 72,365
Total men called from St. Albans - 212
Number of families who received aid to soldiers' families between 1862 and 1865 - 151

Capt. Adelbert Andrews, Francis Austin, Daniel Austin, Claudius B. Albee, John Atkins, Henry Atkins, Constance Bates, Seth Braley, John Braley, William Braley, Rufus Badger, Nathan Badger, John W. Buzzell, Samuel L. Buzzell, Charles L. Bigelow, Nelson Bigelow, Calvin Bigelow, Melvin Bigelow, Wilson Bigelow, Fred A. Brown, Henry W. Boston, Abner Brooks, George Batchelder, Stephen Bradford, Jessie Berry, Harrison T. Clough, George Cook, Charles A. Cook, Robert Cook II, Richard K. Champion, Charles B. Church, Stephen Chase, Charles H. Chase, Fred A. Chase, Chas. W. Cooley, George H. Cooley, Nelson T. Cooley, Melvin Cooley, Elisha Cooley, Trustum Cooley, George Crocker, John A. Chadwick, David H. Chandler, William H. Clifford, G. A. Dunlap, Wm. Davis, George E.

Dillingham, Sylvanus Emery, Carren E. Emery, Augustine Emery, John F. Ellis, Elisha D. Emerson, Albert Frost, William Emerson, Charles W. Frost, Curtis Frost, James Frost, Aaron Frost, Gilman Frost, L. B. Frost, Edmond Frost, Emanuel L. Frost, James S. Foss, Thos. B. Foss, Nathaniel Foss, Mayhew C. Foss, Levi Foss, William Fernald, Benjamin Field Jr., Fred Field, William B. Field, Francis Field, William Freeborn, Alonzo E. Fuller, James Fuller, James Footman, Daniel A. Goodwin, George W. Goodwin, Henry Gordon, Frank Gordon, Isaiah L. Gordon, Hiram C. Gage, Frank Goddard, George H. Graffman, Asa Grant, Chas. H. Grant, William Goodale, Kelsey L. Glidden, William B. Getchell, William Godsoe, Francis Given, Robert Given, Samuel Hanson, Andrew G. Hanson, Stephen Hall, Sampson Hart, John Hartwell, Samuel S. Holbrook, George Hersom, Chandler Hopkins, Renaldo Ireland, Benjamin Ireland, Sullivan Johnson, James T. Johnson, Asa Judkins, Corridan Ireland, Melben Lothrop, Daniel W. Lothrop, Abial Lancaster, Alden Lander, William R. Leach, John B. Leathers, Frank Lambert, Franklin B. Luce, Samuel Lowell, Sullivan Maxim, Charles Maxim, Cyrus Maxim, George H. Magoon, E. J. Magoon, James F. Magoon, George W. Martin, Hiram Martin, Job Mellows, Cyrus Matthews, William H. Moore, James Moore, Harrison Moore, Henry Mower, Jessie Merrill, Miner Merrill, James W. Nickerson, Russell M. Nye, George Nye, Henry S. Nickerson, James Nichols, Samuel Nutter, Fred Overlook, John S. Parker, Edwin A. Parker, John Parker, Simeon S. Parker, Aaron Parker, Lyander H. Parker, Charles P. Parker, Orin Parkman, J. C. Pheland, Freeman Philbrick, James M. Philbrick, George W. Pennell, Bennett Palmer, Frederick Palmer, Levi Powers, Elbridge H. Page, Jedidiah Prescott, Thomas Ray, John W. Russell, Stephen Russell, Milford Russell, R. J. Ryerson, Rufus Robertson, James S. Ridley, Hiram Raymond, Isaac Raymond, Charles Richards, Ansel B. Snell, Hosea B. Snell, Ormandal M. Snell, Eben M. Snell, Samuel S. Snell, Franklin Snell, William Snell, Charles A. Southard, Belden Southard, Joseph Sturdavant, Arthur Stewart, Hiram G. Steward, Benjamin Steward, William H. Steward, Samuel Steward, William H. Sewell, William H. Smart, Marquis Smart, Elizer Smith, Benjamin R. Smith, Edmond K. Smith, Edward K. Smith, Lorenzo M. Stinchfield, Earl S. Stinchfield, J. M. Stone, Leonard Stone, Richard Shorey, John M. Skinner, Alden Sampson, George H. Sampson, Cyrus Sampson, Gustavus B. Sampson, Allen Sprague, Frederick Stafford, Danforth Snow, Earl Stilson, Jr., Harrison O. Turner, Otis Turner, Timothy Tucker, Luther Tripp, John Tripp, Roscoe Trivett, Abithar B. Taylor, N. B. Thorne, Henry C. Vining, Amos Wells, Sylvanus B. White, John White, James White, Amaziah W. Webb, Converse L. Webb, Converse Webb, Jr., John R. Webb, John O. Welch, Joseph W.

Welch, Charles Welch, Henry P. Wood, Daniel Weeks, F. M. Wilkins, Amos Wells, John York, James M. York, Sylvester York, Thomas Whitney

Substitutes:

George E. Dillingham - Army - July 29, 1863
          3 years principle - Benjamin R. Dillingham

William Fernald - Army - July 30, 1863
          3 years principle - Luther Webb

Thomas O. Whitney - Army - August 14, 1863
          3 years principle - Nathaniel H. Vining

A total of 238; 26 names found besides those given in the Adjutant General's list.

## WORLD WAR I (1914-1918)

Rosters of Maine Vol. 1-2
Somerset County - In World War  by Florence Atwood
St. Albans Cemetery Records - Charles Boyd

**Army**

| | |
|---|---|
| Nelson Atwood | Wilbur Nichols |
| Charles Batchelder | Howard Noble |
| William Bradford | Verne A. Merrill |
| Carl Baird | Albion Neal |
| Sumner Jessie Bragg | Ralph Pratt |
| Joseph Buker | Horace E. Parker |
| Nathan Bragg | Carroll J. Patten |
| Percy Bragg | Earl L. Patten |
| William G. Cooley | Cecil R. Peasley |
| Jessie Cooley | John E. Peakes |
| Chester Carson | Frank Palmer |
| Fred Leroy Chase | Orin Parkman |
| John Crocker | Clarence Scamman |
| William Clyde Cook | Elwyn H. Seekins |
| Francis Curtis | Herbert L. Seekins |
| Fred Clark | Alvin A. Southard |
| Charles Eastman | Fred Vassar |
| Frank Fellows | Harold Wheeler |
| Philip Fraser | Guy White |
| Frank Green | Frank Woodbury |
| Alton Hilton | Clifford Wilkins |
| Donald Johnson | Elden E. Wilkins |
| Robie Linnell | Harold Wing |
| William Linnell | Clarence M. Russell Jr. |

Karl Martin

Reuben McLean
Corey Bubar

**Navy**

Grover C. Baldwin
Joseph Badger
Clyne W. Bigelow
William Bigelow
Frank Clark
Clyde Carson

Willis H. Carson
Clarence B. Cole
Floyd O. Matthews
Charles W. Thompson
Donald Raymond

Karl L. Martin

The only casualty in World War I was Private Karl L. Martin, son of Ervin and Minnie (Emery) Martin, born in St. Albans, Maine on Feb. 28, 1893. Owing to frequent changes in residence made necessary by the father's business and later by family health of the father and little brother Francis, the boy received a somewhat cosmopolitan education having attended school in St. Albans, Pittsfield, and Lewiston, Maine, Boston, Massachusetts, and Ashville, North Carolina. In 1914 he studied piano tuning with his father who at the time conducted a class in St. Cloud, Florida. After Mr. Martin's death, which occurred at the old home in St. Albans, Karl entered the employment of F. E. Tainter Co. Lewiston, Me., a tuner and salesman. He made a home for his widowed mother and invalid brother. When he would have responded to his country's call, home ties barred him. Francis, given up by physicians, was taken back to St. Albans. Very soon after his brother's death, Karl entered the service, leaving for Camp Devens the twenty-sixth of July, 1918. He was first in the 47th Co. 12th Battalion Depot Brigade, but soon transferred to Co. D-35th Machine Gun Battalion, where he served until he died of pneumonia at Camp Devens, Sept. 25, 1918. Karl's natural musical ability and inherent good nature won him many friends, and although he enlisted from Lewiston, his native town claimed him as her own, and the only World War I Gold Star flag of St. Albans is for Karl L. Martin.

## RED CROSS

The St. Albans Red Cross, a member of the Waterville Chapter, was organized in June 1917 with 10 members. At the close of World War I there was a membership of 100. Until the local Red Cross Societies were taken over by the state officers, the organization was very active. During 1918 the St. Albans group sent as their contribution to the men in service 34 sweaters, 58 pairs of socks, 50 comfort pillows, 105 fracture pillows, 27 pajamas, 48 wristlets, 32 pairs of thumbless mittens, and 13 mufflers. In addition, innumerable bandages, hot water bottle covers, wash cloths, and other articles were included. At this time Mrs. Joseph Welch was Chairman, Mrs. Osgood Robertson, Secretary, and Mrs. Alfred Bigelow, Treasurer.

During World War II there was a different kind of activity with emphasis placed on preparedness. Marjorie Heath Mower, R.N. who had served in World War I in England and France was the devoted Chairman of the Red Cross in St. Albans until it ceased to be a local organization. She conducted several well attended classes in First Aid and Community Safety regulations. Ruth Powers and Edith Lary gave a course in First Aid and Swimming Survival. During the last decade the Red Cross has become state oriented with all activities directed from a central office. The enthusiasm for personal service in the Red Cross is a thing of the past.

Edwina Mower, born February 28, 1891 graduated from MCI and Bliss College in Lewiston. She served with the American Red Cross for one year traveling to Italy, France, England, and Switzerland. In 1921 she served as Secretary for the Y.W.C.A. in Austria, Germany, Russia, Turkey, Siberia, and other European Countries.

**Army Nurse Corps** — Marjorie Heath Mower

After graduating from Malden Hospital joined Camp Devens, New York City Army Nurse Corps as a Reserve Nurse. Left from base hospital at Camp Devens, Mass. and proceeded to Nurses Mobilization station N.Y.C. Left for embarkation point at Hoboken, N.J. Arrived in England first then sent to Trier, Germany to Mesves evacuation hospital No. 3 for duty. Sent to hospital Center Remaucourt, France, there to U.S. General Hospital Builtmore, North Carolina — Discharged.

For years Marjorie Mower served her friends and neighbors in St. Albans. If and when an emergency arose and a family needed to locate a member of their family in the service, or bring him home, Marjorie Mower was there. Her expertise helped many a family through a difficult time.

**Army Nurse Corps** — Velma Badger

Velma Badger born and brought up in St. Albans enlisted as an army nurse in World War I. She served at Camp Devens, Massachusetts. At the close of the war she became a civilian nurse in New York State where she married Burk Bradbury. She made her home in Schenectady, New York.

### WORLD WAR II (1939-1945)

| | |
|---|---|
| Austin, Edmond | McLean, Verne L. |

24

Austin, Erroll R.
Baird, Philip
Ballard, Donald H.
Ballard, Harry Jr.
Ballard, Sheldon O.
Birkmaier, Theodore A.
Braley, John A.
Breed, Harlan J.
Bryant, Cedric W.
Bubar, Earle Benjamin
Bubar, Wendall G.
Burpee, Harold R.
Butler, Harold
Cook, Charles C.
Cook, Charles Clayton
Cooley, Charles E.
Cooley, Clifton S.
Cooley, Harold E.
Cooper, Fred
Dewey, Arthur E.
Dewey, Donald I.
Dickey, Evelyn
Dirga, John
Edwards, James A.
Elderkin, Charles
Emery, Keith
Field, Donald - Capt.
Fowler, Hartley T.
Goodwin, Harold
Griffin, George W.
Hanson, Gareth M.
Harding, Harold
Harding, Lionel
Harris, Ray A.
Hart, Carroll J.
Hartwell, Leon
Heath, Earle
Hilton, Edward L.
Hughes, Carroll
Hughes, Lauren
Hughes, Paul A.
Knowles, Lowell
Knowles, Robert D.
Larrabee, Lewellyn Calvin

Merrill, Clifford F.
Merrill, Clayton
Merrill, Shirley
Merrow, Mahlon Richard
Merrow, Myron George
Mower, Edwin H.
Nason, Richard N.
Nelson, Edward
Nichols, Clyde
Nichols, Everett B.
Nutter, George H.
Nutter, Walter T.
Page, Linwood
Parker, Archie
Parker, John L.
Parkman, Henry Adrian
Parsons, Albert Burchard
Patterson, Carroll E.
Patterson, Durwood
Pease, Basil H.
Pease Clifton O.
Pease, Mansford A.
Perkins, Robert
Phillips, Reginald J.
Powers, Harlow Eugene
Pratt, Lyndon Grant
Robertson, Gerald O.
Ross, Charles E. Jr.
Salley, Harry R.
Sawyer, Maurice Elmer
Sinclair, Robert F.
Smith, Clarence N.
Smith, Edward Donald
Smith, Elmer H.
Smith, John B.
Spencer, Joseph
Springer, Victor L.
Stone, Joseph R.
Thorne, Bertram E.
Thorne, Raymond Burgess
Waldron, Charles
Waldron, Robert W.
Walker, Charles
Walker, Clarence

Lawrence, Amos Anthony
Learnard, Richard Kenneth
Lewis, Carroll
Libby, Everett R.
Littlefield, Arthur F.
Lombard, Curtis N.
Lovely, Ransford E.
Lucus, Richard
Martin, George E.

Webber, George B.
Wentworth, Kenneth
Wentworth, Evan
Wentworth, Wallace
Wiers, Alfred J.
Wiers, Dean Morris
Wiers, Kenneth Pennell
Wilkins, Freeland
Wood, Merlene

**Carroll I. Patterson** — World War II
Carroll I. Patterson, Motor Machinists Mate Second Class — U.S.N. Died 1946 in a California hospital. He was the son of Vernon and Pearl Joy Patterson. On November 1, 1946 the World War II Victory Medal was awarded posthumously to his family in his honor.

## KOREAN WAR — (1950-1953)

Bailey, Norman Ellis
Bishop, Donald Sylvan
Blanchard, Frank Isaac
Brooks, Darrell Alton
Bubar, Keith E.
Butler, Ernest D. Jr.
Carson, Chester E. Jr.
Emery, Merlon
Field, Oral Colby
Glavine, John Cyril
Hanson, Brian Ashley
Harris, Sherman Lee
Hughes, Kenneth Arden
Jones, Frederick Richard Jr.
Jones, Maurice Wesley
Knowles, Francis Dale
Lucas, Raymond Dumont
Lucas, Richard

McLean, Earl Vincent
McNichol, Paul Bradley
Martin, Harvey Glenwood
Neal, Blaine Alden
Neal, Paul Irving
Nichols, Clarence Eugene
Nichols Frank Wallace
Nichols, Kenneth Harland
Nichols, Roger Ivan
Peasley, Charles Edwin
Sinclair, LaForest Edgar
Springer, Lawrence Curtin
Thorne, Allan Marsh
Webber, Vernon Roland
Adams, George Lewis
Caron, Jean Paul
Mills, James

**James Wilfred Mills**

James Wilfred Mills, an engineer was killed aboard the U.S.S. Bennington, April 1953, Korean War. Enlisted in Navy, September 1950 — Boot training at Newport, Rhode Island. He also served at Bainbridge, Maryland, Norfolk, Virginia, and Brooklyn, New York.

Born May 22, 1929 in St. Albans; son of Mr. and Mrs. Thomas

Mills, graduated from Hartland Academy; Home on furlough late January of 1953, being shipped out shortly after he returned to duty.

**Richard Lucas**

Son of Minot and Leona Dumont Carson Lucas; born July 3, 1927; killed in the Korean War 1953 at age 26. Educated in St. Albans schools and graduated from Hartland Academy, also graduated from University of Maine — Alpha Gamma Rho Fraternity (Agriculture) has a plaque in their building for him.

Enlisted in Medical Corps when infantry called for officers — took Officers' Training. Was killed in the last days of war; received Korean medal, Good Conduct medal, and Silver Star medal.

(After graduation from University of Maine — Lippman Poultry inspector from Blue Hill to Lincoln.)

Headquarters                                              5th October 1955
Infantry Division
DPO 7

SECTION 1

Award of the Silver Star - by direction of the President, under the provisions of the Act of Congress, approved 9 July 1918 (WD Bul. 45 1918) and pursuant to authority in AR 600-45, the Silver Star for gallantry in action is awarded posthumously to the following named officer: Second Lieutenant Richard F. Lucas 01935199, Infantry, United States Army, a member of Company K, 17th Infantry, distinguished himself by gallantry in action near Sokkangas, Korea. On 9 July 1953 Lieutenant Lucas and his men were engaging in an assault up the slope toward the hostile forces. Although Lieutenant Lucas was entirely exposed to enemy observation and fire, his only concern was in leading his men against the enemy. Lieutenant Lucas moved throughout the fire-swept area encouraging his men to advance and direct their fire. At this time enemy machine gun fire became increasingly heavy and Lieutenant Lucas was fatally wounded. Lieutenant Lucas' constant direction of his men's fire and actions enabled his unit to successfully complete the assigned mission. The gallantry displayed by Lieutenant Lucas reflects great credit on himself and is in keeping with the highest traditions of the military service. Entered the Federal service from Maine. By command of Major General Trudeau official:

J. E. Bastion Jr.
Colonel Chief of Staff

Stephen Henley
1st Lt. 17 GC
Asst. Adj. General

## VIETNAM

Anderson, Alton Dwight
Arnold, Dennis Lawrence
Beer, Winifred Ann
Brown, Frank William
Bryant, Frank Whyndam
Bubar, Dean Allen
Carlow, Glen Arthur
Chambers, Dennis Ivan
Chambers, Kenneth Michael
Cloutier, Edgar James
Cooper, Dana Bigelow
Crocker, David Ivan
Crocker, Michael George
Emery, Galen Kenneth
Emery, Ralph Linwood
Field, Harold Lee, Jr.
French, Robert Allen
Harding, Fred
Holt, Timothy Eugene

Jones, David Scott
Jones, Richard Paul
Lary, Terrance Edmund
Neal, Ronald Freeman
Parent, Richard Joseph
Patten, Bruce Earl
Patten, David Charles
Patten, Ernest Edward
Price, Curtis
Robinson, Aubrey Francis
Smith, Ernest Alden
Smith, Gary Wayne
Tasker, Duane Clair
Vicnaire, Maynard Eugene
Viles, Kenneth Ledford
Weeks, Dennis Marshal
Weeks, Earle Osborne
Welch, Alfred Newton, Jr.
Welch, Francis Howard

## CIVIL DEFENSE ORGANIZATION

In 1952 following the use of the atomic bomb in World War II, Civil Defense Committees were formed in the United States. This group planned protection against fall-out from bomb attacks, evacuation of schools to bomb shelters, medical needs, mass feeding, and fire and police duties. Everett Graham was appointed by the Civil Defense Office in Augusta as Director and Ruth Powers became Women's Civil Defense Chairman. Among the citizens who served in this effort were Maurice Sawyer, communications; Oren Neal, fire; Bennie Melanson, Police; Ellen Cooper, Shelter Survey; Frances Seekins, Public Information; Helen Finson, Mass Feeding; Lewis McLeod, Engineering; and Walter Butler, Relay Communications.

The organization adopted an evacuation plan designed to deliver all school children to their homes within thirty minutes of an enemy attack. Fortunately, it was never necessary to carry out these Civil Defense duties and after a few years the group became inactive.

## TRAFFIC CONTROL STATION

Looming above the woods and ledges near the top of St. Albans Mountain are the four 60-foot towers of the Air Traffic Control Sta-

28

tion, one of 24 such installations in Region One of the Civil Aeronautics Administration Service. On land leased from Reginald Phillips, Peter Hargoadon, Carl Cutlip, and Robert Keenan, the station was completed in 1958.

A small building complete with plumbing, electricity, and telephone is available for watchers around the clock should this be necessary. Because he is constantly visiting the project, Mr. Philip Magill of Bangor, the supervisor of Site R.C.A.G. Remote Control Air to Ground, says, "The St. Albans Mountain site seems like a second home to me."

There are 16 receivers and transmitters constantly reporting the activities of commercial and military aircraft, all remote controlled from Nashua, N.H. and passed on to Boston headquarters. The site has its own electricity generator to be used if needed.

Although our towers are outwardly quiet in their seclusion, their inner activity sends important messages far and wide.

## A CIVIL WAR DIARY

Written by Cyrus Mathews from January 1, 1865 to Dec. 25, 1865

Cyrus Mathews (1821-1886) was 44 years old when he began his diary on New Year's Day of 1865. When he joined the army to fight for the Union of the States, he left behind in St. Albans his wife Loantha Steward Mathews (1827-1895) and three sons, Elwyn (1851-1943), Walter (1855-1873), and Benjamin (1858-1932). Following his marriage Benjamin moved to Pittsfield where he lived the rest

The Matthew's House was built by Cyrus Matthews

of his life. Elwyn and his wife Alice Osborn Mathews (1866-1949) remained in the family home. They had three sons: Evan died in infancy, Walter was for years a lawyer in New York, and Floyd became a doctor. Before his death in 1966, Walter sold the home to William and Glenna Bartlett. Mrs. Bartlett found the diary in the attic, and it is through her generosity that it has become a part of this history of St. Albans.

## DIARY:
### Cyrus Mathews

**January, Sunday 1, 1865**

Cold. I went to the caisons. Wrote to my wife. Saw Hannibal Powers. Wrote to Tobys (Folks). All quiet on the line.

**Monday, 2**

Pleasant and cold. Worked on tent. Read letter from my wife. We remain about four miles left of Petersburg.

**Tuesday, 3**

Worked on tent. Stormed afternoon and snowed. Taped one pair of boots. Wrote to my wife in the evening.

**Wednesday, 4**

Cold, two inches of snow on ground. Sent the letter I wrote yesterday. Washed two shirts, two prs. feeting and drawers.

**Thursday, 5**

Pleasant. Went into the woods. Split some pine for floor and bunks. It split nice and we built our bunks. Some cooler tonight.

**Friday, 6**

Rainy day. Laid floor in tent and moved in too. Supper in new tent. Three men shot near here today. Letter from wife.

**Saturday, 7**

Cold and windy. Nothing of importance today. E. Whittier came back to Battery. Had a cold night.

**Sunday, 8**

Cool morning but very pleasant. Had an inspection of clothing. Have written to wife. Rec'd old letter from wife, also two dollars.

**Monday, 9**

Quite pleasant. Have been cobblin today. Was turned out this morning by picket firing in front.

**Tuesday, 10**

Rainy all day, Had thunder shower. Cobbled some, wrote to wife.

**Wednesday, 11**

Fine day. Rec'd letter from wife. Have been cobblin. Saw Hannibal, he is well.

**Thursday, 12**

Pleasant. Done some cobblin, made a stool. John Parker came up to see me. I worked for U.S. one year.

**Friday, 13**

Pleasant. Six boys mustered today. Have written to my wife. O. G. Nutting left battery. Rec'd letter from wife. 3 stamps and ten envelopes.

**Saturday, 14**

Cold wind. Repaired a pr. boots. All remains quiet here yet. Bought a paper. The news was good from Sherman and Thomas.

**Sunday, 15**

Cold and Pleasant. I went to battery H Ohio to see Hannibal. Found him well.

**Monday, 16**

Wrote to wife. Pleasant day. It is said the Jonies are marching to the left of our line. Orders - be ready to march. Sent diary home.

**Tuesday, 17**

Cool. Have been washing and made a stew. I hear the firing of a salute. It is rumored Fort Fisher is taken.

**Wednesday, 18**

Cloudy. Read letter from wife. Wrote to wife. Saw Hannibal. Ordered to the Ambulance Corps. Rec'd paper home.

**Thursday, 19**

Cool and cloudy. I have been to the Ambulance Corps for examination by the surgeons. Windchester stretcher bearer.

**Friday, 20**

Cool and pleasant. We had an inspection today. I have been ordered to the caisons. Taped one pr. boots.

**Saturday, 21**

Rainy day. Ordered to the caisons, in a poor tent. Rec'd letter from wife.

**Saturday, 28**

Cold and windy. Tried for a furlow but did not get any. Have written to Geo., written B. S. Steward. Have mended boots for Clark. Many died.

**Sunday, 29**

Cool and fair. All quiet today. Dreamed of home this night.

**Monday, 30**

Pleasant. Have spent the day cobblin. Borrowed five dollars of Hannibal. Earned 1.85

**Tuesday, 31**

Pleasant day. Have been cobblin all day. I have earned 1.90 today. All quiet. Everyone talks of peace.

**February, Wednesday, 1**

Cloudy, At five o'clock turned out to pack up. At two o'clock nicked up but unharmed. Cobblin today. Did not move.

**Thursday, 2**

Quite warm. Have cobbled some. Saw D. Lothrop and S. Johnson. Read letter from wife and went to meeting and saking Mary death.

**Friday, 3**

Warm. Has stormed some. Have been cobblin all day. Bought 10 lbs. flour. Baked cake and beans. Wrote to Ellwyn.

**Saturday, 4**

Warm, pleasant day. Cobbled some. Went to meeting in the evening. Heavy firing on the right.

**Sunday, 5**

Fine and windy. The 2nd, 5th and 6th corps have orders to march and have gone to the left. We drove the Rebs 7 miles and took cattle and sheep.

**Monday, 6**

Cool. Rec'd letter written the 26th January from wife and 3 stamps. Cobbled some. Wrote letter to wife. Sent 50 cents. A large lot of infantry came in.

**Tuesday, 7**

Stormy day, cold and rainy. Hard fighting on the left. We turned out and hitched up early this morning. Have not moved.

**Wednesday, 8**

Cool. Have been cobblin today. I hear heavy cannonading on the right this evening.

**Thursday, 9**

Cold and windy. Done some cobblin. No letter yet. Jones baked beans.

**Friday, 10**

Cool and pleasant. Cobbled all day for Maine sharpshooters. Have had all I could do today.

**Saturday, 11**

Fine morning. 31 in 3a Maine moved in here. Rec'd letter from Geor. after returning home from river.

**Sunday, 12**

Cold and windy. All quiet today.

**Monday, 13**

Cold and windy. Ordered to pack up to move then ordered to unpack. Taped one pr. boots. Hannibal was here evening.

**Tuesday, 14**

Pleasant. Taped 3 prs. boots. Bought flour and potatoes. Wrote to wife. Sent one dollar.

**Wednesday, 15**

Rainy day. Have been taping all day. Earned three dollars. Did not get a cent of it.

**Thursday, 16**

Fine day. Cobbled some this day. The captain has returned.

**Friday, 17**

Stormy. I washed my clothes. Not much to put down.

**Saturday, 18**

Fine and pleasant. Rec'd letter from wife. Have written to wife. Cobbled some.

**Sunday, 19**

Fine day. Rec'd two letters, one from my wife, and one from B. S. Steward. I have been frying donuts.

**Monday, 20**

Pleasant day. Taped 2 prs. boots. Hear Columbia is taken by Sherman.

**Tuesday, 21**

Fine day. Wrote to Leo and boys. Wrote to Clara.

**Wednesday, 22**

Pleasant. Have played ball some. Packed and harnessed up at night. They thought the Jonies would make a charge on the city.

**Thursday, 23**

Rainy. Wrote to Lantha and to B. S. Steward. Received my paper and envelopes last night.

**Friday, 24**

Yet it rains. Received letter from wife. Bought stamps, 50 cents worth. Have written to wife. Bought a paper.

**Saturday, 25**

A rainy day. Washed and done some cobblin. Boxes for the boys came today.

**Sunday, 26**

Rainy. Two o'clock turned out and got ready to move. Received letter from Esther Tobey. Wrote to Esther Tobey. The frogs are out.

**Monday, 27**

Fine. Paid off for four months amount $64. Played some ball. Greenbacks are plenty. Received letter from wife.

**Tuesday, 28**

Rainy. Some have been mustered for pay in the rain. Wrote to my wife. Sent $10. Have done some cobblin.

**March, Wednesday, 1, 1865**

Cloudy day. Have cobbled a part of the day. Had our guns new bushed. Bought a paper.

**Thursday, 2**

Rainy day. Have been cobblin today. Received letter from my wife.

**Friday, 3**

Rainy day. Cobbled all day. Wrote to my wife but could not send it.

**Saturday, 4**

Squally day. Cobbled all day. Sent letter wrote yesterday with twenty dollars enclosed.

**Sunday, 5**

Fine. Nothing new today. Received letter from wife this morning. Wrote to wife.

**Monday, 6**

Pleasant. I cobbled in the forenoon. In the afternoon done a little by way of luggin wood.

**Tuesday, 7**

Pleasant. David Hanson was here to dinner. Received letter from wife.

**Wednesday, 8**

Rainy. Washed and cobbled today. Wrote letter to my wife. Also received one from my wife.

**Thursday, 9**

Cloudy day. Wrote to my wife. Have been cobblin today.

**Friday, 10**

Rained in forenoon. Cobbled all day. The mud is deep. No news tonight.

**Saturday, 11**

Fair. All quiet along the line. Hannibal came back to battery. I done some cobblin.

**Sunday, 12**

Cool and pleasant. All quiet here. Wrote to my wife. Received letter from my wife. Received another letter.

**Monday, 13**

Fine day. On guard today. Patched one boot. Wrote to my wife. Sent ten dollars.

**Tuesday, 14**

Fine day. On police duty. Orders to pack up. We yet remain.

**Wednesday, 15**

Fine. Taped and capped one boot. Reported to headquarters. Have not moved.

**Thursday, 16**

Windy. Things remain as usual. Done some cobblin. We had 15 recruits.

**Friday, 17**

On guard. Pleasant but windy. Received letter from my wife and An Tobey. Ordered to the train. Wrote to wife, ten dollars.

**Saturday, 18**

Fine day. Went to the train. Sent letter I wrote yesterday with ten dollars and fifty cents enclosed.

**Sunday, 19**

Pleasant. Done some police duty and wrote a letter to wife.

**Monday, 20**

Fine day. Done some police duty. Went to the battery. Received letter form wife with valentine and lock of hair.

**Tuesday, 21**

The sun rose clear and warm. It was till about noon, then it commenced to rain and rained hard. Saw Hannibal. Wrote to wife and was down to battery.

**Wednesday, 22**

Very windy. Detailed for wood. In forenoon hurt. A man died in hospital. A sarg in 1 N.J. Battery. Strained my back.

**Thursday, 23**

Windy, very. It uproots trees and blows down tents. Tremendous wind all night. My back is lame.

**Friday, 24**

Very windy. Received letter from wife this morning and wrote to wife this afternoon. I am not very well just now.

**Saturday, 25**

Cloudy. The Jonies commenced firing about two o'clock at night and broke the line of 9 Corps and we took 3000 rebs. killed 2500. Some 200 threw down and arms. Ordered to battery.

**Sunday, 26**

Cool. Ordered to train again. Feel sick. Took some oil, no appetite to eat. Eight of our boys buried. Killed in fight.

**Monday, 27**

Pleasant but cool. Do not think I am any better. Taking more medicine. Letter from Joseph. Wrote him in return. Wrote wife.

**Tuesday, 28**

Fine day. Getting ready for move. Wrote to An Tobey. Did not move. Hospital packed up all ready.

**Wednesday, 29**

Cloudy. Done some harness repairing. Feel some better. 24 Corps on the left today. In evening firing on the right.

**Thursday, 30**

Rainy. Repaired mule harnesses. Hard fighting on left or on south side road all day. Received two letters from wife.

**Friday, 31**

Rainy. Hard fighting commenced early. Fighting all day. Wrote to wife. Hear Sheridan drove the Jonies ten miles and took 21 pieces artillery.

**April, Saturday, 1**

Fair day, And still they fight. Ordered to the battery in evening. Fighting began about ten o'clock and kept up all night. 9 Corps took five forts.

**Sunday, 2**

Fine. Our boys manned the guns in the forts and turned them on the Jonies. The 6 Corps is coming up in rear of them. Our troops entered Petersburg. Received letter from wife.

**Monday, 3**

Fine morning. Moved at one o'clock. Encamped near city point. Saw any amount of dead. Richmond surrendered at light this morning.

**Tuesday, 4**

Pleasant. Fixed our tent a little. I hear that Lee is taken with 3000 prisoners. 2000 based here. Wrote to wife. The story of Lee is not so.

**Wednesday, 5**

Pleasant. The 6 Maine Battery came in today. Sent the letter I wrote yesterday. Nothing new.

**Thursday, 6**

Sprinkle some. Received letter from Beny. One from Clara, one from wife. Have writted wife and Clara.

**Friday, 7**

Sprinkled. Moved about one mile. Went into park, built tents. Saw 900 prisoners pass 2½ miles from city point.

**Saturday, 8**

Pleasant and fine. Everything quiet here. Wrote to Beny. The boys are fixing over their tents. Received letter from my wife. All well.

**Sunday, 9**

Pleasant and windy. Wrote to my wife and sent ten dollars. Received letter from Eunice Allen. The surrender of Lee.

**Monday, 10**

Rainy day. Salutes have been fired in every direction. Wrote Eunice Allen. Have written to my mother. Bought flour.

**Tuesday, 11**

Rainy. Got a paper stating of Lee's surrender. Charles Frost went to Petersburg. Could not send letters wrote yesterday.

**Wednesday, 12**

Cleared off. Have been fixing tents today and putting up evergreen. Saw 1600 prisoners and 8000 more 2 squads. Letter from wife.

**Thursday, 13**

Rainy. Cleared off at noon. Wrote to wife, sent ten dollars. Turned in 24 horses. Did not send the letter I wrote.

**Friday, 14**

Fine morning. Sent letter I wrote yesterday. Washed jacket. Ordered to report to roll call. Ordered to move toward city. Paint tomorrow. A Lincoln shot, Pres.

**Saturday, 15**

Rainy. Ordered to pack up but did not move. On guard today. Received letter from wife. 7 boys mounted and went after gurilly (gorilla).

**Sunday, 16**

Fine. On guard till five. Heard that Lincoln was dead. Wrote letter to wife but did not send it. Baked beans.

**Monday, 17**

Fine. Packed up early and moved inside the works. Sent the letter I wrote yesterday. Received letter from wife dated April 4.

**Tuesday, 18**

Pleasant, windy. Wrote letter to my wife. Ohio moved along side. Saw heavy set man that was in Bat. 10.

**Wednesday, 19**

Pleasant. On detail. Washed shirts. Hear good news from Mobile of its surrender and a report that Johnston has surrendered. Went to meeting evening.

**Thursday, 20**

Cloudy morning. Saw a Negro shot for attempting to kill his officer. Warm night. Do not get any letter.

**Friday, 21**

Warm and pleasant. Received letter from wife and one from Tobey's father. Have written to wife and Tobey's father.

**Saturday, 22**

Fine. Had a mounted drill. Received letter from wife dated 12th, letter from J. M. Powers. Wrote to J. M. Powers.

**Sunday, 23**

Cool. The 31st reg came in and the 9 Corps is being transported Washington. Wrote to wife. Received letter from wife. Saw Hanson and David.

**Monday, 24**

Cold morning. Pleasant day. Policed a little and cobbled a little. Not anything of importance to write.

**Tuesday, 25**

Pleasant. Had a drill mounted. Ivory Hanson took dinner with me. Wrote to my wife. Went to the 7th Maine in evening. (Battery)

**Wednesday, 26**

Fine morning. This day is set apart as a day of mourning. Firing at head quarters all day. 7th Maine Battery moved.

**Thursday, 27**

Fine and cool. Drew horses. Policed the ground where 9 Corps lay. Went to the meeting in evening.

**Friday, 28**

Fine. Received letter from wife and B. S. Steward. Wrote to wife. Wrote to B. S. Steward. Got news of Johnston's surrender. Booth dead.

**Saturday, 29**

Pleasant. I done some cobblin and took care of a pair of horses. Bought a paper stating how Booth was taken.

**Sunday, 30**

Fine. Had an inspection and mustered for pay. On guard today. On guard tonight maybe. Two deserters return from Canada.

**May, Monday, 1**

Fine and cool. On guard. Expect to move soon. Made pudding for supper. Cool night. Letter from wife.

**Tuesday, 2**

Cold. Washed this afternoon. Turned over ammunition. Wrote to wife.

**Wednesday, 3**

Pleasant. Got up at 4, marched at 8, crossed Appomotax at 10, crossed the James at 1, went in park about 3. Looked at the Reb works.

**Thursday, 4**

Fine. Marched a ¼ before 7, marched through Richmond, went into park at 2. We passed through Mecanicsville. 15 mile march.

**Friday, 5**

Rainy. Marched near cold harbor. Moved at half past 6, parked at twelve near Hanover Court House. Received letter from wife. Wrote to wife. Passed Court House. Stopped at 2.

**Saturday, 6**

Fine. Waiting. Moved about 2, crossed Pomun (1:00) River. Moved one mile. Went into park.

**Sunday, 7**

Cloudy and cool. Marched at half past 4, passed Milford Station. Boarded the Matripona, arrived at Bowling Green. At 5 went into park for the night. 25 miles.

**Monday, 8**

Warm day. Moved at 5 and marched to Frederick City. Went back two miles. Went into park for the night.

**Tuesday, 9**

Started at 4 in morning, marched through Fredericksburg. Rained all day. Mud deep. Crossed Acquise Creek and parked.

**Wednesday, 10**

Cloudy. Moved about 9 in morning. Bad road. Marched some ten miles. Passed Dumfruse and went on a piece and parked.

**Thursday, 11**

Fine day. Marched at five. Crossed Ocquecon River and to Fairfax Station and Fairfax Court House and about 3 miles and parked. Heavy shower.

**Friday, 12**

Cold and pleasant. Laid in park all day. Received 2 letters from wife, one from Beny, one from Mother and Naomi.

**Saturday, 13**

Fine. Letter from Esther. Moved about five miles. Went into park near Fairfax Seminary. Drew hay for horses.

**Sunday, 14**

Pleasant. Received letter from wife and wrote to wife and sent it. Also sent one written some days ago.

**Monday, 15**

Fine day. Got our ammunition chests. Bought ½ dozen eggs paid 25 cents. On guard tonight.

**Tuesday, 16**

Fine day. Melvin Lothrop and wife and sister were here today from Washington.

**Wednesday, 17**

Pleasant and warm. Went in swimming and had a wash. Also washed my clothes. Asked the captain for a pass to Washington. Letter from wife.

**Thursday, 18**

Fine day, Went to Washington. Had a good time. Took dinner with me. Lothrop got wet on the return.

**Friday, 19**

Wrote to my wife. Rained some.

**Saturday, 20**

Some rainy. Monthly inspection. Turned in spare caissons. Drew blouse and haversack.

**Sunday, 21**

Rainy day. Heavy showers. It is very muddy. Wrote to my wife. On guard tonight.

**Monday, 22**

Cloudy, but a fine day. Sent the letter to my wife. Quite a stir in the Army. Move my round for review.

**Tuesday, 23**

Fine day. Quite a number of boys went to review. Letter from my wife.

**Thursday, 25**

Fair. Frank Magoon, Levi Foss, Ivory Hanson and S. Johnson were here.

**Friday, 26**

Rainy day. A wet nasty time for soldiers.

**Saturday, 27**

Rainy some and very muddy. On guard tonight.

**Sunday, 28**

Fine day. On guard. Had an inspection.

**Monday, 29**

Pleasant day. John Parker and George Crocker were here today. Nothing to do. Baked beans.

**Tuesday, 30**

Fine day. Orders to turn in everything tomorrow. Letter from wife.

**Wednesday, 31**

Fine. Turned over our pieces at Washington. Wrote to wife.

**June, Thursday, 1**

Warm day, Turned in horses. I expressed a bundle. We had a great time in evening. Boys felt nicely.

**Friday, 2**

Warm and dry. Three broke camp and started.

**Saturday, 3**

Fine but cloudy. Turned out 3 o'clock. Marched to Washington. Took cars to Baltimore and then to Philadelphia.

**Sunday, 4**

Took breakfast at Philadelphia there, crossed the River and took cars again to S. Amboy. Here we took boat for New York and boat again to New London.

**Monday, 5**

Arrived in New London half past four morning. Here took cars for Boston. Arrived in Boston at 3 o'clock afternoon.

**Tuesday, 6**

In Boston till half past four. Took the (left out) for Hallowell.

**Wednesday, 7**

Foggy. Arrived in Bath at seven. In Augusta at one. Took dinner, got a pass and came home. Arrived at nine. All right.

**Thursday, 8**

Went round some and saw some friends.

**Friday, 9**

Passed as the day previous. Went up to Benny's.

**Saturday, 10**

Rained some. I was moving round the village.

**Sunday, 11**

Fine day. Had some company. Stayed at home all day.

**Monday, 12**

Fair. Went to Augusta. Found Morril Mathews. Went home with him and stopped for the night.

**Tuesday, 13**

Fair. Returned in morning. Went to Franklin House and hired my board.

**Wednesday, 14**

Fine. Not mustered out. Get feel. Anxious to get home.

**Thursday, 15**

Fine day. In Augusta, nothing done yet. Ordered to report at 9 o'clock in morning.

**Friday, 16**

Mustered out. This forenoon took the cars for home and came to Pittsfield and walked home.

**Saturday, 17**

Very warm. Remained at home. Arba Powers and wife came up on a visit to see me.

**Sunday, 18**

Cloudy and warm. Went to church to hear.

**Monday, 19**

Warm. Returned to Augusta. Sick all night. Received letter from B. S. Steward.

**Tuesday, 20**

Cloudy. Some better today. Discharged and paid. Come to Waterville.

**Wednesday, 21**

Warm. Left Waterville and went to Toby's. Left here after tea and went to St. Albans.

**Thursday, 22**

Warm. Went up to Levi's to see Walter. Stopped till after dinner. Walter went down to the Meeting House.

**Friday, 23**

Stopped with Elisbeth last night. Take the cars at Clinton, came to Hartland, Paid Dr. Blake.

**Saturday, 24**

Fine, at home. A free man once more and with my family. Got a pig.

**Sunday, 25**

Pleasant. Stayed at home all day.

**Monday, 26**

Went up and took supper with mother and spoke for a team to go to the River.

**Tuesday, 27**

Fine. Hannibal and Texas were Here. Took Buker's team, went to harmony and Athens and to Madison. Cool, nice time to ride.

**Wednesday, 28**

Cloudy, cool. Looks like rain. Took dinner at Noah Merrill's and went down to Sth Athens and stopped all night.

**Thursday, 29**

To Tobey's today.

**Friday, 30**

At Clinton and made a visit.

**July, Saturday, 1**

At Pittsfield and came home.

**Sunday, 2**

At home.

**Monday, 3**

At home. Morrill Mathews called.

**Tuesday, 4**

At home.

**Wednesday, 5**

At home.

**Thursday, 6**

Worked for J. C. Goodwin part of the day. Commenced at nine.

**Friday, 7**

Worked part of the day for Goodwin, four hours and a half.

**Saturday, 8**

Made shoes for Ellwyn

**Sunday, 9**

At home all day.

**Monday, 10**

Commenced to hay some.

**Tuesday, 11**

Cloudy. Made a hay rick. Ellwyn worked hoeing for John in afternoon.

**Wednesday, 12**

Hauled in two loads, mowed, and put up some. Repaired boots for John Goodwin.

**Thursday, 13**

Rained some. Mended boots for Baxter and began shoes for wife. John worked on his stable.

**Friday, 14**

Got in two loads. J. C. G. was sick.

**Saturday, 15**

Hauled four loads in and put up what we had down.

**Sunday, 16**

At home. Do not feel very well. Drove the cow up to Tutles.

**Monday, 17**

Rained. Made shoes for Lo and repaired boots for John Goodwin.

**Tuesday, 18**

Mowed and worked on hay.

**Wednesday, 19**

I was haying. Let J. C. Goodwin have 300 ft. plank.

**Thursday, 20**

Rained in forenoon. Worked for James Tracy in the afternoon mowing.

**Friday, 21**

Dull but mowed some in forenoon and repaired shoes for George Clark's wife afternoon.

**Saturday, 22**

A nice hay day, haying all day.

**Sunday, 23**

Fine day. Hauled in two loads of hay for the weather looked bad.

**Monday, 24**

Mowed and raked. Very fine and warm.

**Tuesday, 25**

Finished haying on the Vining farm. Mowed some at home. Very fine.

**Wednesday, 26**

Rainy. Went down Lothrop and got some Aid money. Moved in shop.

**Thursday, 27**

Finished mowing. Made a saw handle. Had showers; wet my hay.

**Friday, 28**

Fine. Finished haying made a saw handle and filed saws.

**Saturday, 29**

Rained some. Worked in shop in the afternoon.

**Sunday, 30**

Pleasant and cool. At home all day.

**Monday, 31**

Fine day. Worked for G. A. Parsons.

**August, Tuesday, 1**

Pleasant. Worked for Parsons.

**Wednesday, 2**

Fine. Worked for Parsons.

**Thursday, 3**

Hot day. Worked for Parsons.

**Friday, 4**

Poor hay day. Sick today. Heavy showers.

**Saturday, 5**

Fine day. In shop make shoes for Walter A. Smith and wife called in a few minutes.

**Sunday, 6**

I went up to mothers a little while in the afternoon.

**Monday, 7**

Worked in afternoon Austin.

**Tuesday, 8**

Fine day. Worked for Austin.

**Wednesday, 9**

Bought half heifer and butchered. Commenced to saw slabs.

**Thursday, 10**

Helped C. Smith shingle.

**Friday, 11**

Cobbled boot for Joe.

**Saturday, 12**

J. Pape buy 13 1/9 ft. leather 2.97
    buy 15 1/9 ft. up leather 3.57
Went to Hartland. Mended boots Mel Morse.

**Sunday, 13**

At home.

**Monday, 14**

J. Billing buy 31 lbs. S. leather 10.23

**Tuesday, 15**

Fine day. Worked in shop some.

**Wednesday, 16**

Worked for B. Ireland until five o'clock then showered.

**Thursday, 17**

Worked for B. Ireland until five o'clock

**Friday, 18**

Worked for B. Ireland.

**Saturday, 19**

At home. Bought flour.

**Sunday, 20**

Fine day, went to church and at home the rest of day.

**Monday, 21**

Worked for Edwin Parker. Had Showers just at night

**Tuesday, 22**

Worked for E. Parker. Sawed slabs.

**Wednesday, 23**

Worked for E. Parker.

**Thursday, 24**

Worked for E. Parker a part of the day to make up for lost time.

**Friday, 25**

Worked at home.

**Saturday, 26**

Worked at home.

**Sunday, 27**

Went to church.

**Monday, 28**

Worked for G. Avery till five o'clock.

**Tuesday, 29**

At Avery's as before.

**Wednesday, 30**

Worked for Avery.

**Thursday, 31**

Worked for Avery.

**September, Friday, 1**

Worked for Avery.

**Saturday, 2**

Worked for Avery. This was a hot day.

**Sunday, 3**

Went to church. Arba and Naomi took dinner with us.

**Monday, 4**

Worked for J. Parker on his shop till five o'clock.

**Tuesday, 5**

Worked for J. Parker till five o'clock then quit.

**Wednesday, 6**

Worked for J. Parker all day. Drove cow up to Joel's.

**Thursday, 7**

Worked for J. Parker all day.

**Friday, 8**

At home. Commenced to dig a well.

**Saturday, 9**

Worked in well. Mr. Smith helped me. Had 500 clapboards of Avery to balance my work.

**Sunday, 10**

At home in forenoon and went up to B. Allen's in afternoon.

**Monday, 11**

Worked in the well.

**Tuesday, 12**

At home digging potatoes.

**Wednesday, 13**

In well. Mr. Smith helped me.

**Thursday, 14**

Worked in the well. Mr. Smith helped me.

**Friday, 15**

Stoning well. Seth Emery helped me.

**Saturday, 16**

Finished my well.

**Sunday, 17**

At home.

**Monday, 18**

Worked for B. Allen on ditch.

**Tuesday, 19**

Worked for B. Allen till four in afternoon on ditch.

**Wednesday, 20**

Worked at home.

**Thursday, 21**

Worked at home.

**Friday, 22**

Worked for B. Allen on ditch. Hard heavy noise.

**Saturday, 23**

Hauled slabs.

**Sunday, 24**

At home.

**Monday, 25**

Worked for B. Allen with Walter. Digging potatoes.

**Tuesday, 26**

Worked for B. Allen, myself and Walter. Digging potatoes.

**Wednesday, 27**

Worked for B. Allen, Walter and I till 4 o'clock digging potatoes and hauling in corn.

**Thursday, 28**

Worked for Parsons shingling on stable.

**Friday, 29**

Went to Hartland. Filed my saws, seamed up one boot and lashed a pair.

**Saturday, 30**

Worked for Skinner in forenoon and C. Foss afternoon.

**October, Sunday, 1**

Went to Deacon giving funeral.

**Monday, 2**

Worked for H. Hawse.

**Tuesday, 3**

Worked for H. Hawse.

**Wednesday, 4**

Worked for H. Hawse.

**Thursday, 5**

Worked for H. Hawse.

**Friday, 6**

Finished my boots.

**Saturday, 7**

Worked for B. Allen in forenoon.

**Sunday, 8**

Went to Babcocks.

**Monday, 9**

At home in forenoon. Worked for the miller afternoon and bought flour.

**Tuesday, 10**

Worked some for miller in forenoon. At home in afternoon.

**Wednesday, 11**

B. Allen helped me.

**Thursday, 12**

B. Allen worked for me.

**Friday, 13**

B. Allen worked for me.

**Saturday, 14**

B. Allen worked for me till 4 o'clock.

**Sunday, 15**

At home.

**Monday, 16**

B. Allen worked in afternoon.

**Tuesday, 17**

B. Allen helped me.

**Wednesday, 18**

B. Allen worked for me.

**Thursday, 19**

Rainy day. Repaired shoes.

**Friday, 20**

B. Allen worked in afternoon.

**Saturday, 21**

J. Goodwin painted for me in afternoon.

**Sunday, 22**

Morrill Mathews was here.

45

**Monday, 23**

I worked for H. Hawse.

**Tuesday, 24**

Worked for H. Hawse.

**Wednesday, 25**

Worked for H. Hawse.

**Thursday, 26**

Worked for H. Hawse.

**Friday, 27**

Worked for H. Hawse.

**Saturday, 28**

Stayed at home and put in sidelight.

**Sunday, 29**

At home.

**Monday, 30**

Worked for H. Hawse.

**Tuesday, 31**

Worked on my house.

**November, Wednesday, 1**

Worked on my house.

**Thursday, 2**

On my house.

**Friday, 3**

On house.

**Saturday, 4**

On house, rained.

**Sunday, 5**

Went up to Joel's

**Monday, 6**

At home.

**Tuesday, 7**

At home.

**Wednesday, 8**

Moved mother down to Smith's

**Thursday, 9**

Worked in shop.

**Friday, 10**

In shop, at work.

**Saturday, 11**

In shop.

**Saturday, 11**

In shop.

**Sunday, 12**

At home.

**Monday, 13**

In shop.

**Tuesday, 14**

In shop.

**Wednesday, 15**

In shop.

**Thursday, 16**

In shop.

**Friday, 17**

Worked for E. Smith

**Saturday, 18**

Worked for E. Smith.

**Sunday, 19**

At home.

**Monday, 20**

Worked for E. Smith

**Tuesday, 21**

Worked for E. Smith

**Wednesday, 22**

Worked for E. Smith

**Thursday, 23**

Worked for E. Smith

**Friday, 24**

Worked for E. Smith

**Saturday, 25**

Worked for E. Smith

**Sunday, 26**

At home. Phillip and wife were here.

**Monday, 27**

Made boots for Ellwyn.

**Tuesday, 28**

At home.

**Wednesday, 29**

Worked for E. Smith.

**Thursday, 30**

Worked for E. Smith.

**December, Friday, 1**

At home. Fixed up stall.

**Saturday, 2**

Worked at home.

**Sunday, 3**

Arba and wife were here.

**Monday, 4**

Worked for Joel making boxes. Got my pung.

**Tuesday, 5**

In shop. Made boots for Philbrie.

**Wednesday, 6**

In shop, at work.

**Thursday, 7**

Thanksgiving went to Pittsfield. Very mild, good wheeling.

**Friday, 8**

In shop.

**Saturday, 9**

In shop. Joel went to Pittsfield.

**Sunday, 10**

At home.

**Monday, 11**

In shop.

**Tuesday, 12**

In shop.

**Wednesday, 13**

In shop.

**Thursday, 14**

Put up stairs in house.

**Friday, 15**

Put up mother's clock. Skated some.

**Saturday, 16**

Went up to H. Hawse for straw rye and corn. Mended shoes Mell Morse.

**Sunday, 17**

At home.

**Monday, 18**

At home.

**Tuesday, 19**

At home.

**Wednesday, 20**

Worked for J. C. Goodwin.

**Thursday, 21**

Worked for J. C. Goodwin.

**Friday, 22**

Worked for J. C. Goodwin.

**Saturday, 23**

This day not much done by me. Paid Halway for team.

**Sunday, 24**

At home. It snowed all day.

**Monday, 25**

Loafing.

**Tuesday, 26 - Sunday, 31**

Nothing written.

# CHAPTER IV

## EARLY ROADS AND TRANSPORTATION

The town lines of St. Albans, known then as Fairhaven Township, were run in 1806 by the famous old time surveyor, Samuel Weston of Skowhegan. Getting from one place to another was a major concern during the early days. For years the people of the town covered the area on foot or horseback following bridle paths through the woods.

Several mountain settlers had left families in Harmony and Ripley and visits to relatives presented traveling problems. There were steep hills and deep woods to negotiate between St. Albans and Ripley to the north; from Harmony on the west it was necessary to follow Main Stream down to The Falls to find a safe place to cross. In later years this crossing became the Wild Goose Club Landing. Today we recognize and appreciate the ingenuity, the planning, and skill of our forebears when we realize that many of the roads we use every day follow the pattern laid out so long ago by the early builders of our town.

Every part of St. Albans Mountain has a story to tell - some true, some fictitious, all conducive to either happiness or sadness. Of the old discontinued roads on the mountain, only caved in cellars and rail fences can be seen today.

Capt. Ambrose Finson who was born in Danville, Maine 1789 removed to Hartland in 1816 where he helped to lay out roads and townships, so no doubt he was one of the early surveyors in St. Albans.

St. Albans in the 1820's was divided into Highway Districts and men were named in town meetings to be responsible for the roads in each district. It was necessary to widen and smooth the path so as to make them accessible to vehicles.

In 1840 wagons were introduced and although they didn't have springs, they were considered to be a great improvement over the previous mode of travel. Before that time, the only vehicles had been sledges and clumsy homemade carts. Around 1850 spring wagons were seen in the town.

Gladys Bigelow recalls hearing stories of her grandfather, Isaac Osborn, who traveled to Bangor once a year taking his produce to market. He was gone from his home approximately a week or longer. In return, he often brought calico and raisins. His diet along

Isaac Osborn, Aged 90 years; Hiram Hawes , Aged 91 years.
(Photo taken Sept. 1909 at the Wing farm on St. Albans Mountain)

the way consisted of boiled eggs and fried pies. Fried pies were made of a biscuit dough filled with mincemeat and dried apple and fried in deep fat.

According to an old newspaper clipping (found in the Augusta State Library) there was a regular old time blizzard that swept through Somerset County in January 1881. It took seven yokes of oxen, one pair ahead of the other, to break the road between Skowhegan and Norridgewock. Dr. Brown followed this procession and upon his arrival in Norridgewock delivered his patient's baby on schedule. All roads in Somerset Co. according to the newspaper clipping were blocked. Our ancestors of St. Albans, no doubt, had a few experiences of their own, including Alfred Bigelow, who stayed in Augusta for several days before he could return home.

I'm sure it's not difficult for the older citizens of our town to recall this scene - several pairs of horses plunging through deep drifts, men guiding them with long reins, other men going ahead with shovels at times to make a track for the horses.

In those days a large plank covered roll was used to compact and level off the snow.

St. Albans Old Cleatrac (Operated for many years by Harry Finson)

## PLOWMAN'S WIFE

A plowman's wife has a story to tell
  It's only a bit of her private hell.
She's awakened at night when the wind starts to blow
  For she knows that the temperature could be twenty below.

She says a prayer that the wind will cease
  So her man can get home for a little sleep.
Bad weather's his job and his job is grim
  And it's hard to picture a man like him.
For he's always out when the storm first starts
  To spread the salt is only a part.
For the plowing starts with 3 inches of snow
  And the banks grow higher as the wind starts to blow.

It gives him a lift when the roads are clear
  But thanks is a word he'll never hear.
He's hungry and tired, he's been out all night
  But when he gets home everything's alright.

                by R. K.

It would have been interesting if more records had been kept and town reports printed before 1880.

An item found in the St. Albans Town Report of 1880 under Highway Taxes, Sum raised $6,000.00 Rate 17.5 Mills "This was committed to the highway surveyors and God knows what has become of it."

Town Report - 1889

Road Commissioners Report - Expended on the roads

| | |
|---|---:|
| in summer | 877.47 |
| For Wire | 100.00 |
| In winter to Feb. 24, 1891 | 979.72 |
| | ———— |
| TOTAL | 1,957.19 |

Town Report 1980

| | |
|---|---:|
| Winter Roads | 35,162.00 |
| Summer Roads | 14,948.00 |
| Garage | 2,394.00 |
| Trif. | 4,635.75 |

## THE GOOD OLD DAYS HAD PROBLEMS WITH AUTOS

(Voice from the past)

The following letter appeared in the columns of the Lewiston Journal in the spring of 1907, and was reprinted in 1947.

To the Editors:

Since Legislature opened, I have been reading all the leading daily papers and have been greatly interested in all of the doings -the removal of the State House, the appropriations for N. of M. and "many others", the investigation of the Judge Chapman case, also that of W. W. Stetson, and last but not least, the Automobile Question, comments on which appeared in Sunday's Boston Post. I think five miles an hour too slow, but eight miles an hour should be the limit in the State of Maine, for the safety of all concerned, and that from every Saturday noon until Monday at 6 a.m. they should not be allowed to run.

The penalty for violating this law should be, for the first offense, $100 and 60 days in jail.

We find throughout the State of Maine perhaps one automobile to 500 teams, and the people who own and use teams are the ones who have built and who keep the roads in repair, and I believe they ought to have proper protection.

I have traveled for the last nine years through the states of Maine, New Hampshire, Massachusetts, and Vermont, and I should say that Massachusetts is the most suitable state for the automobile to be run in; while Maine is utterly unfitted for the rapid running auto. Its roads are narrow with many hills and sharp curves, which give anyone with a nervous horse no chance to turn out. It is my opinion that if the voters of Maine had the privilege of voting on the speed of automobiles, they would either limit them to five miles an hour or to exterminate them from the state.

While I want to be fair and just to the men who run the automobiles, I feel it is my duty and the duty of every just, manly man to say a few words in behalf of the ninety and nine who have not and never can have an automobile. There is not any commercial benefit derived from the automobile. They are only a source of pleasure to the few who are able to own them.

I most sincerely hope that this present Legislature will not adjourn without giving the people of Maine some better protection against the automobiles.

Melvin Bigelow

Comments by the Lewiston Journal

How many local people are there who can remember when the fore-going sentiments were widely expressed at the time this letter was written? They were not the views of crackpots either. Many a sober-minded citizen firmly believed the "horseless carriage" was only a novelty, never to come into general use.

## THE RAILROAD THAT MIGHT HAVE BEEN

There were 492 miles of single track in the State of Maine in 1860, 37 miles of this in Somerset and Kennebec counties with ten stations.

In those days the railroads greatly enhanced the value of property.

It's difficult to pinpoint what year the selectmen of St. Albans refused permission to the Maine Central Railroad to run a branch through St. Albans. According to the stories handed down the Central Maine Railroad planned to make Newport rather than Pittsfield the junction for their proposed line. This would have gone through St. Albans.

Hartland Station (1916)

This same picture perhaps could have been taken in St. Albans instead of Hartland in the early 1900's.

# CHAPTER V

## AGRICULTURE

Much can be said and written respecting a farmer's occupation. They are members of one great brotherhood. Today agriculture leads in the industrial life of St. Albans as it did many years ago.

The pioneer farmers of this community as in other Maine towns were hardy men, strengthened and toughened by hard work and constant exposure to the elements.

### This They Found (In St. Albans, Me.)

Logs for a cabin,
Wood for a fire,
Moonlight for dreaming,
Land for desire.

Pine for a cradle,
Oak for a plow,
Black earth and sunshine,
Breeze on the brow.

Dawn and day ending
In flame on the skies,
Sunlight for laughter,
Stars for their eyes.

Time and the season
Set by their toil,
Strength in blue distance,
Pride in tilled soil.

Peace like a prayer,
Unbroken sod,
Where man walked along
And listened to God.

                                    Ramona Vernon

Going back to the year 1816 there were in St. Albans 19 horses, 27 oxen, 54 cows, 47 head of two and three year olds, 22 houses, and 21 barns. The number of voters was 40, and there were 83 children in town. The largest farmer in St. Albans was John Lyford, Esquire.

He had 20 acres in mowing field and 20 acres in pastures. The largest number of cows 4, oxen 4, horses 3, young stock 10, and barns 3.

The orginal John Lyford property is owned today by Kenneth and Phyliss (Knowles) Chambers. The Chambers operate the largest farm in town. What was then 12 farms in the area make up their property.

This same year in history brought about some strange weather in Maine known as the year without a summer. Everything except rye was injured by the frost. This naturally brought about severe privation throughout the state, especially during the winter of 1816-1817.

In those early days it was necessary to combine crop raising with dairying. The wheat crop in 1837 yielded 10,294 bushels.

By 1860 the population had increased to 1808. Valuation 2,810.44, horses 285, milking cows 533, working oxen 319, other cattle 688, sheep 2,565, swine 376, 853 bu. of wheat, 447 bu. of rye, 7,429 bu. of Indian corn, 14,010 bu. of oats, and wool 6,700 lbs.

A disastrous year for the crop farmers of this region was 1870 (known as the "Grasshopper Year"). One farmer in town was more fortunate than many. His name was Thomas Ray, who purchased a farm in St. Albans in April 1870. That spring Mr. Ray planted six acres of wheat among other crops. The wheat crop flourished, and then the grasshoppers descended upon his wheat fields. He immediately thought of his large flock of turkeys penned under the barn. Thomas Ray and his son Jesse let out the turkeys and drove them through the wheat fields. The turkeys ate the grasshoppers and the Rays had a bountiful wheat crop as well as a nicely fattened flock of turkeys.

Among the most extensive farmers in town by 1913 were E. G. Crocker with a dairy herd of 40 or more cows. Frank Hanson owned one of the largest farms in the county and confined himself to general farming without having a specialty. David Grant also had an expecially fine estate and was one of the most extensive farmers in Somerset County. George Merrill, C. P. Coolidge, Frank Vining, Charles Mason, F. W. Wilkins and Nathan Richards were all conspicuous as big farmers and sterling citizens.

In 1915 Ralph Hanson started farming in St. Albans, operating a farm here as well as another in the town of Burnham. It was not long before his name as a Commission dealer was known throughout the state. From the Burnham stockyards Hanson shipped two or three carloads of stock each week to the Brighton Market, Mass. One week 13 carloads left Burnham. The business brought employment to these small communities as the stock not only had to be cared for but loaded into railroad cars. For many years on Monday nights at 11:45 p.m. Mr. Hanson would step aboard Pullman Car No. 226 and make his way to lower five, which he'd find already made up for him. Tuesday mornings you'd find Mr. Hanson in Brighton, Mass., where he conducted his business, disposing of the cows, bulls, and calves that had been entrusted to his care.

Earl Patten was another name known over a wide area as a buyer and seller of cattle. In 1920 Ralph Hanson with Earl Patten as a partner started a meat shop in the village. In 1937 Mr. Patten sold his interest in the business to Guy Smith of Oakland, California. They became known throughout a large area as Hanson and Smith. A new modern up-to-date meat shop was constructed and opened in March 1959 doing a wholesale and retail business, supplying meat to many surrounding communities.

As the years passed, farmers in St. Albans were increasing their dairy herds. One to specialize in raising purebred registered Gurnseys was Eleazor Crocker. Cory Bubar who came to St. Albans in 1926 started to specialize in purebred Gurnseys buying two from Nate Richards and four from Harry Hilton. At one time Cory Bubar and his son Wendall owned the largest Gurnsey herd in town and today it is known to be the oldest registered Gurnsey herd in existance in the state.

Farmers with large herds in 1960 were George Webber, Manley Pease, George Crocker and son Ivan, Cory Bubar and son Wendall, Elmer Chambers and son Kenneth, Sidney Mower and sons Blaine and Richard, Byron Wiers, Burnes Nelson, Jessie Merrill Sr., Ellis Thorne, Arthur Bowman, Robert Sinclair, Irving McNally, Cedric Bryant, Edward Patten, Hugh Cooney, Richard Lachance (farm previously owned by Mansfield Harris).

In 1963 Elmer Chambers and son Kenneth operated their farm with the largest herd of cattle, which consisted of 172 milking cows and 100 dry cows and young stock. Others that year with large herds were Burnes Nelson and Sidney Mower and Sons.

Crop farming has also been widely done in St. Albans. Leonel Warner moved here in 1949 from Aroostook County. He raised potatoes for several years, planting over one hundred and eighty acres. Other potato farmers were Ellis Thorne and John Webber.

In the early years the first effort in an agricultural region was the growing of the staple crops. Fruit growing has been a comparatively late development in any region, but this was not necessarily true of St. Albans as this area possesses special adaptabilities for fruits.

There is a science in the art of fruit growing, and among those who possessed this knowledge either through experience or reading was Irving Parkman, who raised apples, pears, plums, and cherries. Mr. Parkman also had the expertise needed in making maple sugar candy which was sold throughout New England. The Parkman farm is presently owned by Curtis Lombard who is interested in pursuing the same endeavors. Another apple orchard in town is owned by Harold Bishop.

Raising strawberries for local markets for many years were Bernard and Lottie Weymouth.

There are at least two who are doing market gardening today. They are Mr. and Mrs. Arthur Vicnaire and Mr. and Mrs. Harold Bishop.

Farmers in St. Albans in 1982 are Byron Wiers and son Stephen, Dana Leavitt, Sidney Mower and sons Blaine and Richard. Bruce Ballard, Kenneth Chambers, Wendall Bubar and son David, Jessie Merrill Jr., Gerald Robertson, Edward Patten, Irving McNally, Frank Sargent, Dana Hartford, Fred Massow, Byron Ballard, Earle Davis, Hugh Cooney, and Gene Cooley.

Poultry farmers — Larry Wintle and Newman Gee.

Egg Farmers — Victor Richards and Al Thurston.

Among the farmers in St. Albans that set down roots on the rolling hills that overlooked Indian Pond or settled on the crossroads comprising this small town are families who still remain on the land that was cleared by their ancestors.

One such family is that of Sidney Mower and his sons Blaine and Richard, a great-grandson of Eleazor Crocker, who made the trip from Greene, Maine back in 1820. His blood still runs through the veins of the men who make their living on the farm today. The Mowers also own and operate a maple grove which annually yields approximately 300 gallons of maple syrup.

Farming became a way of life to many other families in St. Albans. Working on the farms of either their father or grandfather or following the same line of occupation are: Gerald Robertson, Bruce Ballard, Kenneth Chambers, Byron Wiers and son, Wendall Bubar and son, Jessie Merrill, Jr., and Hugh Cooney.

# St. Albans Farms (1982)

Byron Wiers & Son

Dana Leavitt

This document was supplied by Newton Smith.

St. Albans — February 6, 1838

I DO HEREBY CERTIFY, That I have raised during the year eighteen hundred and thirty-seven twenty-two and a half bushels of well cleaned Wheat, for which I claim the bounty provided by law therefor. I further certify, that said Wheat is my property and has never received a bounty from the Treasurer of any town or plantation whatever.

John Lord     22½<br>x 6<br>$215

COUNTY OF Somerset    SS.

On this sixth day of February 1838 personally appeared before me the above John Lord and made solemn oath that the above certificate is true.

Thomas Smith, Justice of the Peace

HEREBY CERTIFY, That I have assisted in cleansing and measuring Wheat raised by John Lord and that there is twenty-two and a half bushels, and that I verily believe that said Wheat was raised by the said Lord during the year 1837.

Tobias Lord

COUNTY OF Somerset    SS.

On this sixth day of February 1838 personally appeared the above named Tobias Lord and made solemn oath that the above certificate by him subscribed is true.

Thomas Smith, Justice of the Peace

# CHAPTER VI

## ST. ALBANS POSTAL SERVICE

In the very early 1800s and for some years following, the nearest post office was located in Bangor. Letters were given to any dependable individual who happened to be in Bangor and were gladly distributed to neighbors and friends by the traveler.

In 1818 a mail route was established to cover the area between Bangor and Skowhegan. Mr. Hayden of Skowhegan was appointed mail carrier. For the first few years, the mail was carried on horseback over roads that were often difficult to negotiate and in the spring of the year dangerous when the spring freshets washed out bridges and covered swampy roads. Mr. Hayden's contract expired in 1822, and he was succeeded by Colin Campbell of Corinna and Calvin Osgood of Garland. The route traveled by the mail carrier started in Bangor and ended in Skowhegan. The towns covered were Glenburn, Kenduskeag, West Corinna, Exeter, Garland, Dexter, Ripley, Harmony, Athens, and Cornville. On his return trip he passed through the towns of Canaan, Pittsfield, Hartland, St. Albans, Palmyra, Newport, Etna, Carmel, and Hampden to Bangor.

In 1822 the post masters appointed to distribute the mail in each town included Mark Trafton, Bangor; Moses Hodgton, Kenduskeag; Richard Palmer, Corinth; Reuben Bartlett, Garland; Dr. Gilman Burleigh, Dexter; John Todd, Ripley; Mr. Bartlett, Harmony; John Ware, Athens; Thomas Smith, Cornville; John Wyman, Skowhegan; Mr. Tuttle, Canaan; Mr. Foss, St. Albans West Village (now Hartland); Dr. French, North St. Albans; Will Lancey, Palmyra; Mr. Sanger, Newport; Hollis Friend, Etna; Deacon Ruggles, Carmel; and Mr. Stetson, Hampden.

By 1826 the roads had been sufficiently improved to admit the use of a two-horse wagon. This change allowed the carrying of passengers between the towns on the mail route. This was a common service over the years until the automobile became popular. The stage carrying mail and passengers left the St. Albans Post Office around 5 a.m. A stop was made at the Hartland Post Office and shortly after 6 a.m. mail and passengers boarded the train which came puffing into Hartland depot from Harmony. Monday morning passengers were for the most part boys and girls from St. Albans and Hartland returning to MCI after a weekend at home. The travellers were warmed by a large glowing stove while waiting in the depot and kept thawed out by a smaller stove at one end of the passenger car. Although there was little traffic at that hour of the morning, the train's whistle sounded loudly as a warning at both road crossings in Palmyra.

In the town of St. Albans in 1850, Nathan Douglas kept the post office in his home. Benjamin Ireland (1802-1875) became post master in 1853. In 1863, a small building was erected on the northern edge of the present War Memorial site. The Irelands lived in the house now owned by Chrystal Goforth. The flat space between the post office and the Ireland home was made into a croquet ground and became a popular gathering place for community croquet players. Benjamin Ireland's daughter Lydia, born in 1836, was a skilled seamstress at 17, and worked at this trade until at age 27 she became assistant post mistress to her father. She held this office until 1870 when she was appointed official post mistress. Never married, she cared for her parents until their deaths and continued as post mistress until 1887 when she retired because of ill health. The Irelands, father and daughter, had served the public in St. Albans Post Office for 34 years. Daniel Frost succeeded Lydia Ireland and remained in office several years until a change of administration replaced him with Peter Folsom Emery. During World War I Minnie Martin was post mistress followed by Robert Martin, Thomas and Ruth Mills, and Freeman Mills. Earle Robertson was postmaster immediately preceding our present post mistress Hilda Chadbourne, who took office in 1941. On June 16, 1981 Mrs. Chadbourne received a certificate from the Postal Section Center in Auburn in recognition of her 40 years of service in the St. Albans Post Office. Marjorie Martin Chisholm, Joyce Sinclair, and Barbara Leavitt have been assistants over the years. RFD carriers during this period include Roy Chase, Bert Hilton, Maurice Emery, Clifford and Verne Merrill, Harlow Powers, and the present carrier, Robert Weaver.

In January 1957 the Batchelder building which housed the post office was destroyed by fire. Mrs. Chadbourne, aided by volunteers, saved all the office equipment and records and deposited them across the street in Hanson's Store. Here the mail service continued with no interruption until a vacant building on the Batchelder property could be made suitable for a temporary post office. Our present post office, an attractive modern building, is located on the original site.

From this facility, mail is distributed to 305 RFD boxes and 100 post office boxes. However, the number of customers served is much larger, as many of the boxes are used by more than one family.

The poem, The Rural Postman, was composed by Verne Merrill, a great-grandson of the first St. Albans postmaster, Nathan Douglas. It vividly describes some of the trials and tribulations endured by these faithful servants of the public in days gone by.

St. Albans Post Office (1913)

## The Rural Postman

In the cold and blustery weather
When the frost is on the rail,
Would you love to face a blizzard
With a half a ton of mail?

In the biting blizzard weather
When the snow comes to your knees,
Would you love to fish for pennies
While your feet and fingers freeze?

When the gleaming snow is drifted
Underneath a foot of sleet,
Would you love to have the chilblains
In your elbows and your feet?

When outdoors the wind is blowing
And the air is full of snow,

63

Would you love to have a jitney
    And the blamed thing wouldn't go?

Yes, I'd love the good old fireside,
    Sipping coffee from a pail,
But I have to buck the snowdrifts
    'Cause the farmers want their mail.

I don't mind the frozen snowdrifts
    When my knees are stiff with cramps,
If you keep the bloomin' pennies
    Buy a quarter's worth of stamps.

I get snow mixed in my whiskers
    And I get it in my socks,
But it never hurts my feelings
    Like loose pennies in the box.

By Verne Merrill

# CHAPTER VII

## ST. ALBANS MINES

In 1855 mining was going on in many areas of the State. We find over a period of twelve years the revenue to the state totaled $840,000. Some of these mines were located in St. Albans.

Of the fifty states comprising the U.S. of America, thirty-two have reported the existence of gold in sufficient showings to interest the casual collector, and although gold mining has not been important in Maine's extensive mineral industry, the yellow metal has been reported in streambed and bench gravels in many parts of the state.

We are reminded of the stories of how Maine Indians mined lead for musket balls and sold the precious metal for hunting and warfare to the colonists and Revolutionaries. White men tried in vain to learn the location of their mining sites.

The Indian strikes held remarkably rich ore, a near pure sulfide which could be worked by rude tools and melted over wood fires.

Dr. Thomas C. MeCoy of Waterville claimed in an interview with the Sunday Telegram in 1952 that he had discovered an Indian lead mine, located in Somerset County near Great Moose Pond, where Indians camped on the shores of the pond back before the Civil War.

In the book, "We Walk on Jewels" by Jean Blakemore; we find the following: "Pittsfield Quadrangle, St. Albans Township Map 4 -Farnum, French, Gould, Indian Lead, New St. Albans, New York, and New England, Orient, Porter and St. Albans Quarries -Reported: galena (lead) here and there silver, copper, and at St. Albans Mine, gold trace."

"Gold Hunters Cuido Book" by Jay, Ellis, Ransom tells where to find gold in the U.S. Somerset County - "Areas along Gold Brook; (a) in Chase Stream Tract Twp; placers; (b) in T5 R6 and Appleton Twps, numerous placers; (c) along the Smith branch of the Penobscot River, especially in Sandy Bay, Bald Mt., and Printess Twps - placer gold. St. Albans, the St. Albans mine, primarily lead - gold traces."

The new St. Albans, New York, and New England mine is now owned and operated by Earle Davis. The business has been incorporated and is called "Try Hard Mines, Inc."

It is said of the St. Albans mine the silver lead (or genliferous galena) obtained here was, according to one reputable account, of good quality.

## GRANITE QUARRY

The granite quarry on St. Albans Mountain was probably mined in the mid to late 1800's as we find it wasn't being operated in 1905. Joseph H. Baker was one of the early operators. Later, it became the property of the Lynn estate.

The rock, specimen 1-4 1-9, collected by Dr. George Otis Smith is as follows - a quartz diorite with conspicuous black particles on a more bluish then yellowish white ground and of medium to coarse, even ground texture with flow structure predominating.

It consists, in descending order, of an abundance of a translucent milk white soda - line feldspar (algoclase), very slightly smokey quartz, black mica (bistite), black hornblende, and accessory titanate and megnetite. Some of the feldspars cloudy, some in citient alteration.

Years ago, granite was an article everywhere in demand for architectural purposes, and while southern and western states are totally destitute of it, Maine possesses many quarries.

## BRICK YARD

A brick yard was being operated in 1850 by a Maloon family. In 1860, this property was owned by William Davis and later by E. N. Grant. The yard was located on the hill between Clark Brook and the E. N. Grant homestead. The clay certainly was suitable for making brick, for the brick used in the brick schoolhouse came from here.

Another brick yard was located on the Baird property. Bricks from here were used to build the St. Albans Academy.

## GLENWOOD MINERAL SPRING

A flourishing industry of the late 90's was the promotion and sale of water from the Glenwood Spring.

Dr. Charles A. Moulton commenced his medical career in St. Albans shortly after his graduation from Bowdoin Medical School in 1884. He became interested in the spring when he observed that many of the townspeople found the water healthful and pleasant to drink. With the cooperation of S. O. Matthews, owner of the spring, the young doctor had the water analyzed. After some vigorous advertising, the Glenwood Mineral Spring became a thriving business. For two decades regular deliveries of the water were made in St. Albans, Hartland, and Pittsfield.

For many years there was a well house built over the spring to protect it from animals and debris. A dipper hung nearby the spring to provide refreshment for those who came to drink or fill their jugs with the cool pure water.

As the years passed, interest in the project waned, the spring house collapsed, and sand choked the bubbling spring. An attempt to modernize resulted in damage to the original vein of water causing a decrease in the flow which is now intermittent. There are now few who visit the spring or remember its old activity.

Perhaps in years to come some other ambitious young man will restore the facility and Glenwood Mineral Spring will once again become a valuable asset to our town.

### Glenwood Mineral Water

A natural alkaline magnesia water of absolute purity and great medicinal value - the king of table waters, delightful in taste and healthful to all, nature's remedy for many ills. It restores the affected, prevents disease, and purifies the system. Glenwood Mineral Spring Co. — Proprietors - St. Albans, Maine.

1. What is Glenwood Mineral Water and where is it found?

The Glenwood Spring, as the name appropriately indicates, is situated in a quiet, pleasant spot surrounded with the beauties of nature in the town of St. Albans, Maine. Here a stream of water, having its origin in the depths of the earth, bubbles up through a stratum of clean gravel at the rate of a barrel per minute. Throughout the year this stream remains constantly the same, not affected in quantity by wet and dry weather or in temperature by the changes of the seasons. Through the centuries it probably has never ceased flowing, maintaining by its pure flood a sparkling, bubbling brooklet, coursing downward to the lake beneath - but like other beauties of nature, freely offered but not observed, it has been waiting to be discovered and appropriated.

2. Tried and found valuable

The discovery of the remarkable quality of this water has not been a sudden or accidental matter. It has grown out of the long and logical processes of experience. For years many of the inhabitants of the locality have believed that the water possessed remarkable qualities. By degrees this belief asserted itself more and more strongly until it was finally forced upon the attention of those who were able to make scientific investigations. During the last three or four years, it has been put to a practical test by application to a variety of diseases and with constantly increasing evidence of its remarkable properties.

3. What is the nature of the water?

Chemical analysis has simply revealed what would be expected of experience. The following is the analysis in detail: (Grains per U.S. gallon)

| | |
|---|---|
| Silica | .174 |
| Oxide of Iron | .116 |
| Alumina | .116 |
| Carbonate of Lime | 1.455 |
| Carbonate of Magnesia | 2.037 |
| Free Ammonia | .001 |
| Albuminated Ammonia | .000 |
| Total | 3.899 |

It will be seen that it contains no impurity, that it is remarkably soft, that the nature of the mineral contents renders it alkaline, and that among these the preponderating substance is carbonate of magnesia, so that it may be properly described as an alkaline magnesia water.

General information and recommendations: No other Spring like Glenwood: A Remarkable Remedy: An ideal table water. These were followed by testimonies. The testimony of a physician: Dr. C. A. Moulton, after giving his reasons for testing the spring, and speaking in general of the effect on his patients, Dr. Moulton writes, "I have used it exclusively in my own family with an apparent lessening of the usual summer and autumn diseases. In the case of my little girl who was ill every previous season, troubled with indigestion and diarrhea, there has been this year an entire freedom from any tendency to that difficulty, which I attribute to the pure water she has been drinking." Nov. 5, 1894

1/ From Hon. D. D. Stewart, Nov. 17, 1894. "I have been acquainted with the Glenwood Spring many years and use its waters constantly in my family. I know of no better or purer water."

2/ For indigestion from N. B. Turner, Esq., Manufacturer of Shovel Handles, November 1894. Dear Sirs, Last winter I was greatly troubled with indigestion, and this, together with hard work, caused me to fail in health rapidly. I became very weak, losing flesh continually and was finally confined to my room and even to my couch. About this time I heard of the Glenwood Water and, obtaining some of it, found that it relieved my thirst and in a great measure for the distress of the stomach. Often when waking up in the night with a very uncomfortable feeling, a drink of this water would relieve me so that I could easily go to sleep again. I believe that the use of this water has had a great deal to do with bringing about almost a complete recovery. I have always considered that I had one of the best wells of water in town but of late have not been able to drink the water without causing a bad feeling. On the contrary, I have always been able to drink the Glenwood Spring water with comfort and satisfaction. I have heretofore been much troubled with constipation, but find that the use of the Glenwood water regulates the bowels perfectly. N. B. Turner

3/ For the weak stomach, St. Albans, November 5, 1894

Glenwood Mineral Springs Co. Gentlemen: On account of the distress it would cause, I have for several years been obliged to avoid the use of all drinking water. While at a recent visit to the Glenwood Spring, the appearance of the water was so enticing that I made up my mind that I would have one good drink: although I would have to suffer for it. After drinking a good quantity of the water, I was surprised to have no uncomfortable feeling whatsoever. Since that time I have been able to drink of the Glenwood water continually all that is required without any difficulty. Lucretia F. Tyler


Pittsfield, Maine
Nov. 10, 1894
Glenwood Mineral Spring Co. Gentlemen: I have for some time been troubled with indigestion and other stomach difficulties. Although thirsty, all drinking water has been distasteful to me until I received the Glenwood. I enjoy it and it agrees with me perfectly. Very truly yours, Mrs. C. I. Healey

For Catarrh of the Stomach
Hartland, Maine
November 2, 1894
Glenwood Mineral Spring Co. Dear Sirs, Last winter I had an attack of catarrh of the stomach. Although suffering a great deal from thirst, I was unable to drink any water since this would be followed by nausea and distress. With the advice of my physician, I tried the so-called Glenwood water. This was immediately effectual in relieving my thirst and causing no nausea at all. I have used the water constantly since then. Mrs. Frank McCausland

For Nausea and Acid Stomach
St. Albans, Maine
November 6, 1894
Dear Sirs, I have for a long time been suffering with a lung and stomach difficulty. For three years I have been troubled about drink-

ing water as it would cause nausea and when drank in the afternoon would cause acid stomach and vomiting. I recently began using the Glenwood water and found that all these difficulties were immediately relieved. It is a source of great enjoyment to be able to drink all of the water that I desire at all times without causing discomfort. Mrs. Annie Cook

For Gastric Fever
Hartland, Maine
November 12, 1894
Glenwood Spring Co.   Dear Sirs, In January 1894 I had an attack of "grip" followed by gastric fever. For five weeks I was unable to take food or water without causing distress and vomiting. I continually suffered great thirst but no water had been found which my stomach could retain. The family physican prescribed Glenwood water, instructing me to drink 1/3 of a glass. As soon as that water was received I drank that quantity and afterwards a like quantity at intervals with entire freedom from discomfort. Ever after this I drank the water freely without causing the distress or vomiting. My subsequent recovery seemed to date from the first drink of the Glenwood water. Mrs. Albert Waldron

For Kidney Troubles
St. Albans, Maine
November 13, 1894
Gentlemen: In February 1893 I was very ill with attacks of gravel, complicated with inflammation of the kidneys. My physician prescribed Glenwood water and I believe that my entire recovery and freedom from attacks since then has been due to the habitual use of that water. I have not felt so well before for three years. Lydia Bowman

Hartland, Maine
November 8, 1894
Glenwood Mineral Spring Co.   Gentlemen: I have been suffering from general disease of the kidneys and general dropsy. I have had a severe distress in the stomach after eating or drinking. Trying the Glenwood water, I found I could drink it without any distress. I am now much better in all respects. I believe the improvement is largely due to the use of that water. Mrs. George Wheeler

St. Albans, Maine
November 14, 1894
Dear Sirs: I have for years suffered with kidney troubles and lum-

bago. I have had frequent attacks so severe as to compel me to abandon my work entirely for several days at a time. Last spring I began to use the Glenwood water and since then have had no repetition whatever of the dreaded pains. L. P. Southard

St. Albans, Maine
November 16, 1984
Gentlemen: Some time ago while suffering with a kidney trouble, I consulted my physician and obtained a prescription to relieve it. Before I began to take it my attention was called to the Glenwood water by the large number of people who were resorting to the spring. Trying the water I at once began to be relieved, and by using it continually since then, have never had occasion to take the prescribed medicine. Mrs. J. O. Matthews

For Rheumatism
St. Albans, Maine
November 6, 1894
Dear Sirs: I have for a long time been affected with a kidney trouble and rheumatism. Last spring I began using the Glenwood water and in consequence of this, have been better during the past summer than for many years before. John Bowman

St. Albans, Maine
November 13, 1894
Glenwood Mineral Spring Co.   Dear Sirs: I have for some time past been affected with chronic cystitis. I have used the Glenwood water for several months past and find it agrees with me better than any other I have tried. J. F. Butler V.S.

The Hotel
St. Albans, Maine
November 12, 1894
Dear Sirs: I have used the Glenwood water as a table water for several months past. Transient guests notice the water at once and remark that it is the finest that they ever drank. From my own personal experience I will say that two years ago I had an attack of gravel which left me with chronic cystitis from which I suffered more or less until a short time ago. I have recently been drinking the Glenwood water and as a result am now free from any trouble of the kind. E. C. Buker

The Boarding House

St. Albans, Maine

November 14, 1894

Glenwood Mineral Spring Co.    Gentlemen: We have used Glenwood water upon the table during the past summer. Our boarders who have once drank it would not be satisfied with any other water.

Mrs. D. R. Longley

For Domestic Purposes

St. Albans, Maine

November 12, 1894

Dear Sirs: I have used the Glenwood water during the past summer for the table and for other purposes. When used in preparing tea and coffee, it adds a perceptable and agreeable flavor. The water is a great addition to our domestic comfort.

H. C. Prescott
Ex-Postmaster of St. Albans

Boston, Massachusetts

July 6, 1894

The freedom of this water from organic and other impurities renders it a most excellent water for medicinal or domestic purposes.

S. S. Bradford, PH. C.

At present the property of Jennie Springer, the spring, of late years has become less productive. The spring house and the cement foundation deteriorated with time and attempts to repair it with tiling were unsuccessful. Now only a few take advantage of this excellent water which still continues to bubble up from the "Stratum of clean gravel".

# CHAPTER VIII

## STORES AND STOREKEEPERS

For some years there have been only two general stores in St. Albans with the emphasis on groceries, meat, and a few incidentals such as cards and school supplies. Each has its specialty: Dick's Market owned by Mr. and Mrs. Richard Dunham produces pizzas and Italian sandwiches and has an excellent meat department; the General Store owned and managed by Mr. and Mrs. Albert Barrows and Mr. and Mrs. Thomas Roach sells ice cream cones, coffee and hot dogs, and has a supply of health foods, grain, herbs, and flowering plants.

In 1851 three merchants are listed in the Maine Register: P. R. Webber, C. B. Tracey, and Sullivan Lothrop. Mr. Lothrop's store was in the Tannery section of the town, the others located where the present stores are. The lower store was built by T. B. Seekins and the upper or corner store was located in the building owned by D. D. Stewart whose law office occupied the second floor.

By 1882-83 the register still listed Sullivan Lothrop but Prescott and Hurd were proprietors of the upper store with Matthews and Wilbur down at the bridge; another general store built where the War Memorial is now was being run by Calvin and Melvin Bigelow. This store was burned in 1900 and was not rebuilt. At the time of the fire two young men, Alfred Bigelow and Othello Goodwin, were the proprietors. During these years both stores sold hardware, dishes, dress materials, and other yard goods, and a variety of small wares. When Edward Bridgham kept the lower store in the 90's, his wife Myra, daughter of T. B. Seekins, had a millinery shop in the large room over the store. The 1915-16 register lists the owners of the two stores as C. C. Hanson and W. H. Watson.

During the early 1900's Stephen Prescott was storekeeper and he was succeeded by his son Halvor in partnership with O. W. Bigelow. C. C. Hanson purchased the store from these two young men. Except for a time in the mid-twenties when Ervin Parkman was the owner, the corner store was the property of the Hanson family. Glenn and Vera Hanson were proprietors of what was known as Hanson's Store. Following her husband's death in 1957, Mrs. Hanson carried on the business until the mid-seventies.

In the 90's and early 1900's there were almost no packaged foods on the merchants' shelves and canned products were few. Canned oysters and Vienna sausages were considered luxuries to be

73

purchased only for special occasions. Most meat, vegetables, and fruits were thriftily grown and preserved at home. Sugar and flour were bought by the barrel, vinegar and molasses by the keg. Oranges and lemons were occasional treats and when a bunch of bananas was purchased by one of the storekeepers they were sold one or two at a time and frequently eaten on the premises. The custom of eating watermelon on the 4th of July has been kept over the years and was a holiday delicacy. For the younger purchasers, jaw breakers, licorice sticks, lemon drops, and peppermints were available. Strong rivals of these sweets were dill pickles, kept in a keg behind the counter. For 2 cents the young purchaser was allowed to choose his pickle which was speared by the storekeeper and presented cold and dripping to the customer.

Times and manners and purchasable goods have changed with the years, but St. Albans is fortunate in having two grocery stores whose proprietors have a goal not only of making sales but of making friends.

St. Albans General Store (1912)

Dick's General Store (Purchased from James Seekins)

Bigelow & Goodwin — 1800's
Left to right, Edson Buker, A. P. Bigelow, Othello Goodwin, unknown, Melvin Bigelow
Daniel Frost, Henry Prescott on bicycle.

# CHAPTER IX

## INDUSTRY: MILLS AND MANUFACTURERS

St. Albans has never been a manufacturing center. No large mill owners built here. For many years the American Woolen Mill in Hartland gave employment to St. Albans people as the Irving Tanning Company does today. With the use of the automobile, workers find distance less of a problem and mills and factories in Dexter, Newport, Corinna, and Pittsfield provide employment to home owners in our town.

However, since the earliest days of our settlement many small mills have played an active part in the life of our community. As the need arose individual settlers constructed their own small mills for dealing with the products of their farms and wood lots. They accommodated themselves and their neighbors by serving different areas of the town.

Hayward's New England Gazeteer published in 1839 says in its description of St. Albans: "The town contains a large and beautiful pond, the outlet of which forms a good mill stream, a branch of the Sebasticook River."

There were two centers of activity in the early mill development; one in the village proper between the two dams, the other further down the stream in the area known as the Tannery or by its less complimentary name of Shakerag. Sullivan Lothrop was Justice of the Peace, merchant, tanner, dealer in hides and leather. He served as selectman for 23 years, his last term 1878-1879. He was town clerk in 1869-1870. He and his wife, Susan (Bigelow) Lothrop built and occupied the house now owned by Harold Bishop. It was from this house that he supervised the settlement built on Indian Stream. Besides the tannery and a drying house, a grist mill was also built near the bridge. Between the Hartland road and the mill site Mr. Lothrop built seven houses and a store to accommodate his workmen. The town lost some of its records when the store burned. Three of the old houses are still standing.

In 1830 Holman Johnson came to St. Albans and built a grist mill on the east shore of Indian Stream just across from the Grange Hall and the Town House. In the early 1840's he built a factory for the manufacturing of shovel handles on the same site. These were made by hand. In 1848 he bought the Bartlett Turning Lathe and Punch, a welcome innovation to the patient workmen. In 1853 Holman decided to go to Wayne, Maine to establish another wood working factory and sold out to Napoleon Bonaparte Turner Sr., a St. Albans native. Napoleon was the son of William Turner born in 1797 who came to St. Albans about 1820 and raised thirteen children. Napoleon, the third child, was born in 1824 and died in 1896. His son Napoleon Bonaparte Jr. operated the mill until 1903 when it was leased to the Ames Shovel and Tool Company of North Easton, Massachusetts. In 1904 $15,000 worth of shovel handles were shipped to Massachusetts. Much of the continued success of the undertaking came from the skill and devotion of Otis Turner, a family member, and the faithful and careful work of the employees, all of whom were local men. At the close of the shovel handle era for about 20 years the building was used for a repair and carpentry shop by George and James Martin and John Goodwin. The last owners, Calvin Southard and William H. Watson, sold to C. A. Batchelder. Mr. Batchelder built a sprawling three-story building on the west side of the river opposite the original factory, connecting the two by a cat walk which enabled the 40 employees to cross the stream quickly from one building to the other. In these two buildings were manufactured shoetrees, artificial limbs, and wooden novelties. Following Mr. Batchelder's death in 1945, Ralph and Ted McNichol came from Massachusetts, purchased the mill and merged with the Leader Last Company also of Massachusetts. The name Selwell Products Co. Inc. was given to the merger. The business prospered, giving local employees a payroll of $1,100 weekly. This lucrative project ended in 1947 when the larger building was completely destroyed by fire. In 1950 Harold Bishop who with his brother Kenneth had a saw mill on the Bishop farm, bought the original shovel handle factory. Here he manufactured cedar fencing which he shipped to Boston. This building burned in 1967. With this sad occurrence was ended more than a hundred years of industrial activity on the village mill stream.

In 1887 Lucius Phinney came from Portland and built a corn factory near where Victor Springer's mill now stands. As the Baxter Brothers Canning Company this was for many years an active part of our comminity. During the late summer and fall loads of corn were brought in by horse drawn hay racks and farm wagons, and dumped in great heaps under a large shed. Daily these piles were surrounded by local men and women who husked the ears, filling bushel baskets which were transferred to the factory proper for testing, cooking, and putting into tin cans. These were sealed and taken in large trays to a shed to be labeled after the active corn season was over. For many women the five cents a basket earned during the corn canning weeks made most of their Christmas gift money. A quick husker could easily earn $2 a day at the height of the season.

Another task which often lasted well into November was the labeling and packing of the corn. Boxes were made at the factory and women were employed in marking the cans with labels provided by the firms to which they were sent. It was a matter of amusement that the S. S. Pierce can labeled "superior" and those destined for the less pretentious Great Atlantic and Pacific Tea Company were the same product. After string beans and peas were added to the canning program and with expansion in mechanical processes, the Baxter activities were moved to Hartland and Corinna where the Snow Flake Canning Company flourished for many years. On the land vacated by the Baxter factory, Charles E. Mower established an extensive lumber yard and saw mill. This was damaged by fire in 1954. Restored by the owner who retired in 1956, the plant was bought by Victor Springer who had been associated with Mr. Mower. The Victor Springer Building and Lumber Co. enlarged and improved is now a flourishing business providing many building supplies as well as lumber.

At the present time active sawmills are operated by Timothy Ballard, Andy Lawrence, and Sidney Mower and Sons Blaine and Richard although none are located on Indian Stream.

A glance at some of the Maine State Yearbooks shows the status of industry in St. Albans and the changes made over the years.

In 1861 — Sullivan Lothrop, N. B. Turner, Benjamin Ireland, and Thomas A. Whitney are listed as "mill men" dealing in lumbering, tanning, and carriage making. John Smith was the only blacksmith.

In 1882-83 — there were three blacksmiths; John Parker, Henry Murray and Benton Parkman; N. B. Turner, Shovel Handles; Volney H. Bragg, doors and sash; J. S. Martin, shingles; Sullivan Lothrop and Charles Philbrick, lumber; Millard Metcalf, tailor and barber; Darius Emery, grist mill; Edson Buker, harnesses.

In 1915 — there were still three blacksmiths - Herbert Cyphers, A. E. Bradford, and Herbert Foss. The Snowflake Canning Company and the C. A. Batchelder factory were at their height of production. The St. Albans Cheese Association with David N. Grant was still in operation.

In 1927-28 — Snowflake Canning Company and C. A. Batchelder are still listed; C. E. Mower, saw mill; Earl C. Weeks was the only blacksmith. For the first time the summer camp industry was listed with Elva Parker as proprietor of Camp St. Albans at the head of the lake. During this period the Weeks family of Hyde Park, Massachusetts, conducted a summer camp for boys on Picnic Point, now the location of the Martin camps. Melvin H. Martin is listed as a dealer in automobiles.

Over the years dairying has been a major industry in our town. Probably the first organized creamery and cheese factory was owned and managed by I. O. Winslow in the 1800's. This enterprise was carried on in a building Isaac constructed on the property of his father William near where Elwood Allen now lives. About 1890 a cheese factory was owned by a stock company made up of W. H. Watson, Pres.; Frank Varney, Sec.; and Albert T. Hurd, Treas. Located on the Todd's Corner Road on land now owned by Edward Patten, the factory closed in 1907.

In the 1880's and through two decades of the 1900's it was considered a matter of course for families to "keep a cow". Those who had no means or desire to do so were supplied by their neighbors and were charged five cents a quart. Any in the village who had no land available took their cows to a neighboring pasture early every summer morning and led them home at night. Each cow was equipped with a bell in case she strayed, but usually they were waiting at the pasture bars ready for the leisurely stroll home. Later, milk deliveries were made from home dairies. Dana Martin conducted a successful dairy operation for many years, making daily milk deliveries in St. Albans and Hartland.

Gradually as government regulations increased and technology geared us to speed and efficiency in production, individual enterprises became fewer. Although progress has brought many things to make our lives easier and more varied, the virtues of independence, responsibility, and neighborliness fostered by the early settlers of St. Albans must never be forgotten.

Baxter's Snowflake Canning Co. (1900's)

Batchelder's Wooden Products.
Shovel Handle Factory (Burned in 1947.)

# CHAPTER X

## HARTLAND AND ST. ALBANS TELEPHONE COMPANY

A member of the Telephone and Data System, Inc. serving 2,069 customers in Harmony, Hartland, Palmyra, St. Albans, and West Ripley, the Hartland And St. Albans Telephone Company has come a long way from its beginning in 1893.

Dr. Charles A. Moulton felt the need for a means of communication in the area he served as a family doctor and with local backing he started the St. Albans Telegraph Company.

The company was formed by John P. Baxter Jr., Dr. Charles A. Moulton, Napoleon Bonaparte Turner, David Dinsmore Stewart, and A. T. Hurd. At first second-hand telegraph instruments were used to make contact between the two towns, St. Albans and Hartland. The Board voted to give Stephen B. Prescott, proprietor of what is now St. Albans General Store, 2.5 cents for taking and sending each message. The rate to Hartland was 10 cents a message.

On July 23, 1894 Dr. Moulton took over the company, replacing the telegraph instruments with telephones. The telephone was still located in the Prescott Store but free use was allowed, although the 10 cent rate to Hartland was still kept. The first telephone directory listed twelve customers, for the most part business firms. All the telephones were on one line so no operator was needed!

It was in 1903 after the Moultons moved to Hartland that the company was incorporated as the Hartland - St. Albans Telephone Company with the office located in an upstairs room in the Moulton home. One of the early operators was Congressman Clyde Smith, late husband of Senator Margaret Chase Smith. Another operator, Beulah Rowe, for many years served the telephone patrons, not only in her official capacity but as a general source of information, advice, and social communication. In case of an accident, need to contact a family member, or telling the right time, her cheerful and efficient response added much to the well being of the community. Mrs. Rowe was an employee of the company until 1968.

The Telephone Company has remained in the same location over the years, expanding its quarters and modernizing the service. From the crank telephone on the wall to the dial system, from the "party line" and single operator to an elaborate and impersonal computer-run operation, the Hartland and St. Albans Telephone Company has continued to serve an ever widening area. Dr. Moulton was president of the company until his death in 1946 at the age of

86. His son, Dr. Arthur Moulton, succeeded his father as president of the company. In 1971 when the company became a part of the new telephone holding company, Telephone Data Systems, Inc., Dr. Arthur Moulton commented, "People won't even know the company has changed hands." This assurance is largely justified because of the continued service of the company employees, all local citizens.

In 1981 these are Carl Palmer, Palmyra, Manager; Geraldine Cole and Carolyn Wheeler, both of Hartland, Service Representatives; Donald Nichols, Hartland, C.O.E. Technician; Dana Carr, Hartland, Construction Foreman; Robert Giggey, Hartland, Curtis Lombard and Harvey Martin both of St. Albans, Installers, Repairmen, and Linemen.

# CHAPTER XI

## BIRTHDAYS AND HOLIDAYS

Before the days of the automobile, the national holidays of Memorial Day and the Fourth of July were celebrated at home.

In the early 1900's, May 30 began with the small procession of Civil War Veterans and school children led by Franklin Luce playing the flute he had used in the War. Bearing their sprays of flowers and small American flags, the boys and girls marched to the village cemetery for the playing of taps and a prayer by the Union Church minister. Many drove in from the farms to watch the parade and eat picnic lunches while visiting with friends in the village. In the afternoon all gathered at the Town Hall to salute the flag, sing **America,** and listen to an address by a Maine political, legal, or religious dignitary. One special celebration of Memorial Day took place on Sunday, May 28, 1944, when the St. Albans Roll of Honor was dedicated. A large audience enjoyed the afternoon programme.

| | |
|---|---|
| Parade of Organizations | Fairfield H. S. Band |
| Invocation | Rev. J. Kenneth Holliday |
| National Anthem | |
| Salute to Flag | Chairman Verne Merrill |
| Lincoln's Gettysburg Address | Chester E. Carson |
| Presentation of Honor Roll | George C. Crocker |
| Unveiling of Honor Roll | |
| A Rendezvouz with Death | Harlow Powers |
| Solo | Guy R. Smith |
| Memorial Poem | Mrs. Lottie E. York |
| | (State Grange Lecturer) |
| Address | Senator R. Owen Brewster |
| America | Fairfield H. S. Band |
| Benediction | Rev. J. Kenneth Holliday |

Committee:

Verne A. Merrill, Lura L. Crocker, Roy Chase, Mansfield J. Harris, George C. Crocker, Marjorie Mower, Marjorie Martin.

On the Fourth of July the day began at midnight on the third. At that hour the Church bell and the school bell rang for half an hour with the young men of the town taking turns at the bell ropes. Noise, shouting, and general activity went on until dawn when everyone went home to get a little sleep before the day's celebration. Again there was a parade, this time for fun with all taking part wearing laughter-provoking costumes. At night the Hartland-St. Albans Band gave a concert in the bandstand located on the hill above the post office. A spectacular display of fireworks from the same location ended the celebration of Independence Day in St. Albans.

## CENTENNIAL

St. Albans celebrated two birthdays in the 1900's. On June 13, 1913, the town was 100 years old. For months preceding this date, committees worked. Their efforts were rewarded by a big turnout of visitors on a perfect June day. From Dec. 12, 1912, through April 16, 1914, the Centennial treasurer, A. P. Bigelow collected $656.54 to pay the expenses of the celebration. Eighty-eight contributions were made ranging from 50 cents to $10. This sum paid for the music, $104.20, beans for the free dinner, $18, and bunting and flags to decorate every building in the village, $104.

Following is a copy of the programme used at the Centennial Celebration on June 13, 1913:

### PROGRAM OF THE DAY
Salute of Cannon at Sunrise

9:00 a.m.   Band Concert, Waterville Band.
9:30 a.m.   Tent-pitching Drill, Co. A, 2nd Infantry, N.G.S.M., Pittsfield.
10:00 a.m.  Civic and Industrial Parade.
12:00 noon  Dinner. Beans baked in the ground, coffee or lemonade free.
1:30 p.m.   Band Concert
2:00 p.m.   Literary Exercises. Meeting called to order by O. W. Bigelow, Chairman Program Committee. Prayer, Rev. Roland A. Farnham, No. Vassalboro. Address of Welcome, Fred Lucas, 1st Selectman. "Why We Celebrate," S. H. Goodwin, Chairman afternoon exercises. Sketches of Town's History, Mrs. Anna L. Vining, Mrs. Myra Goodwin. Vocal Solo, Mrs. Ada Southard Lombard, Windsor, VT. Address, Gov. William T. Haines.
"Recollections of My Old Home", Daniel Lewis Esq., Skowhegan
"The Church", Rev. Albert W. Frye, Pastor M. E. Church
"The G.A.R.", F. W. Paige, Palmyra.
"Progress of a Century", George H. Morse Esq., Bangor.

Reading, Mrs. Vivian Laughton James, Berlin, N.H.
Address, Hon. D. D. Stewart.
"Our Schools", Harriet E. Fortier, Supt.
Vocal Solo, Goodwin Parker, Lewiston.
Original Poem, "Echoes From Hackett Hill", S. H. Goodwin
"The Doctors", Dr. F. O. Lyford, Farmington.
"The Grange", Hugh F. Goodwin, Master St. Albans Grange.
"Strawberry Art Club", Mrs. Addie Emery.
Letters from Absent Ones, Mrs. Susie J. Lucas.
Vocal Solo, Mrs. Wynifred Staples Smith, Rumford.
Miss Mable C. Johnson, Accompanist, Lewiston.
Singing, "America", by the audience.

4:00 p.m.   Battalion Drill, Co. A, 2nd Infantry, N.G.S.M., Louis O. Haskell, Capt.
4:30 p.m.   Running races and other sports.
5:00 p.m.   Band Concert.

## PROGRAM OF THE EVENING

7:45-8:15   Concert by Drew's Orchestra, Waterville.
            Reading, Mrs. Vivian Laughton James
            Vocal Solo, Mrs. Wynifred Staples Smith
            Piano Solo, Miss Mable C. Johnson
            Reading, Mrs. Vivian Laughton James
            Vocal Solo, Mrs. Wynifred Staples Smith
10:00 p.m.  Grand Centennial Ball/Music by Drew's Orchestra
            Order of Dances:

| | |
|---|---|
| 1. Waltz | 8. Round Dances |
| 2. Lady of the Lake | 9. Quadrille |
| 3. Quadrille | 10. Boston Fancy |
| 4. Waltz and Schottische | 11. Schottische and Two-step |
| 5. Spanish and Hop | 12. Chorus Jig |
| 6. Hulls Victory | 13. Quadrille, Lancers |
| 7. Waltz and Two-step | 14. Waltz |
| INTERMISSION | EXTRAS |

Floor Directors: W. O. Hilton and F. N. Vining
Aides: M. H. Martin, O. W. Bigelow, H. F. Goodwin, and H. E. Prescott

# TOWN OFFICERS
## St. Albans, 1913
* * *

FRED LUCAS, 1st Selectman
DANIEL L. FROST, 2nd Selectman
LEWIS B. JOHNSON, 3rd Selectman
C. C. HANSON, Town Treasurer
DANIEL L. FROST, Town Clerk

* * *

## SOCIETIES AND OFFICERS, 1913
### GEO. A. GOODWIN POST, G. A. R., No. 23
H. O. Turner, Commander    Sullivan Johnson, Adjutant

* * *

### WOMAN'S RELIEF CORPS, No. 25
Mrs. Rebecca Martin, President

* * *

### ST. ALBANS GRANGE, No. 114, P. of H.
Hugh F. Goodwin, Master    Verne Merrill, Overseer
Mrs. Addie Emery, Lecturer

* * *

### WOMAN'S CHRISTIAN TEMPERANCE UNION
Mrs. Martha Boynton, President

* * *

### HELPFUL WORKERS
Mrs. Anna Prescott, President

* * *

### EAST ST. ALBANS LIBRARY ASSOCIATION
Mrs. Nettie Mower, Librarian

* * *

### STRAWBERRY ART CLUB
Mrs Minnie C. Southard, President

86

# CENTENNIAL COMMITTEES

\* \* \*

STUART H. GOODWIN, Chairman General Committee
HENRY C. PRESCOTT, Secretary
ALFRED P. BIGELOW, Treasurer

\* \* \*

**Historical Committee**
Hon. D. D. Stewart
Mrs. Anna L. Vining
Mrs. Myra Goodwin

**Committee on Correspondence**
Hon. Milton L. Merrill
Mrs. Susie J. Lucas
Mrs. Mabel Bigelow

\* \* \*

**Committee on Program**
Oscar W. Bigelow
Lincoln Merrick
Mrs. Lena Mebane

**Committee on Decorations**
Walter O. Hilton
Preston W. Libby
Mrs. Martha Brawn

\* \* \*

**Reception Committee**
Mr. and Mrs. Fred Lucas
Mr. and Mrs. D. R. Longley
Mr. and Mrs. H. O. Turner

Mr. and Mrs. Hugh F. Goodwin
Mr. and Mrs. Daniel L. Frost
Mr. and Mrs. Lewis B. Johnson

\* \* \*

**Committee on Refreshments**
C. C. Hanson
Chas. S. Hilton
Chas. E. Mower

**Committee on Parade and Sports**
Frank N. Vining
C. J. Worthen
M. H. Martin

\* \* \*

**Committee on Souvenirs and Badges**
W. H. Watson
Miss Stella Emery
Mrs. Gladys Avery

**Committee on Printing and Antiques**
Albert F. Hurd
Elwyn N. Grant
Selden J. Martin

## SESQUICENTENNIAL

\* \* \*

On June 15, 1963, St. Albans celebrated her Sesquicentennial. Below are listed the Sesquicentennial committees formed for this special celebration and also the program of the day.

## GENERAL COMMITTEE

Fred Cooper, Chairman     Frances Seekins, Assistant Chairman
James Seekins, Assistant Chairman     Ellen Cooper, Secretary
Everett Graham, Treasurer

\* \* \*

### Historical Committee
Lura Crocker
Vertine Ellis
Ellen Cooper

### Correspondence Committee
Gladys Bigelow
Gertrude Robinson
Mildred Patten

\* \* \*

### Program Committee
Elmer Fisher
Meredith Fisher

### Antique Committee
Pearl Merrill
Helen Finson
Guy Smith
Madalene Smith

### Honorary Members
Oscar Bigelow
Lena Richards

\* \* \*

### Printing and Advertising Committee
Helen Springer     Frances Seekins
Ellen Cooper     Gordon Woodman
Marilyn Wiers     Emma Williams
Rebecca Gilkey

\* \* \*

### Souvenir Committee
Marjorie Martin     Mary Helen Thorne

Brian Hanson    Crystal Robertson
Harlow Powers  Gladys Wilkins,HonoraryMember

\* \* \*

## RECEPTION COMMITTEE
Kenneth Hughes  Byron Ballard
Dorothea Hughes  Doris Ballard
Hugh Goodwin, Honorary Member

\* \* \*

## DECORATION COMMITTEE
Ivan Crocker  Brian Hanson
Charles Boyd  Maurice Sawyer

\* \* \*

## REFRESHMENT COMMITTEE
Walter Butler    Arthur Smith
Verne Merrill    Oren Neal
Guy Wood
Charles Mower, Honorary Member

\* \* \*

## PARADE COMMITTEE
Herbert Wentworth  Allan Thorne
Fred Cooper  Gordon Woodman
James Seekins  Edna Wood
Robert Landry

\* \* \*

## SPORTS COMMITTEE
Clair Russell  Laurence Springer
Everett Holt  Harlow Powers

\* \* \*

## TRAFFIC AND POLICE COMMITTEE
Ben Melanson

## CANNON SALUTE COMMITTEE
Harold Seekins
Harry Finson

## PROGRAM OF THE DAY
### Salute of Cannon at Sunrise

| | |
|---|---|
| 9:30 a.m.-11:00 a.m. | Parade |
| 11:00 a.m.-12:00 p.m. | Open House at Union Church |
| 3:00 p.m.- 5:00 p.m. | Open House at Union Church |
| 11:00 a.m.- 2:00 p.m. | Antique and Relic Exhibit at Chatterbox Club Rooms |
| 3:00 p.m.- 5: p.m. | Antique and Relic Exhibit at Chatterbox Club Rooms |
| 11:00 a.m.- 1:30 p.m. | Dinner - Barbecued Chicken |
| 11:00 a.m.- 1:30 p.m. | Bowling - Town Hall Yard; Horseshoe Pitching - Town Hall Yard; and Beano -Grange Hall |
| 1:30 p.m.- 2:00 p.m. | Band Concert - Hartland Academy Band |
| 2:00 p.m.- 3:00 p.m. | Literary Exercises |
| | Meeting called to order by Fred Cooper, chairman Sesquicentennial |
| | Prayer - Rev. Charles F. Talmadge |
| | Flag Salute |
| | Band and Community Sing - Star Spangled Banner |
| | Dedication War Memorial - Colonel Lawrence Webster, Assistant Adjutant General |
| | Sketches Town History - Gladys Bigelow |
| | Chorus and Parade of Costumes |
| | Trumpet Trio |
| | Letters from Absent Ones - Barbara Patten |
| | Music - Hartland Academy Band |
| 3:00 p.m.- 6:00 p.m. | Pony Pull - Consolidated School Yard |
| 3:00 p.m.- 8:00 p.m. | Beano - Grange Hall |
| 7:30 p.m.- 8:30 p.m. | Band Concert - Hartland Academy Band |
| 9:00 p.m.-12:00 p.m. | Street Dance. |

Now we look forward to the year 2013 when on a sunny June day, a new group of St. Albans citizens will gather to celebrate the completion of 200 years in the life of our town.

### HAPPY BIRTHDAY!

# CHAPTER XII

## THE SCHOOLS

The little red schoolhouse, like the buffalo and the horse and buggy, has become a dim historical memory. Once upon a time it was the hub of the community, the haven of learning, and the wellspring of all the virtues.

They were of a pattern, clapboards or brick painted red or white. The schoolhouse was not designed to make rosy the road of learning - a big pot bellied stove in the center aisle, a row of desks on either side, the teacher's desk up front on a little platform with a blackboard behind, and always a lot of chalk. There were hooks along the back wall for clothes. There too was the water pail, with a big long handled dipper, an A, B, C chart by the teacher's desk, maps hanging from the wall, and a globe to show the world was round.

Education came the hard way; you didn't take it lightly, and it stuck with you.

Dr. Henry Suzzallo, in his monograph "The Rise of Local School Supervision in Massachusetts", has shown how school supervision was developed and legalized in the Colony laws for education up to and through the period of the beginnings of schools in Maine.

The law of 1647 placed the responsibility for schools upon the town as a whole and had resulted in the town meeting attending to two of the most fundamental acts for the establishment and maintenance of a school, the choosing of the schoolmaster, and the providing for his support. The law of 1693 placed the responsibility in two places, upon the selectmen and upon the inhabitants as a whole of such towns.

The law of 1701-02 placed the power of certification of the grammar schoolmaster in the hands of a majority of the ministers of the town. This law showed a strong tendency toward the use of school committees before the practice became legalized in the law of 1789. Much of this development except the legalization of the school committee had taken place before Maine became a part of Massachusetts in 1692.

The early schools of St. Albans, like those of other Maine towns, were established under the most difficult circumstances, but were nevertheless established upon a basis that has developed school systems as successful as any in the state. As we look back today over the progress of our school system, we dwell with pride upon the record it has made. But this system, like all others, was expected to advance, and it has advanced. This town has, in common with other towns, reared the homely structures on the hillsides and at the crossroads, hired male teachers at $10 to $15 a month, and female teachers at 75 cents to $1.50 a week, and this with the board around- provision.

"When the first schoolhouse was erected in St. Albans, or where the building was located, we are unable to state, ("The Hartland and St. Albans Register 1904" compiled by Mitchell, Remick and Bean,) but after considerable research we feel it was the Tracy schoolhouse built in 1815 on the mountain.

We find St. Albans supported 17 schools, besides the school in the village. All of the schoolhouses were made of wood, except the Brick schoolhouse which is still standing and is approximately 152 years old. These schools included the Lang, Hopkins, Tannery, Tracy, Parker Dow, Lyford, Dixie, Merrill, Lucus, Magoon, Five Corners, Pond Rd., Town Farm, Lothrop, Chambers, Brick and Mountain.

Taken from - A Record of Legal Proceedings of District No. 3
1837-1882
(Kept in the safe at the Augusta State Library)

To Parker Dow, School Agent for District No. 3

You are hereby required in the name of the State of Maine to summons and notify the inhabitants of School District No. 3 in said town to assemble at Parker Dow's dwelling house in 3 District on Thursday the eleventh day of April at six o'clock p.m. to act on the following articles:

1. To choose a moderator.
2. To choose a district clerk.
3. To see if the district will agree to build a schoolhouse in 3 District and determine where the same shall be built to locate.
4. To raise a sum of money to build a schoolhouse.
5. To choose a committee to superintend the building of said house and pass such articles relative to building p. house and expending money as may be deemed necessary.
6. To determine what sum of money shall be expended in a school taught by a mistress this summer.
7. To determine where this school shall be kept this summer

and pass such votes relative to the same as they shall think proper.

Given under our hand this third day of April A.D. 1837.

Peleg Haskell
Sullivan Lothrop
Selectmen of St. Albans

A true copy - attest - Nathaniel Tenny, District Clerk

Pursuant to the above warrent District No. 3 in St. Albans were legally notified to meet December 10, 1837. Vote:

1. For Parker Dow for moderator.
2. For Nathaniel Tenney, Clerk of the District, who took the oath of office from the moderator.
3. Voted to build a schoolhouse for the district.
4. Voted to set the schoolhouse nearest the center of the district on the most convenient spot.
5. Voted to raise a sum of money to build a schoolhouse.
6. Voted for the purpose one hundred eighteen dollars.
7. To assess this sum on the next year's valuation of 3 District.
8. Voted a committee to superintend the expending of the money.
9. Voted the committee:
   1. Mark Buzzell
   2. Thomas Philbrick
   3. Dennis Philbrick
10. Voted to adjourn the meeting to next Thursday evening at six o'clock at Parker Dow's house.

December 23 - Thursday evening at six o'clock met according to adjournment. Voted to:

1. Locate the schoolhouse on the line between the land of Mark Buzzell and Nathaniel Tenney on the new road leading from the center of town by P. Buzzell's house.
2. Build a schoolhouse twenty-two feet square and to set up the work in lots to be struck off to the lowest bidders.

The framing of the house to be well underpinned with common stones struck to H. Lancaster for sixteen dollars 25 cents to be completed the first of June next.

Boarding and funding nails to D. Devereaux at fourteen dollars 75 cents by the tenth of June.

Making and sitting window frames to Th. Philbrick, 2nd of June at three dollars. Making a hanging outside door, double boarded, iron box lock, and four panes of glass over it.

Five dollars 50 cents E. Devereaux, June 15 - outside trimmings with the stuff except saddleboards. James Rogers, six dollars 50 cents, June 20 - Furnishing materials and shingling roof; J. Rogers, twelve dollars, July 1.

Double floor top spraid - Mark Buzzell, seven dollars, July 10. Sash and glass, J. Rogers, ten dollars 40 cents, July 12. Clapboarding walls, J. Rogers, seventeen dollars.

Funding materials and fitting for locking, P. Dow, eighteen dollars 75 cents, October 15.

Latching and plastering and funding materials, J. Rogers, eight dollars and 75 cents, October 25.

Seats and desks including teacher's desk, Th. Philbrick, eighteen dollars and 75 cents, November 1.

A true transcript - Nathaniel Tenney, Clerk of District

1838, Mark Buzzell was school agent. The money that year was expended in a winter school taught by Julia Ann Rowe. The school was kept fourteen weeks at $1.25 per week. Board was furnished by Nathaniel Tenney.

1839, Scholars in district reported:

| | |
|---|---|
| Thomas Philbrook | 5 |
| R. Dexter | 5 |
| M. Buzzell | 4 |
| J. Rogers | 3 |
| T. B. Tenney | 2 |
| N. Tenney | 2 |
| Elisha Devereaux | 2 |
| Dennis Devereaux | 2 |
| Chandler Dow | 1 |
| Jere Chessley | 1 |
| Haze Lancaster | 1 |
| Total | 28 |

A village school was constructed in 1832 - John Marble of Harmony, Mr. Weston, and Ozias Millett were among the early teachers. The school attendance then averaged eighty pupils. This building burned in 1843 and was replaced with a two story structure in 1846. The first term of the primary school downstairs was taught by Miss Araminta Merrick. The Grammer school upstairs was taught by Hon. D. D. Stewart. Miss Merrick afterwards became Mrs. Stewart.

You will note in the manuscript written by Rena L. Winslow, "A Quaker Family in Maine", she refers to a two story building in the village in 1874, which documents the two story structure built in 1846.

Some years after 1874 the St. Albans Village school burned in the night. Because of a dense fog, the Mountain Road children started to school as usual, unaware of the fire until they arrived in the village to view only the smouldering ruins of their school.

The beginning of the St. Albans Village school as we know it today was constructed in 1883. This building consisted of two rooms with coat rooms on either side. The height of the rooms was sixteen feet, making it impossible to maintain an even temperature.

To many it will be of interest to learn this building served as a free high school, playing an important factor in the educational system of this town, and proved immense value to those who were unable to attend an instruction of higher grade. This free high school served the town until approximately 1912. This is not to be confused with Hartland Academy, Incorporated Feb. 11, 1832 as St. Albans Academy, which at that time was located in St. Albans.

The following document was contributed by Brian Hanson, a great-grandson of Daniel Hanson.

Specifications of School building to be erected in District 11 town of St. Albans.

Main Building 30 x 50    /30 from east to
Front Annex 8 x 25  west to
Rear 10 x 12    50 from north to south

FOUNDATION

Building to be underpinned with split stone 18-inches wide as follows: commencing on west side of Main Building 8 ft. from south end, running to north end, across north end, on each side to Annex around Annex, and on East side to within 8 ft. of south end. The ground shall be leveled, and the underpinning set on good stone, same as foundation of old Schoolhouse. The remaining 8 ft. of south end be excavated 6 ft. below the sills for basement. There shall be two stone blockings under each cross sill, one under the middle of front sill of main building. The Basement shall be underpinned same as Main house. Frame of sound hemlock or strait grained spruce. All sills shall be 8x8 square of sound hemlock. There shall be 3 cross sills in Main Building besides the end sills and one cross sill in Front Annex. Also four tie sills in center of Main Building.

Sleepers 3x6 not more than 2½ ft. from center. To have two rows of bridging sill and plates. All door, window, and corner posts, to be 4x6. Studding to be 2x4 in not more than 16 inches from centers.

End Beams 6x8 inches and all others 3x8. Beams locked down over plates 1 inch and extend far enough to form a 14 inch joint.

Plates 3x4, Beams to be more than 2½ ft. apart. Rafters to be 2½x5 inches to be placed over beams. Pitch of Roof 19/30. Rafters and Beams to be supported by 2x6 inch joints, as shown in detail. Gable end studding 2x4 inches. Walls to be boarded with seasoned hemlock boards. Roof to be close boarded and covered with extra No. 1 cedar shingles not more than 4½ inches to the weather. Valley where roof of annex joins main house to be laid up one piece of pine to each course of shingles of sufficient size to make tight roof.

Outside trimmings to be sound pine free from large knots.

Corner boards to show 7 inches.

Clapboards - 8 inches.

Gut to be finished with moulded cornice.

Windows, Lip sash 12x18 glass. Eight lights to a window. Glass to be bedded. 17 windows to be put in as shown in plan of main house and front annex. Window frame to be nailed into studding. Width of trimmings - 5 inch plasters, 7 inch lap, doors outside - 3x7 ft. 1 3/4 inch thick.

Inside doors - 2 ft. 8 inches x by 6 ft. 8 inches and 1½ inches thick. Outside doors to be of No. 1 pine and to be hung with 4½ inch acorn butts, 3 butts to each door, and fastened with knob and good stone-lock. Inside doors to be of No. 1 Bass and hung with 3½ inch acorn butts and fastened with latch. Pilasters for outside doors 6 inches, width of cap 8 inches. Outside door trimmings same as those on windows. All caps to be 1 3/8 inches thick, and zinc over outside caps. All door stools to be of birch. Doors to be put in according to plan. Walls to be covered with good felt sheathing paper put under all trimmings. Walls to be covered with extra 6 inch spruce. Clapboards 4 inches to the weather. The partitions dividing the school rooms shall be double i.e. two sets of studding so set that there shall be the space of 1 inch between each wall and the opposite studding. The studding is to be 2x4 inches and 16 inches apart from centers and where the blackboards are to be put in double. Partitions across front annex to correspond with plan.

Tarring overhead 1x3 inches not more than 16 inches apart. The plastering to be 2 coats not less than 3/8 inch thick. Top of window sills shall be 3 ft. above top of sills and the walls shall be sheathed outside with plastering up to the window sills, with matched Bass well seasoned. Cap on top of sheathing to correspond with stool cap. Windows shall be supplied with suitable springs, two for upper sash and one for lower. A door shall be put in the center partition of front annex with common lock. Front annex shall be plastered and sheathed same as school rooms and be supplied with wardrobe hooks.

The building shall be painted outside and inside with pure white lead and linseed oil. Three coats of such colors as shall be selected by the Building Committee. The plastering of walls to be painted, one coat sizing and three coats lead and oil. Blackboards shall be put in with slating to the area of 150 square feet according to the directions of the Building Committee.

Floors - The lower floor shall be laid close and well nailed. The upper floor shall be laid with sound, thoroughly seasoned and planed spruce boards, nailed down with 12 d. nails. Behine brand sheathing paper shall be between the floors. Top floor to break joints over lower floor.

Rooms to be seated with Buffalo School Furniture Company's new paragon school desks - 24 double desks and 4 rear seats in each room. Desks made of maple and cherrywood and finished in three coats of best hard oil. Warantee for 10 years.

Chimney shall start 3 ft. below ceiling in center of partition which crosses main house, and shall be laid 3 bricks. Chimney to be well plastered inside and topped out with the best topping brick. New brick shall be used throughout. It shall be not less than 6 ft. above ridgepole.

Stoves - A stove shall be put in each room. Size 31x21x18 inches of the best material and make for the radiation of heat. 7-inch funnel used.

Rear annex sills 8x8 posts 8 ft. long 4x4 inches walls to be sheathed with bass same as other rooms. i.e. in the water closets. Hall not to be finished. Water closets to be finished according to draught. Stairs leading from rear hall to wood basement to be covered in with window on one side. The door to hall from outside shall be double matched boards, hung with strap hinges fastened with bolt and latch. Walls to be covered with same kind of clapboards as main building. Roof to be shingled with extra No. 1 cedar shingles. Two windows shal be put in south side of basement. Six lights in each of 8x10 glass.

The school room shall be ventilated by a 15x10 inch register in ceiling with ventilator in gable end of annex as shown in draft.

A face shall be built where the front wall or underpinning meets the basement. Sufficient to hold the grading around front wall. The ground shall be graded around the building so that the underpinning even with bottom of sill. North platform to have steps on side and end. South platform steps on end with rail. Steps to be made of sound 2 inch plank. A door 4x4 ft. shall be put in front end of basement, hung on inside with strap hinges, a rough board partition on back side of basement.

Belfry shall be 6x6 ft. square hip roof, timbered and built as shown in detail and draft. A steel Amalgam bell shall be hung in the belfry which shall be 25" in diameter and weigh 140 pounds. This bell shall have yoke and wheel so arranged that the teacher can ring the bell in the dressing room of the grammar schoolroom.

Seats sized by Building Committee.

All work shall be done in a thorough and workmanlike manner and to the acceptance of the Building Committee. The Committee will hold the right to make any changes in the minor details which they may deem necessary which shall not increase the expense or as they may agree with the builder.

S. A. Martin
D. Hanson
A. Bean
Building Committee

I hereby accept the above plan and specifications for a school building in District No. 11 - St. Albans, Maine.

E. A. Bean, Supervisor of Schools
St. Albans, Maine

Village School House, St. Albans, Maine. (1883)

Village School (1903-1904)
The following students are in this early photo. Back row, Gladys Bigelow, Ben Bowman, Carrie Goodwin, Ola Parker, Ethel Moore, Winslow Brigham. Teacher Vivian Laughton (James).
2nd row. Lewis Wright, Clyde Cook, Elsie Frost, Clyne Bigelow, Ella Ray, Stella Emery, Herman Parker.
3rd row. Leon Turner, Arthur Moore, Glen Hanson, Earl Patten, Marion Emery, Mary Hanson, Carroll Patten, Homar Ray, Vivian Bigelow, Helen Hanson, Thelma Worthen.

It was the recommendation of the school board in 1904 that the Village Schoolhouse be moved to a larger and more suitable lot and there thoroughly repaired, as it was not only dangerous to health, but also to bodily injury.

In 1913 major repairs were done on the building, which included a new floor, pipes, registers, and an entire new top. The cellar was also drained and extensive repairs made on the wood furnace.

From the town reports, we find the following repairs made on the Village Schoolhouse: 1928 - East Roof shingled; belfry repaired; cellar wall and south side rebuilt. 1930 - East Roof covered with steel - Cost $147.50. 1935 - The underspinning straightened at the Village Schoolhouse. Only four of the district schools were still open. These included Five Corners, Hopkins, Merrill, and Pond. 1938 -Through the aid of W.P.A., a grant from the government and the voters of St. Albans, a two story addition was added. While construction was going on, it was necessary to evacuate the building and move the students to the Town Hall and the Friends Church. William G. Springer was then the Supt. of Schools.

In 1947 two more rooms were added upstairs to the St. Albans Village School. The construction was done by Charles Mower.

That same year through the efforts of Oscar W. Bigelow, Principal, the C. A. Batchelder Memorial Playground was given to the school by Mrs. C. Batchelder.

In 1953 Gladys Bigelow gave to the children of St. Albans a field adjoining the school playground. This has been used by the school and especially by the Little League.

In the 50's and 60's towns all over Maine were beginning to feel a need to consolidate, and in 1963 under the supervision of Supt. Llewellyn Churchill, the towns of St. Albans, Hartland, Palmyra, Harmony, and Athens formed Union 63.

In 1964 Omar Norton became the Supt. of Schools, and S.A.D. 48 was formed Dec. 31, 1965 with Hartland, St. Albans, Palmyra, Corinna, and Newport.

The joining of District No. 48 brought to an end as a secondary school Hartland Academy after 133 years. This building continues to serve as a Junior High for the students of St. Albans, Hartland, and Palmyra. Our high school students attend Nokomis Regional High School in Newport, Me.

Our present Supt. of Schools, Hartland Cushman, was elected May 17, 1966 as Assistant Supt. and elected March 7, 1967 as Supt. of S.A.D. 48.

The first directors were Elmer Fisher, Fred Cooper, Richard

Jones, James Smith, Homer Woodward, Richard Banton, Lewis Harper, Claude Fisher, James Louder, Jerome Emerson, Meredith Smith, Minette Cummings, Rae Jean Knowles, Lucille Gilbert, Goodwin Gilman and Clair Lewis.

Directors of SAD No. 48 (early members), First Row (left to right) - Richard Banton, Minette Cummings, Goodwin Gilman, Rosco Arno, Rae Jean Knowles, Lucille Gilbert. Second Row — (left to right) Meredith Smith, James Lowder, Jerome Emerson, Richard Jones, Louis Harper, James Smith, Fred Cooper and Elmer Fisher (Chairman).

The following is a copy of the first organizational meeting of the Board of Directors of S.A.D. 48.

December 31, 1965

The organizational Meeting of the Board of Directors of School Administrative District 48 was held on December 31, 1965 at 1 P.M. at Newport High School.

The following members were present: Mr. Jones, Mr. Emerson, Mrs. Smith, Mrs. Knowles, Mrs. Gilbert, Mr. Arno, Mrs. Cummings, Mr. Gilman, Mr. Woodward, Mr. Banton, Mr. Lewis, Mr. Harper, Mr. Cooper and Mr. Fisher.

The notice of the meeting as directed by the State Board of Education was read by Mr. Norton.

The oath of office was read to each director by Mr. Ernest Kurt, a Notary Public from Palmyra. The Directors gave Mr. Kurt a vote of thanks for volunteering his services for this occasion.

The term of each director was determined by lot as follows:

Corinna -     Mr. Jones - 1 year
              Mr. Louder - 2 years
              Mr. Emerson - 3 years
              Mrs. Smith - 2 years
Hartland -    Mrs. Knowles -1 year
              Mrs. Gilbert - 2 years
              Mr. Arno - 3 years
Newport -     Mr. Cummings - 1 year
              Mr. Gilman - 3 years
              Mr. Woodward - 2 years
              Mr. Banton - 1 year
Palmyra -     Mr. Lewis - 3 years
              Mr. Harper - 2 years
St. Albans -  Mr. Cooper - 3 years
              Mr. Fisher - 1 year

Mr. Elmer Fisher was elected Chairman of the Board of Directors of School Administrative District No. 48, and Mr. Homer Woodward was elected to serve as the Vice Chairman.

Mrs. Minnette Cummings was elected to serve as Secretary Protempore to record the election of a superintendent of schools.

The Directors voted to elect Mr. Omar Norton as the Superintendent of Schools at a salary rate of $12,000 per year. While Mr. Norton stated he would not be available for this position for an extended period of time, he agreed to act as Superintendent until the services of a successor could be secured. A Screening Committee to survey applicants for this position was appointed by Chairman Fisher and consisted of: Mr. Woodward, Mrs. Knowles, Mr. Harper, Mr. Cooper and Mrs. Smith as Chairman.

Mr. Guy Fish was designated as the assistant Supt. of Schools.

The Directors voted to accept responsibility for the operation of School Administrative District No. 48.

It was voted to schedule regular meetings of the Board of Directors on the first and third Tuesdays of the month. In line with this policy, the next meeting will take place next Tuesday, January 4, 1966 at the Palmyra Consolidated School at 7 P.M.

The by-laws were accepted as presented, subject to review at the next meeting.

The Directors voted to allow resident pupils attending schools outside the District to finish this school year with tuition paid by the District.

The Directors voted to have Chairman Fisher appoint a Committee to: (1) investigate school property now held by the individual municipalities or other agencies and negotiate the transfer of this property to the School Administrative District and (2) serve as a Building Committee. The following persons were appointed to this Committee: Mr. Jones, Mr. Arno, Mr. Lewis, Mr. Cooper and Mr. Gilman who will serve as Chairman.

The Directors voted to elect a finance Committee composed of Mr. Fisher, Mr. Banton, Mr. Harper, Mrs. Gilbert with Mr. Louder serving as Chairman.

This Committee was also charged with the responsibility of seeing to it that the proper authorities of school district or municipal officials be directed to transfer liabilities and assets and sinking funds to the School Administrative District, the same to be set aside for payment of indebtedness which has been assumed by the School Administrative District. Futhermore, this Committee was authorized by the vote of the District Directors to request each town in writing that the unexpended balances remaining in the School Accounts as of December 31, 1965 be paid to the Treasurer of the School Administrative District.

The Directors voted to authorize the Supt. of Schools to purchase necessary books and supplies for the operation of the District. It was voted in addition to authorize the Supt. to issue truancy notices, hire substitute teachers, and teachers for handicapped pupils (home instruction).

It was voted to fill teaching vacancies occurring during the year or for a new school year by having the Supt. nominate a candidate or candidates with the Directors empowered to elect said candidate(s).

The Directors voted to continue the lunch programs and milk programs now in operation.

The Supt. was directed to incorporate the Martell System of financial accounting in the District.

A Budget Committee was appointed by Chairman Fisher and consisting of the following members: Mr. Emerson, Mrs. Gilbert, Mr. Harper, Mr. Cooper and Mrs. Cummings as Chairman. This Committee was further empowered to investigate the possibility of hiring legal counsel and report back to the Directors at a future meeting.

The meeting was adjourned by a unanimous vote of the Directors.

Respectfully Submitted

Omar Norton
Superintendent of Schools

*    *    *    *    *    *

In July 1978 the Building Committee of S.A.D. 48 met at the St. Albans Consolidated School with Hartland L. Cushman, Supt. of Schools. This meeting was requested by director Ruth Knowles for the purpose of either remodeling the existing school building, or applying for necessary funding for a new school. Peter Duncombe, St. Albans director, pointed out many of the structural problems of the old building to the Committee, assisted by Roland Wortman. Principal of the St. Albans Consolidated School, and Hartland L. Cushman, Supt. of Schools.

The Building Committee felt if renovating the existing building was too costly, they would recommend the possibility of looking into a new school for St. Albans.

On October 5, 1978 the S.A.D. 48 School Directors approved the request for a new school and authorized Mr. Cushman to proceed with the necessary paperwork. On October 18, 1978 the initial application was submitted and notification received November 20, 1978 to complete education allocation, space allocation, and select an architect. On July 9, 1979 the Directors voted to employ Allied Engineers of Gorham for architectural work on the new building.

On July 11, 1979 the State Board met and approved the final funding. Then a citizens' committee was formed to assist with the site selection, building reviews, etc. Members of that committee were Byron Wiers, Bruce Hughes, Everett Graham, Lowell Knowles, Richard Dunham, Diane Dunham, Elizabeth Wiers, Dennis Smith, Philip Bowman, Ethelyn Bowman, Louis Leal, Albert Barrows, Lewis MacLeod, and many other citizens who expressed interest and concern.

The building is a one-story structure located 7/10 of a mile from the village on 29 acres of the Harold Bishop property. There are nine classrooms, a cafeteria-auditorium, two conference rooms, and a library, besides the office space.

Without the support of Hartland L. Cushman, Supt. of Schools, and his untiring efforts and labor; Elwin Littlefield and James Smith, Chairmen of the Building Committee, and all the members of the

Board of Directors of S.A.D. 48, this building could not have become a reality.

St. Albans Consolidated School — 1981

## PRESENT FACULTY

Roland Wortman . . . . . . . . . . . . . Principal Grade 6
Ruth Powers . . . . . . . . . . . . . . . . . . . . . Secretary
Darlene Wintle . . . . . . . . . . . . . . . . . . . Grade 5
Mary Helen Thorne . . . . . . . . . . . . . . . . . Grade 4
Pricilla Dean . . . . . . . . . . . . . . . . . . . . . Grade 3
Mary Hatfield . . . . . . . . . . . . . . . . . . . . Grade 2
Christina Gee . . . . . . . . . . . . . . . . . . . . Grade 1
Velma Walker . . . . . . . . . . . . . . . . . Kindergarten
George Perkins . . . . . . . . . . . . . . . . . . . . Janitor
Margaret Williams . . . . . . . . . . . . . . . . Lunchroom
Ethelyn Bowman
Margo Springer . . . . . . . . . . . . Teacher Associates
Jane Palmer
Shelia Berry . . . . . . . . . . . . . . . . . . . . Special Needs
Glen Richardson
Jack Clifford . . . . . . . . . . . . . . . . . . . . . . . . Music
Special People: Beverly Ball, Connie Allen, Kerry Martin

105

## EXCERPTS FROM SUPT. REPORTS

1894: There is no uniformity of text books in this town. There seems to be no regularity to them. There should be order and system and especially in so important a matter as this. It was deemed desirable to change the psychology in use for a more desirable one; consequently, the "Pathfinder Series" published by the instigation of the National Women's Christian Temperence Union was adopted, and the results thus far have been very satisfactory.

Let no local prejudices or sectional animosities divert us from the determination to give to our scholars the best preparation for the duties of life - a thoroughly practical education.

E. P. Dyer
Superintendent of Schools

1895-96: Our schools compare very favorably with the schools in surrounding towns. They will continue to improve so long as we continue our interest in them. We can all do something to make our schools better. Parents should visit our teachers and our school. They should encourage and aid their children at home. They are doing this to a great extent, and our schools are growing better every year.

Rosa Harding
Superintendent of Schools

1903: The chief aim of our public schools should be to teach our boys and girls that virtue, honor, and integrity should be their highest aim in life -Add to this a good, practical education that will fit them for the social and business affairs of life, and we need not fear for the future of our nation.

E. A. Harding
Superintendent of Schools

1923: By vote of the teachers, part of last fall's entertainment receipts was used to put a Bible Story book in each school. Hurlbuts Story of the Bible was chosen. No use has been made of the book to which anyone could reasonably object, and we feel that its influence is very wholesome.

H. B. Clifford
Superintendent of Schools

1947: Like every other community you have a building shortage. Your school has been consolidated ahead of your present housing facilities. However, the church alleviates the overcrowding for the present.

You have fine teachers handling nine grades and 200 pupils which is way out of reason.

Harvey B. Scribner
Superintendent of Schools

1965: The past school year has witnessed an event which will influence educational policies in this area for years to come. The event to which I refer is naturally the formation of S.A.D. 48. This reorganization of schools should most certainly result in an improved educational program at a more reasonable cost to the town of St. Albans.

Omar Norton
Superintendent of Schools

# CHAPTER XIII

## ST. ALBANS CHURCHES

### ST. ALBANS UNION CHURCH

As in most New England communities, the Congregational denomination played an active part in the beginning of the growth of the church in St. Albans. Prior to the completion of the Union Church in 1856, services were held in the Town Hall and in the Merrill Schoolhouse. As early as 1845 there are accounts of neighborhood gatherings for worship.

Levi J. Merrill who came from Madison to St. Albans in 1820 purchased the land from Merrill's Corner one mile north and two miles east, known as Merrill's Ridge. He with four of his sons settled on this tract of land. These four men, Levi, Joseph, Nathaniel, and James Merrill, were instrumental in building the Union Church.

From the beginning the organization was in fact as in name a Union Church. Four Sundays of each month were evenly shared by the Congregationalists, the Baptists, the Free Baptists, and the Methodists. Frequently the fifth Sunday was delegated to a Quaker or Friend, already established in their own church home. Regardless of creed, frequently non-church oriented, the citizens of the village worked together to build the church, furnishing materials and labor, and best of all enthusiastic support of the project. The cash needed came from the sale of pews in the new church, with each citizen contributing $18 receiving a deed of ownership. All were the same:

Know all men by these presents - that I Nathaniel Foss of St. Albans, County of Somerset and State of Maine in consideration of $18 paid by John Smith of St. Albans aforesaid (the receipt whereof I do hereby acknowledge) have remised, released, and forever quit-claimed, and do for myself and my heirs by these presents remise, release, and forever quit-claim unto the said John Smith, his heirs and assigns Pew No. 44 in the meeting house recently erected in St. Albans village. To have and to hold the afore mentioned premises, with all the privileges and appurtenances thereto belonging to the said John Smith, his heirs, and assigns forever; so that neither I, the said Nathaniel Foss nor my heirs or any person or persons claiming them or under me or them or in the name, right, or stead of me or them, shall or will by any way or means have, claim or demand any right or title to the aforesaid premises or their appurtenances or to any part or parcel thereof forever. In witness whereof, I the said Nathaniel Foss together with wife, in token of her relinquishment of her right to dower in the afore granted premises, have hereunto set my hand and seal this 17th day of July in the year of our Lord one thousand eight hundred and sixty-five in the presence of S. Lothrop -Nathaniel Foss. Somerset SS to be his free act and deed before me July 17, 1865.

Then the above named acknowledged this instrument by him subscribed.

Sullivan Lothrop, Justice of the Peace

In 1981 Doris Seekins Ballard sits every Sunday in Pew No. 4 purchased so long ago by her grandfather James Darius Emery. With her sits her daughter Diane Ballard Landry and her grandchildren Adam and Lisa Landry. So the terms in the deed "to his heirs and assigns forever" are being carried out to this day.

It was not until 1882 that the church had a permanent pastor. At this time the church became affiliated with the Methodist Church in Hartland and this friendly connection continued until 1952. Services were held in the forenoon in Hartland and in the afternoon in St. Albans. It was a custom in the Methodist denomination to change pastors every two years and our roster of ministers is long:

| Pastor | Year |
|---|---|
| A. W. C. Anderson | 1882-1884 |
| James Biram | 1884-1886 |
| Elisha Skinner | 1886-1888 |
| George H. Hamilton | 1888-1890 |
| W. H. Denmark | 1890-1892 |
| P. A. Smith | 1892-1894 |
| Elisha Skinner | 1894-1895 |
| I. H. Lidstone | 1895-1899 |
| C. E. Peterson | 1899-1901 |
| C. H. Johonnett | 1901-1904 |
| William C. Baker | 1904-1906 |
| Charles E. Southard | 1906 |
| J. H. Gray | 1907-1910 |
| F. W. Brooks | 1910-1911 |
| J. O. Rutter | 1911-1912 |
| M. S. Hill | 1912-1913 |
| A. W. Frye | 1913-1914 |
| C. C. Jones | 1914-1916 |
| W. R. Patterson | 1916-1918 |
| E. J. Webber | 1918-1920 |
| E. S. McMahon | 1920-1923 |
| W. J. Bennett | 1923-1925 |
| W. Crosby Hamilton | 1925-1927 |
| W. P. Bender | 1927-1928 |
| Frances Adams (Batchelder) | 1928-1931 |
| Alexander Stewart | 1931-1933 |
| Willard Rand | 1933-1935 |

| Roy S. Graffam | 1935-1937 |
| Guy Smith | 1937-1939 |
| Charles Stanton | 1939-1941 |
| Robert Holcomb | 1941-1943 |
| F. Ernest Smith | 1943-1946 |
| Barbara Chandler (Huse) | 1946-1951 |
| Frank Moffett | 1952-1955 |
| Charles Talmadge | 1955-1965 |
| Donald Minnick | 1965-1966 |
| Sidney F. Whitehouse | 1966-1972 |
| William Freiheit | 1972-1975 |
| Earle Jewell | 1975-1977 |
| Douglas Dinsmore | Jan. 1, 1978-Aug.11, 1978 |
| Earle Jewell | 1978-1980 |
| Leonard Whitman | 1981- |

Milestones in the life of the Union Church

1952 - Incorporated as an independent church

1952 - Rev. Frank Moffett called as minister

1953 - Memorial week-end May 30 and 31, parish supper at Grange Hall Saturday evening followed by hymn singing at the church. Homecoming service Sunday morning.

1956 - Purchased Brock House. At town meeting in 1956 the citizens agreed to allow the church to make this purchase.

1956 - On May 26 and 27 a celebration of the 100th birthday of the Union Church. Saturday evening a special service was held to dedicate the electric organ, a gift from the Thorne family in memory of their parents, Emma J. and Ellis M. Thorne. The gift was made "with the sincere hope that the music furnished by this instrument will bring much enjoyment to congregations in the years to come." Our organists, Edith Talmadge, Elvera Whitehouse, and Barbara Patten have carried out this wish faithfully.

At the Sunday morning service Mrs. Pauline Lombard sang "Face to Face"; Verne Merrill read the Church history, and Mrs. Vertine Ellis read her poem.

St. Albans Union Church — 1982

### The Little White Church 'Cross The Way

I'm sitting tonight in the gloaming
Thinking of old time songs,
And my heart is filled with sadness
When I think of the ones who have gone.

The village has changed for the better.
The houses don't look just the same,
But the little white church that is near me
Is beautiful in sunshine or rain.

The voices I heard in the choir
Are now in the silent land,
And new ones have taken over
The care of the church and the plans.

The little white church is still standing,
Robed in its snowy white,
An emblem for us to follow
As a shining example of light.

I love to look at the picture.
It helps to brighten the day,
And I wish we could all be as spotless
As the little white church 'cross the way.

by Vertine Ellis

111

Reverend Charles Talmadge preached on Building For Eternity. On both days the church held open house with an exhibition of family Bibles, historic church furnishings, and refreshments.

1955-1965 - Brock House was sold; four Sunday School rooms were added to the west side of the building, and the parsonage bought.

1972 - Funding for the present Lowheit Wing was commenced in 1972 during the pastorate of Rev. William Freiheit. This became a community project with lumber donated by Dana Leavitt, finished by Sidney Mower and sons Blaine and Richard, and monthly contributions by members and friends. Sherburn Lary and Terrance Lary completed the wing in 1975. The painting of the wing was the gift of Kenneth Hughes, Joseph Tripaldi, and Walter Butler. The wing has a large room for social gatherings, two toilets, and six classrooms. During the coldest weather it has been used for church services. A monthly blood pressure clinic is held here and Released Time Bible Classes meet twice a month during the school year. On June 15, 1975 the wing was dedicated. Joseph Tripaldi, Chairman of the Board of Trustees, presented memorial plaques honoring former members, and Gladys Bigelow gave a history of the church.

1977 - On March 18 a continuing scholarship fund was established by Reverend Harry Randall, Newport, R.I. and Halston Randall of Vacaville, California in memory of their parents, Mark Halston Randall and Sadie Alice Buzzell Randall, both devoted members of the Union Church. From the dedication:

"The purpose of this fund shall be to provide financial aid to young people of the church and community for Christian summer conference experiences or scholarships for post-highschool formal education at accredited schools of learning.

Though the memory of these faithful Christian servants shall diminish with time, their influence will be nourished by the Holy Spirit in the lives of God's children until Christ comes again."

Beneficiaries so far are Vaughn Martin and Nolan Leavitt.

1980 saw the purchase of a new organ, again supported by the Thorne family, with a gift from Meredith Fisher and contributions from members and friends. A $2,500 bequest from Halvor Prescott, a descendant of Seth and Hannah Bigelow Emery, made it possible to complete the purchase.

1981 - Given incentive by a generous gift from Meredith Fisher in memory of her parents, Charles and Ada Mower, and her husband Elmer Fisher, a carpet fund has been started. Increased by monthly contributions from church members and community friends, the worn out floor covering will soon be replaced, adding to

112

the comfort and beauty of our church.

Our church by-laws state the purpose of the Union Church of St. Albans is to provide a place of worship and fellowship for all who believe in Jesus Christ as their Savior from sin, and who desire to live an obedient, effective Christian life. It is on this principle that after 125 years the Union Church is still a living force in our community.

## THE QUAKER CHURCH

Although the Quaker or Friends Church was active in St. Albans only from 1830 to the early 1900's, the influence of these devoted Christians was very great. Their ideals of brotherly love and peaceful coexistence with their neighbors created a strong feeling of unity and good will in the community.

The following birth and death records of Quaker families in St. Albans were found in the safe at the Augusta State Library. This material was donated to the library September 18, 1964 by Vertine E. Ellis, a member of the old St. Albans Quaker Church.

**Hawks:**   Moses Hawks, b. April 20, 1787 - d. October 26, 1853.
Anna Hawks, b. July 6, 1793.
Nathaniel Hawks, b. May 29, 1817.
Joseph S. Hawks, b. May 26, 1822.
Sarah Marie Hawks, b. February 4, 1826.
Elizabeth Hawks, b. June 17, 1823.
Moses Hawks, b. September 3, 1845.
Ebline Hawks, b. April 27, 1849.

**Estes:**   Isaac Estes, b. May 26, 1778.
Stillman Estes, b. December 13, 1818.
Irene Estes, b. December 4, 1819.
Helen M. Estes, b. March 16.
James T. Estes, b. February 17.
Horace A. Estes, b. August 27.
Philena Estes, b. May 26, 1847.
Horace Estes, b. August 19, 1849.
Amy E. Estes, b. September 5, 1850.
Henry Minot Estes, b. May 29, 1853.
Daniel Shepherd Estes, b. May 10, 1855.

**Estes:**   Valentine Estes, b. April 3, 1815.
Amy Estes, b. November 19, 1817 - d. 1845.
Sarah Estes, b. May 19, 1817 - d. April 13, 1887.
Joseph L., b ?

Charles Henry, b. January 16, 1848..
Edwin D., b. March 31, 1850..
Horace, b. 1854.
Rosa Bell, b. 1856.

**Dudley:** David Dudley, b. April 15, 1794.
Eunice B. Dudley, b. July 8, 1796.
Anstry Dudley, b. February 5, 1818.
Almira Dudley, b. March 1, 1820.
Sarah Dudley, b. March 18, 1822.
Chandler A. Dudley, b. May 24, 1824 - d. June 9, 1847.
Daniel Dudley, b. August 14, 1826.
Edwin Dudley, b. August 12, 1828 - d. August 8, 1849.
Mary Dudley, b. October 25, 1830.
Dorcas Dudley, b. July 27, 1833.
Maria J. Dudley, b. October 1, 1835 - d. June 29, 1850.
Eliza Dudley, b. February 4, 1838.
Susan H. Dudley, b. November 7, 1840.

**Jones:** Ephraim Jones b., February 1776 - d. January 22, 1851.
Suzannah Jones, b. December 1778.
Hannah Jones, b. May 5, 1821 - d. August 26, 1841 at
    Corinna.
Silas Jones, b. March 27, 1800.
Lois Jones, b. July 16, 1808.
George Jones, b. February 7, 1828.
Sarah Jones, b. December 10, 1829.
Joseph Jones, b. August 29, 1837.
David D. Jones, b. June 2, 1839.
Charles W. Jones, b. December 30, 1840.
Phoebe Jones, b. November 7, 1843.
Nelson Jones, b. January 16, 1847.
Mary Elizabeth Jones, b. December 6, 1848 - d.
    December 28, 1848.
Byron Watson Jones

**Vining:** Joseph Vining, b. April 10, 1785 - d. February 14, 1859.
Esther Vining, b. October 10, 1787 - d. February 27,
    1879.
Sarah Vining, b. December 25, 1811.
Louisa Vining, b. November 13, 1813.
Jacob H. Vining, b. November 20, 1815.
Abigail Vining, b. July 16, 1817.
Esther Vining, b. February 13, 1820 - d. 1852.
Josiah Vining, b. September 22, 1822 - d. 1843.
Ruth Vining, b. December 12, 1824.

John Warren Vining, b. May 19, 1827 - d. 1838.

William Francis Vining, b. December 22, 1831.

**Magoon:** Daniel Magoon, b. January 11, 1783 - d. 1860.

Phebe Magoon, b. January 15, 1785 - d. 1851.

Charles Magoon, b. August 19, 1810.

Martha Magoon, b. April 3, 1812 - d. 1847.

Charles H. Magoon, b. May 5, 1837 - d. January 1851.

William A. Magoon, b. December 4, 1840.

Ephraim J. Magoon, b. November 20, 1842.

Lindsey H.Magoon, b. June 25, 1844.

Martha Bailey Magoon ,b. July 2, 1847.

Moses Bailey Magoon,b. July 2, 1847 - Twins.

Daniel Magoon, b. August 4, 1850 - d. 1851.

Mary Magoon, b. May 21, 1852.

Esther Magoon, b. March 12, 1812 - d. 1884.

Josiah Magoon, b. April 8, 1792 - d. 1854.

Mary Magoon, b. April 14, 1789 - d. 1855.

Hugh Magoon, b. October 10, 1815 - d. 1819.

Benjamin Magoon, b. July 14, 1817.

Josiah Magoon Jr., b. July 25, 1820.

Alfred Magoon, b. January 21, 1822.

Elizabeth Magoon, b. June 17, 1823 - d. February 15, 1851.

Franklin Magoon, b. April 11, 1825.

Mary W. Magoon, b. June 10, 1827 - d. Nov. 8, 1850.

George H. Magoon, b. August 1830 - d. August 11, 1850.

Benjamin Magoon 2nd, b. August 22, 1788.

Harrison Magoon, b. October 23, 1813 - d. in Africa.

**Partridge:** Thomas Partridge, b. February 9, 1808.

Sarah W. Partridge, b. June 6, 1818.

Mary Elizabeth Partirdge, b. April 7, 1838.

Ann Elisa Partridge, b. June 4, 1840.

Joseph Pratt Partridge, b. May 4, 1843.

James Reed Partridge, b. March 23, 1847.

Eunice D. Partridge, b. June 22, 1849.

**Steward:** Randall Steward, b. July 10, 1818.

Sarah Marie Steward, b. February 4, 1826.

Eulyssa Steward, b. February 7, 1845 - d. 1849.

Chelsea Steward, b. August 8, 1847.

Adella Steward, b. July 26, 1849.

Eulyssa Steward, b. April 15, 1851.

Anna H. Steward, b. March 29, 1853.

Eleanor Steward, b. June 12, 1855.

**Perkins:** Ebenezer F. Perkins, b. December 16, 1837 - d. June 10, 1865.

**Getchell:** Isaac Getchell, d. 1864.

**Davis:** Sarah Davis, d. February 27, 1867.

**Butler:** Joseph Butler, d. December 27, 1868.

**Crowell:** Edmond Crowell, d. December 12, 1864.

**Chase:** Linus Chase, b. January 16, 1810 - d. 1877.

**Bean:** Ezekiel H. Bean, b. July 2, 1797.

**Burton:** John Burton b. September 2, 1767 - d. 1842
Peace Burton, b. September 1772 - d. 1849.

**Weeks:** Phear Weeks, b. September 22, 1757 - d. May 24, 1847.

**Dill-**
**ingham:** Edward Dillingham, b. June 1, 1772 - d. 1857.
Hannah Dillingham, b. May 7, 1782 - d. Feburary 16, 1847.
Esther Dillingham, b. July 14, 1803.
Deborah Dillingham, b. October 28, 1804.
Nathan Dillingham, b. May 24, 1807.
Olive Dillingham, b. August 4, 1808 - d. September 4, 1809.
Mary Ann Dillingham, b. January 18, 1811.
James W. Dillingham, b. September 24, 1814.
Eliza Dillingham, b. October 7, 1817 - d. 1818.
Lucy Dillingham, b. May 30, 1821.
Allen W. Dillingham, b. September 20, 1823.

**Nye:** Ebenezer Nye, b. June 11, 1780 - d. March 10, 1869.
Elizabeth Nye, b. July 25, 1784 - d. 1863.

**Fair-**
**brother:** Moses Fairbrother, b. August 5, 1804 - d. 1871.
Syrena Fairbrother, b. March 28, 1812 - d. 1865.
Daniel Fairbrother, b. July 6, 1844 - d. 1851.
Margaret Fairbrother,b. February 4, 1846 - d. August 26, 1849.
Moses Alfred Fairbrother, b. April 6, 1847 - d. 1849.
Phebe Fairbrother, b. August 31, 1849 - d. 1849.
Margaret Ann Fairbrother, b. January 12, 1851.
Phebe Catherine Fairbrother, b. March 16, 1852.
Joseph Fairbrother, b. January 1, 1802.
Susannah Fairbrother, b. August 8, 1806.
Henry Fairbrother, b. August 5, 1827.
Browning G. Fairbrother, b. December 11, 1830.

Isaac Fairbrother, b. April 11, 1840.

Joseph Fairbrother, b. August 17, 1845.

Henry Fairbrother, b. August 5, 1827.

Avis Fairbrother, b. November 24, 1820.

Ella Eunice Fairbrother, b. June 29, 1852 - d. 1853.

Oscar W. Fairbrother, b. June 29, 1857.

**Bailey:**    Daniel Bailey, b. December 13, 1815 in Winthrop.

Phebe Bailey, b. November 5, 1815 in Falmouth - d. December 10, 1848 in St. Albans.

Samuel L. Bailey, b. July 22, 1839 in Winthrop.

Hannah Bailey, b. January 15, 1841 in Fairfield.

Charles Bailey, b. April 27, 1842 in St. Albans - d. May 30, 1842.

George Bailey, b. October 8, 1843 in St. Albans.

Eunice Bailey, b. January 8, 1845 in St. Albans.

Twins born March 11, 1848 in St. Albans - both died.

**Winslow:** Daniel Winslow, b. March 31, 1789.

Irene Winslow, b. November 15, 1793.

William Prince Winslow, b. January 20, 1836.

Nancy Maria Winslow, b. March 8, 1839.

Martha Emma, b. April 5, 1862.

Maria Adelia, b. September 16, 1865.

Rosanna, b. May 9, 1867.

Robert Winslow, b. May 28, 1831.

Phebe Winslow, b. October 12, 1831.

Charles Augustus Winslow, b. September 8, 1859.

Elizabeth Irena Winslow, b. May 4, 1861.

Mary Abbie Winslow, b. September 16, ,1864.

**Douglas:** David Douglas, b. July 16, 1796.

Chloe Douglas, b. December 27, 1800.

Lydia Ann Douglas, b. September 10, 1820 - d. July 10, 1841.

Hannah Douglas, b. May 20, 1822.

Eunice Douglas, b. March 4, 1824.

John Henry Douglas, b. November 27, 1832.

Robert Walter Douglas, b. November 11, 1834.

David Cornelius Douglas, b. January 5, 1840 - d. 1843.

Joseph Winslow, b. May 9, 1824.

P. Carter Douglas, b. April 1859 - d. April 1881.

Esther Douglas, b. February 17, 1770 - d. April 1865.

John N. Douglas, b. November 15, 1820.

Sarah Douglas, b. December 10, 1829.

|         | Maria Douglas, b. November 24, 1847.        |
|---------|---------------------------------------------|
| Cook:   | Elijah Cook, b. September 23, 1790.         |
|         | Judith Cook, b. December 31, 1811.          |
|         | Albert Cook, b. February 17, 1827.          |
|         | Almira Cook, b. May 23, 1828.               |
|         | Sarah Jane Cook, b. July 11, 1829.          |
|         | Rachel Cook, b. March 24, 1831.             |
|         | John M. Cook, b. June 14, 1834.             |
|         | Edward H. Cook, b. May 17, 1836 - d. 1848.  |
|         | Elijah Cook Jr., b. June 5, 1839.           |
|         | Ebenezer Cook, b. March 29, 1841.           |
|         | Hanson Cook, b. June 10, 1844.              |
| Hoxie:  | Allen Hoxie. b. April 11, 1797.             |
| Beal:   | Samuel Beal, b. January 30, 1773.           |
|         | Lois Beal, b. December 5, 1798.             |

The Winslow families were especially active in the educational life of St. Albans. Martha, Maria, and Rosanna, daughters of William and Nancy Winslow, graduated from the Moses Brown School in Rhode Island and taught in St. Albans. While Rose was teaching in the Lucas School, she was bothered by a mischievous scholar. After she had administered a good spanking, she said kindly but forcefully, "Now if thee will behave thyself, thee and I will be good friends".

Isaac Winslow and his wife Sarah had four daughters and a son all of whom were active in the field of education. The son, Oscar, and his sister, Elma, were superintendent of schools in St. Albans in the 1870's. Julia taught in Brooklyn, New York and Clara in Rhode Island. Rena was employed for many years in the State House in Augusta. The essay "A Quaker Family in Maine" written in 1953 is in the Maine Historical Society Library in Portland.

## A QUAKER FAMILY IN MAINE
### By Rena L. Winslow

Our earliest American ancestor, Kenelm Winslow, a brother of Governor Edward Winslow, came to America from England in 1629. His son Job, who married Ruth Cole, had 13 children, and the fourth child, James, was the first Quaker in Falmouth, Maine. He married Elizabeth Carpenter and had 7 children. Benjamin, his fourth child, married Hope Cobb and had nine children, of whom my great-grandfather William was one. The house in which he lived on Blackstrap is still standing, but somewhat remodeled. He had 18 children. The

15th child, Daniel, my grandfather, after his marriage to Irene Briggs of Winthrop, lived in West Gardiner for a time, and my father was born there. The family later moved to East Fairfield and formed a settlement known as Winslow's Mills, later called Larone, its present name. There my grandfather built and operated, with his sons, several mills, including a sawmill, a grist mill, and a tannery. Of his 11 children, Phebe, the oldest, married Dr. Bailey of Winthrop. Benjamin was a sea captain, with a home in Mattapoisett, Mass. Mary married Levi Wing, after his death David Tuttle of St. Albans, and later in life, left a widow again, married Josiah Magoon of Larone, whose first wife was another daughter, Hannah. Moses married Eunice Pinkham and lived in Larone. He died when his children were young and his widow kept the Post Office in her house for several years. That house, still standing, on the banks of a beautiful stream, was purchased by a granddaughter in recent years and remodeled into an attractive home and gift shop. Joseph and William bought farms in St. Albans, and Robert and Charles went West, settling in Iowa. The other son died in infancy.

I remember my grandfather as a mild mannered, pleasant man, a good executive and an untiring worker. I was more impressed with my grandmother, who was a very strong, energetic woman. She raised a family of ten children, weaving the cloth and making their garments, spinning the yarn and knitting their stockings, and in addition to all her household duties, sometimes helping in the grist mill. Farmers in that section used to tell how, when they drove up to the mill with bags of corn containing two bushels each, my grandmother used to take a bag, sling it over her hip, carry it into the mill and empty it into the hopper, with apparent ease. My father told of an instance when, working on a farm about a mile away, he needed new trousers. He went home at night and his mother cut a piece from goods on the loom, made a pair and had them ready for him in the morning.

Father and mother lived with his parents until after my oldest brother and sister were born, then moved to a small farm a short distance away. There he supplemented his farm income by making harnesses and doing surveying, - "running lines" for the town's people. Here the family lived until I was eight years old. The soil in that section was very sandy, and I think my favorite recreation was making houses in a large sand pile near the house. The school house was a few rods from our house. It was a small building with a wood stove in one end, the stove pipe running the length of the building overhead. The teacher in those days was usually my oldest sister or a cousin, and I began going to school at four years of age. Our meeting was four miles away, at North Fairfield, but the family were always present except for some unsurmountable obstacle.

When I was six years old a severe epidemic of Scarlet Fever swept through the community, taking many lives. All of our family except father were stricken. The doctor was four miles away but came to us as often as possible. No nurses were available, but an aunt came to us from China, and through the kindness of neighbors and father's devotion we all recovered without lasting ill effects except my three-year-old brother who died within 36 hours after taking the disease. My father never left us, neighbors doing all his farm chores, and his patience and gentleness with us at that time seem to me quite remarkable.

The first Christmas after that illness a friend of my mother presented me with a wonderful doll, a large China doll with red cheeks and black, shiny hair, and surprisingly, a red plaid dress with lace trimmings. Our dolls had been rag dolls or small China dolls with plain, sober dresses. This doll was treasured for years, in fact it held a prominent place in my possessions until my 86th year.

On the road between our house and grandfather's lived an "Old Maid" in a small weather-beaten house. We children were a little afraid of "Lydie Ann", as sometimes she would be in an irascible mood, especially when teased by the boys. But at other times she would call us in and give us cookies. When she was in the seventies she suddenly married a man who had recently appeared in the neighborhood. When some one asked her why she took such a chance at her age, she said "if he is a good man he was worth waiting for, and if he isn't I shall have long enough to live with him.".

In 1874, as the death of David Tuttle had left Aunt Mary alone on a farm in St. Albans, Maine, at her earnest request father took his family up to live with her. He purchased some land to add to this small farm, and had many farm animals, which then had a greater attraction for me than dolls. The very young pigs had a large, low pen in which they could run, and whenever I was missing mother would first look in this pen, where she usually found me, playing games with the little white pigs. I would pull them around by the ears or tails and tell them, "Thee stand here", or "Thee go over there", and the little pigs didn't seem to mind being pawns in the game. I also had a pet lamb of which I was very fond, and unfortunately she was very fond of me. The school was three-fourths of a mile from our home, and frequently when I was a short distance on my way the lamb would suddenly appear, and I would have to go back with her and get mother to shut her up while I hurried to school. She was very much afraid of thunder and lightening, and at the onset of a thunder shower would find her way into the house and patter across the floors until she found me.

The school in St. Albans was a two-story building, the primary school on the lower floor and the grammar school on the second floor. We took our lunches to school, I think usually in a lard pail. I had for a seat mate a very agile, venturesome girl, Carrie Vining, and during the noon hour, after our lunches were eaten, she would lead me on some escapades. A stream ran through the village and it was her delight to run across the dam or out to an eel trap in the stream, on a narrow board which led to it from the bank. I was more clumsy but persistently followed her everywhere. One day we safely reached the eel trap, but on coming back I lost my balance and fell into 6 or 7 feet of water. When I came to the surface I managed to get hold of the board and Carrie finally, with much difficulty pulled me out. I went all the way home dripping wet and she went back to school. Ironically, I suffered no ill effects while Carrie took a very bad cold from sitting in school with wet feet. That incident, to my dismay, put an end to my visiting the stream.

The house in St. Albans had a large fireplace in the living room, but this was later replaced by a soapstone stove, which would hold the heat longer. Large pieces of wood were put in at night and coals would be found in the morning. Wood was burned in the kitchen stove, also. It was our only fuel until we moved to Winthrop 25 years later. Candles and oil lamps were used for lighting. One of my chores was to tie the wicks in the candle mold, ready for the hot tallow. We girls also had to do our stints of sewing or knitting before we could go out to play, - so many times around the stocking or so many squares of patchwork. We were early taught to knit and sew and many quilts were made of different patterns, one a log cabin quilt. The aprons which we wore were called ty-ers. They were made with high neck and sleeves and were buttoned in the back, thus completely protecting the dresses. They were not usually worn to school.

The second floor of the house was unfinished when we moved in, and the first winter my sisters and I slept in the "open chamber" with the snow sometimes blowing in through the cracks. But with feather beds, soapstones, and warming pan we were always warm during the night, and in the morning would dress in the warm living room. There was no plumbing and our baths were taken by means of large wash bowls. But father was not satisfied with that method of bathing and he had a tin bath tub made especially for him, the sides soldered on to the bottom by a tinsmith.

The house was banked with evergreen boughs to keep the cellar, where the apples and vegetables were stored, from freezing.

The farm furnished us plenty of food. In the fall a pig was usually killed, the lard tried out, sausages and "head cheese" made, the fat pork cured and packed in brine, and some of the lean meat frozen and packed away for winter, sometimes in a barrel of oats. A beef animal was also butchered in the neighborhood and our portion was either dried or frozen for winter use. Poultry was always available, roosters from the spring hatching or hens that had ceased to lay. Also, a lamb was killed occasionally. A good garden furnished plenty of green vegetables, for summer eating and canning for winter, and potatoes, beets, turnips, carrots, squash and pumpkins to be stored for winter use. Eggs, butter, and other farm products were exchanged for flour, sugar, and other necessary groceries. The milk was set in large pans, the cream skimmed off and churned into butter and the skim-milk fed to the calves and pigs, until a creamery was established in the town, after which some of the whole milk was sold to the creamery.

My mother was a very good cook, but we had mostly plain food. Her beans and brownbread, pies and doughnuts, were excellent. And we were very fond of an Indian pudding, baked several hours, with pieces of sweet apple in it; also of her "biscuit doughnuts" made from unsweetened biscuit dough, fried in deep fat and eaten with dishes of maple syrup. A corn cake which I learned to make with white corn meal, which was then in the market, was also much liked by the family. Mother's steamed apple dumplings, with a sugar sauce flavored with nutmeg, was another favorite dessert.

Mother had little use for recipes, seldom using a cook book, and consequently had some difficulty in teaching us to cook. When Julia was trying to make a cake, mother gave her the ingredients but not always the quantities. "How much flour?" Julia would ask. "Use thy judgement," mother would say. "But I haven't any judgement," was the reply. One Saturday mother was away and baking the beans was left to Julia. Mother had told her what to put into the bean pot, but omitted to tell her the quantity of beans. Julia remembered that the pot was usually full when it came from the oven, so she filled it with the dry beans. Soon the beans began to swell and the pot to overflow, and I think nearly all our baking dishes were put in requisition and the family must have lived on beans largely for the next week.

Father had a keen mathematical mind and was a good student, but had no opportunity to acquire a broad education. Boys on the farm could be spared for school for only a few weeks in the winter, and the country schools were not very well equipped. The school to which father went had no blackboard, the sums being done with chalk on a brick fireplace. He soon found that the teacher could not help him much in mathematics, and he must work the problems out himself. So he put his mind on then and did every problem in his arithmetic and algebra. His children always knew where to look for help in this line. While his solutions were not always in accordance with text book methods, the results were always correct.

Our Meeting House at St. Albans, about three-fourths of a mile from our house, was a low, wide, wooden building, with unpainted pews and two rows of facing seats, one row slightly raised. These seats went across the whole width of the building, but in the center of the building was a frame for shutters which could be closed, dividing the room into two parts. The men sat on the right side, the women on the left. In meetings for worship the whole room was open, but in business sessions the shutters were drawn, the men and women holding separate meetings. On the higher facing seat, on the men's side, my Uncle Joseph usually sat first, then Lindley Magoon when present, then father and Uncle William. On the women's side Aunt Eunice (Uncle Joseph's wife) sat first, then mother. On the lower facing seat some prominent members of the meeting usually sat. There was no program, no music, and of course considerable silence. When Lindley Magoon spoke we always enjoyed his messages. He was a very eloquent speaker and a fine man, but unfortunately after a time he became mentally unbalanced and had to be cared for by the meeting. Then my father was the principal speaker. Mother frequently had short messages and Uncle William offered prayers, I do not think many of the "lay" members took part in the meetings, although anyone was at liberty to speak if the "Spirit moved". A very ignorant man from a nearby town sometimes came and spoke briefly. A few words which he once said cling to my memory: "The question haint whether or no you daresn't, not by no means." These meetings were somewhat of an ordeal for a child and I remember watching Uncle Joseph quite anxiously, to see when he would turn and shake hands with the one nearest him, thus closing the meeting. The First Day and the Fifth Day meetings were always attended, no matter how pressing the farm work may have been. After the First Day Meeting we would all go to the Union Church, a short distance away, for Sunday School. This was the only other Church in the Village and was composed of Methodists, Free-Will Baptists and Congregationalists. The Quakers co-operated fully with them, when possible; in all community work. Lindley Magoon taught a class in this Sunday School for some time.

Family worship, Bible reading and prayer, in the morning, was never neglected. I considered this an indispensable part of the day. Even my pet cat seemed to recognize the devotional period, as he always came and sat in my lap with his front paws on my shoulder at this time. One morning the family was unexpectedly called away before devotions, leaving only myself and a hired man at the table. When an older sister came back, she found me trying to read a chapter in the Bible, with the hired man, his chair tilted against the wall, patiently listening. He was probably not much edified but may have appreciated this shortening of his day's work.

Our outdoor winter recreation was usually coasting, as there was no pond or lake near for skating. On a "double runner" with some neighbor's older boys to steer there would be some exhilirating rides down a steep hill near our house. And spring mornings, when the snow was crusted over, was the favorite time for using my sled. A field on the hill offered a fine opportunity. One morning I stayed a little too long; the crust had melted in spots. In the middle of the descent suddenly the sled sank into the snow and I went on, striking on my face in the crust. For some days my face was a patchwork of court plaster. We used to take our sleds up into the pasture, where father had tapped some maple trees, and gather the sap for boiling in the large iron kettle into delicious light-colored syrup.

For indoor games we played checkers, dominoes, authors, and jack straws. Cards were not allowed. We went to a few children's parties, but dancing was strictly forbidden. We seldom missed any school days. Attired in warm coats, leggings, mittens and hoods, we could breast almost any kind of weather.

In planting time we dropped corn for father to cover (5 kernels to a hill, 3 to grow and 2 for the crows), and we sometimes helped to cut the potatoes for planting. Rainy days in spring, which I usually dreaded, were often devoted to picking over beans for planting. In the summer picking strawberries and raspberries was more to my taste, as I loved the out-of-doors. The country air kept us so healthy that a doctor was seldom called. A few medicines were kept on hand, belladonna, rheubarb mixture, hoarhound syrup for coughs, and sulphur and molasses for a spring tonic.

My father was fond of traveling, delighted in seeing new scenes, but his family cares and his finances did not permit much gratification of this trait. In those days Friends whose gift in the ministry had been acknowledged were sometimes given a "Minute" by the meeting to visit other meetings in distant places, When I was about ten years old father took such a Minute to visit Quaker meetings in Iowa, where two of his brothers lived, and the next year a similar Minute to visit meetings in Canada. I have no doubt that his "concern" for these meetings was genuine, but he combined duty with pleasure. Mother was a home body and did not care much for these journeys but she dutifully accompanied him, as he would go nowhere without her. During these absences Aunt Mary was in charge of the house, and as she was anxious that the usual progress should be made in the farm work, we were kept busy gathering apples, husking corn, and doing other chores.

Mother's ancestry included a Quaker family, John Hanson of Dover, N.H. who married Elizabeth Meader and had six children. In September, 1724, a band of 13 Indians came to the home, when they knew the husband was absent, killed two of the children and carried Elizabeth and the other four children to Canada, to be sold to the French. Elizabeth was sold for 600 livres. Not long after this her husband went to Canada and succeeded in ransoming her and one of the daughters. A second attempt to ransom another daughter failed, and John Hanson died in 1727. The ransomed daughter Elizabeth married Ebenezer Varney, who was, I understand, my great, great grandfather. My grandfather, Ebenezer Varney, came to Albion, Maine, from Dover, about 1800. The goods came in an ox cart and my grandmother on horse back. They had 8 children. Mary, Elizabeth and John married and settled in China, Jedediah went to Unity, Margaret to Windham, and William Penn went to Aroostook County and was Pastor of the Friends Meeting in Maple Grove until his death. Lydia married Henry Robinson of Windham, and their son, Dr. Edward F. Robinson, was a renowned physician in Falmouth.

We children were sometimes taken to visit the aunts and uncles in China and Unity. My most vivid remembrance of such a visit was at Aunt Elizabeth's in China, when most of my time was spent in playing with some guinea pigs, a new pet to me. On a visit to Aunt Mary's Clara was taken and was to be left for several days when father would go after her. There were some Seventh Day Adventists in the neighborhood and unfortunately a girl from one of the families came to play with Clara and told her the world was coming to an end in two days, and her people were all going up onto a hill nearby and be taken up to Heaven. Clara thought she would prefer to be with her father and mother in such an event, and while she did not tell Aunt Mary the real reason, she was so unhappy and homesick that she had to be taken home before the date set for the advent.

My Grandfather Varney died before I was born, but I have a picture in my mind of my grandmother Lois, sitting in the chimney corner at Aunt Elizabeth's, with the Quaker cap and kerchief on.

My brother and three sisters were sent to the Friends Boarding School in Providence, R. I., later known as the Moses Brown School, but father's financial ability did not go beyond that. The oldest sister, Elma, the flower of the family, taught for a few years after her graduation, in country schools and in the Boarding School. Then she had three years of happy married life with Dr. Seth K. Gifford, then Head Master in the School and later for long years its Principal. Elma died at the age of 26 with spinal meningitis.

My brother, Isaac Oscar, worked his way through Brown University by teaching evening school and tutoring in the daytime. This left him little time for study, but he finished his college course with good marks, was elected to the Phi Beta Society and a little later got his A. M. degree. He secured at once a position as Principal of a Grammar School in the City, which he kept for a few years. Then he had a longing for country life and a vision of much greater remuneration in business than in school teaching and went back to St. Albans for a few years, living with his parents and investing quite largely in farming and creamery operations. But business ability was not a trait of the family, and his enterprises were not successful financially, to his great sorrow. During his stay in St. Albans he was on the Board of Selectmen of the Town, and served a term in the State Senate at Augusta. He returned to Providence about 1854 and the remainder of his active life was spent in educational work in that city - Principal of Grammar School, then Assistant Superintendent of Schools and for 15 years Superintendent. He had very strict principles and performed his duties "without fear or favor." There were some corrupt politicians on the School Board in those days and he had some severe fights to gain what he deemed best for the schools. One member of the Committee was very insistent that his daughter be given a certain teaching position. She was not qualified and it was refused. He used to say that he wondered why he was able to retain his position. However, the leading newspaper in Providence and public opinion were in his favor, and the schools attained some eminence during his term of office. I remember when some educators from western states came to visit them.

The following is taken from resolutions passed by the School Committee at the time of his death: His high scholastic attainments, his conscientious devotion to duty, his continued efforts to raise educational standards to a higher level, his unusual ability both as an educator and an administrator, won for him the respect and admiration not only of his teachers and administrative associates but also of the general public in the community at large. A pioneer in many fields, he was the author of several text books and was responsible for the introduction of vocational guidance into the Providence Public Schools. His leadership in the field of education received national as well as local recognition and gained for him the esteem and admiration of leaders in various fields of endeavor.

I also quote a few of the words spoken at his funeral by the Pastor of the Congregational Church: "Quietly, earnestly, faithfully he lived and labored in this community, helping to make it a better place in which to live. This he did in part by unconscious influence. I doubt if he had any idea of the good he did simply by being the kind of man he was. Then he helped the whole community by helping its boys and girls to be good citizens, enabling them as best he could to achieve health of body and mind, with spiritual strength adequate for useful, happy living. He was a true public servant."

Notwithstanding his troubles with the schools and domestic difficulties, with an invalid wife who was in bed many years, he somehow found time to write 3 volumes of Arithmetic, introducing the spiral method, several geographical text books and a treatise on Agriculture.

My sister Julia was very ambitious to obtain an education. Possibly some of this characteristic was inherited from our mother, who said when she was a small child that she was going to learn all that was to be learned in the World. Julia worked her way through Colby College by alternating a term at Colby with a term of teaching. The most of the teaching was done at the Erskine Academy in South China. Then she had one year in the State Normal School in Providence, and the following two years taught in the Coburn Classical Institute at Waterville. There she lived in the family of Dr. Small of Colby, who had a German wife. The conversation was usually in German and Julia acquired a fluency in that language. In the fall of 1889 she went to Brooklyn, N.Y., having secured a position in the Girls' High School, which she held for 40 years. In the early years of her teaching she still pursued some of her studies, taking private lessons in French and other subjects. In 1900, having a Sabatical Year, she took a six months' course in the American Institute at Rome, Italy. The remainder of the year was spent in traveling in Greece, Italy, Austria, Germany, and France, and in that year she saw the Passion Play at Oberammegau. During her summer vacations three trips abroad were taken, one spent mostly in England and Scotland, another in Switzerland, and the third on a Mediterranean cruise, visiting Egypt and Palestine.

She was always loyal to the Friends Church, and had discussions in regard to its underlying principles with a favorite cousin, Rufus Jones. After her retirement from teaching, in 1929, she was quite active in the Friends Church at Oak Street, Portland, for some years being a member of the Committee on Ministry and Oversight.

My sister Clara, after graduating from the Moses Brown School, taught for a few years in that Institution, then married Eugene Mumford of Winthrop Center, having her home there until the death of our father in 1905, when she came, with her husband and child, to live at our home which was then on the shore of Lake Cobosseecontee in East Winthrop. There for many years she faithfully cared for mother until her death at 92, and for Aunt Mary, who lived to be 96.

Clara was a conscientious, loyal Quaker, active in the work of the Church. For many years she held offices in the monthly and quarterly meetings and was assistant clerk for the New England Yearly Meeting of Friends and on some of its important committees.One of these was the Committee on the Lincoln School in Providence, R. I. After her death the following letter was received from the Board of Trustees of that School: "Lincoln School has just lost a valuable friend and a faithful member of the Board of Trustees in the death of Mrs. Clara W. Mumford on September 16, 1943. She has served for many years as a trustee, as a member of the School Committee for Moses Brown and Lincoln Schools and on the Scholarship Committee. Her interest in young people, her fairness in evaluating character and need, her cheerful outlook through pain and suffering, her many splendid qualities of heart and mind, have endeared her to us and she will be greatly missed."

My education, outside of country schools, was at the Girls' High School in Providence, where I lived with my brother. After a few years at home, I spent the rest of my active life in clerical and stenographic work: 2 years with Davis and Soule, Promoters, in Waterville, 27 years in the State House at Augusta, and 13 years with the Union Central Life Insurance Company in Portland. A few interesting trips were taken in vacations, to Bermuda and one to Nova Scotia.

During the first 6 years in Portland I lived in an apartment with a cousin, Lois Varney. In 1929 Julia retired from teaching and purchased a home on Seeley Avenue and we went to live with her. Clara, whose husband had died the previous year, joined us and we all lived there until the death of the others left me alone in 1953. Five of those winters were spent by Julia in St. Petersburg, Florida. Clara was with her one winter and she and I were there together for three winters.

\*     \*     \*     \*     \*     \*     \*

During the 90's, the church increased in numbers and activity

128

and outgrew its modest building. In 1897 this building was purchased by Melvin Bigelow and moved across the road, where it became a dwelling house. Through the efforts of the local ministers, Mrs. Hannah Bailey, and other Friends in Winthrop aided by the National Society of Friends, a new church was built. It was occupied in 1898. This building served the area as a central meeting place for the Association during the early 1900's. One pastor during this period was Reverend Horace Hall, a former missionary in Africa, who adjusted to a New England village with surprising success. Following him was Reverend Osborne J. Hoffman, also active in promoting youth services, prayer meetings, and evangelistic meetings. Because the site was central, the tent meetings were held on the Union Church property, welcomed by the Methodist congregation and attended by all. When the Friends Church held its quarterly meetings, members gathered from all over Central Maine for two days of revival meetings, business sessions, and special speakers. Those from away were lodged and fed by members of the community, not necessarily members of the congregation, but neighbors of those who were. Fellowship dinners Saturday and Sunday were served in the dining room above the meeting room. This room was also used to accommodate the overflow from the meetings in the main church when the doors were open so all could see and hear.

With the decline of the Quaker group in Maine, the death of many local members, and greater competition with other denominations, the Society of Friends finally closed the church as a place of worship. During the 1940's the building, now owned by Alonzo T. Williams, was used for living quarters. In 1946-1947 the church was rented by the St. Albans School Board to house the kindergarten pupils. In 1955 the Chatterbox Club purchased the building from Mr. Williams. Behind the Chatterbox Club, there are still traces of the old Quaker cemetery. Possibly because of the limited space, the following transaction is found among the records of the Society:

*Taken from "Old Quaker Church in St. Albans Played Part in Town's History" - By Vertine E. Ellis

Know all Men by These Presents: That I, Phineas Parker of St. Albans in the County Somerset, State of Maine, consideration of twenty-five dollars paid by Daniel Shepherd and Thomas Partridge, as overseers of the monthly meeting of the Society of Friends in the town of St. Albans in said County (the receipt whereof I do hereby acknowledge), do hereby give grant, sell, and convey unto the said Daniel Shepherd and Thomas Partridge as overseers, as aforesaid, and to their superiors, a certain parcel of land situated in said St. Albans and bounded as follows, to wit: beginning on the north side of the grave yard belonging to the inhabitants of St. Albans, in lot No. 12, range 2, four rods and four links and ½ link from the northwest corner of the fence around the graveyard 80° East by the compass, ten rods to a stake and stone, N. 10° East, four rods to a stake and stone, N. 80° West, the rods to a stake thence south two degrees, West (S. 10° W) to the first named bounds containing 40 square rods.

To Have and To Hold The Same. To the said Shepherd and Partridge and their superiors for their use and benefit forever and I do covenant with the said Shepherd and Partridge and their superiors and assigns that I am lawfully seized in fee of the premises, that they are free from all incumbrances, that I have good right to sell and convey the same to the said Shepherd and Partridge and their superiors and that I will warrant and defend the same to the said Shepherd, partridge, and superiors and assigns forever against the lawful claims and demands of any person.

In Witness Whereof I, the said Phineas Parker, and my wife, Lois Parker, whereby for the aforesaid consideration she relinquishes her right of dowry in the premises, have hereunto set our hand and seal this 20th day of March in the year of our Lord one thousand eight hundred and forty-nine.

Signed, sealed, and delivered in the presence of S. Lothrop and L. R. Bailey. Phineas Parker and Mrs. Lois Parker. Somerset 66 -March 19, 1849, Then the above named Phineas Parker acknowledges this instrument by him subscribed to be his free act and deed before me: Sullivan L. Lothrop, Justice of the Peace.

Deed Recorded Phineas Parker to Daniel Shepherd, etc. May 18, 1849 11 a.m. paid $100.

\* \* \* \* \* \* \* \* \* \*

With the building of the new church many of those buried in the small plot were removed to the northwest portion of the village cemetery set aside for them so many years before.

So we see in the history of the Quaker Church the birth, the active growth and accomplishment, and the gradual decline of an institution for many years a power for good in our town.

# CHAPTER XIV

## CLUBS AND ORGANIZATIONS

In the early 1800's, the pioneer families of St. Albans had little time or energy for social gatherings. They cleared land, they built homes, and they bore children. As their families increased, they enlarged their houses. They produced their food by their own efforts.

As the boys and girls came to school age, the men found time to build a schoolhouse in each neighborhood centrally located so all the children could walk to school. These one room schoolhouses became the social center for the families in the area. Frequently they were used for Sunday School; sometimes neighbors gathered on Saturday nights for a spelling bee, a candy pull, or a sing-along. The last day of school brought parents and friends together for a program of songs and recitations.

The Grange Hall, St. Albans, Maine

### THE GRANGE

In 1875, however, interest was aroused among farm families all over the nation. The Civil War had been over for ten years. Men had come back to their farms with an appreciation of the importance of cooperation and support for one another. Consequently when the Patrons of Husbandry, known informally as the Grange, was organized in Washington, D.C. in 1867, farmers in Maine were eager to become involved. Not long after this, A. E. Walker organized the

Eastern Star Grange No. 1 in Hampden, Maine. When I. W. Patten, a member of Eastern Star Grange No. 1, was sent to St. Albans in 1874 to recruit new members, he found an eager listener in Nathaniel Isaac Vining, 37. A canvass of his farmer friends brought an enthusiastic response and on February 28, 1875 Deputy George Brennan of Norridgewock officially organized St. Albans Grange P. of H. No. 114.

Charter members were Mr. and Mrs. Nathaniel Vining, Mr. and Mrs. E. C. Buker, Mr. and Mrs. Lloyd C. Dillingham, Mr. and Mrs. A. J. Plummer, Mr. and Mrs. William Hussey Goodwin, Emma Goodwin, Mr. and Mrs. J. H. French, Mr. and Mrs. J. C. Lyford, Mr. and Mrs. Charles B. Philbrick, Mr. and Mrs. E. B. Ramsdell, J. W. Grant, Mr. and Mrs. J. M. Wilkins, Mr. and Mrs. A. B. Tyler, Stephen Knight, Mary Knight, Mr. and Mrs. John S. Parker, Mr. and Mrs. C. G. Mower, Mr. and Mrs. W. W. Wilkins, Mr. and Mrs. Levi Lucas, Mr. and Mrs. Melvin Bigelow, Mr. and Mrs. J. L. Field, Mr. and Mrs. Seth Emery, Hannah Lucas, Mrs. H. K. Goodwin, Nellie Bigelow and Susan Emery. Levi Lyford Lucas was the first Master.

For five years the Grange met in Buker's Hall, a large room at the back of E. C. Buker's Hotel. One evening a skunk wandered in through the open door. There was a quick evacuation of Grangers through the exit leading into the hotel with no questions asked!

The Grangers met in the Town Hall until 1884 when 28 members representing 13 families decided to build a hall of their own. The building located on Water Street not far from the Town Hall, was started April 20, 1885. On November 7, 1885 the dedication of the Grange Hall was held. The building cost $1,000. J. L. Field was worthy Master.

In 1910 while the hall was being enlarged, the Grange met in the Town Hall. They lost their Bible, their piano, and their working paraphernalia when the Town Hall burned in 1910. On Washington's Birthday in 1911 the Grange Hall was re-dedicated with Lincoln Merrick as Master. At this time Ripley Grange presented a Bible to replace the old one, and this is in use today.

During the first decade of the 1900's, the Grange flourished, often having more than a hundred in attendance. It was during this period that a unanimous vote was taken to send the Congress of the United States a formal declaration favoring Women's Rights. The members also sent a signed paper to the State of Maine Legislature protesting the removal of the State capital from Augusta.

In 1913 the Centennial Committee had a collection of historical objects in the hall, an exhibit of antiques and a float in the Centennial parade. Those on the committee were D. S. Emerson, Hattie Blaisdell Emerson, Charles Martin, Verne Merrill, Grace Webb, and Rose Robertson.

April 20, 1917 was a gala occasion celebrating the payment of all notes held against the Grange. Frank Vining, son of the Grange organizer, Nathaniel Vining, lighted a candle. In its flame his mother, Anna Vining, burned the notes.

For many years the Grange held a Harvest Fair with horse pulling, contests of strength and skill, a parade, and a display of prize vegetables. Following a baked bean dinner, there was always a Baby Show often with 40 babies to be admired and judged. Each baby received a prize donated by the merchants in the area.

With the decline of the family farm and the wider field of activity made possible by the automobile, the Grange is no longer the center of the social life in the community. However, it is still very much alive and a vital part of St. Albans. One open meeting each year is devoted to honoring those who have been faithful members over the years. On May 8, 1980 Joseph Libby of Waterville received the 75 year certificate; his wife, Rose Libby, Ruth Robertson Bubar, and Sidney Mower received the 70 year awards. In August 1979 Irene Libby Mayo came from Portland to celebrate her 70th year as a member. At the same time, Pearl Varney Merrill completed 65 years and her sister Esther Varney Chambers completed 55 years. Another annual event is the serving of the Town Meeting dinner, a tradition of many years. Officers for 1980-1981 are Master - Marie Lombard; Lecturer -Curtis Lombard; Treasurer - Rosalie Bowman; Secretary - Doris Fuller; and Chaplain - Cory Bubar.

Closely allied with the Grange is the Matrons' Circle, organized on January 14, 1959 by Helen McLean, an active member of the Grange. Meeting twice a month at the homes of the members, the Circle combines work with pleasure, frequently enjoying pot-luck dinners followed by an afternoon of quilting or making articles for the annual Christmas Fair. 1980-1981 officers are President -Crystal Robertson; Secretary - Rose Boyd; Treasurer - Rosalie Bowman; and Chaplain - Ruth Bubar.

Another still active organization is the Extension Group, once a part of the Farm Bureau. These women have for years held meetings devoted to the activites of the farm and home. In the 1950's a large membership holding monthly meetings gave programmes on Laundering, Health in the Home, Quick Meals, and Home Gardens. The members of the 1980-1981 organization have considered Types of Lingerie, Safe Use of Wood Stoves, Figure Flattery, Cooking with Herbs, and Drugs Over the Counter. The contrast in programmes shows the broadening field of interest among women. Present officers are: Chairman - Marian Spalding; Secretary - Rose Dinsmore; Treasurer - Martha Nabors; Publicity - Helen Bowman; Programmes -Elizabeth Wiers.

## 4-H CLUB

For many years the St. Albans Indians 4-H Club sponsored by Byron and Marilyn Wiers was very active. The boys and girls raised animals for exhibition and sale and became skilled in farm activities. In 1966 a member of the Indians, Michael Wiers, represented Maine in the State Leadership Award programme. After a citizenship training programme in Washington, D.C., Michael was chosen as a delegate to the National 4-H Club Congress in Chicago. In 1980-81 the 40 members are divided into groups covering Care of Small Animals, Household Duties, Dairy Farming, and Horseback Riding. Leaders include Mary Jane Sorenson, Teri Hart, and David Bubar.

## W C T U — GOOD TEMPLARS

Although these two organizations are no longer in existence, they are worth mentioning here because around the turn of the century their influence in the community was outstanding. In 1886 the St. Albans Women's Christian Temperance Union was organized by Mrs. J. C. Hamilton. The first president was Hattie Philbrick; the secretary was Anna Vining; Zilpha Foss was treasurer. Frances Chandler, Eva Turner, Sarah Winslow, and Martha Lucas Boynton were active members. These ladies were instrumental in starting and supporting the East St. Albans Library. Portraits of two temperance leaders, Frances Willard and Neal Dow, were presented to the two rooms of the Village School. Inspired by these portraits, each spring the older boys and girls were required to write biographical essays not only extolling the characters of the two temperance leaders, but the virtues of temperance as a way of life.

A popular addition to the work of promoting temperence in St. Albans in the early 1900's was the organization of Good Templars. The boys and girls met Friday evenings at the Town Hall. A feature of the weekly meetings was the hearty singing from the Good Templar Songbook. The hall rang with the singing of the selections Drinking Gin, Hurrah For Temperance, and Shun the Bowl. The formal meeting usually ended with the enthusiastic singing of Hurrah For Temperance. Oscar Bigelow, the principal of the Village School, and Lena Richards, a teacher, acted as chaperones. Following the business meeting, Oscar played the piano and the young people rollicked through Trim The Willow, Haymakers, Chase the Squirrel, and Drop The Handkerchief. Although these were in fact contra or country dances, because of the strict decorum of the community, they were labeled games by the young Templars.

## STRAWBERRY ART CLUB

This group of twenty young married women was started by Mrs. Mary Snell, whose daughter Susie Cooper Lucas was the first member. Their meetings held every two weeks were purely social and devoted to working on embroidery or delicate sewing, conversation, and delicious and elaborate refreshments.

STRAWBERRY ART CLUB

Minnie Southard, Flossie Hanson, Bertha Longley, Susie Lucus, Annie Murphy, Addie Emery, Lena Merrill, Myra Bridgham, Eva Fairbrother, Louise Emery, Louise Patten, Katherine Bigelow, Cora Watson, Emma Worthen, Mabel Bigelow, Bertha Hilton.

At the St. Albans Centennial on June 13, 1913 the club members in white dresses rode in a decorated hay rack drawn by four horses. They were awarded first prize in the parade.

The last member of this group, Mrs. William Bigelow of Pittsfield, died in 1971 at the age of 95.

## CHATTERBOX CLUB

On December 13, 1922 a group of young women met at Vera Hanson's to begin meetings of a club which is very active today. Those at the first meeting were Bessie Hanson, Ena Emery, Ruth Robertson, Ethel Libby, Nellie Patten, Clara Chase, and Mary

Parkman. They chose the color yellow, the yellow daisy, and the motto "Work Together" as symbols of their organization. With an increasing membership in 1929, they commenced to meet over the General Store where they held mid-week dinners, Saturday night suppers, and card parties. A family club, playpens, toy boxes, and cribs were in constant use.

In 1955, feeling the need for larger and better equipped quarters, Meredith Fisher, Marjorie Martin Chisholm, and Elsie Vining Kinney negotiated the purchase of the Friends Church building from Alonzo Williams for $600. Over the years great improvements have been made, perhaps the most outstanding a fully equipped modern kitchen, complete with freezing units, storage cupboards, and facilities for catering. The Chatterbox Club has become a popular place for wedding and anniversary receptions and is the meeting place of the Hartland - St. Albans Lions Club.

Over the years the Chatterbox Club has been active in the life of St. Albans. In 1931 they engaged and sponsored Grace Rogers of Pittsfield to teach music in the St. Albans School. Miss Rogers taught for two years. Every year a $200 scholarship is given to Nokomis, a week at Camp Fair Haven is given to a Union Church Sunday School student. The members plan an annual summer trip and over the years have visited the State House and Blaine Mansion in Augusta, Bar Harbor, Cabbage Island, Blue Hill Potteries, Maine Maritime Academy, the Black Mansion, and other historic Maine sites. The club's one money-raising project is the annual spring smorgasbord in late April or early May. This affair is a high spot for many, not only for St. Albans people, but for a large area of central Maine. Besides the enjoyment of good food the occasion gives to many the opportunity for greeting friends and pleasant visiting.

The club meets for supper Wednesday nights during most of the year, omitting the summer months. For some weeks during the winter, Saturday night baked bean suppers and card parties are held for members and their friends.

Officers for 1980-1981 are President, Meredith Fisher; Vice President, Doris Ballard; Secretary, Noreen Willey; and Treasurer, Gladys Kerr.

### CHRISTMAS CLUB

Save your pennies, save them one by one,
Save your pennies, see what you have done.
They have grown to dollars and the interest to the same
We will freely use it in the Master's name.

This song opens every meeting of the St. Albans Christmas Club. The club was started in 1920 with a membership of twelve women. Each contributed one dollar and one Christmas gift at the monthly meetings. At the end of the year, the $12 and the twelve gifts were used for Christmas. It was not long before the membership grew, and as it did, the members decided to work for Christmas cheer for others as well as themselves. For many years the wrapping meeting, held in December, has been devoted to sending gifts of clothing, food, books, and fruit to shut-ins, older citizens, children, and nursing homes. The membership has increased from 12 to 31. In 1980 the club deposit was more than $2,000. Besides the Christmas giving, the Club pays for the December lighting of the church and sends one Sunday School child to Camp Fair Haven each year.

Meetings are held the third Thursday of each month with the annual meeting in October. This is a dinner meeting at which the members receive their deposits and elect officers. 1980-81 officers are President, Chrystal Goforth; Vice President, Jennie Springer; Secretary, Helen Bowman; Treasurer, Ruth Springer; and Chaplain, Reverend Barbara Huse.

### HELPFUL WORKERS

In the early 1900's a group of women in the St. Albans Union Church organized the Helpful Workers with the purpose of financially supporting the church. During the early years, money was raised from baked bean suppers, strawberry festivals, house to house soliciting, and an annual fall fair. Until the mid 40's besides making needed repairs on the church, the Helpful Workers helped support the minister, paying $10 a week toward his salary.

Gradually money raising centered on the fall fair. On October 29, 1931 adults paid 50¢, children 35¢ for the chicken pie supper. For entertainment following the supper, the fair flyer announced "two side-splitting farces," Cohens Divorce and The Fascinators given by local talent; several "interesting exercises" by the school children, and a performance by the Waterville Sentinal Orchestra of 15 pieces with three soloists. Tickets for this programme were adults, 25¢, children, 15¢.

In 1921 $200.25 was realized from the fair and supper. In 1980 $1,250.00 was added to our treasury.

From secretarys' records we get a glimpse of the Association's service to the Union Church over 70 years:

April 22, 1913 - voted to pay $2 for the presiding elder's claim.

Sept. 5, 1913 - voted to pay H. C. Prescott $5 for care of the Church for six months.

Nov. 25, 1913 - from a gift of $10 from D. D. Stewart and $88.96 realized from the fair, it was voted to give the minister $35

July 21, 1914 - paid Leland Welch $1.50 for "putting in wood at the Church and piling same"

March 16, 1915 - Voted to assess each member 50¢ to be paid directly to the minister

Nov. 8, 1916 - voted to pay Edward Burton 50¢ a Sunday for building the fire

Jan. 16, 1924 - voted to pay $5 toward the board of our minister at the Methodist Conference

June 17, 1926 - new hymn books, $7.25

Forty years later with 35 active members, the Helpful Workers still support the Union Church attending to special needs. There are three major money raising projects each year: the annual fair and chicken pie supper in the fall, and the spring and fall rummage sales and coffee breaks. In 1980 adults paid $4 for the supper; children under 12 paid $2. The proceeds from the sale held upstairs at the Grange Hall and the supper were $1,231.69; the fall rummage sale netted $711.13.

Of late years the Helpful Workers have taken the full responsibility for repairs and upkeep of the parsonage. Among the gifts to the church during the last ten years are the complete kitchen and floor covering of the Lowheit Room, complete insulation of the Church building, repair and repainting of the steeple, and in 1981 the shingling of the south roof. The meetings are held the first Thursday of every month except in July and August. The 1980-81 officers are President, Wilda Tripoldi; Vice President, Doris Ballard; Secretary, Gladys Bigelow; Treasurer, Ruth Springer; and Chaplain, Doris Ballard.

## CROCKER CEMETERY ASSOCIATION

A unique organization still active after more than 60 years is the Crocker Cemetery Association. On land once owned by the Crocker family, this well-kept cemetery is located on the Dexter road next to Sidney Mower's property and is still in use as a resting place for the descendents of the original owners.

On the afternoon of September 11, 1915, eight East St. Albans citizens met with Nettie Mower to discuss starting a neighborhood cemetery. The meeting was called to order by G. G. Mower. The first officers were President, G. G. Mower; Vice President, P. W. Libby; Secretary, Carrie E. Fisher; Treasurer, C. M. Page; Executive Committee, C. G. Mower, P. W. Libby, Carrie E. Fisher, C. M. Page, E. G. Crocker, Mrs. C. M. Page; Entertainment Committee, Nettie Mower,

Hattie Smith, Hattie Bragg, Lucy Crocker, Lillie Libby. The first meeting was held at the East Saint Albans Library on Oct. 22, 1915. Clifford Bragg was added to the Executive Committee. Monthly meetings were to be held on the Thursday evening nearest the full moon. The meetings were to open at 7:30 sharp and were to be followed by a social hour. Yearly dues of 25¢ were decided upon. The group voted to mow the cemetery twice a year.

Surrounded by a neat iron fence, this peaceful plot is a tribute to those early families who began the project and to their decendents who have so faithfully met annually to preserve it.

Besides the officers elected at the first meeting, the membership list included: H. W. Cole, E. E. Badger, Mr. and Mrs. T. W. Smith, H. B. Fisher, John Page, Mrs. G. Page, Mrs. Flora Blanchard, Mrs. May Higgins, and Mrs. S. B. Crocker.

Members in 1980-81 are Ivan and Evelyn Crocker, Philip and Muriel (Crocker) Nelson, Winfred and Phyllis Wiers, Sidney Mower, Eva Springer, Victor and Ruth Springer, Zala Nelson, Wendall Patterson, Blaine and Nellie (Crocker) Tibbetts, Norman and Arline Cain. 1980-81 Officers are President, Blaine Tibbetts; Vice President, Wendall Patterson; Secretary, Muriel Nelson; Sexton, Joseph Tripoldi.

## ST. ALBANS FIRE DEPARTMENT

Until 1956 St. Albans depended on the Hartland Fire Department for aid in fighting fires, paying the sum of $500 yearly for the service. In May 1956 Horace Ervin Parkman, a lifelong resident of St. Albans, presented a $9,000 fire truck to the town. Mr. Parkman, who never married, was born in St. Albans on April 2, 1878, the son of Richard and Flora Libby Parkman. Always a successful farmer he became well known for his fine apples, pears, cherries, and maple syrup. His large farmhouse where he died June 3, 1958 overlooks Big Indian Lake and is owned by Curtis and Marie Lombard. Included in the gift were an extension ladder, auxiliary pumps, hose, and other equipment. At once a volunteer fire department was organized with 25 members led by local grocer James Seekins as chief. Almost at once a second hand tank truck was presented to the town by an anonymous donor.

The problem of housing the new equipment was soon solved. A piece of land on Water Street was procured and fill donated; local landowners contributed 1600 feet of standing timber. This was cut and yarded by members of the fire department. Blaine and Richard Mower and Carroll Chambers did the sawing without charge and Charles Mower milled the lumber as his contribution. The hall was built entirely with volunteer labor, Philip Mower, a local carpenter, offering his professional services as foreman for the workers.

The actual cost of the building including wiring, heating, and two expensive doors was $2,500. $2,000 was borrowed; the dedication supper, the Firemen's Ball, food sales, raffles, and donations, with all members of the community helping, covered expenses and allowed the note to be paid off in June 1957. The Fire Department is a valuable asset to the town. Their faithfulness and skill as fire fighters promote security and their service in burning grass, chimney inspection, and quick response to calls for help are appreciated by the entrie community.

Meetings are held every Monday evening. 1981 membership is 30. The officers for 1980-81 are Fire Chief - Peter Duncombe; First Asst. Fire Chief - Alver Snowman; Second Asst. Fire Chief - Alan Curtiss; Captian - John Michaud; Lieutenants - Harley Cooper and David Crocker; Secretary - Wendall Patterson; Treasurer-Elaine Crocker.

At the town meeting in March 1981 money raised for the Fire Department included another truck, physical examinations for the firemen, repairs and making the fire hall more energy efficient. The sum raised was $26,200.

The whole community recognizes the value of the excellent fire fighting facilities and is thankful and proud of the organization and its service to our town.

### BIG INDIAN FISH AND GAME ASSOCIATION

This association was developed in 1964 by several local men interested in hunting and fishing, and for a while was called The Rod and Gun Club.

In 1967 the group became organized under the name Big Indian Fish and Game Association. Sherman Harris was the first president; William DeWolfe, Secretary; Glenna Bartlett, Financial Secretary; and Kenneth Dunton, Treasurer. By this time the membership had increased and interest quickly spread through the community.

A piece of land was purchased from Arthur Vicnaire; lumber and labor was contributed and a club house was built. Bonzy and Weeks donated the well to the endeavour. The roadside sign was the gift of the Pride In Maine Committee of St. Albans Grange. The association was active in developing the Public Boat Landing near the Club House, stocking the lake with brown trout, and repairing the dam in the village.

Over the years the club house has been frequently used for anniversary and wedding receptions and the club's meetings are held there. The members sponsor trap shooting during the summer months. Every year the association raises money to keep the club house repaired and to carry on their activities, conducting two fishing derbies, one in mid-summer, the other at the peak of the ice fishing season.

Officers for 1980-81 are President - Brent Ireland; Vice President -Bud Drew; Secretary - Treasurer, Lonnie Drew.

## SNO-DEVILS SNOWMOBILE CLUB

### Away We Go

Over the mountain and through the snow
Devil's Head is the place to go.
The sleds are ready and the lunch is packed
At the top of the mountain you'll eat your snack.
You glance behind you as you glide along
Everyone's coming, there's nothing wrong.
At the top of the summit you're off your sled
To kindle a fire and heat your bread.
The food was delicious, the company good
Even the children went after the wood.
On to the sleds and away you go
To the granite quarries down below.
Nothing to stop you, you ride and ride
Who's that lady by your side?
Sno-sledding started right here in our town
Now it's a virus going around.
I'm sure that you've caught it, it's now in your blood,
So stop in and join us, you'll enjoy our club.

R.K.

Inspired by interest shown at a public meeting on Jan. 27, 1971.

In March 1971 a group of area snowmobiling enthusiasts began planning a snowmobile club. The planners were Dana and Barbara Leavitt and Curtis Lombard of St. Albans, Harry Nutter of Ripley, and Diane Taylor. At once the idea became a reality with ten families as charter members. The first officers were President, Harold Russell; Vice President, Alver Snowman; Secretary, Harry Nutter; Treasurer, Barbara Leavitt. For a while the Sno-Devils Snowmobile Club held their meetings at the Big Indian Lake Fish and Game Club House. In the summer of 1971 the club bought land on the Todds Corner Road, and at once began the building of the present club house. The money for land and building materials was raised by auctions and pony pulls. Members volunteered for the construction and clearing of the land. Bonzy and Weeks drilled a well for their gift to the enterprise. On November 7, 1971 with 56 families present, Open House celebrated the opening of the completed Sno-Devils Club House.

In 1973 the club was awarded a Rupp Snowmobile as first prize for outstanding accomplishment in Maine Snowmobile Club activity.

On March 18, 1977 a large group gathered at the club house to burn the mortgage, the loan having been completely repaid in five years. Although the last two winters have provided less snow than the Sno-Devils could wish, the club has been active and there are Beano games each Friday evening; money-raising affairs for an annual scholarship for a high school student, and participation in the Pine Tree Society's fund raising program. Every year the club gives a dinner in appreciation of the cooperation of the land owners in the area over whose property the trails are made.

Officers for 1981-82 are President - Harold Russell; Vice President - Everett Graham; Secretary - Rose Dinsmore; Treasurer - Barbara Leavitt; M.S.A. Director - Dorothy Dubois; M.S.A. Alternate -Walter Dinsmore; Trail Master - Harold Nutter; and Beano Chairman - Emile Dubois.

## STAMP CLUB

Since 1948 many St. Albans boys and girls have enjoyed collecting stamps, working together to enlarge their collections, exchange stamps, and learn of our country's history. Frequently the first generation members have passed their collections down to their own children who have become members in later years.

Meetings are held once a month. A busy afternoon is spent adding to collections, making scrap books, preparing duplicates for the National Association of Hospitalized Veterans, and becoming familiar with the new issues. The meetings this year have included preparation for Boy Scout Merit badges in stamp collecting. At many meetings notes are sent to our generous friends. Besides many local donors, stamps come regularly from Sweden, Germany, Guatamala, Brazil, Indiana, New York, and Massachusetts.

The Stamp Club could not have been active for 35 years without the support and encouragement of parents and the generosity of our many friends.

Leaders: 1948-1960; Gertrude Robinson; 1960-1969, Sadie Randall; 1970-1981, Gladys Bigelow.

The present members are Christopher Ballard, Kevin Dunham,

Roger Giggey, Adam Landry and Randy Plourde.

## THE BROTHERHOOD CLUB

This small organization active during the 1930's and 40's was composed of several semi-retired men, all old friends, who gathered to play whist. They were incorporated and held a five-year lease on the second floor of the D. D. Stewart building, now the General Store. Over a period of ten years they gathered several times a week to play and were notably skilled in the art of playing whist, occasionally trying out the new fashioned game of bridge.

Their bylaws numbered fourteen. Although many were routine dealing with payment of dues and general organization, several were indicative of the standards of their generation and of their own character. All were unanimously adopted and obeyed.

1. There will be no gambling.
2. No liquor will be allowed on the premises.
3. No angry disputes will be tolerated.
4. Each member is to be given a key to the club room. This key will be used only by him, by his wife, or another member.
5. There will be no card playing on the Sabbath.

Charter members were:

| | |
|---|---|
| Closson C. Hanson | Harry Hilton |
| Samuel W. Green | Melvin Martin |
| Alfred P. Bigelow | Frank Hersey |
| Clarendon J. Worthen | Edward King |

Gradually members moved away or died and the group dissolved but not one ever forgot those years of friendly competition when they were the Brotherhood Club.

## THE SCOUTS

Two organizations which play an active part in our community are the Boy Scouts and the Girl Scouts.

With their leader Dennis Smith, Boy Scout Troop 404, meets every Monday night at the St. Albans Consolidated School. This is a self supporting organization, providing for their needs by conducting bottle and paper drives. Besides carrying out their Scout activities recognized twice a year at their Courts of Honor, the boys have helped paint the Grange Hall and cleaned the boat landing as community projects.

The 40 Brownie and Girl Scouts have an active program under the leadership of Mrs. Velma Walker. Mrs. Diane Landry leads the Scouts; Mrs. June Vicnaire the Brownies. They meet Thursdays.

An outstanding event in this year's program was a Christmas dinner given by both groups to 50 St. Albans Senior Citizens. The affair was held at the Chatterbox Club at noon on December 13, 1981. The Scouts served the turkey dinner; the Brownies sang carols during the meal. This was a joyful occasion for all those who participated in the celebration.

A spring excursion to the Planetarium at the University of Maine was an exciting experience. A joint meeting of the Scouts was held in April at which Albert Worden of the Nokomis High School faculty spoke on the dangers of drugs and alcohol. Mr. Worden who teaches Social Studies spoke with authority about the drug and alcohol problem and the boys and girls gained much from the meeting.

On the Sundays dedicated to the Scouts the members attended the St. Albans Union Church sitting together and taking part in the service.

St. Albans is fortunate to have these two flourishing groups and the devoted leaders who make their organizations definite assets to the community.

# CHAPTER XV

## EAST ST. ALBANS LIBRARY

The only library building our town ever had was the East St. Albans Library in the original Crocker homestead. After the family outgrew the small house, it remained vacant for many years.

After Edwin and Nettie (Richardson) Mower built their home beyond Five Corners, the old house was moved to its present site opposite the Mowers. It was not long before Nettie Mower, always an active member of the East St. Albans community, decided it would be beneficial for the children as well as the adults in the neighborhood to have a library. The Crocker house was chosen to fill the need.

Her efforts were successful. Contributions of books and labor made it possible for those who wished to have access to reference books and recreational reading not possible before.

For years Mrs. Mower was librarian, always ready to go across the road to serve those who came to borrow books. The library was very popular with the summer occupants of the cottages on Indian Pond who made weekly trips to the library, leaving with arms full of books to be enjoyed during the leisurely summer afternoons. Frequently several ladies would gather on a piazza to do fancy work or mending while one of the group read aloud.

Most of the books in the East St. Albans Library were novels of romance, western adventure, or mystery by Kathleen Norris, Grace Livingston Hill, Zane Gray, Agatha Christie, Dorothy Caufield Fisher, and Emilie Loring. The guardians and patrons of the library believed that reading should be an edifying and pleasant diversion; that world problems and social ills could be dealt with in libraries serving a larger clientele.

The Library was a source of inspiration and pleasure for many years but in time the radio, television, and automobile made the pleasure of quiet reading less attractive. The consolidation of the schools with their more adequate resources made the need of the library less important. Gradually Mrs. Mower became less active in her role as librarian and fewer and fewer books were used. The automobile made the libraries in Dexter and Hartland more accessible.

Probably the East St. Albans Library will never again be a living part of our town. However, the sturdy little brown building still fitted with shelves remains a symbol of good days to be remembered with pleasure and appreciation.

# CHAPTER XVI

## ST. ALBANS PROGRESS
### FAIRHAVEN TERRACE

Primary concern for the Elderly Citizens Housing need was made known to a Planning Board meeting on November 21, 1975. Present at that meeting: Walter Butler, Richard Lachance, Garnet Bubar, Charles Boyd, Kenneth Hughes. Alternate: Hobart Kemp. Visitors: Gladys Bigelow, Michael Wiers, John Webber, James Martin. Mr. Martin representing the State Human Services Dept. explained the Elderly Housing Program. Subsequently seven members formed the corporation and temporary officers were elected — Walter Butler, Chairman; Michael Weirs, Vice Chairman; Kenneth Hughes, Sec. Other members — Charles Boyd, Richard Lachance, Gladys Bigelow, and Hobart Kemp.

The St. Albans Housing Corporation was legally formed Dec. 1, 1975 and temporary officers named for the remainder of the year, the annual meetings to take place in January of each year.

On Dec. 8, 1975 Farmers Home Administration in Newport started plans to build 16 units of Elderly Housing under F.H.A. Financing in St. Albans.

Three pieces of property were viewed for the housing site, the Patten lot, Porter lot, and Merrill lot.

On Jan. 13, 1976 it was voted to give Pres. Walter Butler authority to sign an option on behalf of the St. Albans Housing Corporation on land of Pearl Merrill.

The architects interviewed were Prentiss and Carlisle Co., Inc., Bangor, Kleinschmidt & Dutting, Pittsfield, and Eaton Tarbell Associates of Bangor. The corporation hired Eaton Tarbell Associates.

"Difficulties soon became the name of the game."

1.  The townspeople voted against raising the seed money for the project at the annual town meeting. (Seed money being .02 of the total project)

2.  Farmers Home Administration turned us down on March 29, 1976. The reasons cited were that there are no banks, no shopping centers, no hospitals in St. Albans.

On May 10, 1976 a letter requesting that Farmers Home Administration reconsider the application with a list of interested and qualified tenants was submitted. A succession of meetings followed. It was only due to the persistent hard work and efforts of those early members that the four buildings of four apartments each located on a hill overlooking St. Albans village became a reality.

Eaton Tarbell brought the plans that had been finally approved by Farmers Home Administration to the annual meeting on January 11, 1977. These plans were on exhibit and discussed in great detail. The following members elected at this meeting were Walter Butler, Kenneth Hughes, Michael Wiers, Angilee Seekins, Hobart Kemp, Ruth Knowles, and Gladys Bigelow.

At Eaton Tarbell's office on August 18, 1977 sealed bids for the construction of the project were opened. The lowest bidder was Bowman and Littlefield.

The Security Agreement with Farmers Home Administration was signed September 15, 1977.

Ground Breaking was a time of rejoicing as officials from Farmers Home, Eaton Tarbell Associates, town officials, and members of the St. Albans Housing Corporation met on October 13, 1977 to break ground. Special guest was Pearl Merrill former owner. The land had been in the Merrill family for many years.

Another commemorative day for the St. Albans Housing Corporation was an Open House on August 6, 1978. Visitors totaling 234 signed the guest book. Refreshments were served by Angilee Seekins, Ruth Knowles, Cynthia Hill, Barbara Leavitt, Elizabeth Wiers, and Laura Smith. In charge of the guest book were Gladys Bigelow and Dorothea Hughes.

OPEN HOUSE AUGUST 6, 1978
Left to Right: Kenneth Hughes, Ruth Knowles, Barbara Leavitt, Angilee Seekins, Michael Wiers, Walter Butler, Andrew Redmond, Donald Hall, Andy Muench

Andrew Redman, Dorothea Green, Marjorie (Martin) Chisholm, Vera Hanson, Pearl Merrill, Angilee Seekins, Barbara Leavitt.

The well for the project was drilled by Bonnsey & Weeks.

The name Fairhaven Terrace was given to the project because of its association with the history of St. Albans.

Present members of the St. Albans Housing Corporation are: Walter Butler, President; Michael Weirs, Vice President; Ruth Knowles, Secretary; Kenneth Hughes Treasurer; Barbara Leavitt, Angilee Seekins, and Hobart Kemp.

Present tenants at Fairhaven Terrace are Mr. and Mrs. Charles Boyd, Mr. and Mrs. George Bowman, Mr. and Mrs. Roland Huse, Ethel Fox, John Kneeland, Vira Moor, Leaman McFarland, Emma Williams, Stella Carr, Mr. and Mrs. Lloyd Temple, Marion Martin,

Ethel Butler, Deborah McAllister, Laura Amee, Stela Sellars and Grace Grace.

The love and care the tenants have shown one for another has proven beyond a doubt that the dream held by a few people when the Corporation was formed was worth every bit of the effort that went into this project.

## SEBASTICOOK FARMS

A small group of parents, grandparents and friends formed an association in 1962, in Pittsfield, Maine, for the purpose of gaining knowledge and interacting experiences, with others who had children with special needs. The group was responsible for sponsoring the first school in the area to provide educational programs for the trainable retarded children. The school opened in September of 1964, in facilities provided by the First Baptist Church of Pittsfield with an enrollment of five students. Mrs. Ruth Parkhurst was employed as a teacher.

In 1965 the Town of Pittsfield authorized the use of the former Hartland Ave. School building by the association. The school was dedicated as the Marie Bradford School honoring Mrs. Marie Bradford a longtime public health nurse, then retired. Mrs. Bradford had devoted her services to the welfare of children and was directly interested in promoting help for the retarded in the area.

In 1973 the Marie Bradford School in Pittsfield became a part of School Administrative District No. 53 thus terminating the long involvement of the association. It was at this time the Sebasticook Association for retarded citizens directed its attention to serving young adults and providing realistic work programs as well as housing.

In 1974 plans were formulated to start a boarding home in a farm oriented atmosphere. Mrs. Kay Simon was employed as executive director. It was at this time that Mrs. Judith Worcester made the home of her mother Mrs. Ruth Lawrence in St. Albans available at an attractive price for the purposes of the association, providing a memorial to her mother.

In 1976 Lawrence Acres became a reality for the adult handicapped people of the area.

Mr. Lester Parkhurst was executive director and Dr. Robert Carignan was president. From this humble beginning Sebasticook Farms has become a major source of development for St. Albans.

Members of the board were: Mr. and Mrs. Lester Parkhurst, Dr. and Mrs. Robert Carignan, Mrs. Glenna Carmichael, Mrs. Judy Worcester, Mr. Jack Dyer, Mr. Gerald Dott.

Today the Sebasticook Assn. is being managed by Larry Wentzil.

## THE ARTS

The cultural history of Maine has been an uneven one due mainly to the lack of financial support for the arts.

Maine has long been a favorite of artists, especially painters, and St. Albans is no exception.

Raymond Clark, who is known nationally as a country singer, has contributed many fine paintings and his work is found in nearly every home of this small community.

Others whose work has been displayed throughout the area are Marjorie Martin Chisholm and Charles Boyd.

## BUSINESSES 1982

| | |
|---|---|
| **Lawyer** | Michael Wiers - Esquire<br>office located in Hartland |
| **Patent Lawyer** | Wolfgang Fasse - Esquire |
| **Building Contractors** | Bowman & Littlefield, Inc.<br>Philip Bowman<br>Elwin Littlefield |
| **Building Materials** | Victor Springer |
| **Construction Contractors** | Lowell E. Knowles, Inc.<br>Earthmoving, Landscaping,<br>Sand, Gravel, Loam, Crushed stone |
| | Lewis McLeod<br>Earthmoving, Landscaping,<br>Sand, Gravel, Loam |
| | Michael Snowman<br>Earthmoving, Sand,<br>Gravel, Loam |
| **Foundation Contractor** | Edward Walker |
| **Plumbing & Heating** | Terry Parker |
| **Trucking & Wood Products** | Andy Laurence |
| | Philip Russell |
| | Donald Reynolds |
| **Tool Sharpening** | Douglas Parkhurst |
| **Sawing Lumber** | Timothy Ballard |
| | Andy Laurence |
| | Sabasticook Farms Assn. |
| | Sidney Mower & Sons |

151

| | |
|---|---|
| **General Stores** | St. Albans General Store<br>Al & Val Barrows<br>Tom & Lynn Roach |
| | Dick's Market<br>Richard Dunham<br>Diane Dunham |
| **Snowmans Garage** | Alver Snowman |
| **Electricians** | Gilpatricks Electric |
| | Harold Whitney |
| | Leslie Campbell |
| | Peter Duncombe |
| **Carpenters** | Sherburn Lary |
| | Peter Duncombe |
| | Harlan Cooper |
| | Terrance Lary |
| **Cattle Dealer** | Bernard Charrier |
| **Antiques** | Norman Bailey |
| **Beauty Shops** | Glenice Hanson |
| | Fay Laurence |
| **Ceramic Shop** | Glenna, Gary, & Mary Bartlett |
| **Camp Albans** | Brian Brooker |
| **Lehr Agency** | The Kenneth A. Hughes & Son Agency, Inc.<br>began in 1946. Recently the business was<br>sold to the Lehr Agency. |
| **St. Albans Trailer Sales** | Hobart Kemp<br>located in Newport, Maine |

# CHAPTER XVII
## PERSONAL GLIMPSES

### DAVID DENSMORE STEWART ESQ.

David Densmore Stewart was born Oct. 2, 1823 in Corinna, Maine. His only formal education was acquired in the common schools of his native town and the academies of St. Albans and Charleston. He never ceased to be a student and was recognized as a man of culture.

He was admitted to the bar in 1845 and began his practice in St. Albans. D. D. Stewart occupied the same small law office on the second floor of the St. Albans General Stone for more than sixty years, and remained in active practice until he was nearly ninety years old.

D. D. Stewart enjoyed more than a local reputation. He had one of the keenest intellects of any lawyer in Maine. His knowledge of the law was exceptional. He is said to have been the only practioner of his day to secure the reversal of a decision of the Maine Law Court by the Supreme Court of the United States.

Excerpts taken from the Lewiston Journal Magazine August 3-6 1910

D. D. Stewart, lawyer of St. Albans, is no different today as the richest man in Maine than he was six months ago when a plain, ordinary country squire with a moderate fortune.

He stops and gossips with his country neighbors, leans on the board fences which surrounded their places and discusses the crops, the political situations, religion, and local affairs just as he has all the years of his life.

The fact that he has more millions than any other person in the state weighs on him in but one way. It brings him a grist of absurd letters each day from people who imagine that he is going to scatter the great wealth which has come to him to the four winds, regardless of whether it will do good or not. Mr. Stewart will obey the command of his brother's will and dispose of the money, but in doing so, will seek to dispose of it in the manner which will bring benefits to mankind. That is the Stewart method.

Today this wealth is not confined in the strong vaults of a bank. To many this will be news, no doubt, for they seem to think that it comes to this delightful old gentleman in the shape of national bank notes and gold coins. Nothing like it. For the most part, every dollar is represented by valuable real estate in the city of Minneapolis.

Mr. Stewart, who is 84 years of age, comes into this large fortune, which is estimated at from $6,000,000 to $15,000,000 through the death in the western city on May 3 of his brother, Levi M. Stewart, who ammassed it through prudent investments, covering a residence of 54 years in Minneapolis. The will which makes D. D. Stewart heir to his brother's estate provides that he must dispose of it by gift or will during his lifetime. It is this provision which brings Squire Stewart the volume of mail which now disturbs the otherwise even tenor of his ways.

It is a question if ever a legacy attracted so much attention in Maine as has this. Many times in the past there have been stories of wealthy Maine people. Most of them have proven under investigation to be myths or much less in size than at first stated.

The Stewart estate is different. None is able to judge its amount. In the city where it is, they can give you but a single answer. That answer is that it can't be a cent less than $6,000,000 and to show that they are correct, they will take you out and point out buildings and land, the known value of which is more than that amount.

A year or two ago, Levi M. Stewart said that he did not know by a million dollars how wealthy he was. Because the estate is large and further because it is to be given away, people have taken a great interest in the matter.

The will itself, was written by Levi Stewart, for he was a lawyer of great ability - Its bequests, summarized are:

| | |
|---|---|
| $50,000 — | to the Home for Children and aged women of Minneapolis |
| $50,000 — | to the Home for Aged Women of the Little Sisters of the Poor of Minneapolis |
| $50,000 — | to the Stewart Memorial Library, Corinna, Maine |
| $20,000 — | to Miss Lillie M. Crafts, Minneapolis, assistant librarian at the University of Minnesota |
| $20,000 — | to Dr. Leo M. Crafts, Minneapolis |
| $25,000 — | each to several relatives |
| $20,000 — | each to three relatives |
| $15,000 — | to one relative |

The rest of the estate to his brother D. D. Stewart of St. Albans with the request that after he has retained for himself such portions as he may deem best, he distribute the remainder among such persons or institutions as in his judgement will do the most good. This he is requested to do by gift before death and in his will.

One thing in connection with this matter, which seems to have escaped the attention of many, is that it did not require the inheritance of a great fortune to make the name of David D. Stewart known in Maine. That name has been known throughout the length and breadth of this state for many years for he has been one of the shining stars of the bar of Maine these many years. He frequently had cases which took him to Washington to argue before the Supreme Court of the United States and the number of times the decision was his way far overbalances those cases he lost.

He was a teetotaler. This he no doubt inherited from his father who made the first temperance speech in Maine. Mr. Stewart once said that if he had ever permitted himself to drink beer, he could not have accomplished what he did during his lifetime.

## SIMON WING — CANDIDATE FOR PRESIDENT

Not many small New England towns have produced a candidate for President of the United States. St. Albans can claim this distinction even though Simon Wing was no longer a St. Albans citizen at the time of his candidacy.

Simon Wing was born on St. Albans Mountain August 29, 1826 and joined the Averys, the Osborns, the Frosts, and the Bigelows in boyhood activities. As a young man he and Isaac Osborn opened a photographer's establishment in St. Albans where they made tintypes for the local clientele. In the mid fifties Simon moved to Massachusetts and finally settled in Charleston, Massachusetts.

Here he introduced an improved camera and set up a manufactory for producing his invention.

In 1892 Simon helped organize the Socialist-Labor Party and in the election of that year became the Party's Presidential candidate. There were five men in the Presidential race. Democrat Grover Cleveland won his second term as President with 5.5 million votes: Benjamin Harrison, Republican, was second with 5.1 million votes: third was People's Candidate, James Weaver, and John Bidwell represented the Prohibition Party: Simon Wing, Socialist and Laborite, was last with 21,000 votes. It seems incredible that the great and powerful labor movement of today should have had its beginnings in part through the efforts of a man born and raised on St. Albans Mountain.

Simon Wing died in Charleston, Massachusetts in 1910 and came home to join his wife, Mary Bigelow Merrill Wing (1830-1885) in the peace of the Village Cemetery in St. Albans.

## FRANK J. ROBINSON, M.D.

Frank J. Robinson, M.D. was an able and successful physician of Fairfield. He was born in St. Albans, Me., January 23, 1850, the son of John and Mary (Nutter) Robinson.

Frank J. Robinson in his youth attended the St. Albans High School and the Corinna Union Academy. His medical studies were inaugurated at the Maine Medical School, Brunswick. They were continued in New York City at Long Island College Hospital, from which he graduated in the class of 1875. His practice in Fairfield was recognized and appreciated by his fellow townsmen for many years.

## HON. MILTON L. MERRILL

Hon. Milton L. Merrill attended St. Albans Academy at Hartland, graduated from Farmington Normal School, receiving his diploma from Gov. Chamberlain. He was a Representative in 1891, served two terms as Senator from Somerset County, was County Commissioner from 1902-1908, Trustee for State School for Boys 1907-1911. Mr. Merrill is best known in connection with the subject of taxation, having been a member of the Special Tax Commission in 1891. Mr. Merrill was a member also of the Special Tax Commission appointed by Gov. Cobb in 1907. He served at many of the sessions of the legislature as one of the Grange Committee, more especially taking up the question of taxation so that he became recognized as one of the best authorities on the equalization of taxes in Maine.

## HON. SULLIVAN LOTHROP

Hon. Sullivan Lothrop was widely known. His time was given to business matters and he took an active interest in public and political affairs. He filled many positions of public honor and trust: Selectman of St. Albans for some 30 years, member of the Court of County Commissioners from 1841-1854, and repeatedly represented his constituents in both branches of the Legislature.

Mr. Lothrop and Mr. Jones, a neighbor, built a tannery and were in business together. Mr. Lothrop also kept a store near his home. When the tannery and store burned, some of the town books were destroyed. He rebuilt both places of business.

While making his yearly settlement with Harris Garcelon, who was one of the traders, Mr. Lothrop said, "That settles all my accounts for this year." Elden Osgood who was present asked if he had squared accounts with the devil, Mr. Lothrop replied, "I have no dealings with him, so I have no accounts to settle."

## TIMOTHY GREEN DOUGLAS

Timothy Green Douglas born November 10, 1825, son of Nathan Douglas, and grandson of Nathan Douglas, went to New Haven, Conn. with his father to enter into the rubber business. After a few years they sold out, the father returning here, and the son going to Edinburgh, Scotland to engage in the same business. There he added to it the making of celluloid. He amassed quite a fortune and died at the age of 80 years. The father made two trips to his native country to visit relatives.

## CHARLES A. SOUTHARD

Reverend Chas. A. Southard, born in St. Albans on February 9, 1844, was educated in the common schools. In July 1862 he enlisted in the 20th Maine Regiment where his hip was shattered during the Battle of Antietam early in the war. His life was saved only because the bullet was deflected by a canteen hanging on his hip. Another St. Albans boy, John S. Parker, stood by his side and helped remove him from the battlefield. In 1864 he married Abbie Hanes Goodwin. As he was unable to do heavy work for some time after his discharge, he returned to Hartland Academy where he graduated in 1872. In 1874 he began to preach the Gospel after receiving a minister's license from the Presiding Elder in the Methodist Church. His first church was in Brownville. After joining the Eastern Maine Methodist Conference he had charges in Hampden, Brewer, Oakland, Newport, and Orono; later he preached in Bradford, Livermore Falls, Lewiston, and his home-town St. Albans. For some years he was District Superintendent in the Methodist Church in Maine.

He was always a loyal member of the GAR and in 1888 was Department Commander of the Grand Army of the Republic. Charles Southard had a fine baritone voice and was in great demand at GAR gatherings, always being asked to sing "The Army Bean", a song popular with the troops. With the same zeal he sang "Onward Christian Soldiers" and "The Battle Hymn of the Republic" in his churches, gaining the title "the fighting Parson." Because of failing health, he retired to his home in St. Albans in 1907. During five years of invalidism he never lost interest in living. He died Sept. 12, 1912, a loyal warrior for church and country.

## CLARENDON J. WORTHEN

C. J. Worthen and his horses in front of his home

A colorful figure of the early 1900's was C. J. Worthen known over New England as a successful dealer in horses, first in St. Albans, then with a large stable in Bangor. For years he bought and sold horses, frequently dealing with Canadian horse dealers as well as New England sources. He resold the horses frequently to out of state customers often disposing of two and three hundred yearly.

Each year "Can" held a day long horse auction at his stable in St. Albans located where his granddaughter Ellen Cooper and her family now live. Dealers came from miles away sometimes bringing horses to add to the sale. There were "bean hole" beans for customers and onlookers with brown bread, doughnuts, and coffee to feed those who had brought no lunch.

For years C. J. Worthen was an ardent harness racing driver and a very good one. Every fall he made the round of the fairs, often driving one of his own horses. His son, Dana Worthen, was also a skillful driver and frequently they competed against each other on the race track. The fans enthusiasm ran high when these two St. Albans men, father and son, raced neck and neck down the home stretch to the finish line.

C. J. Worthen made many friends especially in Masonic circles during his long life. He died at 84 on May 2, 1955 and is buried in St. Albans Village Cemetery.

## A. P. BIGELOW — CITIZEN

Alfred Payson Bigelow was born June 3, 1870, on his father's 300 acre farm on the north east slope of St. Albans Mountain. When he was nine years old, his mother died and from that time he had no regular schooling. His father left the farm to become proprietor of a village store and Alfred helped in the store and looked out for his younger brother, William, and sister, Jennie. At sixteen he went to Augusta where he attended Dirigo Business College for two years, doing chores to earn his board. With a partner, Othello Goodwin, he took over the store which burned in 1897. After working at making boxes for the Baxter Company and doing other odd jobs, he became a wholesale flour salesman for Ansted and Burk Co., Springfield, Ohio where he continued to work until his retirement in the 1930's. Following the Bank Holiday during the great depression, he was elected president of the First National Bank in Pittsfield, retiring in 1948.

He traveled extensively over the United States, visiting California, Florida, and Alaska but he always returned to St. Albans with pride and satisfaction. Once he was persuaded to run for State Representative on the Democratic ticket. Although he was beaten by his opponent, he was always proud that he "ran ahead of his party" on the ticket which meant that many of his Republican friends crossed party lines to vote for him.

From the time he retired from his salesman's work, he became involved in community affairs. He served the town as selectman; for some years he was chairman of the Red Cross; although not a member of the church, he attended regularly and took the responsibility for raising money for repairs. He received government recognition for his successful selling of Liberty Bonds.

During his long life, 1870-1951, Alfred Bigelow had cause to be proud of his New England background, his success as a business man, and the respect of his associates.

## DR. CHARLES A. MOULTON

He was born in Concord, Maine, on March 12, 1860, the son of Larenzo and Sarah Piper Moulton. When Charles was five years old, his mother died and his father moved from Concord to North New Portland where his son attended local schools. His father remarried, taking Charity Strickland of Embden for his second wife. Charles became half brother to Larenzo Edward, Carrie Moulton Healey, Adelbert H. and Ethel with all of whom he kept a close relationship over the years.

Charles completed his early education at Westbrook Seminary in 1881 and graduated from Bowdoin Medical School in 1884. In June 1885 he married Abbie Lunt of Brunswick, Maine, and in July 1885 he commenced his practice of medicine in St. Albans where he remained until 1897 when he moved to Hartland.

In more than a half century of medical practice, Dr. Moulton was not only physician but friend and advisor to hundreds of patients and friends in the area. For many years he traveled day and night, summer and winter to visit his patients, always encouraging them to come to his Hartland office for periodical health check-ups. After he had an automobile, he added caterpillar treads to his wheels in order to travel more efficiently through the winter snow and ice. Babies were delivered at home and the doctor had delivered more than 3,000 babies before his retirement.

In 1933 Dr. Moulton started the Scott-Webb Memorial Hospital, which for many years was an active and valuable asset to all the towns in the area.

Dr. Moulton served as president of the Maine Medical Association in 1923, and received that organization's 50-year medal in 1934. He also served several terms as president and secretary of the Somerset County Medical Association, and served more than a score of years as school physician.

He died at the age of 86 in December 1946. He left to our community a legacy of memories of his devoted and faithful service as a doctor and a friend.

## DR. PAUL R. BRIGGS

A newspaper article written in 1961 describes Dr. Paul R. Briggs as Scott Webb Memorial Hospital's "Guiding Light", a title well deserved after years of devoted service not only to the hospital but to the entire community. Coming to Hartland from Massachusetts in 1935, he at once became a valued member of both Hartland and St. Albans as well as a large surrounding area.

Dr. Briggs was born in Ashland, Massachusetts. As a young man he played professional football, giving up that activity when he entered Tufts Medical School. Following his graduation and internship, he practiced in several hospitals including Boston City Hospital, the Connecticut Veterans Hospital, the Polyclinic Hospital in New York City, and the Cook County Hospital in Chicago, Illinois.

From a small inadequately equipped hospital accommodating a dozen patients, Scott Webb became a 60 bed facility. Under Dr. Briggs' administration a new wing was added to the original building, an elevator installed; a blood bank, sprinkler system, and X-ray department.

Dr. Briggs became an honored figure in the field of medical research and modern techniques. He is a Fellow of the American Academy of Hospital Administrators and the Association of Medical Writers having had several articles printed in Medical Journals. He is also a member of the International College of Surgeons.

As an obstetrician Dr. Briggs has a remarkable record. During his career at Scott Webb he delivered 8000 babies. Especially in the early days of his practice many of these babies were delivered at home. Accompanied by a nurse, the doctor went anywhere at any time of day or night, summer or winter, covering an area of twenty-five miles. One of his long-time associates said of him and his service - "He never refused aid to the stricken and we don't know of a soul Dr. Briggs ever turned away."

Although no longer connected with a hospital or formal medical facility, Dr. Briggs has an office in his home. Here he and his wife Ida, a talented registered nurse, welcome the many who feel confidence in the wisdom and friendly concern of this wise and dedicated physician.

## CAPTAIN SHIRLEY MERRILL WARREN, RN U.S. Navy

Captain Shirley Merrill Warren is a descendant of one of the most active first families in St. Albans.

Born and brought up in St. Albans, she had decided to be a

nurse long before she graduated from Hartland Academy. She was admitted to the five-year course in nursing at Simmons College in Boston, graduating with honors. She received a Masters Degree in Nursing from the University of Washington.

Although offered administrative work, Shirley chose regular hospital nursing, serving in various hospitals and acting as community health nurse in California. In 1950 Captain Warren was commissioned in the U.S. Navy and became Captain in October 1980. Her navy career has taken her to seven Naval Hospitals or Naval Regional Medical Centers including Naval Hospital Kadiak, Alaska; Naval Hospital Subic Bay, Phillipines; and Naval Hospital Guantanamo Bay, Cuba. She served twice at the Naval Hospital in Portsmouth, New Hampshire. She is now head nurse at the Joel T. Boone Branch Clinic, Little Rock, Virginia. Her duties include supervision and training of military and civilian nurses, orientation and training of Hospital Corps personnel and CPR Training of all Boone Clinic staff members, along with directing a weekly in-service programme for all enlisted personnel.

Captain Merrill and Herman R. Warren were married on Feb. 12, 1981 and now live in Virginia Beach, Virginia.

Shirley is owner of a piece of land in St. Albans. Her friends and neighbors hope that after her retirement from active duty she will return to her home town.

# CHAPTER XVIII

## PEOPLE, PLACES AND THINGS

### AN ANCIENT VIOLIN

In a farmhouse on a high scenic ridge at Lyford's Corner near the village of St. Albans I chatted with an old-timer who has happily fiddled his way through life on an ancient violin carrying the mark of Stradivarius and the date, 1724.

He was unimpressed when I told him that a Strad of a year's later date was recently sold for the sum of $60,000, and he said he would not part with his instrument for all the gold in the world. But one would expect such an answer from Elden Wing, seventy-seven years old, whose whole life has portrayed him as an idealist. More than a half century ago he purchased the violin from an aged pioneer in Aroostook County, and at the time he had no knowledge of the significance of the name of the maker. But before long he sensed that the voice of this instrument was sweeter and more haunting than anything he had ever heard before, and almost at once the violin became an inseparable part of his life.

In his younger days he played it at numerous dances in Somerset and Aroostook counties, and later as age crept upon him he played the old fiddle in the barn after long hours of milking; invoked tender music from it in the shade of a gnarled apple tree after sweating labor haying or plowing; drew solace from its strings winter nights beside the kitchen fire when snow drifted against the door, and impish winds played tag up and down the chimney.

Now the ravages of rheumatism have taken from this old man of the farm the pleasure of rhythmic communion with this old Strad but ever and again he carefully removes it from its age-worn case, and sounds a few chords on it. I have seen a few real Strads in my time and when he reverently passed the old violin to me I felt reasonably certain that I was holding one of Antonio Stradivari's instruments which for tone and finish have never yet been excelled. The name of Stradivarius and the date, 1724, were dim with age but they were clear enough to be deciphered. The instrument appeared to have the composition of all Strads - sycamore for the back, neck, and sides, the belly of deal and the finger-board and tail-piece of ebony.

Upon Elden Wing's request I handed the instrument to his daughter, Mrs. Bernice Nelson, who played "Money Musk" to give me an idea of the tone. The chords which she drew from the old violin flooded the old farm kitchen with harmony, and wistful, haunting music brought to Elden Wing's mind memories of long ago when his fiddling brought joy to hundreds. Later, I listened to the yarns he spun for me of his life in Somerset and Aroostook counties. He spoke with a native simplicity that added to the genuineness and the charm of these tales of rural life of the past.

"There were twelve children, eight boys and four girls in the family," he said wistfully, "and I'm the only survivor. Father's farm comprised 160 acres and all of us twelve children had to get out as soon as we were old enough and help out with the work. I was seven years old when I milked my first cow. We children attended classes at the Rand district school house. For fifteen years Lorinda Robinson was a teacher at that school and her influence for good helped to guide the lives of many of her pupils toward the better things of life. Also, we had a man teacher who was a terror when it came to harsh discipline. He used to stand a half dozen boys against a wall with their feet thrust forward, and then he would kick their feet out from under them so that they sprawled yelling on their backs. But I think that the prize stunt of this teacher came when he spanked a sixteen year old girl for passing a love note to a boy. In front of the whole class he put her over his knee and lustily paddled her with his bare hands. And how that girl yelled and struggled with her braids dangling against her tear-streaming cheeks. It was a long time before that girl lived down the public spanking in the old Rand school house.

"I paid three dollars for my first fiddle when I was eighteen years old. Money was scarce then, and I earned the purchase price doing odd jobs for neighboring farmers. Soon after acquiring the fiddle I began playing around at kitchen dances with Bill Hume and Theodore Smith of St. Albans. Those St. Albans kitchen dances were very orderly affairs, and there was very little drinking, but things were a bit different when I played at Mars Hill, Blaine and Easton in Aroostook. Those rugged pioneers of what is now the nation's potato empire liked their rum red and fiery, and they brought their rum jugs to the kitchen shindigs and imbibed with the abandon of healthy men, fired with vision and enthusiasm for a new frontier. They didn't think that the Lady of the Lake could be danced properly unless everybody was half-swizzled and when they spun their partners they stayed spun, I can tell you that. I had just acquired my Strad when I began playing at these Aroostook dances, and Ernest Murphy, the best waltzer in Aroostook a half century ago, followed me around from dance to dance so he could shake a leg to the accompaniment of my violin. He used to say, 'Elden, I don't know what it is but that violin of yours has a voice such as I never heard before.' "

"The Aroostook pioneering fever got into my blood and with my brother Orrin I took up a tract of one hundred acres near Mars Hill, and built a log house, a part of which is still standing. With much labor we cleared fifty acres and planted beans and potatoes around the stumps. After five years we sold out, and I returned to St. Albans where I bought a shingle mill on Weymouth Pond. I conducted the mill for twenty years and then I bought this farm, and settled down to farming for the rest of my life. Although I can't play the old Strad any more it gives me a lot of comfort to take it out of the case and look at it now and then."

*Taken from "Assignment Down East" written by Henry Buxton, used with permission.

## ST. ALBANS - "ROCKY DUNDEE"

More than 100 years ago Harmony had in its town a little settlement of three houses and the locality was called Rocky Dundee.

It was a crossroad going from Mainstream to St. Albans road about two miles from Mainstream and on the right side.

According to the 1850 census on the right hand side of the crossroad was the home of B. F. Hurd and past the place the road forked: on the right fork was the home of H. Reed, and on the left fork of the road was the home of T. H. Dugan.

This was on the town line of St. Albans and the nearest neighbor was Jacob Raymond in St. Albans. This road went about a mile or more from the main road and for years has been overgrown with trees and bushes. Only the cellars remain to be seen and the three or four graves near the building that are now forgotten.

Percy Baine, 82, of St. Albans who lived near this locality as a boy, remembers the road as rough and rocky and without doubt it was named Dundee by someone who remembered the Dundee of Scotland perhaps their former home.

Brought before the Somerset County Court in 1856 was Betsy Dugan who lived in Rocky Dundee, accused of the murder of Jane Dugan by beating her with a wooden club.

The jury brought in a verdict of not guilty and Betsy was acquitted later of another murder in this locality, that of Betsy's husband, who was found with a breadspoon pushed down his throat. Betsy was placed under arrest. The warrant was made out by Cleopas Boyd, a lawyer in legal practice in Harmony. The accused woman sought the services of D. D. Stewart of St. Albans and again Betsy was cleared of the crime laid to her door.

165

Another episode in Betsy's life was due to a colored man named William White, who lived in the Mainstream section of Harmony. He sold his farm for $600 and left with a neighbor whom he had engaged to take him to Bangor. But with a quart of whiskey and two gallons of old cider, they decided to visit Betsy Dugan. The neighbor didn't come home for some time. He said they filled up at Betsy's and he didn't come to life for nearly two days. White had disappeared. The old residents of Harmony said, as the story goes, that Betsy was flush with money. No action was taken and finally Betsy died and is buried beside her husband under an apple tree near her home.

Written by Vertine Ellis — October 28, 1959

## NOTES ON THE 1850 CENSUS TAKEN BY NATHAN DOUGLAS

The disease called disentary or cholera morbus has made ravages on this town this past year. While I am writing its attacks are renewed with great violence and mortality. Local causes are not easily detected.

\*    \*    \*    \*    \*    \*

The rocks are blue limestone, mingled with a soft oily substance. The water hard for washing cooking utensils ferred up. Oxides of iron and copper are very prevalent. Marine shells embedded in the rocks.

\*    \*    \*    \*    \*    \*

Forest trees, same as Harmony, Rock Sugar Maple. Spruce and Fir, Birch and Beech. Hemlock and Cedar.

## CEMETERY INSCRIPTIONS

Lang Cemetery
John Currier, July 31, 1888
"I have fought a good fight
The race appointed I have run
The combat is over, the prize is won.
And now my witness is on high
And now my records in the sky."

Mary J. Malbon of Malbons Mill — died February 5, 1899
"I have a heritage of joy,
Tis hard to part with mother dear,
Whose love we shared so long.
Her toiling hands and voice so clear
Expressed her love so long."

166

Maloon Cemetery
Ella Bragg — died January 31, 1871 Wife of John W. Grant
"My Partner kind, my child so dear
I am not dead but sleeping here.
And as we lived on earth in love
So may we dwell in Heaven above."

Eliza Bethan, wife of Lysander Hartwell — died 1842
"I will not live always so welcome the tomb.
Since Jesus has lain there, I dread not its gloom.
Here sweet be my rest til He bid me arise."

Ebenezer Rollins, April 22, 1872.
No pompous marble to my name we raise
This humble stone bespeaks thy praise
Parental fondness did my life attend
A tender father and a faithful friend.

Charity Holway, wife of Dan Holway — died May 29, 1897 Age 82
Many daughters have done virtuously,
but thou excelled them all.

Martha Merriman, wife of Thomas Merriman, whose death took
place May 10, 1840.
"Lo soft remembrance drops a silent tear,
And holy friendship sits a mourner here."

## MARGARET PACKARD STORY

This was read by Mrs. Percival at a Fisher Get Together. There
were two terms of school a year, June 1, the other December 1. The
length of the term depended on how long the money held out.

I remember when the snow was deep the first winter I went to
school. Some of the big boys used to carry me home in their arms.
One day my mother had just made up her spare bed all clean and
had said, "There, I hope we don't have any more company for a
while to stay overnight." That night George Mower brought me
home, and when he put me down he said, "There, I have brought you
home. Can't you invite me in?" I said, "Yes, but you mustn't stay all
night 'cause mother doesn't want you to."

He always teased me about that for years afterward. I
remember the day he came home from the war. He came to Newport

167

on the train and drove from there. I was sitting out by the steps as he went past. He stopped and spoke to me. I was seventeen then. He said, "Well! When the boys take you home now, do you tell them they mustn't stop?"

## ST. ALBANS EARLIEST TRADER

Thomas Skinner was a very influential man in the early days of our town. He was the first trader in the village and kept a plentiful supply of what was believed to be necesssary, rum and molasses. He was thought to be a temperance man at heart. An anecdote is told of him to illustrate his reluctance to see a man drinking more than was good for him. One of his patrons had been for some time increasing the size and frequency of his drinks until the merchant became alarmed and determined to give him a hint. The next time he came in and called for a glass of rum, he threw down three cents, the customary charge, in payment for the same. To his surprise, Mr. Skinner pushed back one cent. "Why?" said he. "What's that for? Isn't rum three cents a drink?" Skinner replied, "That's my retail price, but when I sell it wholesale, I make a discount." It is said the man put his good sense to work and made up his mind he had better go out of the business entirely.

## JOHN WOODCOCK

A laughable incident of long ago was that of John Woodcock of Ripley. Woodcock had his name changed to Goodale, but didn't get his wife's name changed. Boys who saw them out driving would say, "Here comes old Goodale with old Woodcock's wife."

## AARON RANDALL

Aaron Randall died in St. Albans at a great age. He purchased his coffin, paid for it in gold, and kept it under his bed several years before his death.

Before he died, he left a paper with Daniel Frost in which he requested no preaching at his funeral, that the slate slab under the kitchen stove be used for his headstone, and that the four pall bearers and driver of the hearse at his funeral be Democrats. To each one of them he left a silver dollar. Daniel Frost was a Democrat and to be trusted. There were very few Democrats in the State of Maine at that time.

## ITEMS OF INTEREST

John Rand Jr. is credited with building the upper dam in St.

Albans, and also the stone mill in Dexter. He made the first clearing on Rand Hill in St. Albans.

*  *  *  *  *  *

The earliest marriages in town of which we have found record begin in 1813-1814 and were recorded by Nathan Douglas, town clerk. He was a Congregational minister.

### Poem written upon the occasion of the
### Golden Wedding Anniversary
### of
### Mr. and Mrs. Frederick Richards
### St. Albans, Maine
### March 10, 1911

'Tis fifty years since these two wed
   And cast their lots together,
And promised to love and cherish
   Thro' wintry winds and pleasant weather;
And when into this home she came,
   A loving, cheerful wife,
It was with every thought intent
   To make a happy life.
For the aged parents who lingered there
   She gave tireless, unremitting care.
She cared for neighbors and more distant friends
   In sickness and in health;
She soothed the aching head and heart,
   And wiped the dews of death,
And when the son was born or daughter given,
   Arriving safely from the gates of heaven,
'Twas she who clothed with their first attire
   Without money and without hire.
From their homes o'er the hills and the valleys,
   From the farms and the mills far and near,
With warm hearts fraternal and friendly
   Come kind friends to meet with you here.
And we meet on this joyful occasion
   With you, brother, and with you rejoice
For the fifty years full of happiness
   You have passed with the wife of your choice;
And we greet you, kind and worthy brother,
   And the wife who sits by your side,
You have cherished and cared for her truly,
   Since a maiden she came as your bride,
And as you have journeyed together

169

In the sunshine and shadows of life
You have not felt regret for a moment
Being united as husband and wife.
And in fifty years looking backward
Over life which will not come again,
Come memories that fill you with gladness,
While some have the shadows of pain.
Our life is not always all sunshine,
But it is made up of hopes, joys, and fears;
And you in your joys were united,
And in sorrow could mingle your tears.
The children came, fair household treasures,
And you felt that you never could part
From the loved ones you held so closely
To the depths of your large loving heart,
But the kind Father said to one "Come up higher,"
And then there came sorrow and pain
Of having a loved one go from you
Never to see them again.
But with all truth you could say
"The Lord giveth and He taketh away."
And in your home life with each other,
So kind, so devoted and true,
That the home has had joy at the fireside
Made happy and joyous by you.
Oh blessed, indeed, are the memories
Of those who have followed the plan
Of being kind, forbearing and pleasant,
And a true help to his fellow man;
And in your long life as patrons
Much honor we feel is your due;
For you have stood by its colors staunchly
And to its principles ever been true.
May life still grow brighter before you
For many long years that may come,
May yours be true hearted happiness
And on you shine brightly life's sun,
And brighter for you grow life's evening
When now you are growing old,
Nearing the portals of glory,
And the city whose streets are of gold.
Then for all a kind word and cheerful,
To the children so kind and so true,
Andy may joy dwell with you forever

Is the wish that we all wish for you.
And as the years in their passage go onward
  We hope we more often shall meet,
Renewing the true bond fraternal,
  'Tis a tie that is sacred and sweet.
Now as each says good bye to these friends,
  And take up their separate ways,
We leave our best wishes with you
  On this fiftieth anniversary day.

Mrs. A. L. Vining

## ALBERT'S PLEASURES AND TROUBLES

Where is the pen, and now where is the ink
Now for the verses Ah! just let me think
Oh! Why can't I think of something to write
Some subject that would be witty or bright.

Little, my friends, do I of rhyming know
As these few lines will evidently show;
By daring to write down my simple thought
Where wittier, worthier, wiser pens have wrought.

Of the subjects that came to my mind
Among them a sketch from real life I find,
It's of Albert S. these lines I will pen
Writing it down here as it happened then.

One night as the stars shone brightly above
Albert went to call on his lady love;
Rosie G. received him with much delight
And wore one of her brightest smiles that night.

As he was seated by the lady's side
He thought he would like to call her his bride;
And wishing the time would quickly pass away,
He longs for the dawn of their wedding day.

With pleasure her company he enjoyed
While his mother at home was being annoyed.
It being cold she thought it was his desire
That she should sit up and keep a good fire.

She said "Some ill has happened to my son"
As the clock on the shelf pointed to one;
"Oh! Where can he be?" she said, with dismay,

171

"Surely it soon will be the dawn of day."

"Obed and I will inquire for to know
In what direction he was seen to go."
With a lighted lantern they went and gained
The information they sought to obtain.

Being very frightened and sad hearted
With their lighted lantern they departed;
Having obtained information at last,
Through the dismal darkness they traveled fast.

Albert saw the light come over the hill.
With dismay there came to his heart a chill;
For he quickly recognized his mother;
By her side with the light was his brother.

Immediately on the front door they thumped,
While out of the back door he quickly jumped;
He got over the fence and ran ahead -
When they arrived home they found him in bed.

Author unknown

## ST. ALBANS

St. Albans, fairest town you are
    In the pinelands of old Maine;
'Tis now I long to come home
    To your loved haunts again.

And roam once more among
    Thy verdant valleys and rugged hills,
To wander through the meadows fair,
    Or pause beside thy rills.

Beside the streams I long to stand
    And see them glide along,
And on their banks of velvet green
    To hear the blue birds' song.

On the lake's rough shore I seem to see
    Its water by the breezes fanned;
Play through swamps of lilies fair
    Or lick the shining strand.

In the distance looms the mountain
    Towering dark and high,

While o'er its snow capped summit
  The fleecy cloudlets fly.

On a gently sloping hillside
  Flocks and herds at pasture roam;
While on another amid its shade trees
  Is sitting my old home.

I love you, old St. Albans,
  Each twig and foot of ground
From the distant mountain summit
  To the lowest spot in town.

And as kind a people dwell
  Within your borders wide
As ever tilled the soil
  Along a country side.

No matter where I wander,
  Be it far or be it near,
Thy landscape and thy people
  To my heart are ever dear.

Author unknown

## DESOLATION

I walk in the valley of long ago.
The tide is out and the water low,
Waiting my ship from a foreign shore
That sailed away in days of yore.

I stand on the top of the highest cliff
O'er the rockbound shore and ocean drift;
The damp seaweed and shifting sands
Make me seem afar from haunts of man.

My eyes are dimmed by falling tears
And weary watching of many years;
I pray that my ship will return to me
But all I hear is the moaning sea.

by Vertine Ellis

# BREVITY IS THE SOUL OF WIT

Lo! From the northeast corner of the town
There came to us a cheerful sound
From Bro. Frost and his good wife,
"Come up and see us and come now."

"Come up to the T. Farm and look it o'er
And see if you ever saw the like before;
Come try the cheese and the butter view
And have a good time and an oyster stew."

"Come view the sheep and the lowing kine,
The horses, poultry, and the swine.
See how things are kept and how they look
And see if Sister Frost isn't a good cook."

So when the rain came pouring down
Brother Frost rode around the town
And says "Come in; we won't mind the pour
If it don't thunder 'n lighten, we're going sure."

So Melvin and Clara forth they started
Not being in any way faint hearted.
For knowing Brother Frost would go with great speed,
They hurried up their faithful steed.

And when they arrived at the town farm door
They found no one had come before.
They were warmly greeted by Brother Frost and wife
And sat themselves down to enjoy life.

Soon Brother Vining and wife came straggling in,
Saying to be out in such rain was surely a sin.
Then Daniel and Zilpha were next to arrive
Saying "You played a game on us sure as I am alive.

For we harnessed our horse, we put on our wraps,
And down we sat and folded our hands in our laps.
To wait for the rest and all go together
Regardless of wind, regardless of weather.

I looked at Zilpha and she looked at me
Saying "Where they are I cannot see."
Then Zilpha took her knitting and knit, knit, knit
And I went to the village as fast as I could git.

When I got there I learned, alack,
They all had gone so I started back,

And here I am at this time of night
But if you haven't been to supper why I'm alright."

Next Brother Merrill and wife with a show of power
Came strolling in at the eleventh hour.
Soon some neighbors came dropping in
While the elements kept up a furious din.

Then Brother Turner and his brilliant wife
Came drizzling in, yet full of life.
Then I. O. Winslow last but not least
Made the company complete in time for the feast.

Stories were told about cats and bees,
About going beech nutting and climbing trees,
About one sparrow stopping a team,
And Mrs. Winslow's method of testing cream.

Then Brother Frost held our attention
By telling how he got through a convention;
By putting on cheek and wading in
He went the whole figure without any pin.

Then Brother Foss, he took the cake
And a great laugh he did make
By telling how he to Bangor went
And all they had with no evil intent.

Potatoes, onions, beef steak, and bread,
Pies, cake, and doughnuts before him fled
And twelve cups of coffee was all he drank
He said he didn't like it because 'twas rank.

And when he walked up and called for his bill
They asked him if he was sure he'd eaten his fill.
Then they opened the door and told him to retreat
And never come there for anything more to eat.

So Brothers and Sisters, I warn you all
Never to give that place a hungry call.
For if you from St. Albans come,
They'll open the door and tell you "Be gone!"

When supper was announced all were there.
Oyster stew was served with the greatest care.
Pies, cakes, and cheese served by Sister Frost
Were partaken without price or cost.

175

Such nice food you'll seldom find
Everything just to your mind.
Sister Frost knows how to cook
Equal to anything found in a book.

I will not tell who the most did eat,
Or how they tried each other to beat
But who got the least, why, surely 'twas I,
Now, Brother Bigelow, don't you cry.

While the ladies washed the dishes
The Brothers gave them their best wishes.
Then up the stairs they all did grope
And I know they went up to smoke!

At twelve o'clock they all went home
Feeling glad they each had come.
Saying they had enjoyed it much
And wishing for many more such.

by S. Lothrop

## HERE IN OUR MAINE STATE LAND

But the shimmering dark blue water
Placed by the unseen hand
Flowed onward down through the village
Just as the Maker planned.
I love to look at the picture
It is gorgeous to behold,
But I cannot write the description
For its beauty can never be told.

And oft when I sat by my window
When the moon rose over the hills
The rosy light was reflected
In every rippling rill.
And the water looked like silver
In the quiet hush of the night
And it seemed that the lake was sleeping
Under a rosy light.

Don't travel away from St. Albans
To other parts of the State
To see some other landscape
And your own home to await:

176

The springtime will bring its beauty
Along by the peaceful shore
And Big Indian Lake will be wonderful,
More than ever before.

by Vertine Ellis

# CHAPTER XIX

## GENEALOGY

This section of genealogical information has been compiled in order to acquaint the present generations with the part their ancestors played in founding the town of St. Albans and protecting their American heritage.

We have used every available source of information to make this possible. First of all, we have tried to get some handle on your immigrant ancestor, searching the libraries for possible genealogies, town histories, census records, and ship passenger lists to find some clue to the region or country he came from.

In spite of our best efforts, the genealogy contained in this town history will not be entirely accurate. We wish we had the time and space to publish genealogies on all the early families of St. Albans, but this is impossible. Nevertheless, we prefer not to give more significance to one family than another, as all are equally pertinent to the development of the town. We find that St. Albans families in general have been honest and respected members of their community.

### Your Name

You get it from your father
It was all he had to give,
So it's yours to use and cherish
For as long as you may live.
If you lose the watch he gave you,
It can always be replaced,
But a black mark on your name, Son,
Can never be erased.
It was clean the day you took it
And a worthy name to bear,
When I got it from my father
There was no dishonor there.
So make sure you guard it wisely;
After all is said and done,
You'll be glad the name is spotless
When you give it to your son.

Author unknown

## THE SHIPS THAT CARRIED OUR ANCESTORS

Between 1630 and 1643 it is estimated that 20,000 people of all ages and walks of life were carried in 200 ships from England in search of a new life in the New World.

The spirit in which would-be emigrants faced the future in the country about which they knew so little is described by William Bradford, a Mayflower passenger in his "History of the Plymouth Plantation."

The ships which carried emigrants to the New World had not been built to accommodate passengers, and it must have been hard, indeed, for men and women who may never have seen the sea before. It has been estimated that on the Mayflower voyage each person might have had space no more than the size of a small single bed in which to live, sleeping and waking, while a pile of possessions was all that divided one family from the next.

No particulars are recorded of tonnage or size of the Elizabeth Bonaventure in which the first party from Hingham is known to have sailed, but other ships carrying emigrants to the New World in the years following the voyage of the Mayflower averaged between 150 and 185 tons, were from 54 to 65 feet long, 24 to 26 feet broad, and about 12 feet deep.

When the Winthrop Fleet sailed in 1630, carrying the founders of the Massachusetts Bay Colony, the fare for each adult was 5 pounds.

Even a simple household must have taken several tons of baggage. Besides their furniture, there were items that could not be left behind. The travelers had to remember to store enough food which they would need on the voyage itself, as well as for the future. The voyage might last from six to twelve weeks or even longer if the ship was blown off course.

Certain items like salt, for which there were so many uses, must be taken in good supply, as must oatmeal and rye meal, smoked and salt beef and pork, smoked hams and herrings, dried ox tongues, spices and raisins.

When it came to packing their clothing, a great deal of thought must have been given. Children's clothes were copies in miniature of those worn by their elders. A good supply of boots and shoes would be of the greatest importance. One passenger on the Mayflower included 126 pairs of shoes in his luggage, as well as many pairs of boots.

Certainly books would not have been overlooked by those who possessed them. Few families would have gone without a Bible

-Hornbooks for the children, so called because they were mounted on wood and covered with thin horn to prevent tearing.

Many ancestors of St. Albans families arrived on these early ships. Whenever possible in the genealogies, we have given the name of the ship on which your ancestor sailed to America.

Perhaps a few families in St. Albans can trace their ancestors back to these immigrants whose names appear in the Hingham Register. The following is a list of people known to have emigrated in search of religious freedom beyond the seas. This information was supplied by a cousin of Lowell Knowles, Mrs. John C. Leeds of Silver Springs, Maryland, who visited the church at Hingham, England in 1980.

Not all these immigrants arrived in the Elizabeth Bonaventure. John Folsom and Mary Gilman according to the Folsom genealogy by Elizabeth Knowles Folsom sailed April 20, 1638 on the ship Diligent of 350 tons burden. Nineteen families and six or eight single adults along with Rev. Robert Peck joined the others at Hingham, Massachusetts.

**Beal (Beale)**

John: Marriage, Baptism of children
Nazareth: (Hobart) Baptism, Two marriages
Caleb: Baptism

**Buck**

James: Baptism of child
John: Baptism

**Chamberline (Chamberlyne)**

Henry: Baptism of children, Burial of two children
John: Baptism
Robert: Baptism
Henry: Baptism

**Cooper (Coop, both spellings given in one entry)**

Anthony: Marriage, Baptism of children, Burial of wife
John: Baptism
Anthony: Baptism
Jeremye: Baptism

**Cooper**

Thomas: Baptism of children
Rachel: Baptism
Elizabeth: Baptism

**Cushing (Cushinge)**

Matthew: Marriage, Baptism of children
Nazareth: (Pitcher) Marriage

Daniel: Baptism
Jeremye: Baptism
Matthew: Baptism
Deborah: Baptism

## Foulsham (Folsom) (Alias Smith)

John: Marriage
Mary: (Gilman) Marriage

## Gates

Stephen: Marriage, Baptism of child
Anne: (Weare) Marriage
Mary: Baptism

## Gilman

Edward: Marriage, Baptism of children
Mary: (Clark) Marriage
Edward: Baptism
Sarah: Baptism
John: Baptism
Jeremye: Baptism
Moses: Baptism
Daniel: Baptism

## Hawke

Adam: Baptism
Stephen: Baptism

## Hubberte (Hubbert, Hubbard, Hubbart, Hubert)

Edmond: Marriage, Baptism of children
Margaret: (Dewe) Marriage, Burial of child
Edmond: Baptism, Marriage
Elizabeth: (Elmer) Marriage
Peter: Baptism
Thomas: Baptism
Alice: Baptism
Rebecca: Baptism
Joshua: Baptism
Sarah: Baptism

## Jacob

Nicholas: Baptism of children
John: Baptism
Mary: Baptism

## Lincoln

Daniel: Baptism
Samuel: Baptism

**Ludkinge**

George: Baptism of child Burial of another
Aron: Baptism

**Peck**

Joseph: Marriage, Baptism of children, Burial of wife
Rebecca: Baptism
Joseph: Baptism
Nicholas: Baptism

**Peck (Pecke)**

Robert: (Minister Clerk) Baptism of children, Burial of wife
and a child
Anne: (Lawrence) Burial after return to England
Annie: Baptism
Robert: Baptism
Thomas: Baptism
Joseph: Baptism

**Tower**

John: Baptism

# AVERY

I. **William Averill,** the first of the family in America, settled at
Ipswich, Massachusetts, before March 1637, the date on which
he received his first grant of land from that town, and also on
which his name is first recorded in the Town Proceedings. He
appears there as William Avery. It is evident from this and
other records that he was born about 1611 or earlier, and that
like many others who came to the shores of New England at
that time, he was a simple husbandman, young, and with small
means.

His wife's name was Abigail (surname unknown) and she appears to have been the mother of all his children.

We could not establish his name on a passenger ship list, but
a year later one hundred settlers came, which included the
names of the Dudleys, Winthrops, Bradstreets, Lyfords,
Philbricks, Jacksons, and Andrews.

1
II. **William Averill** (William), b. probably in England about 1632.
He married Hannah Jackson on July 31, 1661; 14 children:

2    1
III. **Job Averill** (William, William), b. Jan. 1, 1666 or 1667 at
Topsfield, Mass. He was m. Feb. 1, 1702 to Susanna Brown. He
inherited his father's grist mill; seven children:

IV. **Israel Averill** (Job³, William², William¹), b. April 21, 1713 at Topsfield, Mass. He m. first Mary Kinney, daughter of Daniel Kinney, a famous ironmonger of Mass.; eight children: m. second Mary (Lee) Hilton, widow of William Hilton.

V. **Israel Avery** (Israel⁴, Job³, William², William¹), b. 1756; m. Jane Clark of Pownalboro, Me. He was a surveyor of highways 1787 in Pownalboro, Me. The family later moved to Clinton, Me.; six children:

VI. **Israel Avery** (Israel⁵, Israel⁴, Job³, William², William²), b. Jan. 6, 1790 at Sheepscot, Me. and lived at Harmony and St. Albans, Me., where he made a permanent home out of the wilderness. Children:
  1. Seth, b. June 12, 1812; Hallowell, Me.; m. Nancy Dorr.
  2. Julia, b. Mar. 3, 1814; St. Albans, Me.; m. William Southard, a mill owner. Their children were:
    1. Rev. Charles S. Southard who was at one time Commander of the GAR for the State of Maine.
    2. Calvin S. Southard, m. Melissa Marble.
    3. Leander Southard
    4. Daniel Southard
    5. Warren Southard
  3. Jane, b. Oct. 18, 1816; St. Albans, Me.; m. Jacob Raymond.
  4. Drusilla, b. Apr. 2, 1818; Harmony, Me., lived at St. Albans, Me.
  5. Israel, b. Jan. 17, 1820; Harmony, Me.; m. Harriett Brown.
  6. Mark, b. Dec. 1, 1822; at Harmony, Me.; m. first Lucinda S. Russell m. second Mrs. Diantha (Parlin) Lock.
  7. Martha, b. Mar. 20, 1827; St. Albans, Me.; m. Joseph Adams.

VII. **Israel Avery** (Israel⁶, Israel⁵, Israel⁴, Job³, William², William¹) b. Jan. 17, 1820; a farmer at St. Albans, Me; He m. Harriet Brown, daughter of Robert Brown and Tanor Brown; Children:
  1. Almond Avery, b. Mar. 27, 1850; m. Adelaide Anderson.
  2. Wilbra Avery, b. Sept. 4, 1852; m. June 21, 1879 Lizzie Hight.
  3. Eliza Avery, b. Dec. 24, 1862; m. John Wippich.
  4. Junius Avery, b. July 4, 1866; m. first Gusta Nelson; m. second Blanche Ross.

**VIII. Almond Avery** (Israel,⁷ Israel,⁶ Israel,⁵ Israel,⁴ Job,³ William,²

William,¹), b. Mar. 27, 1850; m. Adelaide Anderson; Children:
1. Arthur Avery, m. Mabel Parker Page.
2. Bernard Avery.
3. Lula Avery, m. first William Woodcock; m. second Charles Hilton; children by Hilton:
   1. Marion Hilton.
   2. Edna Hilton m. Newell Philbrick.

**VIII. Junius Avery** (Israel,⁷ Israel,⁶ Israel,⁵ Israel,⁴ Job,³ William,²

William,¹) b. July 4, 1866 at St. Albans, Me; m. first Augusta Nelson, daughter of George Nelson and Jane Matthews; m. second Blanche Ross, daughter of Henry Ross - Children of Junius and Blanche (Ross) Avery:
1. Glenice, b. June 4, 1898.
2. Chalmer, b. Sept. 3, 1902 at St. Albans.
3. Albert W., b. 1909.

**IX. Glenice Avery** (Junius,⁸ Israel,⁷ Israel,⁶ Israel,⁵ Israel,⁴ Job,³

William,² William,¹), b. June 4, 1898; m. 1916 William Augustus Lord, son of William Lord and Caroline (Warner) Lord, Ipswich, Mass. Children:
1. Cyril Augustus Lord, b. Sept. 14, 1916; m. Evelyn Merrow. St. Albans, Me.
2. Erma Mildred Lord, b. Sept. 29, 1917; m. Clyde M. Lewis, Hartland, Me.
3. Grace Francis Lord, b. Apr. 9, 1921; m. Bernard P. Lary, Pittsfield, Me.
4. Margaret G. Lord, b. Aug. 12, 1923; m. Myron Merrow, St. Albans, Me.
5. William Junius Lord, b. Apr. 17, 1925; m. Catherine Cranshaw, b. Nov. 2, 1925
6. Edith Blanche Lord, b. Dec. 11, 1927; m. Sherburn Lary, Pittsfield, Me.
7. Patricia M. Lord, b. July 25, 1928; m. Ernest Killam, Pittsfield, Me.

**IX. Albert William Avery** (Junius,⁸ Israel,⁷ Israel,⁶ Israel,⁵ Israel,⁴ Job,³

William,² William,¹), b. Mar. 26, 1909; m. Mildred Jones of Danvers, Mass. Children:
1. Albert Avery Jr., b. Dec. 23, 1930; m. Estelle Gallant.
2. Phyllis Avery.

# BATES

The Bates family trace their ancestry back to the year 1595 when Clement Bates was baptized Jan. 22, 1595 in Lydd Co.England. He was the sixth son of James and Mary (Moline) Bates, born during the reign of Queen Elizabeth. Clement and his wife Anna had five children. With his family he embarked at London for New England on the ship Elizabeth April 6, 1635. After their settlement at Hingham, a son, Samuel, was born in 1639 and this son concerns our narrative.

I.  **Clement Bates,** m. Anna; 5 children:

1

II.  **Samuel Bates,** (Clement), m. Lydia Laphen, Feb. 10, 1667; 9 children.

2        1

III.  **Samuel Bates** (Samuel, Clement), b. Hingham; removed to Sandwich, Cape Cod; 6 children.

3        2        1

IV.  **David Bates** (Samuel, Samuel, Clement), David Bates is assumed the father of Solomon Bates, pioneer of Greene, Maine. One reason for this is the sequence of names, another that Solomon served in the American Revolution. Dates agree, and that he came from Eastern Massachusetts. This is not a proven statement.

4        3        2        1

V.  **Solomon Bates** (David, Samuel, Samuel, Clement), b. Hanover Mass., in 1741. He married Aquilla Bates, daughter of John and Abigail (Bailey) Bates. Children:
1. Doughty, b. 1761.
2. Levi, b. 1763.
3. Solomon Jr., b. 1765.
4. Abigail, b. 1767.
5. Capt. Samuel, b. 1769.
6. Lucinda, b. 1771.
7. Lydia, b. 1773; m. Abel Crocker. (See Crocker family)
8. John, b. Oct 9, 1774.
9. Caleb, b. 1777 m. Elizabeth Herrick.
10. Alexander, b. 1782 m. Nancy Robinson.
11. Sally, b. 1784.
12. Sylvara, b. 1786 m. Artemas Cushman.
13. Reuben, b. 1788.

VI. **Capt. Samuel Bates** (Solomon, David, Samuel, Samuel,
                        1
Clement), b. 1769 m. first Hannah; m. second Sarah Daggett d.
of Capt. John and Mary Stevens Daggett in 1815. Children by
1st wife:
1. Hannah, b. 1791.
2. Marlin, b. 1794.
3. Lucy, b. 1795.
4. Hetty, b. 1797.
5. Deborah, b. 1800 m. Leavitt.
6. Abigail, b. 1802.
7. Sam, b. 1804.
8. Seth, b. 1807; m. Elizabeth Douglas, daughter of Nathan
   Douglas (See Merrill family).
7. John S., b. 1809.
By 2nd marriage
8. Florentina, b. 1817; m. Claudus Buchanan Albee.
9. Simon Daggett, b. 1819 m. Sarah Mower.
10. Marella, b. 1821.
11. Sarah Jones, b. 1823.

VI. **Alexander Bates** (Solomon, David, Samuel, Samuel, Clement), b.
1782; m. Nancy Robinson. Children:
1. William, b. 1804; m. Malinda Smith.
2. Sewell, b. 1806; m. Allura Crocker.
3. Jane, b. 1808; m. Jonathan Weymouth (See Weymouth
   family)
4. Elizabeth, b. 1810; m. John Smith.
5. Hannah, b. 1812
6. Sally, b. 1814; m. Moses Parker.
7. Calvin, b. 1816.
8. Nancy, b. 1817.
9. Hiram, b. 1819.

The Daggett family made its advent into America after the
Pilgrim band. Savage in his Genealogical Dictionary says: "John
Daggett was in Watertown in 1630. Probably came in the fleet with
Gov. Winthrop." Daggett removed to Martha's Vineyard where he
doubtless went with Gov. Mayhew as a first settler.

# BIGELOW

The name of Bigelow is believed by most authorities to have

been derived from the ancient English surname of Bagaley, which was taken by its first bearers because of their residence at a place so called.

The immigrant John Bigelow (or Bagaley) is said by some family historians to have emigrated to America as early as 1636, and it is certain that he was here before 1642, in which year he was married.

I.   **John Bigelow** m. 1642 Mary Warren, daughter of John Warren of Watertown, Mass. Children:
1. John
2. Jonathan
3. Mary
4. Daniel
5. Samuel
6. Joshua
7. Elizabeth
8. Sarah
9. James
10. Martha
11. Abigail
12. Hannah

II.  **Joshua Bigelow**, (John¹) m. 1676; Elizabeth Flagg, daughter of Thomas Flagg; five sons.

III. **Jonathan Bigelow**, (Joshua², John¹), b. May 22, 1679; m. Elizabeth Bemis, June 11, 1702; five sons.

IV.  **James Bigelow**, (Jonathan³, Joshua², John¹), b. 1712. There is some confusion in the records of this generation as to his date of birth, the genealogy listing 1722. The 1712 date was obtained from the cemetery in Skowhegan. Both the genealogy and the information obtained in "Skowhegan on the Kennebec" agree that his wife's name was Sarah.

V.   **James Bigelow**, (James⁴, Jonathan³, Joshua², John¹), b. Jan. 1, 1743; (Records from Skowhegan) m. Mary Sawyer Jan. 1, 1763. They had ten children. He fought in the French and Indian War.

VI.  **James Bigelow** (James⁵, James⁴, Jonathan³, Joshua², John¹), b. 1766; m. Betsey Davis b. 1777, daughter of Jonathan Davis and Elizabeth Emery, daughter of John Emery and Mary Monroe. Children:
1.   Cushman, b. Dec. 15, 1797.

2. Amasa, b. Sept. 22, 1799.
3. Mary (Polly), b. May 5, 1801.
4. Susanna, b. Dec. 2, 1803 - d. 1891.
5. James, b. Mar. 18, 1805 - d. 1873.
6. Joanna, b. Sept. 21, 1808 - d. 1860.
7. Jonathan, b. Oct. 17, 1811.
8. Betsey, b. Aug. 25, 1814.
9. Sarah, b. Dec. 21, 1817 - d. 1877.
10. Hannah, b. Apr. 27, 1820.
11. Louisa, b. Jan. 23, 1824 - d. 1851.

All of the children of James and Betsey Bigelow were given when they left home: boys - a cow and $100 — girls - a feather-bed and $100.

VII. **Cushman Bigelow** (James$^6$, James$^5$, James$^4$, Jonathan$^3$, Joshua$^2$, John$^1$), b. Dec. 15, 1797; m. Thankful Bowden

VII **Amasa Bigelow** (James$^6$ James$^5$ James$^4$ Jonathan$^3$ Joshua$^2$ John$^1$) b. Sept. 22, 1799; m. Mary A. Davis.

VII. **Mary Bigelow** (James$^6$, James$^5$, James$^4$, Jonathan$^3$, Joshua$^2$, John$^1$), b. 1801 - d. 1830; m. Joseph Merrill March 1827 in St. Albans. Children:
1. James Merrill, b. June 26, 1828 - d. Feb 4, 1851. (See Merrill Family)
2. Mary Elliott Merrill, b. Jan. 14, 1830; m. Simon Wing (Presidential candidate) d. 1885.

VII. **Susanna Bigelow** (James$^6$, James$^5$, James$^4$, Jonathan$^3$, Joshua$^2$, John$^1$), b. Dec. 29, 1803; d. 1891; m. June 22, 1826 Sullivan Lothrop b. 1802 - d. 1882 in Bloomfield. They had eleven children:
1. Amasa Lothrop, b. May 17, 1827; d. San Francisco, California.
2. James, b. May 5, 1828.
3. Mary D., b. Sept. 22, 1829; m. Maxwell; Neenak, Wisconsin.
4. Allen H., b. Mar. 24, 1831; d. Santa Anna, Claifornia.
5. James B., b. Nov. 22, 1832; d. Orovelle, California.
6. Roscoe G., b. Aug. 12, 1835.
7. Olive F., b. Apr. 29, 1837; m. Ford.
8. Esther Emery, b. July 11, 1839; m. Wilson Bigelow; d. Sacramento, California.
9. Daniel Webster, b. May 20, 1841; d. Washington D. C.

10. Millen, b. June 1, 1843; New Orleans, Louisianna.
11. Susan, b. Jan. 27, 1846; d. Oakland, California.

         6     5     4     3     2     1

**VII. James Bigelow** (James, James, James, Jonathan, Joshua, John), b. March 18, 1805 - d. 1873; m. Louisa Abbey b. 1809; d. 1873. Children:

1. James Bigelow, b. May 18, 1827; d. 1873.
2. Betsy Bigelow, b. Aug. 18, 1829; d. 1847.
3. Amos Bigelow, b. Nov. 15, 1831; d. 1858.
4. Melissa Bigelow, b. March 3, 1833; m. Joseph Davis.
5. Alfred Bigelow, b. Oct. 26, 1835; d. 1863; m. Caroline Butler. She died a few days after their son Israel was born so he was brought up by his grandparents James and Louise. (See Emery family)
6. Hannah Bigelow, b. May 20, 1837; d. 1882.
7. Calvin Bigelow, b. Mar. 30, 1829; d. California 1926.
8. Louisa Bigelow, b. June 20, 1841; d. 1927; m. Elbridge Douglas.
9. Joanna Bigelow, b. Oct. 8, 1843; d. 1925; m. Isaac Marble.
10. Melvin Bigelow, b. June 3, 1845; d. 1909; m. first Caroline. Harris; second Clara Buker; third Emma Upham.
11. Jerome Bigelow, b. May 3, 1849; d. 1874.
12. Cushman Bigelow, b. July 10, 1847; d. 1862.
13. Frank Bigelow, b. July 23, 1852; d. 1927.

         7     6     5     4     3     2

**VIII. Melvin Bigelow** (James, James, James, James, Jonathan, Joshua,

1

John), b. June 8, 1845; d. 1909. To know Melvin Bigelow was to love and respect him. For years he had been one of the leading business men of the State and, in fact, of New England. He was large in body, mind, and heart, and his kindly face and manner made him a welcome visitor always.

A representative of a large western flour concern, he established their business on a firm footing in New England.

In Somerset County where Melvin Bigelow was known by almost every man, woman, and child, he was greeted everywhere as "Mell". With his two sons he was frequently mistaken as one of the Bigelow brothers.

m. first Caroline Harris (1846-1879); m. second Clara Buker on March 1, 1883; m. third Emma Upham. Children by first wife:

1. Alfred Payson Bigelow, b. 1870; d. 1951; m. Mabel Frost, b. 1869; d. 1948, daughter of Daniel Frost and Henrietta

Osborn; one daughter Gladys Bigelow, b. 1892. (See Frost Genealogy)
2. Jennie Bigelow, b. 1874; d. 1890.
3. William Bigelow, b. 1876; d. 1939; m. Katherine Smith, b. 1875; d. 1971.

**VII. Joanna Bigelow** (James,⁶ James,⁵ James,⁴ Jonathan,³ Joshua,² John¹), b. Sept. 21, 1808; m. first Howes; m. second Israel Vining. -Children:
1. Rosetta Howes
2. Nathaniel Vining b. 1838; d. 1899.
3. Seldon Vining

**VII. Jonathan Bigelow** (James,⁶ James,⁵ James,⁴ Jonathan,³ Joshua,² John¹), m. Melissa Abby - Children:
1. Aurilla, b. Oct. 27, 1861; m. Oct. 18, 1879 Fred Knowles, b. 1859.
2. Flavella, b. Feb. 4, 1863.
3. Wallace L., b. Mar. 15, 1865.
4. Horace A., b. Nov. 14, 1867.
5. Effie, b. Nov. 20, 1869; m. Charles Jones.
6. Emma, b. Dec. 25, 1871; m. Clarendon Worthen, son of Quimby Worthen and Ellen Stevens. Their children:
   1. Thelma Worthen, m. George Mills, son of Freeman and Cassie Mills.
   2. Dana Worthen, b. 1894; d. 1965; m. Lois Wilkins; one daughter Ellen Worthen. (See Wing family)
7. Granville M., b. April 12, 1873.
8. Oscar W., b. Sept. 17, 1880; d. 1966.

**VII. Betsy Bigelow** (James,⁶ James,⁵ James,⁴ Jonathan,³ Joshua,² John¹), b. Aug. 25, 1814; m. April 20, 1835 to Jabez Foss, res. in St. Albans.
Children:
1. Louise, b. Aug. 22, 1836; d. 1846.
2. Mary Susan, b. Sept. 2, 1838; m. May 12, 1860 Browning. G. Fairbrother, b. China, Me. Nov. 12, 1836. Their children:
   1. Cora, b. Aug. 3, 1861; m. Jan. 5, 1881 to Charles Coolidge.
   2. Eva, b. Nov. 19, 1873.
3. Eleanor E., b. Sept. 14, 1842; d. 1845.
4. Gustave Milton, b. Dec. 5, 1844; d. 1860

5. James Seldon, b. Nov. 7, 1848; m. (1st) Jessie King Nov. 25, 1869; King; m. (2nd) Alice Davis.
6. Edson Samuel, b. Dec. 15, 1849.

              6      5      4      3      2      1

**VII. Sarah Bigelow** (James, James, James, Jonathan, Joshua, John), b Dec. 21, 1817; d. 1877; m. Ira Atwood, son of James and Abbie Atwood - Children:
1. Mary, b. 1850; d. 1905.
2. Horace, b. 1850; d. 1932.

              6      5      4      3      2      1

**VII. Hannah Bigelow** (James, James, James, Jonathan, Joshua, John), b. Apr. 27, 1820; m. Seth Emery - 7 Children: (See Emery family)
1. James D.
2. Augustine
3. Salvanus
4. Ellen
5. Susan
6. Betsy
7. Anna

# BOWMAN

Thomas Bowerman came to the Plymouth Colony in 1633. A descendent Thomas Bowerman settled in Windsor, Maine.

I.    **Thomas Bowman** settled in the town of Windsor. (History of Kennebec Co. Chapter XLIV).

           1

II.   **Dennis Bowman** (Thomas), m. Jennie Cottle; 2 sons known.
1. Isaac, m. Phebe Richards, daughter of Benj. and Alice Adams Richards.
2. Dennis, b. April 11, 1808.

           2     1

III.  **Dennis Bowman** (Dennis, Thomas), b. April 11, 1808; m. Sophronia Richards, daughter of Benj. and Alice Adams Richards. (See Richards family) Children:
1. George (farmer in Windsor)
2. Frank (nursery business)
3. Benjamin
There may also have been other children.

           3     2     1

IV.  **Benjamin Bowman** (Dennis, Dennis, Thomas), m. Jane Hawks, daughter of Hawks and Hannah Burton, a respected citizen of the community and a member of the Old Friends Church St. Albans. Children:

1. John, m. 1st Deborah Woodcock; m. 2nd Lydia Fields.
2. Daniel, m. Lydia Beatty. He was a supervisor of schools for many years. Moved to Iowa. A daughter, Mary Bowman m. Purman. She was a physician. A son of Daniel and Lydia became the Lieutenant Governor of Oregon.
3. Frank (moved West)
4. Elizabeth Ann, m. James E. Gifford.
5. Avis, m. Aaron Whitney.

V. **John Bowman** (Benjamin, Dennis, Dennis, Thomas), m. (1st) Deborah Woodcock; m. (2nd) Lydia Fields. Children:

1. Willie (son of John and Deborah)
2. Oscar (son of John and Lydia, daughter of Benj. & Ruth Ann Leach Fields) 1875-1880.
3. Nellie, 1875-1875.
4. Benjamin, 1890-1931.
5. Winn m. Oneita Osborn.
(Probably more children).

VI. **Willie Bowman** (John, Benjamin, Dennis, Dennis, Thomas), Brought up by his grandparents Mr. and Mrs. Benjamin Bowman. His mother died when he was very young, married Annie Folsom, a descendent of John and Mary Gilman Folsom. (See Lyford family) Children:

1. Linwood, b. Sept. 22, 1906; d. Sept. 24, 1942.
2. George, b. Oct. 10, 1908.
3. Arthur, b. Jan. 9, 1911.
4. Ann, died young.

VII. **George Bowman** (Willie, John, Benjamin, Dennis, Dennis, Thomas), b. Oct. 10, 1908; m. Helen Nichols, daughter of Robert and Elva Ross Nichols. Children:

1. Arnold
2. Erol
3. Lori

VII. **Arthur Bowman** (Willie, John, Benjamin, Dennis, Dennis, Thomas), b. Jan. 9, 1911; m. Rosalie Folsom, daughter of Bert and Iva Dearborn Folsom. Children:

1. Mary, b. Oct. 26, 1936; d. 1968; m. Raymond Springer.
2. Philip, b. May 28, 1939; m. Ethelyn Littlefield.


# BRALEY

The Braleys' ancestors were of English descent. Four brothers came from England to New Bedford, Massachusetts.

David Braley came from Hallowell about 1825 and cleared a farm of approximately 170 acres. He was the father of nine children.

I.  **David Braley**, m. first Mimia Raymond; m. second Martha Raymond Smart - Children found listed in old records:
1. John Braley - (Taken prisoner and died in Anderson Prison)
2. Seth Braley.
3. David Braley.
4. William Harrison Braley.

            1
II.  **Seth Braley** (David), m. first Dorothy Smart; m. second Sophronia Reze; Bradford, Me. - Two children:
1. William.
2. Elwell.

            1
II.  **William Harrison Braley** (David), m. first Francis Frost, daughter of Ephraim Frost.
Child by (1st) wife:
1. Etta, m. George A. Willard. Their children; Clyde, Fredonia, Hazel E., Justina.
m. second Ann Hatch. Children:
2. Calvin (Lived on Mountain).
3. Frank Harrison, m. Mrs. Carrie Sawyer.
4. Evelyn, m. George Emery; their children:
   a. Vera, m. Glen Hanson.
   b. Ena, m. O'Neill Plummer.
5. David, m. Margaret Chase; their children:
   a. Edgar.
   b. Lucille.

Ephraim Braley, m. Dec. 23, 1822 Clarissa Raymond.
David Braley, m. Feb. 13, 1827 Jemema Raymond.

# BUKER

I.  **Edson Buker**, (1827-1897), m. Rebecca Butler (1818-1894) and lived in Searsport, Maine before moving to St. Albans. Their children:
1. Henry.
2. Albion.
3. Alphonso.
4. Frank.
5. Clara.

II. **Henry Buker** (1852-1930) (Edson)[1], m. Elizabeth Stevens, daughter of Bradford Stevens. They were the parents of eight children.
1. Minnie, m. George Goodridge of Pittsfield, son of Alpheas and Lucy Seekins.
2. Celia, m. Albert Cook, son of George Cook.
3. Ida, m. Fred Worth.
4. May, m. Henry Shaw.
5. Earl, m. Ethel Page.
6. Phyliss.
7. Beryl, m. first Justin Bickford; second, Earl Folsom, Cambridge, Me.
8. Doris, m. Bert Marr.

III. **Earl Buker** (Henry[2], Edson[1]), m. (1st) Ethel Page; dau. of Ethel Page and Ida Stevens. Children:
1. Arlene, m. (1st) Everett Holt; m. (2nd), George Senencha.
2. Earl Jr., m. Marie Libby.
3. Francis, m. (1st) Earlene Hughes; m. (2nd) Betty Whitney; m. (3rd) Jackie Hazelton.
4. Edson, m. (1st) (Sept. 22, 1937) Mildred Dyer; m. (2nd) Lucille Tilton.
5. Ida May, m. Ernest Wooster; (2nd) William Meierik.

II. **Albion Buker** (Edson)[1], m. Alice Turner, daughter of John and Diantha Worthen Turner. Children:
1. Frank.
2. Clyde.

II. **Alphonso Buker** (Edson)[1], m. Ella Moody, daughter of Chandler and Sarah (Cooley) Moody. One daughter, Inez.

II. **Frank Buker** (Edson)<sup>1</sup>; m. Grace Sleelbrook; Children:
1. Vance E.
2. Joseph S.
3. Hollis L.
4. Robert R.

II. **Clara Buker** (Edson)<sup>1</sup>, b. 1867 Brighton, Me.; d. 1895; m. Melvin Bigelow, son of James and Louisa Bigelow. (See Bigelow family)

# CROCKER

Two brothers named John and William Crocker were among the first settlers in Barnstable, Massachusetts. William came with Reverend Lothrop and his church October 21, 1639, and John arrived the following spring. John Crocker, the elder brother, left no family, but William's posterity are very numerous. A large majority of all the Crockers in the United States trace their descent from Deacon William of Barnstable.

There was also a Francis Crocker of Barnstable in 1645, but the descendants of Francis are not as numerous.

Deacon William Crocker m. first Alice (surname unknown), mother of all his children; m. 2nd Patricia Cobb Parker. Some of his children are:

1. John Crocker, b. May 1, 1637; m. first Mary Bodfish, daughter of Robert Bodfish; 2 children; m. second Thankful Blish.
2. Deacon John Crocker m. first Mary Walley; 2 children; m. 2nd Hannah Taylor.
3. Josiah Crocker, b. Sept. 19, 1647; m. Melatiah Hinkley, daughter of Governor Thomas Hinkley.
4. Eleazor Crocker, b. July 21, 1650; m. first April 7, 1682 Ruth Chipman; m. 2nd Mercy Phinney.
5. Joseph Crocker, m. Temperance Bursley.

I. **Abiel Crocker** married Lydia Bates, daughter of Solomon and Aqulla (Braley) Bates, Jan. 1800. Children:
1. Mahalia, b. July 9, 1801, died 1845.
2. Wheaton, b. Nov. 1, 1802; died 1804.
3. Eleazor, b. July 8, 1804, died 1883.
4. Carlish, b. May 4, 1808, died 1885.
5. Lovel J. C., b. Jan. 12, 1810, died 1872.
6. Lydia, b. Oct. 8, 1811, died 1877, m. Capt. Joseph Sprague.

7. Arrilla, b. July 7, 1813, died 1862.
8. Aquilla, b.July 7, 1813, died early in life.
9. James Granville, b. March 17, 1815, died age 19.
10. Silenus Granville, b. March 17, 1815, died age 7.
11. Eleanor Jane, b. April 10, 1817, died early in life.
12. Marietta L., b. about 1820, died 1870.
13. Deborah A., b. March 22, 1823, died 1897, m. Alonzo Denning.

Abiel Crocker lived in the north part of the town of Greene. He conducted the old grist mills on Allen Stream, known as Crockers Mills, the first grist mill in town, erected by or shortly before 1786 carrying two sets of stones and doing a good business.

Abiel Crocker removed with members of his large family to St. Albans in 1830. His son Lovel born Jan. 12, 1810 was named for Grandfather Crocker's three wives Lovel Joseph Ramsom Crocker. He lived in New York.

II. **Eleazor Crocker** (Abiel)¹, b. July 8, 1804 became one of St. Albans most prominent and respected citizens. He married Sarah Gray; served as selectman six years; Representative to Legislature two years; State Senate one year; also president of the E. Somerset Co. Agri. Society for several years - 7 children: (1) Solomon W. (2) Silenus G. (3) Georgia (4) Sarah (5) Mary (6) Ruth (7)Maria.

III. **Ruth Crocker** (Eleazor²,  Abiel¹), married Dec. 22, 1855, Granville Mower - Children:
1. Edwin Mower, married Nettie Robertson.
2. Mabel Mower, married Frost. (See Mower Genealogy)

III. **Solomon Crocker** (Eleazor²,  Abiel¹), married Jan. 5, 1859; Sarah Keene - 4  children: (2 listed below)

IV. **Joseph E. Crocker** (Solomon³, Eleazor², Abiel¹), married Edna Leavitt - Children (1) Paul (2) Harold (3) Guy

IV. **Eleazor G. Crocker** (Solomon³, Eleazor², Abiel¹), married Christina Cole, daughter of Dow Cole and Melissa - 5 children:

V. **George Crocker** (Eleazor⁴, Solomon³, Elezor², Abiel¹), b. Sept. 3, 1888, married Lura Libby, daughter of John Libby and Nellie

196

Varney. (See Libby Genealogy) - Children:
1. Eleazor Carl Crocker, b. March 15, 1914; married Winnifred Rines. 2 children
2. Thelma Elizabeth Crocker, b. June 4, 1917; married first Durwood Patterson - 9 children; married second Frederick Smith.
3. Muriel Ruth Crocker, b. June 7, 1922, married Philip Nelson. 3 children
4. Ivan George Crocker, b. April 21, 1926, married Evelyn Dickey. 4 children
5. Jeane Ann Crocker, b. Jan. 21, 1934; married George Martin. 2 children.
6. Nellie Lou, b. Nov. 28, 1935; married Blaine Tibbetts - 4 children.

             4        3       2      1

**V.** **Grace Crocker** (Eleazor, Solomon, Eleazor, Abiel), married Ray Thomas.

             4        3       2      1

**V.** **Marion Crocker** (Eleazor, Solomon, Eleazor, Abiel), married Glenn Nickerson.

             4        3       2      1

**V.** **Lucy Crocker** (Eleazor, Solomon, Eleazor, Abiel), married Frank Davis.

Solomon Crocker son of Eleazor II lived until 1911, passing most of his life in St. Albans. In 1855 he went to Minnesota, and at one time owned a considerable part of the land, on which the city of Minneapolis is now located. It was at that time a village or trading post. Mr. Crocker carried many of the supplies driving with a rifle beside him as a protection against the Indians.

At one time he met a band of warriors who had been on the war path and were returning with their scalps. He succeeded in pacifying them by giving them his supplies. While in the west two of his companions were Levi Stewart and D. D. Stewart.

# COOLEY

John Cooley was born in Holland.

**I.** **Isaac Cooley**, b. Jan. 11, 1811; Carroll Co., N. H.; m. Belinda White, daughter of Timothy White of Ossipee, N. H. Children:
1. Greenleaf
2. Caroline

3. Mary Francis
4. Melville
5. Charles
6. Tristum
7. Chalma
8. Malvina

**II.** **Greenleaf Cooley** (Isaac)¹, b. Oct. 23, 1836 and d. July 27, 1860. On the headstone which marks his resting place in the Crocker Cemetery is inscribed the following:

"And they cried with a loud voice saying, How long O Lord holy and just, dost thou not avenge our blood on them that dwell on the earth."

His death is said to have been due to a severe and undeserved beating by a townsman who went unpunished.

**II.** **Caroline Cooley** (Isaac)¹, b. 1838; m. Charles Thompson.

**II.** **Mary Francis Cooley** (Isaac)¹, b. Aug. 23, 1841.

**II.** **Melville Cooley** (Isaac)¹, b. July 7, 1843; m. Dora Holbrook. Children:
1. Ida
2. William

**II.** **Charles Cooley** (Isaac)¹, b. Feb. 6, 1846; d. Dec. 15, 1926. m. Delia Lunt. Children:
1. Elnora, m. Elmer Pingree
2. Elmer
3. William, m. Celia Johnson.
4. Jennie, m. Lee Schoff.
5. Grace, m. Frank Bryant, son of Horatio and Lura Hanson Bryant. Children:
   1. Velma, m. Dan Hamilton.
   2. Bernice, m. George Parker.
   3. Bertell
   4. Cedric
   5. Thelma
   6. Lura

**II.** **Tristum Cooley** (Isaac)¹, b. May 10, 1847.

**II.** **Chalma Cooley** (Isaac)¹, m. Eva Smith.

**II.** **Malvina Cooley** (Isaac), b. Dec. 3, 1854; m. (1st) Charles O. Ellis; m. (2nd) Julian Nichols, son of Joseph and Elizabeth White Nichols. Children:

1. Vertine
2. Bessie
3. Nena
4. Leroy
5. Clara
6. Vivian

Nichols and Ellis children will be listed.

**III.** **Vertine Ellis** (Malvina, Isaac), daughter of Malvina Cooley and Charles Ellis, m. Charles Ellis son of Sylvester and Nancy Lyford Ellis. One daughter Ruth, m. Charles Bailey. They were the parents of a son, Norman Bailey.

**III.** **Bessie Nichols** (Malvina, Isaac), daughter of Malvina Cooley and Julian Nichols; m. William Magoon.

**III.** **Nena Nichols** (Malvina, Isaac), daughter of Malvina Cooley and Julian Nichols; m. Charles Ross, son of Henry and Lydia Dyer Ross. Children: (see Ross family)

1. Erma
2. Elva
3. Doris
4. Bernice
5. Charles E.
6. Arthur
7. Cleo
8. Elwood
9. Lydia

**III.** **Leroy Nichols** (Malvina, Isaac), son of Malvina Cooley and Julian Nichols; m. Belinda Wing.

**III.** **Clara Nichols** (Malvina, Isaac), daughter of Malvina Cooley and Julian Nichols; m. Almon Nickerson.

**III.** **Vivian Nichols** (Malvina, Isaac), daughter of Malvina Cooley and Julian Nichols; m. Walter Munn.

# EMERY

Anthony Emery, second son of John and Agnes Emery was born in Romsey, Hants, England; married Francis (surname unknown). He landed in Boston, June 3, 1635, in the ship James of London.

He removed to Dover, New Hampshire, about 1640, and October 22 of that year signed the "Dover Combination". When he removed to Kittery, Maine, he was identified with the interests of that town.

During his eleven years' (1649-1660) residence in Kittery, he was juryman for several years, selectman in 1652 and 1659. He was one of the forty-one inhabitants of Kittery, who acknowledged themselves subject to the government of Massachusetts Bay, November 16, 1652. At four different times he received grants of land from the town.

In 1660 he was fined for entertaining Quakers. In entertaining Quakers he obeyed the divine commandment: "Thou shalt love thy neighbor as thy self".

Deprived of the rights and privileges of a free man in Kittery, he turned his footsteps toward a colony in which greater liberty was allowed and was received as a free inhabitant of Portsmouth, Rhode Island, Sept. 29, 1660. From records we know that he had three children, that James was his surviving son.

1
II.  **James Emery** (Anthony), came to America with his father, married first Elizabeth (surname unknown) - seven children. He married second Mrs. Elizabeth Ridge (Newcomb). He had grants of land in Kittery, 1653, 1656, 1669, 1671. He was elected Representative to the General Court, 1693-1695. It is related of him that when he went to Boston his carriage was a chair placed in an ox cart drawn by a yoke of steers. This mode of conveyance was necessary as there was not in Kittery a carriage large or strong enough to carry him safely. He was a large man weighing over three hundred fifty pounds. Eleven children:

2        2
III.  **Zechariah Emery** (James, Anthony), b. 1660; married Dec. 9, 1686; Elizabeth Goodwin, daughter of Daniel Goodwin - two children:

3        2        1
IV.  **Zechariah Emery** (Zechariah, James, Anthony), b. Oct. 5, 1690; m. Sarah (surname unknown). 10 children; m. 2nd Rebecca Reddington, 1 son; Only two sons by his first wife will be listed:
   1. Zechariah, b. Aug. 26, 1716.

2. John, b. Jan. 2, 1724-5.
Zechariah and John have descendants in St. Albans.

**V.** **Zechariah Emery** (Zechariah[4], Zechariah[3], James[2], Anthony[1]), b. Aug. 26, 1716; married Dec. 2, 1741, Esther Stevens. 12 children.

**VI.** **Levi Emery** (Zechariah[5], Zechariah[4], Zechariah[3], James[2], Anthony[1]), b. Nov. 3, 1762, settled in Bloomfield, Maine. He was in Canaan in 1790, married Mindwell Ireland, b. Jan. 6, 1772. Children:
1. Sally, m. Levi Bigelow (See Bigelow family)
2. Esther, m. Solomon Steward.
3. Levi, m. Lydia (Leighton) Flagg.
4. Darius, m. 1st Susan Steward.
5. Eunice,m. Charles Fowler.
6. Zechariah, m. Abigail Cole.

**VII.** **Dea. Darius Emery** (Levi[6], Zechariah[5], Zechariah[4], Zechariah[3] James[2], Anthony[1]), m. Susan Steward daughter of Thomas Steward and Olive Moor, Lunnenburg, Mass. 2 sons:
1. Seth
2. Darius
   Seth's line is continued.

**VIII.** **Seth Emery** 1813-1891 (Darius[7], Levi[6], Zechariah[5], Zechariah[4], Zechariah[3], James[2], Anthony[1]), m. Hannah Bigelow. Children:
1. James D. Emery, m. Hattie Ryerson.
2. Augustine, b. Feb. 12, 1841; m. Racheal Winner.
3. Sylrania, b. Dec. 29, 1843.
4. Ellen, b. 1846; m. Isaac Given, Barre, Vt.
5. Susan, m. Dr. Joseph Jackson, Barre, Vt.
6. Betsey, m. Stephen Prescott, (member of the St. Albans Cheese Association).
7. Anna, b. Oct. 4, 1858; m. Henry Prescott.

**IX.** **James Emery** 1851-1929 (Seth[8], Darius[7], Levi[6], Zechariah[5] Zechariah[4], Zechariah[3], James[2], Anthony[1]), m. Hattie Ryerson daughter of J. R. and Almyra (Durmon) Ryerson of Paris, Me. Children:
1. Flossie Emery, m. S. Wesley Seekins.

2. Ernest Emery

9 8 7 6 5
**X.** **Flossie Emery** (James, Seth, Darius, Levi, Zechariah,
4 3 2 1
Zechariah, Zechariah, James, Anthony), m. Stephen Seekins. Children:

1. Iva Seekins, 1899-1974; m. Gilbert Neal - 5 children.
2. Gordon Seekins, 1903; m. Marion Libby - 4 children.
3. Wyna Seekins, 1905-1913.
4. Joseph Seekins, 1906; m. Erma Sinclair - 3 children.
5. Harold Seekins, 1909; m. Angilee Fuller - 3 children.
6. Jennie Seekins, 1912; m. Delmont Springer - 10 children.
7. Alfred Seekins, 1913-1969; m. Charlotte Waldron.
8. Everett Seekins, 1914-1914.
9. Evelyn Seekins, 1914;m. 1st Howard Prescott - 2 children. m. 2nd Clyde Dickey. 1 child.
10. James Seekins, 1917; m. Frances Waldron - 2 children.
11. Doris Seekins, 1920; m. Byron Ballard - 3 children.

4 3 2 1
**V.** **John Emery** (Zechariah, Zechariah, James, Anthony), m. April 24, 1745 Mary Monroe. He settled in Acton, Mass., afterwards removed to the vicinity of Bloomfield - 13 children (five died young) (The Emery genealogy differs somewhat with the history of Bloomfield on his family) Four sons and three sons-in-law had service in the Revolutionary War.

5 4 3 2 1
**VI.** **Elizabeth Emery** (John, Zechariah, Zechariah, James, Anthony), b. Dec. 25, 1749 - m. Jan. 23, 1773 to Jonathan Davis, son of Capt. Jonathan and Hannah (Preston) Davis. Was born in Harvard, Mass. on Sept. 17, 1756. He was a drummer in Capt. Jonathan Davis Co.
Two children:

1. Joseph
2. Betsy, m. James Bigelow. (See Bigelow family)

5 4 3 2 1
**VI.** **Mary Emery** (John, Zechariah, Zechariah, James, Anthony), b. 1751 m. David Hutchins.

5 4 3 2 1
**VI.** **John Emery** (John), Zechariah, Zechariah, James, Anthony)

5 4 3 2 1
**VI.** **Sam Emery** (John, Zechariah, Zechariah, James, Anthony), b. Feb. 19, 1754, married first April 26, 1781 to Rebecca Wheeler of Carlisle, Mass. (b. Mar. 6, 1752 -d. Sept. 30, 1825); m. second

on Oct. 4, 1826 to Hannah Boston. He was one of the eight months men in the Revolutionary War; first tax collector of Canaan, Me. 1788; lived in Bloomfield, removing to Ripley, Me. The first publishment of marriage in Ripley was that of his daughter Joan Emery to Joseph Butler on April 26, 1817 (Ripley Town Records)

Children:
1. Asenath, b. Aug. 9, 1782; m. John Davenport.
2. Susan, b. April 19, 1784; m. Alvin Bigelow.
3. Infant, d. young.
4. Infant, d. young.
5. Lucy, b. Jan. 13, 1787.
6. John, b. Feb. 18, 1789.
7. Olive, b. March 16, 1791.
8. Lucinda, b. Feb. 4, 1793.
9. Rachel, b. Dec. 13, 1794; m. Edward Leavitt.
10. Rebecca, b. April 1, 1797; m. Benjamin Allen.
11. Samuel, b. April 20, 1799.
12. Joanna, b. March 27, 1801; m. Joseph Butler.
13. Mary, b. May 25, 1803, m. Rufus Greeley.

VII. **Joanna Emery** (Samuel⁶, John⁵, Zechariah⁴, Zechariah³, James², Anthony¹), m. July 6, 1817 to Joseph Butler, (who came from Farmington) 13 children:
1. Rebecca, m. Edson Buker - St. Albans - 5 children (See Buker family)
2. Susan Butler, m. Hiram Bassett - Dexter - 5 children.
3. Asenath Butler died young.
4. Sarah Butler, m. Greenwood Stafford - 6 children.
5. Son.
6. Asenath Butler, m. Myron B. Knowles, lawyer - Residence Greeley, Colorado - 7 children. (See Descendents of John Knowles)
7. Benjamin Butler.
8. Joanna Butler, m. Edwin Ramsdell; lived in St. Albans.
9. John Burleigh Butler, m. Mary Haskell; res. Monson - 6 children.
10. Freeman Allen Butler, m. Drusilla Trafton
    Children:
    1. Eugene, m. Addie Hawes.
    2. Edna, m. Leslie Hartwell.
    3. Lena, m. (1st) William Mebane; (2nd) Nathan Richards.
11. Joseph Butler, m. Amanda Ransom.

12. Caroline Butler, m. Alfred Bigelow - one son Israel.
13. Henry Butler, m. Ella Denning; res.Ripley.
    3 children:
    1. Harry
    2. Bessie
    3. Carrie

# EMERY

I.  **John Emery,** son of John and Agnes Emery of Romsey Hants, England, born Sept. 29, 1598 brother of Anthony, sailed with his brother on ship James of London. m. 1st Mary (surname unknown) who died in 1647. He married Mrs. Mary Webster, widow of John Webster. 4 children:

II. **Jonathan Emery** (John¹), b. Newbury, Mass., May 13, 1652 - married Mary Woodman, daughter of Edward Woodman. He was a soldier in King Philip's War. 10 children.

III. **James Emery** (Jonathan², John¹), bapt. April 10, 1698; married Ruth Watson of Haverhill, Massachusetts. 11 children.

IV. **Jonathan Emery** (James³, Jonathan², John¹), b. Nov. 23, 1722. Haverhill, Massachusetts; m. Jerusha Barron, daughter of John and Hannah Barron, of Dracut, Masachusetts. Jonathan Emery was probably a carpenter and farmer. His home was a stopping place for travelers. In 1755 when Arnold was making his famous expedition to Canada, he made his headquarters at Jonathan Emery's house for two weeks. 10 children.

V.  **David Emery** (Jonathan⁴, James³, Jonathan², John¹), m. Abigail Goodwin. Served as one of General Washington's life guards, discharged at Morristown, N. J. March 1780 - 10 children born at Fairfield.

VI. **Miles Emery** (David⁵, Jonathan⁴, James³, Jonathan², John¹), b. Nov. 29. 1799; m. Mary Delia Nedeau in Tobigue Victoria, N.B. Lived in Fort Kent - 15 children.

VII. **Raphile Emery** (Miles⁶, David⁵, Jonathan⁴, James³, Jonathan², John¹), m. June 1, 1858 Anchemes Plourde - 12 children.

**VIII. Jerry Emery** (Raphile,⁷ Miles,⁶ David,⁵ Jonathan,⁴ James,³ Jonathan,²

John),¹ b. April 6, 1877 in Glazier Lake, N.B. moved to St. Albans; m. Helena Freve, b. 1886. Children:

1. Irene Emery, b. 1903; m. Lance Knowles. 4 children
2. Leonard Emery, b. 1905; m. Grace Perkins. 3 children
3. Maurice Emery, b. 1907; m. Evelyn Bishop. Children: Galen, Betty, Ralph.
4. Lucille Emery, b. 1908; m. John Cummings. 4 children.
5. Fremont Emery, b. 1910; m. Charlotte Ginn. 1 child, Merlon.
6. Aurelia Emery, b. 1912; m. Fred Cummings. 4 children.
7. Infant, d. at birth 1914.
8. Durwood Emery, m. Lydia Ross. 3 children: Duane, Larry, Barry twins.
9. Keith Emery, b. 1919; m. Edna Bane. 2 children: Nelda d. young, Helena.
10. Twin sister to Keith, d. at birth.
11. Colby Emery, b. 1921; m. Althea Dearborn - 3 children.
12. Leona Emery, b. 1923; m. Harold Burpee - 4 children; David, Robert, Sandra, Donald.

Another family of Emerys lived in St. Albans for many years. The connection has not been made, but no doubt it is the same line.

I. David Emery, m. Elizabeth Farrer
II. Jerah Emery m. Hannah Cook. Their children:
1. Owen H. Emery, m. Carrie Hatch.
2. George W. Emery, m. Evelyn Braley.
3. Lula Emery, m. Hatch.
4. Walter Emery, m. Willey.
5. Sylvester Emery.

# FINSON

I. **Thomas Finson** (1) married on December 6, 1716 to Mary Lane; she was born August 8, 1696 and died in 1792. Thomas was killed on June 22, 1724 while on a fishing vessel when three "were taken by the Indians in Fox Harbour viz. James Wallis Senr., James Wallis, Junr. and John Lane," John Lane was Mary's father. Mary married Joseph Thurston on March 9, 1724. He died May 29, 1780. Tradition states, Thomas Finson came from Scotland. 4 children:

1
II. **Thomas Finson** (Thomas), married Sarah; b. July 16, 1720; d. May 13, 1762; 6 children:

2　　1
III. **Thomas Finson** (Thomas, Thomas), married on September 7, 1777; at Sandy Bay to Mary (Molly) Dresser. (Baptized Jan. 15, 1748) 7 children.

3　　2　　1
IV. **Ambrose Finson** (Thomas, Thomas, Thomas), married Elizabeth Jordan; b. June 1, 1789; d. July 5, 1857. Elizabeth was b. April 15, 1788 in Danville, Maine and died August 7, 1858. When Maine was made a state in 1820, he was elected Representative at the First Legislature and was twice elected to the same office by the voters of the district comprising Hartland, St. Albans, and Palmyra. Children:
1. Ambrose, b. Feb. 26, 1811; m. Elizabeth; d. July 5, 1857.
2. Elizabeth, b. Nov. 27, 1812.
3. Thomas Major, b. Feb. 8, 1816.
4. Emeline Jordan, b. Feb. 3, 1818; m. Darius Rand; d. Feb. 19, 1903.
5. James Jordan, b. Feb. 25, 1820, Hartland, Maine.
6. John Dresser, b. July 11, 1823.
7. Amasa Bigelow, b. July 5, 1825.
8. Henry Warren, b. Sept. 30, 1827.
9. Mary Jordan, b. March 14, 1830.
10. Greenleaf Church, b. Sept. 16, 1832.

4　　3　　2　　1
V. **John D. Finson** (Ambrose, Thomas, Thomas, Thomas), m. Jan. 16, 1856 - Sarah H. Homer - Children:
1. Almira
2. Amelia
3. Fred
4. Georgia

5　　4　　3　　2
VI. **Fred Finson** (John, Ambrose, Thomas, Thomas,

1
Thomas), m. MeDora Frostina (Chase) Finson.
Children:
1. Ruth Ellis, b. Nov. 22, 1895; m. June 9, 1916; m. (1st) Earl Robertson;(2nd) Cory Bubar. Children by Robertson:
   a. Marguerite, m. Weston Sherburne.

b. Gerald, m. Crystal Cuddey.

    c. Erlfred, b. 1940; d. 1944.

2. Ellen

3. Winfred, m. Helen Lawrence.

4. Harry A.

                         6     5       4        3        2

**VII.** **Harry A. Finson** (Fred, John, Ambrose, Thomas, Thomas,

    1

Thomas), b. May 9, 1904; d. Nov. 29, 1931; Helen Baird; b. June 7, 1913. 1 child, Ronnie.

## FROST

Edmond Frost was born in County Suffolk, England very early in the seventeenth century.

In the year 1635 he came with his wife and infant son to Massachusetts. Some say that he came in the ship Great Hope; others say in the Defence. Savage's Genealogical Dictionary says "he came in the Great Hope in 1635, from Ipswich, having embarked with Rev. Thomas Shepard, who left that ship and came in one not so good, probably the Defence, from Londs. Matthew's American Armory and Blue Book also says that he came in the Great Hope. Others say that the Great Hope wrecked in 1634 off Yarmouth, England, and that Sheperd's party took passage in the Defence the next year.

Whatever doubt there may be as to the ship that brought Edmond Frost, there is none as to that in which Mr. Sheperd came, since Governor Withrop tells us in his journal of Oct. 6, 1635 that "Here arrived two great ships, the Defence and the Abigail, with Mr. Wilson, Mr. Sheperd. . . and other ministers.

Whatever ship brought him, he arrived in Cambridge in 1635. (Frost Genealogy by Norman Seane Frost)

**I.** **Edmond Frost** - married first Thomasine; eight children; married second Mary (surname unknown); one child.

           1

**II.** **Samuel Frost** (Edmond, Thomasine) b. Feb. 13, 1638 in Cambridge Mass. - married in 1663 to Mary Cole; three children -married again to Elizabeth Miller. Samuel was a physician and also seemed to have been a building contractor. 8 children.

           2           1

**III.** **Thomas Frost** (Samuel, Elizabeth, Edmond), b. Billerica, Mass. on April 30, 1674; married Sarah Dunton - 8 children.

           3        2      1

**IV. Samuel Frost** (Thomas, Sam & Eliz Edmond) m. Nov. 9, 1725 to Margaret Ware; 2 children.

           4      3      2      1

**V. Samuel Frost** (Samuel, Thomas, Sam & Eliz, Edmond), b. April 14, 1728 Billerica, Mass. He removed to Wayne and was livng there in 1790. married first Rachael Adams; married second Ann Clark.

           5      4      3      2      1

**VI. Aaron Frost** (Sam & Ann, Samuel, Thomas, Sam&Eliz, Edmond), b. Dec. 14, 1767 - married Huldah Curtis of North Sandwich, Mass., and after his children were born removed to St. Albans -Children:

1. Ephraim
2. Aaron
3. David
4. George
5. Frances
6. Clark
7. Ellis
8. Elijah
9. James
10. Harriet

Aaron Frost, the ancestor of the Frosts in St. Albans, settled with several of his sons on the south side of St. Albans mountain. Ephraim Frost settled near the top of the mountain and Elijah and Clark, his brother, cleared farms on the Ripley side of the town line. Ephraim Frost had a daughter Francis who married William Harrison Braley. (See Braley family)

           6      5      4      3      2

**VII. David Frost** (Aaron, Samuel, Samuel, Thomas, Samuel,

           1

Edmond), b. 1806; married Patience Ellis. Children:

1. David Jr., b. Sept. 16, 1824; d. 1864.
2. Thomas, b. Jan. 15, 1827; d. 1913.
3. Huldah, b. Sept. 7, 1830' d. 1903.
4. Aaron, b. June 13, 1833.
5. Daniel, b. May 24, 1840; d. 1919.

           8      7      6      5      4      3

**VIII. Daniel Frost** (David, David, Aaron, Samuel, Samuel, Thomas,

           2      1

Samuel, Edmond), b. 1840; married 1862 to Henrietta Osborn; one child Mabel H., b. 1869; d. 1948; m. Oct. 22, 1890; Alfred Bigelow, one child, Gladys.

VII. **Clark Frost** (Aaron,⁶ Samuel,⁵ Samuel,⁴ Thomas,³ Samuel,²
Edmond¹), married Lydia Ellis; married second Jessie Boston.
Children:
1. William m. Cora Pomery
2. Lydia m. Luce.
3. Charles
4. Axen
5. Cordella, m. Nathan Ellis.
6. Sewell
7. Wesley

VIII. **William Frost** (Clark,⁷ Aaron,⁶ Samuel,⁵ Samuel,⁴ Thomas,³ Samuel,²
Edmond¹), born in St. Albans April 23, 1863 - died Nov. 1936. He
married Grace Marsh who was born in Palmyra Nov. 1, 1879.
Three children:
1. Harold Ray Frost; born in St. Albans Nov. 7, 1897 - died
   May 19, 1970. He lived his whole life in St. Albans. He
   married Harriett Lowell. Children:
   1. Gerald, b. Mar. 24, 1929.
   2. Harold, b. Mar. 24, 1929; d. Dec. 18, 1929.
   3. Joyce, b. Aug. 14, 1930 - married Howard Sally.
   4. Wayne, b. Dec. 12, 1937.
2. Gladys Frost: born in St. Albans May 20, 1900; died Jan.
   26, 1958. She married first Wesley Clark; one daughter.
   Lona, b. Nov. 2, 1918; married second Warren White.
3. Lois Frost: born in St. Albans Jan. 7, 1910 - died July 10,
   1960; married Robert Nichols. Children:
   1. Beverly Nichols, b. May 28, 1931.
   2. Kenneth Nichols, b. Mar. 7, 1933.

# HILTON

Edward Hilton came from London in the ship Fortune. He was
the first permanent settler of New Hampshire settling in Dover in
1623. His first wife was the mother of his children. He married 2nd
Catherine Treworthy. Known children:
(1) Edward, b. 1626 or 1630 m. Ann Dudley daughter of Rev.
Samuel Dudley.

(2) William, b. 1628 or 1632. Capt. William died about 1690.

(3) Sobriety, b. ? m. Henry Moulton.

The American Hiltons, like the Drakes and the Webbers have been victims of a missing heir estate in Chancery fraud. The legend went that the last Baron Hilton (of Co. Durham) had died a bachelor and that, as his two brothers William and Edward had emigrated, the estate was in Chancery.

About 1885 Nathan Hilton, a magistrate of Yarmouth, Nova Scotia collected a fund and hired a woman of London to search the matter out (letter of Capt. B. R. Hilton 1924) and the best professional Col. Banks, knew, employed by him when he returned to America, failed to find any trace. They did, however, find over thirty contemporary records supporting the origin of the American emigrant brothers in Northwick Co. Chester. The baronial pedigree was published in the Yarmouth Herald March 22-29, April 5-12, 1898, and will doubtless charm the credulous for years to come.

Our first records of the St. Albans Hiltons begin with:

I.  **Jonathan Hilton**, m. Sarah, Brookfield N.H. (Records from the town office of Brookfield, N.H. give the birth of Jonathan Hilton b. Jan. 16, 1779 as the son of Jonathan & Sarah Hilton) Records St. Albans state Joseph Watson, an early settler of St. Albans, was a cousin to the Hiltons.

                                    1
II.  **Jonathan Hilton** (Jonathan) b. Jan. 16, 1779; married Nancy Stoddard. He came to St. Albans from Brookfield, N.H. in 1806. Children:

  1. Stephen, b. 1820
  2. Betsey Ann
  3. Mary m. Nicholas Bragg
  4. Sarah
  5. Hannah
  6. Orinda
  7. Martha
  8. Jonathan, b. 1827.

                            2         1
III.  **Stephen Hilton** (Jonathan, Jonathan), b. 1820; m. Elizabeth Osborn. Children listed in 1850 census: Charles 11, Alfred 10, others in household were Hannah 29, b. N.H.; Martha 25; Betsey Ann, Mary, Orinda and Jonathan.

                            2         1
III.  **Jonathan Hilton** (Jonathan, Jonathan), b. Sept. 7, 1827; St. Albans; m. Ann Augusta Brown, b. March 11, 1841. Mr. Hilton was formerly engaged in the cattle business, driving large

herds to Brighton, Mass. Children:
1. Walter O.
2. Alfred
3. Herbert
4. Charles
5. Harry
6. Nancy

IV. **Walter O. Hilton** (Jonathan³, Jonathan², Jonathan¹), b. Oct. 18, 1862. m. Jan. 1, 1885; Bertha Smith, b. 1869, daughter of John and Lydia A. (Dunlap) Smith. Walter Hilton was a prosperous dairyman shipping large quanities of butter annually to Boston and Lowell, Mass. A daughter Flossie Hilton, b. Dec. 13, 1886; m. Harry Merrick, son of Lincoln and Lilla P. (Sawyer) Merrick. Children:
1. Madaline Merrick, m. Guy Smith. (2 sons)
2. Theresa Merrick, m. Wilfred Mills. (3 children)

IV. **Alfred Hilton** (Jonathan³, Jonathan², Jonathan¹), b. March 12, 1864; m. Mabel Philbrick.

IV. **Herbert B. Hilton** (Jonathan³, Jonathan², Jonathan¹), b. Jan. 17, 1869; m. (1st) Annie Hanson m. (2nd) Addie Hawes. Children:
1. Myrtle
2. Grace

IV. **Charles Sumner Hilton** (Jonathan³, Jonathan², Jonathan¹), b. Oct. 26, 1872; m. Lula Avery. Children:
1. Marion Hilton.
2. Edna M. Hilton, m. Newell Philbrick.

IV. **Harry T. Hilton** (Jonathan³, Jonathan², Jonathan³), b. Oct. 10, 1875; m. Vesta Wilkins.

IV. **Nancy May Hilton** (Jonathan³, Jonathan², Jonathan¹), b. July 31, 1878; m. (1st) Bert Lambert m. (2nd) Ramsdell.

Other early Hilton marriages found in St. Albans records.
Thomas Whitney, m. 1861 Nancy Hilton.
Christopher Knowles, m. Aug. 23, 1878; Ellen Hilton daughter of Benj. Hoyt Hilton and Cynthia Lane Gusha.
Stephen Hilton Jr., m. July 16, 1862; Mary Robertson.
The 1850 census lists the following. John Hilton 47, Maria 47, Good-

win 17, Elizabeth 16, Nancy 13, Jane Hilton 34, Robert D. 13, Mary 11, Hannah 9, Nathaniel 7, John 5, Christa 1.

# LIBBY

John Libby was born in England in 1602, came to Scarborough, Maine, about 1639.

I. **Matthew Libby**, b. in Scarborough in the year 1663; m. Elizabeth Brown, daughter of Andrew Brown, one of the principal inhabitants of Black Point. (operated a sawmill) 14 children.

1
II. **Lieut. Andrew Libby** (Matthew), b. Kittery, Dec. 1, 1700; m. Esther Furber, daughter of Jethro Furber of Newington, N.H. He became one of the largest farmers in town, but took no part in the town business. He and his wife were both members of the Congregational Church.

2    1
III. **Edward Libby** (Andrew, Matthew), b. in Scarborough, April 10, 1745; m. Feb. 12, 1767; Mary Libby - 3 children.

3    2    1
IV. **Joseph Libby** (Edward, Andrew, Matthew), b. Scarborough, Mar. 6, 1772; m. Anna Plummer, daughter of Jeremiah and Sarah (Eldrich) Plummer. He worked much at teaming, going sometimes as far as Boston, Mass. 14 children.

4    3    2    1
V. **Joseph Frank Libby** (Joseph, Edward, Andrew, Matthew), b. in Pownal, Me; June 16, 1809; m. April 14, 1839; Julia A. Libby, daughter of Zebulon and Dorcus Libby. In April 1834, he removed to Palmyra where he took up a piece of land and lived there until 1846, when he moved to St. Albans near what is known as Five Corners. He built several houses in town. He also helped to build the St. Albans Grange Hall. 12 children, (9 listed).
   1. Edward, b. May 15, 1840; m. June 18, 1871 Narcissa Sampson, daughter of Daniel and Ruth (Boynton) Sampson.
   2. John H., b. April 23, 1843; d. Oct. 4, 1856.
   3. Joseph Francis, b. Oct. 20, 1845; m. Aug. 27, 1870 Ellen, daughter of Josiah and Hannah (Winslow) Magoon of Fairfield; m. (2nd) Mary Prescott; m. (3rd) Emma (Webb) Prescott, daughter of Mr. and Mrs. Henry Webb.

4. Flora A., b. St. Albans, April 19, 1848; m. Feb. 8, 1868 Richard C. Parkman. (See Parkman family)
5. Betsey E., b. Nov. 29, 1850; m. Nov. 17, 1873 Albion Parkman of St. Albans. Children:
   a. George
   b. Frank
6. Albion K., b. July 17, 1853; m. Sept. 4, 1849 Estella M. Lancaster, daughter of Bela and Louisa (Turner) Lancaster. Children:
   a. Laforrest m. Belle Welch
   b. Elmer m. Dora
   c. Fred m. Edith Philbrick
   d. Eva m. Victor Jordan
   e. Julia
7. Preston, b. March 14, 1856; m. Jan. 9, 1877 Violetta E. Knight; m. 2nd Lillie S. Nye - 2 children:
   a. Clarence
   b. Edna
8. Alice, b. March 8, 1858; m. Parkman.
9. John Horace, m. Nellie Varney. Census record 1904 says Hannah E. Varney. Children:
   a. Lura Belle, m. George Crocker. (See Crocker family
   b. Alton Leroy b. Apr. 13, 1885; m. Grace Babb; m. (2nd) Grace Nutter; m. (3rd) Marilla Stone.
   c. Joseph Harris b. Feb. 10, 1887; m. Rose Knight.
   d. Hannah Ada b. May 18, 1889; m. Charles E. Mower. (See Mower family)
   e. Vira Angie, b. Sept. 7, 1892; m. (1st) Fred Thomas; m. 2nd Dr. Charles Norcross; m. 3rd Earl Moor.
   f. George d. young.

VI. **Joseph Francis Libby** (Joseph,[5] Joseph,[4] Edward,[3] Andrew,[2] Matthew[1]), b. Oct. 20, 1845; m. Aub. 27, 1870 Ellen, daughter of Josiah and Hannah (Winslow) Magoon. Children:
1. Lilly, b. June 9, 1871.
2. Mary, b. Aug. 3, 1872; m. Fred Wing.
3. Julia, b. Feb. 1, 1875;
Joseph, m. 2nd Mary Prescott - no children; m. 3rd Emma (Webb) Prescott, daughter of Henry Prescott b. Feb. 26, 1882; Joseph and Emma's children:
1. Leon Francis, b. April 10, 1886, d. Mar. 4, 1919.
2. George, b. April 10, 1891; d. 1952.

3. Irene Agnes, b. March 29, 1895; m. June 28, 1946 Fred D. Mayo.

VII. **Leon Francis Libby** (Joseph,⁶ Joseph,⁵ Joseph,⁴ Edward,³ Andrew,² Matthew¹), b. April 10, 1886; d. March 4, 1919; m. Annie Harvey. Children:
1. Harry Ervin Libby, b. Sept. 26, 1906; m. Emma Varcuise.
2. Dorothy May Libby, b. Jan. 18, 1908; m. Irving Smith.
3. Walter Harvey Libby, b. Sept. 7, 1910; m. Gladys Schmitz; 2 children.
4. Charles Arnold Libby. b. March 9, 1916; m. Sara Murphy; 2 children.

VII. **George Arthur Libby** (Joseph,⁶ Joseph,⁵ Joseph,⁴ Edward,³ Andrew,² Matthew¹), b. April 10, 1891; m. Ethel Welch; one daughter. He was in the grain and farm equipment business. Mary Evelyn Libby b. July 20, 1919; m. Joseph Manley Pease b. Apr. 4, 1915. Their children:
1. Joseph Manley, Jr. b. July 10, 1940; m. Donna Ward.
2. George Libby b. April 3, 1942; m. Shirley Leavitt.
3. Harlow Bruce b. April 14, 1944.

# LUCUS

It may be of interest to our readers whose ancestors came from Ossipee and Wolfeboro, N.H., settling in Corinna, St. Albans, and Stetson, to learn the facts of these places. Wolfeboro is on the northeast side of Lake Winnipesaukee and south of Ossipee.

In the history of Wolfeboro we found that in 1765 Paul Marsh agreed with the committee on settlements to have ten families located in Wolfeboro by spring; each to clear 4 acres of land, and build a house equalling 20 sq. ft. by the succeeding autumn to be given 100 acres in the westerly part if done. In March he was to receive a similar lot. If he failed he would lose his proprietory lot and 25 pounds lawful money; each person was to stay ten years and improve same.

We found the first or easterly lot was 56 rods wide and taken by James Lucus. Associated with him was Thomas Lucus, both being about 50 years old, each with a family. James was moderator of the first town meeting and Thomas a member of the first board of selectmen. They came from Suncook to Wolfeboro and were of Irish ancestry. James had a son Nehemiah and grandson James Lucus III. The third lot of land which was 55 rods wide was taken by Joseph Lary. His wife was the daughter of Lieutenant Charles Rogers, who was the grandfather of the late James Rogers that settled in Stetson about 1840. The Rogers family claimed the Lucus family as cousins probably on the Lary side. We don't know who the father of John Lucus was, but to his son Daniel Lucus and wife Hannah Lyford were born seven children.

I. **John Lucus** m. Jemina Lary (?)

1

II. **Daniel Lucus** (John), m. Hannah Lyford, daughter of Stephen Lyford (See Lyford family) Children:
1. Henry, b. 1813.
2. Sarah, b. 1815.
3. Mary, b. 1817.
4. Hannah, b. 1819; m. Isaac Osborn.
5. Levi, b. 1821.
6. John, b. 1823.
7. Stephen, b. 1825.

2  1

III. **Henry Lucus** (Daniel, John), m. May Libby b. 1818; d. 1852; m. 2nd Mary Jones - 2 children.

2  1

III. **Sarah Lucus** (Daniel, John), b. 1815 m. William Watson - one child Henry Watson.

2  1

III. **Mary Lucus** (Daniel, John), b. 1817; m. James B. Lewis of Wayne, Maine April 1845; lived at Nelson's Corner. The first owner was Stephen Lyford. Children:
1. John Lewis (lawyer Skowhegan)
2. Daniel Lewis (Attorney at Law)
3. Sarah Lewis
4. William Lewis m. Abbie Durgin.
5. Rose Lewis m. Edgar Ramsdell of Ripley - Their daughter Sadie Ramsdall m. S. H. Hopkins.

2  1

III. **Hannah Lucus** (Daniel, John) b. 1819 - d. 1858; m. Isaac Osborn son of Jediah Osborn and Elizabeth Jackson. (See Osborn family). Children:
1. Henrietta Osborn, 1846-1918; m. Daniel Frost; one daughter Mabel Frost; m. Alfred Bigelow.
2. Rebecca Osborn; m. (1st) John Goodwin; (2nd) George Martin, son of Jacob Martin.

215

3. Hannah Osborn; m. Ralph Reed; one son, Benton Reade.
   (See Osborn family)

III. **Levi Lucus** (Daniel,$^{2}$ John$^{1}$), b. 1822; d. Aug. 19, 1898; m. Naomi
   (Marden) Lucus. Their family is told in an old rhyme - - Father,
   Mother, Frank, and Fred, Hannah, Emma, George and Ed.
   Children:
   1. Hannah Lucus; m. C. E. Jones of Ripley Jan. 28, 1879; one
      daughter Jessie Jones m. Harry Seavey; their children:
      1. Marjery Seavey, m. Stanton Ross.
      2. Marion Seavey, m.
      3. Emma Seavey, m. Charles Berry.
   2. Emma Lucus, m. Seavy from Ripley; m. 2nd Alfred Merrill.
   3. George Lucus
   4. Ed Lucus
   5. Frank Lucus 1853-1934 - ran a hotel in Brighton, Me.
   6. Fred Lucus, b. 1823.

IV. **Fred Lucus** (Levi,$^{3}$ Daniel,$^{2}$ John$^{1}$), b. 1865; d. 1932; m. (1st) Ella
   Cook, m. (2nd) Susie Cooper. Children by 1st wife:
   1. Infant, b. 1882, d. at birth
   1. Fay
   2. Flora
   3. Minot
   Children by 2nd wife:
   5. Laura.

V. **Minot Lucus** (Fred,$^{4}$ Levi,$^{3}$ Daniel,$^{2}$ John$^{1}$), m. Leona Dumont Carson April 20, 1926. Children:
   1. Jeanne - adopted.
   2. Richard, b. July 3, 1927; d. 1953 in Korean War.
   3. Raymond, b. Oct. 9, 1929.
   4. Geraldine (Sally), b. April 2, 1932 m. Maynard Deering.
   5. Robert, b. 1933.

Minot Lucus had an old letter dated January 30, 1826 written by
Stephen Lyford to his sister Hannah (Lyford) Lucus concerning the
educational advantages that his sister's family was receiving.

# LYFORDS

The Lyfords arrived in the ship Arbella with the Winthrops,
Dudleys, Philbricks, Bradstreets, and Johnsons.

I.   **Francis Lyford:** m. first in the Old South Church in Boston June
     1671; Elizabeth Smith, daughter of Thomas and Elizabeth
     Smith; married second Nov. 21, 1681 in Exeter, N. H. to Rebec-
     ca Dudley, daughter of Rev. Sam Dudley by his third wife
     Elizabeth, granddaughter of Gov. Thomas Dudley. Francis
     Lyford owned his own ship, the sloop Elizabeth.
     Children by 1st wife:
     1.   Thomas, b. March 25, 1672.
     2.   Elizabeth, b. July 19, 1673.
     3.   Francis, b. May 31, 1677.
     Children by 2nd wife:
     1.   Stephen, m. Sarah Leavitt (daughter of Moses and
          Dorothy (Dudley) Leavitt.
     2.   Ann, m. Timothy Leavitt.
     3.   Deborah, m. Benjamin Follett.
     4.   Rebecca, m. Theophilus Hardy.
     5.   Sarah, m. John Folsom, son of John and Mary (Gilman)
          Folsom. Their names appear in the Hingham Register.

1

II.  **Stephen Lyford** (Francis) married Sarah Leavitt, daughter of
     Moses Leavitt and Dorothy Dudley. Dorothy was the daughter
     of Rev. Sam Dudley, and granddaughter of Gov. Thomas
     Dudley. Stephen Lyford is mentioned in the list of distributions
     of land in Exeter April 12, 1725, as having received 100 acres.
     He was selectman in 1734. His estate, appraised at 1575.10.9
     comprised among other items: negro woman syl. p10, Negro
     gent. Nants, P30
     Children:
     1.   Biley, b. 1716; m. Judith Wilson.
     2.   Stephen, b. April 12, 1723; m. Mercy Pike.
     3.   Moses, m. Mehitable (Smith) Oliver.
     4.   Sam - unmarried.
     5.   Francis.
     6.   Theophilus, m. Lois James (Kinsley.)
     7.   Betsey, m. Joshua Wiggin.

2    1

III. **Biley Lyford** (Stephen, Francis), m. Judith Wilson, daughter of
     Thomas Wilson. Biley Lyford was in Col. Nichols Gilman's regi-
     ment of Militia Sept. 12, 1777. In his will he says, "My will is
     that my two Negroes shall live with any of my children they see
     fit or otherwise to have their freedom as they choose". He also
     leaves Molly and Judith each 100 Spanish milled dollars.
     Children:

1. Rebecca, b. 1744; m. Samuel Dudley.
2. Dorothy, b. 1746; m. James Robinson.
3. Alice, d. young.
4. Mary.
5. Alice (Elsey), m. John Sanborn.
6. Anne, m. Bartholomew Thing.
7. Biley Dudley.
8. Sarah, m. Enos Sanborn.
9. Judith.
10. John.

2    1

**III.** **Stephen Lyford** (Stephen, Francis), m. Mercy Pike, daughter of Robert Pike and Hannah Gilman; granddaughter of Major Ezekiel Gilman and Sarah Dudley.
Children:
1. Sarah, b. 1754.
2. Love, b. 1756.
3. Stephen, b. 1758.
4. Francis, b. 1760.
5. Biley William, b. 1762.
6. Samuel, b. 1765.
7. Robert, b. 1767.
8. Mercy, b. 1770.

3    2    1

**IV.** **Stephen Lyford** (Stephen, Stephen, Francis), b. 1758 - m. Sarah (Lampney) Hilton a widow, niece of General Henry Dearborn
One child: Mary Hilton.
Children by Lyford:
1. Hannah, b. 1785; d. June 30, 1851 at St. Albans, married Oct. 1, 1811; Daniel Lucus (See Lucus-Bigelow family) A daughter Hannah Lucus, m. Isaac Osborn.
2. Stephen Carr, b. 1787.
3. Levi, b. 1789.
4. Theophilus Wiggin, b. 1792.
5. Sarah, b. 1793; m. Jonathan Gage.
6. Betsey, d. 1796 infancy.

3    2    1

**IV.** **William Dudley Lyford** (called Biley) (Biley, Stephen, Francis), m. (1st) Mary Robinson; m. (2nd) Dorothy Blake.
Children by 1st wife:
1. John, b. 1782; m. (1st) Marion Rowe; m. (2nd) Abigail Fogg Baine,(widow).
2. Dudley, b. 1793.
3. James, b. Feb. 25, 1795.

4. Ezekiel, b. 1796.
5. Mary, b. 1798.
6. Epaphras Kibby, b. 1800.
7. Henry, b. 1803.
8. Dorothy, b. 1810; m. (1st) Johnson; (2nd) Lyman Worthen.
9. Washington, b. 1805.

               4      3      2      1

V. **John Lyford** (Esquire) (Biley, Biley, Stephen, Francis), b. June 1, 1782 - Brentwood N. H.; m. 1st Marion Rowe; 2nd Abigail Fogg (Baine) daughter of Samuel Fogg and Ruth Lane, who was a daughter of Joshua Lane and Ruth Batchelder, a second cousin to Susanna Batchelder, b. May 28, 1713; who married Ebenezer Webster, (grandparents of Daniel Webster).

Children by 1st wife:
1. Biley, b. June 22, 1805; m. Catherine Dow.
2. Mary, b. Nov. 30, 1807; m. John Snow.
3. Albert, b. Jan. 26, 1810; m. Phebe Bates.

Children by 2nd wife:
1. John Fogg, b. Feb. 17, 1818; m. Farrena Bean Rowe, daughter of David and Betsey Rowe. Children - Horace, Frank, Vestie, and John. Their son John Fogg Lyford, M. D. m. Ellen Skinner, daughter of Thomas and Sarah Hackett Skinner.
2. James Robinson, b. April 6, 1819; m. Mary Eliz. Ellis.
3. Mary E., m. Ellis; Senica, Ohio.
4. William King, b. April 13, 1820; d. June 12, 1836.
5. Maria Rowe, b. Nov. 13, 1821; d. June 21, 1840.
6. Pamela R., b. Jan. 7, 1823; m. Enoch W. Rollins; m. 2nd Savylla Knowles.
7. Sullivan, b. May 25; d. Nov. 1863.
8. Sarah, b. July 4, 1836; d. 1861.
9. Abigail, b. Dec. 27, 1825; m. Asa Bates.
10. Lois Ann, b. Feb. 5, 1832; m. L. E. Judkins.
11. Francis, b. July 5, 1828; m. Harrison Given.
12. Samuel Fogg, b. May 7, 1830; m. Almeida Robinson.
     The dates differ in the St. Albans records, from those in the Lane genealogy, on the children of John Lyford.

               5      4      3      2      1

VI. **Samuel Fogg Lyford** (John, Biley, Biley, Stephen, Francis), m. Almeida A. Robinson, daughter of Stephen B. and Dolly W. Robinson. Sam Lyford Esquire lived in the family home in St. Albans for many years; which he kept it in excellent condition. Mr. Lyford had a genial disposition and was well liked. Children:

1. Florence, b. 1869 (school teacher) m. Elbert Eaton Knowles b. May 1865; son of David and Aldana Batchelder Knowles.
2. Cora Lyford, m. Fred Costello; one son Harold lived in Fresno, California.

        5     4     3     2     1

**VI. Lois Anne** (John, Biley, Biley, Stephen, Francis), m. Levi Judkins Three children:
1. Charles
2. Annie
3. Marie

Dr. Charles Judkins died in Skowhegan. He practiced in Hartland, before moving to Skowhegan.

        6     5     4     3     2     1

**VII. Florence Lyford** (Samuel, John, Biley, Biley, Stephen, Francis), b. 1869; d. 1923; m. Elbert Eaton Knowles. He was married before having one son, Guy Bertram Knowles, b. Nov. 26, 1888; m. (2nd) Florence Lyford. Children: (See John Knowles genealogy)
1. Dana Lyford Knowles, b. Jan. 19, 1899; m. Minnie E. Bigger Six children; she remarried Dec. 24, 1938; Chester L. Buck, Newport.
2. Elbert Lowell Knowles, b. Dec. 31, 1909; m. Bertie Anderson; seven children.
3. Theresa Knowles, b. Dec. 23, 1905; m. Francis J. Leighton, one daughter.
4. Donald Eaton Knowles, b. Nov. 21, 1906; m. (1st) Emma Genet Maguire (daughter of John and Emma (Lovejoy) Maguire; Children:
1. Robert Donald, b. July 12, 1925; m. (1st) Marilyn Brooker; (2nd) Christine Rines.
2. Lowell Elwin, b. Jan. 5, 1927; m. Ruth McGowan.
3. Patricia, b. March 18, 1929; died young.
4. Francis Dale, b. Aug. 2, 1931; m. Theresa Bovat.
5. Infant, b. Aug. 3, 1933; died then.
6. Donald, b. June 21, 1936; died then.

Married (2nd) Ruth Clement, daughter of Elmer and Lula Allen Clement. Three children:
1. Elton Stanley, b. May 20, 1938; m. Bette Spaulding.
2. Sharon Jean, b. Aug. 17, 1941; m. Philip Holt.
3. Donald Bruce, b. June 12, 1949; m. Elaine Knowles.

# MERRILL

The Merrill family is an ancient and knightly one, originally domiciled in the Province of Aisen, France. They were knighted, both in France and England.

The Merrills are one of the oldest families in New England, having been in this country since the first third of the seventeenth century. Nathaniel Merrill and his brother were among the first settlers of Newbury, Mass. Nathaniel Merrill is the ancestor of all the Merrills in the United States, who can trace their origin to this period, as his brother John had no sons, and other Merrill immigrants are of more recent date.

Nathaniel Merrill born in 1610, Willshire, England married Susannah Wolterton or Willerton.

The lines from Nathaniel Merrill to Levi James Merrill of Madison, Maine and St. Albans, Maine have not been fully documented so our narrative will begin with Levi James Merrill who came to St. Albans in 1820. He purchased all the land from St. Albans village stream to the pond running north one mile from Merrils' Corner and east two miles. Four of his sons settled in the area known as Merrill's Ridge.

I.    **Levi J. Merrill**, m. Betsy Sawyer, daughter of Joseph Sawyer and Mary Steward, daughter of Solomon Steward. Joseph Sawyer was the son of Phenus and Mary Sevey Sawyer. Children:
1. James, b. 1799; m. Pauline Weston.
2. Joseph, b. 1801; m. (1st) Mary Bigelow; (2nd) Sarah Jane Butler.
3. Peter, b. 1804; m. Lovina Bowden. There is some question in our minds concerning Peter belonging to this family. Jessie Merrill, Jr. of St. Albans has been endeavoring to assist us in determining the ancestry of Peter Merrill. The census record of 1810 in Madison is the main reason we have placed Peter in this family, also the close proximity of Madison and Cornville.
4. Serena, b. 1805.
5. Ebenezer Merrill, b. 1808; m. Olive Hayes.
6. Nathan Merrill, b. 1810; m. Elizabeth Ann Walker.
7. Noah Merrill, b. 1816; d. 1 year old.

1
II.   **James Merrill** (Levi James), b. 1799; m. Pauline Weston. Children:

1. Sarah
2. Nathan
3. Ann
4. Elizabeth

II. **Joseph Merrill** (Levi James[1]), b. 1801; m. (1st) Mary Bigelow; m. (2nd) Sarah Jane Bullen. Children by (1st) marriage:
   1. James
   2. Mary, m. Simon Wing.

Children by (2nd) marriage:
   3. Phineas Merrill, b. Dec. 24, 1832; m. Oct. 18, 1858 Mary Elizabeth George, b. Sept. 21, 1833, Newport; d. Nov. 25, 1877. At least one son Dr. George Merrill, Newport.
   4. Francis M. Merrill, b. Apr. 19, 1835; m. (1st) Charles Soule; (2nd) Jessie Chandler.
   5. Sumner Merrill, b. Aug. 25, 1839; m. Enlissa Stewart, 5 daughters, 1 son.
   6. Jessie Merrill, b. Sept. 1844; d. in service Petersburg, Va.
   7. Ella Merrill, b. Aug. 4, 1848, lived in Bangor; m. Dr. Walter Hunt.
   8. Evelyn P. Merrill, b. May 3, 1854; m. Harrison Turner.

II. **Peter Merrill** (Levi James[1]), m. Lovina Bowden. (The 1850 census of Cornville)
Charles-16.
William-14.
Fredelia-7.
John H.-4.
Fredelia-18.

III. **William Littlefield Merrill** (Peter[2], Levi James[1]), b. Sept. 28, 1837; d. Dec. 3, 1917 Bloomfield, Me., m. Aug. 16, 1857; Sarah Maria Bickford, b. Feb. 11, 1839, Norridgewock, Maine; d. Jan. 19, 1871, Mars Hill, Maine.

IV. **Albion Frank Merrill** (William[3], Peter[2], Levi James[1]), b. July 8, 1858 Skowhegan, Maine; m. Jan. 1, 1879; died Dec. 7, 1929 Prentiss, Me. m. Margaret Emmaline Palmer b. Feb. 23, 1857; d. Aug. 22, 1932 Prentiss, Maine.

V. **Jessie Albion Merrill** (Albion[4], William[3], Peter[2], Levi James[1]), b. Dec. 15, 1895 Mars Hill, Maine. May 7, 1917 m. Dora Agnes Chabbuck, b. Feb. 13, 1900, Carroll, Maine. Children:
   1. Elnora Violet Merrill, b. Feb. 5, 1918; Carroll, Me.

2. Eunice Vivian Merrill, b. Sept. 29, 1919; Prentiss, Me.
3. Haley Andrew Merrill, b. Aug. 6, 1921.
4. Clinton Edgar Merrill, b. Apr. 21, 1923.
5. Leta Mae Merrill, b. May 10, 1925.
6. Lois Phyliss Merrill, b. May 23, 1927.
7. Jessie Albion Merrill, b. Oct. 27, 1934; m. May 31, 1969, Lucinda Maureen Reidhead.

II. **Ebenezer Merrill** (Levi James¹), b. 1809; m. Olive Hayes of Norridgwock Jan. 23, 1830. One known son, Harlan.

II. **Nathaniel Merrill** (Levi James¹), b. 1810; m. Elizabeth Ann Walker. Children:
1. Hannah
2. Emily
3. Levi
4. Clara

## 2nd MERRILL FAMILY

I. **Loring Merrill**, b. Dec. 9, 1807; d. Aug. 20, 1883; m. Dorcus, b. Dec. 31, 1814; d. July 25, 1881.

II. **Guy Merrill** (Loring¹), b. Jan. 13, 1835; d. Sept. 26, 1911; m. Lauring Downing, b. Nov. 16, 1837; d. Feb. 11, 1982.

III. **George Merrill** (Guy², Loring¹), b. 1886; d. 1946; m. Lena Hanson, dau. of Lowell Hanson and Sarah (Bates) Hanson. Children:
1. Florence, m. (1st) Harry Plummer; m. (2nd) Fred Patterson.
2. Verne, m. Pearl Varney.

IV. Verne Merrill (George³, Guy², Loring¹), m. Pearl Varney. (See Varney family). Children:
1. Shirley, m. Hermon L. Warren
2. Clayton, m. Anna Vining.
3. Clifford, M. Evangleine Powers.

# MOWER

Richard Mower came from Devonshire, England in 1638 to Salem, Massachusetts in the ship Blessing with two of his sons, John and Samuel. Most of the families in America having that name are descendants of the above, except the Mower family that settled in Pennsylvania.

I. **Richard Mower**

II. **Samuel Mower** (Richard[1]) married Joanna Marshall, daughter of Capt. Thomas and Rebecca Marshall of Lynn, Mass. (Fought in King Philip's War) 7 children.

III. **Samuel Mower** (Samuel[2], Richard[1]), born Sept. 26, 1689 - May 8, 1760 married Elizabeth Sprague of Malden, Mass., daughter of Phineas and Elizabeth (Greene) Sprague. Prominent in the.early affairs of Malden, Mass. - 7 children.

IV. **Jonathan Mower** (Samuel[3], Samuel[2], Richard[1]), born May 5, 1730; died October 12, 1816; married Elizabeth Bemis, daughter of Samuel Bemis of Spencer, Mass. Pioneer settler of Greene (See History of Greene, Me.)

V. **Ebenezer Mower** (Jonathan[4], Samuel[3], Samuel[2], Richard[1]), born May 23, 1769 died August 22, 1857; married first Lucretia Ward of Greene, Me. died July 12, 1793; married second Jane Robinson. -12 children. All will be listed. They were an unusual family in their church relations. Three were Baptist deacons, two, Methodist class leaders.

VI. **Ebenezer Mower** (Ebenezer[5], Jonathan[4], Samuel[3], Samuel[2], Richard[1]), born Jan. 21, 1791 - died July 12, 1842; married Beulah Davis of St. Albans, where they lived. Children:
1. Henry Ward, b Jan. 12, 1816.
2. Artemas, b. Mar. 1, 1819.
3. Ebenezer Davis, b. Nov. 8, 1821.
4. Sterling, b. Feb. 1, 1827.

VI. **Henry Mower** (Ebenezer[5], Jonathan[4], Samuel[3], Samuel[2], Richard[1]), born June 23, 1793; died Jan. 21, 1825; married Lydia Richmond. Children:
1. Cynthia W. b. Mar. 10, 1822.
2. Henry Clay b. Jan. 14, 1825.

VI. **Isaac Mower** (Ebenezer[5], Jonathan[4], Samuel[3], Samuel[2], Richard[1]), born June 23, 1793; died Jan. 21, 1825; married Sally Adams and went to Corinna in 1819. He bought a section of land south from his brother Hiram in the wilderness and lived with him in a log house. These two were the first to settle in this section of the state. Cleared his farm and established his home. Three of his four children are listed with their families.

**VII. Elias Adams Mower** - married Rhoda M. Harlow -Children:
1. Mary F., married Charles E. Conners.
2. Caroline, married William H. Farrer, Ripley, Me.
3. Rhoda, married Frank Hazelton, Dexter, Me.

**VII. Sarah** - married Simeon D. Bates, St. Albans. Children:
1. Samantha - married Z. L. Turner.
2. Isaac - married Nellie Kimball.

**VII. Abigail** - married Edwin Higgins, Dexter, Me.

VI. **Lucretia Mower** (Ebenezer⁵, Jonathan⁴, Samuel³, Samuel², Richard), born April 6, 1797; died May 29, 1834.

VI. **Hiram Mower** (Ebenezer⁵, Jonathan⁴, Samuel³, Samuel², Richard¹), born May 1, 1799; died Sept. 2, 1879; married Sophia Parker, daughter of Benjamin and Rebecca Royal Parker of Greene. Children:
1. Jane, married John H. Gould, Dexter.
2. Ann, married Dea. Aaron F. Mower.
3. Hiram Gustauns Mower.
4. George H. Mower.

VI. **Nancy Mower** (Ebenezer⁵, Jonathan⁴, Samuel³, Samuel², Richard¹), b. Aug. 26, 1801; died Jan. 28, 1892; married Charles Ellms of Leeds on March 18, 1832 and moved to Dexter. Children:
1. Horace Ellms, b. Sept. 7, 1833.
2. Nancy Jane Ellms, b. March 7, 1835.
3. Augusta Ellms, b. Dec. 28, 1838.
4. Charles Ellms, b. Feb. 11, 1841.
5. Albert Ellms, b. Aug. 12, 1843.

Descendants settled in Dexter, Ripley, and the West

VI. **Dan Mower** (Ebenezer⁵, Jonathan⁴, Samuel³, Samuel², Richard¹), b. June 5, 1806; married Mary T. Horn of Ripley - Children:
1. Sarah Jane
2. Amos Horn
3. George Wesley
4. Lucy Ann

5. Maria Louise
6. Flora Ellen

$$\overset{5}{} \quad \overset{4}{} \quad \overset{3}{} \quad \overset{2}{} \quad \overset{1}{}$$

VI. **John Mower** (Ebenezer, Jonathan, Samuel, Samuel, Richard), b. July 29, 1808; married Ellen O. Buxton of Danvers, Mass. and settled in Corinna. Children:
1. Lucy Ann; married Elijah Katon.
2. William
3. Jane Lydia
4. Esther V.
5. Ella L.

$$\overset{5}{} \quad \overset{4}{} \quad \overset{3}{} \quad \overset{2}{} \quad \overset{1}{}$$

VI. **Loring Mower** (Ebenezer, Jonathan, Samuel, Samuel, Richard), b. July 11, 1811; married Elvira Morse; settled in Dexter, Me. Children:
1. Harrison
2. Isaac
3. Clarissa
4. Selena
5. Roscoe
6. Henry
7. Annie

$$\overset{5}{} \quad \overset{4}{} \quad \overset{3}{} \quad \overset{2}{} \quad \overset{1}{}$$

VI. **Bemis Mower** (Ebenezer, Jonathan, Samuel, Samuel, Richard), b. April 11, 1814; married Mary J. Brown; settled in Cambridge, Me. Children:
1. Harriet N.
2. Luella
3. Mary
4. Elmira
5. Irving

$$\overset{5}{} \quad \overset{4}{} \quad \overset{3}{} \quad \overset{2}{}$$

VI. **Warren Mower** (Ebenezer, Jonathan, Samuel, Samuel,

$$\overset{1}{}$$

Richard), b. Nov. 3, 1819; married Louisa Gilmore; settled in Dexter. Children:
1. Emma J.
2. Evelyn E.

$$\overset{5}{} \quad \overset{4}{} \quad \overset{3}{} \quad \overset{2}{}$$

VI. **Deacon Charles Mower** (Ebenezer, Jonathan, Samuel, Samuel,

$$\overset{1}{}$$

Richard), b. Feb. 23, 1804; d. Nov. 6, 1869; married Comfort Coburn; settled in St. Albans, where he cleared his large farm and became prosperous. Deacon in the St. Albans Baptist Church. An excellent bass singer and leader of the choir for

many years. Stood 6 ft. 4 in. in height - Children:
1. Jessie Coburn Mower, b. Feb. 6, 1827.
2. Charles Granville Mower, b. July 3, 1833.
3. Emily Mower, b. Feb. 23, 1843.

                             6       5       4
**VII. Charles Granville Mower** (Dea. Charles, Ebenezer, Jonathan,
    3       2      1
Samuel, Samuel, Richard), b. July 3, 1833; married Ruth Crocker, daughter of Eleazor and Sarah (Gray) Crocker of St. Albans, Dec. 22, 1855. (See Crocker family) Children:
1. Edwin E. Mower, b. 1856.
2. Mabel Mower, m. Frost, Ripley, Me.

                         7       6      5      4
**VIII. Edwin Mower** (Charles, Dea. Charles, Ebenezer, Jonathan,
    3       2      1
Samuel, Samuel, Richard), b. 1856; d. 1891; married Nettie Robertson, daughter of Rufus and Julette (Fuller) Robertson. Children: 5, all continued.

                         8       7      6
**IX. Charles Eleazor Mower** (Edwin, Charles, Dea. Charles,
    5       4      3      2      1
Ebenezer, Jonathan, Samuel, Samuel, Richard), b. April 21, 1822; married Ada Libby, daughter of John and Nellie Libby -Children:
1. Ruth M. Mower - m. (1st) Thomas Mills; m. (2nd) Newton Smith. Children:
   a. James Mills
   b. Marilyn Mills
2. Meredith; m. Elmer Fisher, son of Robert and Gladys (Dickenson) Fisher. Children:
   a. Mary
   b. Allen

                       8      7      6      5
**IX. Philip Edwin Mower** (Edwin, Charles, Dea. Charles, Ebenezer,
    4       3      2      1
Jonathan, Samuel, Samuel, Richard), b. Nov. 4, 1885; married Marjory Heath of Mass., b. 1894; d. June 10, 1971. Children:
1. Edwin Mower; married Irene Berry; 3 children.
2. Priscilla Mower; married Harold Dunn; 1 child.
3. Winifred Mower; married Clair Russell; 2 sons.

                       8      7      6      5
**IX. Sidney R. Mower** (Edwin, Charles, Dea. Charles, Ebenezer,
    4       3      2      1
Jonathan, Samuel, Samuel, Richard), b. Jan. 7, 1890; married Crystal Philbrick, b. June 24, 1905; d. 1972, daughter of

William and Eva Philbrick. Children:
1. Blaine; married Roberta Brawn; 3 children.
2. Richard; married Elaine Brooks; 2 children.

IX. **Edwina E. Mower** (Edwin,⁸ Charles,⁷ Dea. Charles,⁶ Ebenezer,⁵ Jonathan,⁴ Samuel,³ Samuel,² Richard¹),b. Feb. 28, 1891; d. 1944.

IX. **Eleanor Mower** (Edwin,⁸ Charles,⁷ Dea. Charles,⁶ Ebenezer,⁵ Jonathan,⁴ Samuel,³ Samuel,² Richard¹), m. Scott Hanford.


# OSBORN

The first Osborn came from England probably in mid 1700s. The first Isaac settled on Long Island, New York, living there until after the Revolutionary War. He moved to Pownalborough, (now Dresden) Maine where he met Sarah Wyman, the daughter of William and Love Wyman. In 1785 the Wymans moved to Winslow, Maine. Isaac followed and he and Sarah were married in Winslow on November 15, 1787. Isaac settled on a farm in Fairfield in 1792.

I. **Isaac Osborn** m. November 15, 1787 to Sarah Wyman. Children:
1. Jeddiah or Jedidiah, b. Aug. 22, 1788; m. Elizabeth Jackson. Elwoode Osborn of Fairfield, a direct descendent believes Jeddiah is the original spelling.
2. Deborah, b. Dec. 5, 1790; m. Libidee Littlefield.
3. Isaac Jr., b. Sept. 15, 1792; m. Millie Saliner. (last name indistinct in the records)
4. William, b. Dec. 22, 1794; never married and became an herb doctor.
5. Jacob, b. Feb. 15, 1798; m. Lydia Burrill.
6. John, b. July 6, 1800; m. Sally Wing.
7. Sarah, b. Dec. 18, 1802; m. (1st) Humphrey Burgess; m. (2nd) Jonas Burrill.
8. Timothy, b. April 12, 1805; m. (1st) Lydia Burrill Osborn, (Jacob's widow) (2nd) Olivia Haskell.
9. Anna (Annie), b. Nov. 3, 1807; m. Joshua Wing.
10. Mary, b. Aug. 8, 1811.

II. **Jeddiah Osborn** (Isaac)$^1$ m, Elizabeth Jackson; Jeddiah and his wife Elizabeth left the home place in Fairfield in 1825 and settled on St. Albans Mountain.

Children:
1. Alfred, b. about 1815; m. 1841 to Mary Holway.
2. Eliza, b. 1817; m. Stephen Hilton.
3. Isaac, b. 1819; m. (1st) 1841 Hannah Lucus; m. (2nd) 1865 Laura Trafton.
4. Rebecca; m. 1841 Benjamin Burrill.
5. Eunice; m. 1847 William R. Burrill.
6. Sullivan, b. about 1830.
7. Alfriedda, b. 1835; m. Christy, lived in California.

III. **Isaac Osborn** (Jeddiah, Isaac)$^{2\ 1}$, b. 1820; d. 1916; m. 1841 to Hannah Lucus; m. (2nd) 1865 to Laura Trafton. Isaac spent his life in St. Albans. He moved from the mountain to the village after Hannah's death and lived the last of his life in the house now owned by Michael Wiers. He died peacefully having lived a long and active life.

Children by (1st) wife Hannah Lucus:
1. George Benton 1843-1898; never married; went West.
2. Henrietta 1846-1918; m. Daniel Frost.
3. Hannah Eliza 1850-1941; m. Ralph Reade; one son, Benton.
4. Rebecca 1852-1924; m. (1st) John Goodwin; m. (2nd) George Martin, no children.
5. Daniel Lucas; m. 1866 Roxanna Randall.

Children by (2nd) wife Laura Trafton:
6. Alice 1866-1949; m. 1887 Elwin Matthews; two sons.
7. Kate 1868-1889.
8. Vira 1873-1893.
9. Walter 1877-1880.
10. Wallace 1877; m. (1st) Edith Lombard; children Oneita, Arlene; m. (2nd) Lucy McCloud.
11. Laura 1882-1899.

IV. **Henrietta Osborn** (Isaac, Jeddiah, Isaac)$^{3\ 2\ 1}$, b. 1846; m. Daniel Frost, son of David Frost and Patience Ellis; one child Mabel Frost married Alfred P. Bigelow - one daughter, Gladys Bigelow b. 1892.

# PARKMAN

Descendants of Gideon Parkman and Ruth Vining.

I. **Gideon Parkman**, b. 1720 and died in 1789. Moved from Abington, Mass. to Maine, then a part of Massachusetts. Married 1742 Mary Vining, daughter of John and Elizabeth Vining. 5 children. Gideon Parkman and his wife Mary together with their grandson Noah, a lad of 13 or 14, oldest son of Daniel and Hannah (House) Parkman, settled in Old Canaan now Skowhegan, on the north side of the Kennebec River below the Great Eddy. Gideon Parkman, a thorough man, left detailed instruction in his will:

"I, Gideon Parkman of Canaan in the County of Lincoln and State of Massachusetts, sensible that I am, mortal and must soon leave this world and appear before God, my final judge, to receive of him according to the deeds done in the body, and being of sound mind and memory I make this my last will and testament.

"And first I committ my Soul to God as my only portion and refuge thru the merits of Jesus Christ his Son my only redeemer, on whose merits alone I depend for justification and acceptance before God now and in the day of judgement; and my body I commit to the dust to be decently, but not sumptiously buried, in a firm belief that it shall be raised again by the virtue and power of my head Jesus Christ who is the resurrection and the life.

"And as to the small temporal interest God hath blessed me with, I dispose of it in the following manner, Viz:

"First I give to Mary my beloved wife all my household goods and furniture for her use during her life, and after her decease to be equally divided/except a bed Noah Parkman lodges on and a Bible, which I give to Betty Clark, Rhoda Whitman, and Mary Pratt.

"Item - I give to my son Daniel Parkman one pound to be paid by Noah Parkman when he shall be (twenty two) years old.

"Item - I give him, the said Noah Parkman, and to his heirs and assigns, all that tract of land lying in Canaan aforesaid which I bought of Lieutenant Isaac Smith of Canaan together with the house and barn and all the appurtenances hereunto belonging for his and their use forever; after the death of Mary, my wife. But I will and bequeath to the said Mary the sole use and benefit of the aforesaid land and buildings during her life."

Signed by Gideon Parkman in presence of Nathaniel Whitaker, John White, Peter Haywood Jr., and Joseph Watson.

(Added) "Schedule: Before the sealing and delivery of these presents I appoint Mr. Brice McCleveland to be my Sole Executor to this my last will and testament, which appointment was forgot till the above was finished."

The will was probated at Lincoln County Court on September 15, 1879.

II. **Daniel Parkman** (Gideon[1]), b. Sept. 7, 1743; m. April 26, 1766 Hannah House; b. June 10, 1736, daughter of Benjamin and Abigail (Merrill) House. Children:
1. Noah, b. March 15, 1769; m. Hannah Weston.
2. Betty, b. Nov. 9, 1770; m. Seth Lathram.
3. Mary, b. Feb. 20, 1773;
4. David, b. Feb. 13, 1775.
5. Gideon, b. April 11, 1777.
6. Hannah, b. March 17, 1781; m. Joshua Gardiner.
7. Daniel, b. March 14, 1883.
8. John, b. May 8, 1785.
9. Lydia, b. April 5, 1788.

Only John and Noah Parkman's lines will be carried forward.

III. **John Parkman** (Daniel[2], Gideon[1]), b. May 8, 1785; m. Lydia Pratt.

IV. **Benjamin Parkman** (John[3], Daniel[2], Gideon[1]), m. first Mary Higgins; second, Abbie Berry.

V. **Orin Alonzo Parkman** (Benjamin[4], John[3], Daniel[2], Gideon[1]), m. first Esther McLuer; second, Ellen Tracy.

VI. **Jedidiah Parkman** (Orin[5], Benjamin[4], John[3], Daniel[2], Gideon[1]), m. first Mertie Goodwin; second, Bertha Wheeler. Children:
1. Ethola
2. Earl
3. Bertina S. Wheeler.

VII. **Ethola Parkman** (Jedidiah[6], Orin[5], Benjamin[4], John[3], Daniel[2], Gideon[1]), b. Sept. 10, 1893; m. Jessie Earl Lary, b. Aug. 17, 1885, son of Jeremiah and Georgia Etta (Church) Lary. Children:

1. Ruth Evelyn, b. July 20, 1916; m. Victor Springer.
2. Merton Elwood, b. July 21, 1918; m. Doris Ames.
3. Alton Earl, b. April 24, 1919; died 1919.
4. Bernard, b. Jan. 28, 1921; m. Grace Lord.
5. Sherburn, b. March 27, 1924; m. Edith Lord.
6. Kenneth Alonzo, b. Feb. 28, 1927; m. Barbara Brown.
7. William Hershall, b. July 20, 1928; m. Virginia Green.
8. Dana Milton, b. Aug. 20, 1937; m. Brenda Bailey.

6    5    4    3    2    1

**VII. Earl Parkman** (Jedidiah, Orin, Benjamin, John, Daniel, Gideon) son of Jedidiah and Mertie; m. Violet Hart. Children:
1. Henry, m. Phyliss Pease
2. Mertie, m. Winfred Allen.
3. Meredith, m. Ernest Wood; 3 children.
   a. Ernestine
   b. Hazel
   c. Michael

An ancient hand-hewed cradle that has been in the Parkman family as far back as 1810, when it was used by Benjamin Parkman and his children, has been handed down for years in this family.

2    1

**III. Noah Parkman** (Daniel, Gideon), b. March 15, 1769; m. first 1788 Hannah Weston, daughter of Joseph and Eunice (Farnsworth) Weston. Children:
1. Joseph, m. Phebe Niles.
2. Noah, m. Mary Laughton.
3. David
4. Simeon
5. Eunice
6. Mary, m. Charles Osborn.
7. Hannah

Noah married second Mary or Lucy Smith; children:
1. Electa
2. Richmond
3. Everett, m. Nancy Wells.
4. Gridley
5. Alvin

3    2    1

**IV. Everett Parkman** (Noah, Daniel, Gideon), m. Nancy Wells; res. St. Albans. Their children:
1. John, m. Lucy Steward.
2. Sylvia, m. Wadsworth Crocker.
3. Philona, m. Sevey.

4. Philander, m. Clarenda Farrer.
5. Benton
6. Richard

4   3   2   1

V. **Philander Parkman** (Everett, Noah, Daniel, Gideon), m. Clarenda Farrer. Children:
1. Lailand E., m. (1st) Georgianna Nelson; m. (2nd) Lizzie Johnson.
2. Malcolm K., m. Emma Collins.
3. Philona, m. Frank Varney.
4. Philena; m. Ernest Braley

5   4   3   2   1

VI. **Malcolm Parkman** (Philander, Everett, Noah, Daniel, Gideon), m. Emma Collins; Children:
1. Orin, m. Mary Hanson, daughter of Closson Hanson and Florence Hilliker.
2. Bessie, m. Ralph Hanson.

5   4   3   2   1

VI. **Philona Parkman** (Philander, Everett, Noah, Daniel, Gideon), m. Frank Varney; Children:
1. Pearl, m. Verne Merrill. (see Merrill family)
2. Stewart, m. Erma Johnson.
3. Esther, m. first Roy Chase; second, Ivan Chambers.
4. Enzer, m. Preston Lewis.

4   3   2   1

V. **Richard Parkman** (Everett, Noah, Daniel, Gideon), m. Flora Libby; Children:
1. Nora, b. Jan. 3, 1869; m. Parker
2. Horace, b. April 2, 1878.
3. Ernest, b. Oct. 11, 1875.
4. Nellie, b. Nov. 17, 1880.

5   4   3   2   1

VII. **Nellie Parkman** (Richard, Everett, Noah, Daniel, Gideon), m. Seldon Martin, son of Charles Martin and Jennie Collins. Children:
1. Myron
2. Ervin
3. Clyde
4. Dana b. Sept. 6, 1904.

6   5   4   3   2   1

VIII. **Dana Martin** (Nellie, Richard, Everett, Noah, Daniel, Gideon), b. Sept. 6, 1904; m. Marjorie Green, dau. of Wilson and Sarah (Bickmore) Green. Marjorie, m. (1st) Evan Martin; m. (2nd) Dana Martin; daughter by 1st marriage:

1. Pauline, m. Curtis Lombard.
   Children by 2nd marriage:
1. Barbara, m. Edward Patten.
2. Geraldine, m. (1st) Arthur Chadbourne; m. (2nd) Richard Cole.

## PHILBRICK

Thomas Philbrick is said to have come from Lincolnshire in England. Old records state he and his family came in 1630 in the Arabella, in which came Governor Winthrop and others, sailed from Yarmouth April 8, 1630 and arrived in Salem on June 14.

In 1639, the second summer after the settlement of Hampton, N.H., John, son of Thomas Philbrick, moved to Hampton, and it seems that his brother Thomas followed him. We will list all the children of Thomas and Elizabeth, as we believe the St. Albans Philbricks go back to this family.

Thomas Philbrick, by his wife Elizabeth:
1. James Philbrick, m. (1st) Jane Roberts; m. 2nd Ann Roberts; 10 children.
2. John Philbrick, m. Ann Palmer.
3. Deacon Thomas Philbrick, b. 1624; m. (1st) Ann Knapp-4 children; m. (2nd) Hannah French White, widow of John White of Haverhill-3 children.
4. Elizabeth Philbrick, m. 1642 (1st) Thomas Chase; m. 2nd E. P. Garland; m. (3rd) Judge Henry Robey.
5. Hannah Philbrick.
6. Mary Philbrick, m. Edward Tuck of Hampton.
7. Martha Philbrick, b. 1663; m. John Cass.

I. **James Philbrick** b. 1785, d. 1879; m. Mary Pierce b. 1802, d. 1866 James Philbrick came to St. Albans from Wellington in 1826, cleared the farm where Ralph Philbrick lived and moved his family there in 1829. His wife, Mary did spinning and weaving to pay for sawing the lumber to build the first barn in that place. Philbrick was a "root and herb" doctor and traveled around the country selling his medicine.

When eighty years old, he traveled to New Hampshire and sold $175 worth of medicine. He built what was known as the Buker House at the village, and afterward moved there and kept a hotel, leaving his son Newell and wife on the farm. It was later carried on by his son Elwin and then by Ralph whose children make five succeeding generations to live on the farm.

Children:
1. Mary, b. 1821.
2. Naomi, b. 1822.
3. Sarah, b. 1825; m. Americus Morrill.
4. Newell, b. 1827; m. Relief Hurd.
5. Freeman, b. 1829.
6. Hannah, b. 1831.
7. Susan, b. 1834.
8. Louisa, b. 1838.
9. James, b. 1840, d. 1863.

II. **Newell Philbrick** (James[1]), m. Relief Hurd. Children: Elwin H.

III. **Elwin H. Philbrick** (Newell[2], James[1]), m. Parintha Burton. Children:
1. William
2. Eric
3. Ralph

IV. **William S. Philbrick** (Elwin[3], Newell[2], James[1]), m. Eva Dore. Children:
1. Newell, m. Edna Hilton. Children:
   a. Elmer
   b. Thelma, m. Elwood Green.
2. Myrtle, b. June 24, 1905; d. April 27, 1950; m. (1st) Ernest Powers; m. (2nd) Alonzo Williams. Children:
   a. Harlow Powers, b. Sept. 23, 1926; m. Ruth Fox.
   b. Evangeline Powers, b. Sept. 21, 1925, m. Clifford Merrill.
3. Crystal, b. June 24, 1905; m. Sidney Mower. (See Mower family)

IV. **Ralph Philbrick** (Elwin[3], Newell[2], James[1]), m. Winnifred Goodwin. Children:
1. Edith, m. Fred Libby.
2. Ardis
3. Charlotte, m. Kenneth Wiers.
4. Goodwin

Another family by the name of Philbrick were early settlers of St. Albans.

The farm once called the Frank Bishop place on Mill Hill once owned by Manley Pease was first settled in 1798 by Thomas

Philbrick when he first came to St. Albans. He traveled over a bridle path from Palmyra. In the 1850 census we find -Thomas Philbrick b. 1802, 48; Edy b. 1803, 47; Nathaniel 20; Michael 18; Eunice 15; Charles 12; Elijah 10; Lura 6; and Michael Philbrick 84

Charles Philbrick m. Hattie Maxim, b. 1833 and d. 1910. They had two sons, William and Sullivan. William b. 1864; m. Almeda Whittier.

# RICHARDS

The first Richards family to arrive in America was Thomas and Weatheam Richards, who came in the Mary & John, Dec. 20, 1630. It was their daughter, Ruth Richards, who married Gov. Thomas Hinkley of Barnstable, Massachusetts.

If this line is connected to Thomas Richards it was back in England. There is no mention of a connection in the Richards Genealogy to John Richards, who appeared in Newbury, Mass., March 20, 1694.

I. **John Richards** m. first Hannah Goodrich who died in 1695; m. second Sarah Cheney, July 16, 1696.

1

II. **Benjamin Richards** (John), Sarah m. first Mary Staples; m. second Abigail Bradley. Benjamin was a carpenter in Rochester, N.H. moved to Haverhill, Mass. and later built the first dwelling in Atkinson, N.H. in 1727. When the Congregational Church was formed, he was one of the original members.

2   1

III. **Bradley Richards** (Benjamin, John), b. 1748 Norridgewock; d. Dec. 27, 1828; m. Judith Kent of Hampstead, N.H.

3   2   1

IV. **Benjamin Richards** (Bradley, Benjamin, John), first settled in Norridgewock and then moved to St. Albans, Me. He married Alice Adams in Norridgewock, April 14, 1794. Children:
1. David, b. Nov. 7, 1794; m. Abigail Wiggin.
2. Alice, b. Jul. 27, 1799; m. Feb. 22, 1823; Rufus Hodgdon.
3. Benjamin, b. Aug. 15, 1801.
4. Joseph, b. May 9, 1803.
5. Ezra, b. June 18, 1805.
6. Sophronia, b. Jan. 9, 1809; m. Dennis Bowman. (see Bowman family)
7. Phebe, b. May 6, 1810; m. March 10, 1830 to Isaac Bowman.

8. Mary, b. Aug. 2, 1813.
9. Amanda, b. Aug. 13, 1818.
10. Betsy, b. Feb. 8, 1816.

V. **David Richards** (Benjamin⁴, Bradley³, Benjamin², John¹), b. Nov. 7, 1794; d. Jan. 18, 1876; m. Dec. 31, 1815 Abigail Wiggin, daughter of Asa and Abigail (Nud) Wiggin. Children:
   1. Nancy, b. Feb. 12, 1816.
   2. Alfred, b. Dec. 15, 1819.
   3. Abigail, b. June 4, 1821.
   4. Frederick, b. Dec. 22, 1829.

VII. **Frederick Richards** (David⁵, Benjamin⁴, Bradley³, Benjamin², John¹), b. Dec. 22, 1829; m. Margaret Renfrew Whitelaw; b. July 14, 1833 at Greensboro, Vermont; Children:
   1. Jeanette, m. Dondero.
   2. Nathan, m. (1st) Lillian Johnson; m. (2nd) Lena (Butler) Mebane.
   3. George, b. 1873; d. 1880.

VII. **Abigail Richards** (David⁵, Benjamin⁴, Bradley³, Benjamin², John¹), b. June 4, 1821; m. David McGregor Jones; Children:
   1. David Wesley, b. March 24, 1846; m. Nora Turner. Their son, Frederick Richards Jones; m. June 28, 1924, Gladys Weeks. (see Weeks family) Jones Children; Maxine, Earle, Maurice, Frederick, Clarence, Marjorie, Herbert, Ralph, Edwin, Shirley, Fay, David, Richard.


# ROSS

I. **Charles Henry Ross**, b. Bloomfield Dec. 9, 1836; m. Lydia Estelle Dyer, Hartland. Children:
   1. Carrie
   2. Nena
   3. Edith
   4. Charles H.
   5. Lena
   6. Mary
   7. Eugenia
   8. Grace
   9. Vella

II.    **Carrie Ross** (Charles$^1$), b. Sept. 20, 1862, St. Albans.

II.    **Nena Belle Ross** (Charles$^1$), b. Sept. 11, 1864, Garland; m. Theodore W. Smith. Children:
1. Bertha, m. Clifford Goulette.
2. Forest, m. Gladys Sturtevant.
3. Iva B., m. Bailey French.

II.    **Edith Blanche Ross** (Charles$^1$), b. Aug. 6, 1866; m. Junius Avery. Children:
1. Glennice
2. Chalma
(See Avery family)

II.    **Charles H. Ross** (Charles$^1$), b. Jan. 27, 1869; m. July 28, 1896 Nena M. Nichols, daughter of Julian and Malvina Cooley Nichols. Children: (see Cooley family)
1. Erma
2. Elva
3. Doris
4. Bernice
5. Charles E.
6. Arthur
7. Cleo
8. Elwood
9. Lydia

III.    **Erma Ross** (Charles$^2$, Charles$^1$), b. Oct. 2, 1897; m. Carroll Emery of Palmyra. Children:
1. Dorothy
2. Francis
3. Kenneth
4. Nena
5. Laurence
6. Glenice

III.    **Elva Ross** (Charles$^2$, Charles$^1$), b. Mar. 25, 1899; m. Robert E. Nichols, son of Joshua and Emma (Nickerson) Nichols. Children:
1. Willard, b. Nov. 28, 1915.
2. Helen, b. Dec. 20, 1917; m. George Bowman.
3. Ervin, b. Jan. 8, 1920
4. Everett, b. May 27, 1923.
5. Margaret, b. Nov. 8, 1924.
Elva Nichols, m. (2nd) Hermon Parker

**III. Doris Ross** (Charles², Charles¹), b. August 4, 1900; m. Samuel Lyford Fellows. One son, Frances Fellows, b. Apr. 22, 1918.

**III. Bernice Ross** (Charles², Charles¹), b. Feb. 5, 1903; m. Lionel C. Parker, son of Ulysis and Nellie (Nye) Parker. One son, Wilfred, b. June 26, 1923, one dau. Winona.

**III. Charles E. Ross** (Charles², Charles¹), b. Sept. 5, 1906; m. Agnus Wood, daughter of Eugene and Blanche Brown Wood. Children:
1. Barbara, m. Gareth Hanson.
2. Charles

**III. Arthur Ross** (Charles², Charles¹) b. Jan. 13, 1909.

**III. Cleo Ross** (Charles², Charles¹) b. Mar. 9, 1915; m. Cordella Dickey. Children:
1. Robert
2. Beverly

**III. Elwood Ross** (Charles², Charles¹), b. Oct. 14, 1916; d. Oct. 15, 1916.

**III. Lydia Ross** (Charles², Charles¹), b. Aug. 3, 1918; m. Durwood Emery. (See Emery family)

**II. Lena Ross** (Charles¹), b. Oct. 6, 1871.

**II. Mary Ross** (Charles¹), b. April 23, 1875; m. Jepha Bane of Ripley in 1897 - one son, John Marshall Bane m. Gladys Mann. Children:
1. Beverly L., m. Wilmont Grant.
2. Edna, m. Keith Emery.
3. Hugh, m. Atwater.

**II. Eugenia Ross** (Charles¹), b. Sept. 24, 1879; d. early in life.

**II. Grace Ross** (Charles¹), b. Dec. 15, 1883; m. William Cain of Prince Edward Island. Children:
1. Evelyn, b. Jan. 1907; m. Donald Bartlett.
2. Norman, b. May 18, 1915.
3. Lyndall, b. June 3, 1919.

II.   Vella A. Ross (Charles), b. Mar. 26, 1887; m. Fred Hanson.
      Children:
      1.  Winnifred, m. Gardiner Burns.
      2.  Arlene.


# STINCHFIELD


I.    John Stinchfield, b. Oct. 12, 1715 in Leeds, England. Came to
      America in 1735; married Elizabeth Burns.

II.   William Stinchfield (John), b. Jan. 9, 1741 Gloucester, Mass.; m.
      Mary Bordge Farmer, drowned in Little Androscoggin River.

III.  William Stinchfield (William, John), b. July 18, 1770; m. Susan-
      na Smith and resided in Chesterville, Me.

IV.   John Stinchfield (William, William, John), b. July 9, 1793; m.
      Maria Moore. Resided in Hartland, Me. Seven children.

V.    Alphonzo Stinchfield (Johnm William, William, John), b. Dec. 6,
      1816; m. Harriet Briggs; 12 children:
      1.  Henrietta, b. Jan. 3, 1843; m. George W. Knowles. Resided
          in Corinna.
      2.  Lorenzo, b. July 17, 1844; m. Miranda E. Stewart.
      3.  Clarinda, b. Nov. 11, 1845; d. 1850.
      4.  Marilla, b. Feb. 11, 1847.
      5.  Sophia, b. May 9, 1849 St. Albans.
      6.  Clara, b. Dec. 8, 1853; St. Albans; m. Horace K. Lyford.
      7.  Laura, b. April 30, 1854; St. Albans; m. M. T. Morrill.
      8.  Mary, b. July 20, 1855; St. Albans; m. Fred Stinchfield.
      9.  Frederick, b. October 13, 1856; St. Albans.
      10. Edward, b. Oct. 10, 1858; St. Albans.
      11. Harriet, b. April 17, 1862; St. Albans.
      12. Jennie, b. March 16, 1865; St. Albans.

VI.   Harriet E. Stinchfield (Alphonzo, John, William, William, John),
      b. April 17, 1862; m. Alfred Durkee Baird. Their son, Harold E.
      Baird, b. Dec. 20, 1886; m. Etta Bennet and had the following
      children:
      1.  Helen, m. Harry Finson.
      2.  Howard, m. Edna Reynolds.

3. Elsie, m. (1st) Nathaniel Vining; m. (2nd) Lyndon Kinney.
4. Kenneth.
5. Nellie, m. Frank Pooler.
6. Herbert, m. Ena Culley.
7. Webster Baird, m. Ruth Watson.

## STEWARD

The Stewards of this area are descendants of Duncan Stewart, Highland Scot, who came to America in 1650. The family had been Stewart in Scotland and Masachusetts, but all became Steward in Canaan. The children of the early Stewards intermarried with those of other settlers so that it would seem impossible for any St. Albans line having Canaan ancestry to have escaped a Steward line.

I.   **Duncan Stewart**, said to have been born in Scotland, died in Rowley, Mass. age 100; m. Anna.

II.  **James Stewart** (Duncan¹), b. Oct. 8, 1664 Newbury, Mass., d. Rowley, Mass.; m. (1st) Elizabeth (surname unknown). James was a carpenter and a man of considerable means.

III. **Solomon Stewart** (James², Duncan¹), b. July 24, 1698; Rowley, Mass; d. about 1758; m. Martha Farrington June 28, 1727; Andover, Mass. Solomon of Rowley was in military service in 1721-22 fighting Indians under Capt. Harmon in Maine, and tradition states that he was at the distruction of Norridgewock. Children:
1. Solomon, b. Jan. 14, 1730.
2. Phineas, b. March 27, 1732.
3. Daniel.
4. William, bapt. March 14, 1736.
Three of the boys married Ireland sisters.

IV.  **Solomon Stewart** (Solomon³, James², Duncan¹), b. Jan. 14, 1730; m. Elizabeth Taylor. He came to Canaan about 1780. Children:
1. Mary, m. Joseph Sawyer.
2. Betsy, m. Isaac Russell.
3. Rebecca, m. Samuel Bigelow.
4. Solomon, m. Betsy Bigelow; b. Templeton, Mass.

V.   **Solomon Stewart** (Solomon⁴, Solomon³, James², Duncan¹), m. Betsy

Bigelow. Children:
1. Betsy, m. Samuel Jewett.
2. Polly, m. Benjamin Hartwell.
3. Rebecca, m. Isa Weston.
4. Solomon, m. Esther Emery.
5. James, m. Hannah Jewett.
6. Beulah, m.
7. Isaac, m. Jewett.

IV. **Phineas Stewart** (Solomon³, James², Duncan¹), b. March 27, 1732; m. Anne Ireland. Children:
1. Samuel, m. Sally Turner.
2. Anne, m. Capt. Seth Wyman.
3. Phineas, m. Molly Snow.
4. Abraham, m. Sarah McKenzie.
5. Thomas, m. Olive Moore.

V. **Thomas Stewart** (Phineas⁴, Solomon³, James², Duncan¹), m. Olive Moore, Derryfield, N.H. Children:
1. John, m. Mercy Stewart.
2. Susan, m. Darius Emery. (See Emery family)
3. Olive, m. Joseph Cleveland.
4. Asa, m. Sally Parker.
5. Seth, m. Elizabeth Baker.
6. Betsy, m. Sam Dinsmore.
7. Thomas, m. Lucretia Wyman.
8. Cynthia, m. Constance White.
9. Sylvanus, m. Rebecca Goodrich.
10. Paoli, m. Eliza. Wyman.
11. Elijah, m. Sarah Springer.
12. Darinda, m. Capt. William Parker.
13. Anson, m. Pamela Lambert.

IV. **Daniel Stewart** (Solomon³, James², Duncan¹), m. Mary Ireland. Children:
1. John, m. Abigail Whitcomb.
2. Daniel
3. Benjamin
4. Amasa, b. Dec. 18, 1769.
Daniel, Benjamin, and Amasa were all Revolutionary War soldiers.

V. **Amasa Steward** (Daniel⁴, Solomon³, James², Duncan¹), b. Dec. 18, 1768 in Lunenburg, Mass. m. Sept. 1788 Eunice Ireland of Canaan, who died Feb. 4, 1847. This family moved to St. Albans. Children:

1. Lydia died young.
2. Benjamin.
3. Joseph, b. Jan. 23, 1793; m. Sarah Snow.
4. Eunice, b. Dec. 16, 1795; m. Charles Varney.
5. Harriet, b. June 19, 1797; m. Levi Varney.
6. Betsy, b. May 2, 1799; m. Emerson Wardwell.
7. Sophia, b. Feb. 11, 1803; m. Joseph Tuttle, Athens, Maine.
8. Amasa, b. Dec. 18, 1805; m. Mary Spaulding.
9. Hannah, b. March 31, 1807; m. Warren Patten, St. Albans.
10. Asa, b. March 6, 1812; m. Lovina Smith, St. Albans.

                5      4     3     2     1
VI.  **Joseph Steward** (Amasa, Daniel, Solomon, James, Duncan), b. Jan. 23, 1793; m. Sarah Snow. Children:

1. Sarah, m. D. J. Redlon; m. 2nd Valentine Estes.
2. Esther, m. Tobey.
3. Eunice, m. Allen.
4. Elizabeth, m. Ellis first, second Richardson, third Wardwell.
5. Clara, m. Allen first, second Jackson.
6. Lonantha, m. Dec. 3, 1846 Cyrus Mathews.
7. Adeline.
8. Benjamin.
9. Joseph.

                3      2     1
IV.  **Deacon William Steward** (Solomon, James, Duncan), bapt. Mar 14, 1736 at Salem, Mass.; m. Abigail Ireland July 25, 1728. Removed to Bloomfield, now Skowhegan. Children:

1. Abigail, m. George Pooler.
2. Dr. William, m. Sally Hood.
3. Susanna, m. Joseph Cleveland.
4. Jonathan, m. Joanna Jewett; 2nd Olive Moore.
5. James, m. (1st) Hannah Jewett; (2nd) Lucy Pattee; (3rd) Olive (Moore) Steward.

                4      3     2     1
V.  **Rev. Jonathan Steward** (William, Solomon, James, Duncan), b. July 13, 1769 at Fitchburg, Mass.; d. July 23, 1848 at Skowhegan, Maine. He m. first about 1790 Hannah Jewett. She was killed by lightning on August 17, 1795 at Canaan. He married second June 21, 1796 at Winslow, Maine, Lucy Pattee who died in Bloomfield. He married third Dec. 10, 1804, Mrs. Olive (Moor) Steward, widow of his brother Deacon Thomas Steward

of Norridgewock, Maine. She died March 12, 1848. He was one of the first Baptist preachers in central Maine.

VI.  **Rev. David Steward** (Jonathan,$^5$ William,$^4$ Solomon,$^3$ James,$^2$ Duncan$^1$), b. Feb. 22, 1797 at Bloomfield, Maine; died April 6, 1884 at Corinna, Maine. M. first Eliza Merrick; m. second Mrs. Harriet Niles. He was a Baptist minister and pioneer temperance advocate. He served on the school committee and was selectman in Corinna. He was a man of ability and high standing in town. Children:

1   David Dinsmore, b. Oct. 22, 1823 at Corinna and d. Dec. 31, 1917 at St. Albans; m. Mar. 16, 1854 Ariminta Merrick, his cousin.

2.  Eliabeth Merrick, b. Jan. 4, 1825 at Corinna; m. John Winchester, b. Jan. 25, 1822, son of Rev. Benjamin P. Winchester and Elizabeth Knowles, dau. of John Knowles and Lydia Chaplin.

3.  Levi Merrick, b. Dec. 10, 1827 at Corinna and d. May 3, 1910 at Minneapolis, Minnesota; not married.

4.  Charles Miller, b. Apr. 24, 1829 at Corinna and d. unmarried while on a voyage to Australia.

VII.  **Elizabeth Merrick Steward** (Rev. David,$^6$ Jonathan,$^5$ William,$^4$ Solomon,$^3$ James,$^2$ Duncan$^1$), m. John Winchester. Children:

1.  Mary E., b. June 20, 1845; m. Dinsmore Hilliker. Their daughter - Florence Hilliker b. 1869 d. 1956 m. Clossen Hanson b. 1867 d. 1935. To this marriage was born Glen Hanson, Mary Hanson, and Helen Hanson.

# TURNER

I.  **William Turner**, b. Jan. 2, 1797, m. Annie Bullen, b. Apr. 16, 1800. They were of English descent coming to St. Albans in 1820. 14 children:

1.  Putnum
2.  Sarah
3.  Bonaparte N.
4.  Augusta L.
5.  Louise
6.  John

7. Elizabeth J.
8. Susan
9. Hannah M.
10. Mary
11. Harriett
12. Wallace W.
13. Gilbert L.

II. **Putnam** (William)[1], b. Mar. 13, 1822; m. Sarah Gould.

II. **Sarah A. Turner** (William)[1], b. Apr. 11, 1834; m. Enoch French, b 1813; d. 1873. Children:
1. Elizabeth French, b. Nov. 9, 1844; m. David Longley
2. Henrietta French, b. Apr. 11, 1846; m. Daniel Hanson, son of Mesech and Nancy (Tibbetts) Hanson, 3 children, among them Closson Hanson.
3. William French, b. 1847; d. in the Civil War.
4. Mary Elizabeth French, b. 1848; d. unm.
5. John Henry French, b. 1851. (res. Calif.)
6. George Washington French, b. 1855; m. Sadie Garside. (res. Calif.)

II. **Nepoleon Bonaparte Turner** (William)[1], b. Nov. 15, 1824; m. Alice Haines; m. (2nd) Mary (surname unknown). Prominent both in business and socially. In 1854 he bought out the shovel handle factory. 9 children:
1. Mertie Turner, m. Charles Goodwin.
2. Addie Turner, m. Charles Emery.
3. Nepoleon Bonaparte, m.
4. Edgar Turner.
5. Frank Turner.
6. Alfred.
There may have been other children.

III. **Nepoleon Bonaparte Turner** (Nepoleon[2], William[1]) 1 son Leon

II. **Augusta L. Turner** (William)[1], b. Aug. 20, 1825; m. Moses Keene.

II. **Louise C. Turner** (William)[1], b. Mar. 1, 1827; m. Bela Lancaster. Children:
1. Estelle Lancaster, m. Albion Libby.
2. Lille Lancaster, m. Greenwood.

II. **John B. Turner** (William)[1], b. July 7, 1828; m. Diantha Worthen.

Children:
1. Dr. Franklin Turner.
2. Alice, m. Buker.
3. Ada, m. Davis.

II. **Elizabeth Turner** (William)[1], b. Nov. 4, 1829; m. William Lincoln.

II. **Susan M. Turner** (William)[1], b. Mar. 18, 1830.

II. **Hannah M. Turner** (William)[1], b. Aug. 17, 1832; m. John Brackett. 10 children.

II. **Mary Turner** (William)[1], b. May 18, 1834; m. Sewell Whittier.

II. **Harriet Turner** (William)[1], b. May 18, 1834; d. 18 years old.

II. **Wallace W. Turner** (William)[1], b. Jan. 11, 1837; m. Clara Webb.

II. **Gilbert L. Turner** (William)[1], b. May 12, 1839; m. Emma Goodwin.

# VARNEY

I. **William Varney**, b. 1608 in Claydon, Buckinghamshire, England. He came to Ipswich, Massachusetts in 1649, no doubt well educated and medium wealthy, as he owned many books.

On May 4, 1629, he married Bridget Knight Parsons, widow of John Parsons. She was the daughter of Walter Knight, born 1585, an explorer who was reported to have been in Nantucket in 1622. William Varney died in Salem in 1654 about four years after his arrival in this country. For seven generations the Varneys were Quakers.

II. **Humphrey Varney** (William)[1], born 1627, died 1714; married March 1664 Sarah (Starbuck) Austin, daughter of Edward Starbuck. five children.

III. **Ebenezer Varney** (Humphrey[2], William[1]), born 1670; in Dover, N.H. He married Mary Otis, daughter of Stephen and Mary Pitman Otis. Like his father, he became a man of influence and substance. Most of the Varneys in New England are descendents of this family. twelve children.

IV. **Nathaniel Varney** (Ebenezer³, Humphrey², William¹), married Content Gaskell in 1727; ten children.

V. **Silas Varney** (Nathaniel⁴, Ebenezer³, Humphrey², William¹).

VI. **Nathaniel Varney** (Silas⁵, Nathaniel⁴, Ebenezer³, Humphrey², William¹), m. Eunice Stewart. He died 1875; one child, Amasa.

VII. **Amasa Varney** (Nathaniel⁶, Silas⁵, Nathaniel⁴, Ebenezer³, Humphrey², William¹), m. Hannah Stinson Dunlap, daughter of William and Hannah Stinson Dunlap; five children: (All will be listed.)
1. Rose
2. Nellie
3. Angie
4. Frank
5. Horace

VIII. **Rose Varney** (Amasa⁷, Nathaniel⁶, Silas⁵, Nathaneil⁴, Ebenezer³, Humphrey², William¹), m. Osgood Robertson, son of Rufus and Juliette (Fuller) Robertson. Children:
1. Harold, m. Mary Fling - one daughter, Elizabeth. Agent for Ginn & Co.
2. Irving, m. Mabel Badger of Harmony. Graduated from U. of M.
3. Clarence, m. Alzada C. Prescott, daughter of Henry and Anna Emery Prescott.
4. Vera.
5. Earle C., m. Ruth Finson, daughter of Fred and Dora Chase Finson. He settled on his great-grandfather, Isaac Robertson's, farm. Their children: 1. Marguerite, m. Weston Sherbourne. 2. Earle 3. Gerald, m. Crystal Cuddy. (see Finson family)

VIII. **Nellie Varney** (Amasa⁷, Nathaniel⁶, Silas⁵, Nathaniel⁴, Ebenezer³, Humphrey², William¹), m. John Libby, son of Joseph and Julia Lib-

247

by; (See Libby family) Children:

1. Alton, m. (1st) Grace Babb; (2nd) Grace Nutter; (3rd) Rella Stone. Libby children: Earl, Mahlon, Rosalie
2. Joseph, m. Rose Knight, daughter of Stephen and Alvah Knight of St. Albans.
3. Ada, m. Charles Mower, son of Edwin and Nettie Robertson Mower; their children:
    1. Ruth Mower, b. Nov. 15, 1907 m. (1st) Thomas Mills; (2nd) Newton Smith.
    2. Meredith Mower, b. May 30, 1910; m. Elmer Fisher. (See Mower family)
4. Vira, m. (1st) Fred Thomas; (2nd) Dr. Charles Norcross; 3rd Earl Moor.
5. Lura B., m. George Crocker. (See Crocker family)

VIII. **Angie Varney** (Amasa,⁷ Nathaniel,⁶ Silas,⁵ Nathaniel,⁴ Ebenezer,³ Humphrey,² William¹), m. Howard Nutter, son of Joel and Irene Douglas Nutter. Children:

1. Harry, m. Edna Ireland.
2. Mildred, m. Charles Newcomb.
3. Marion, m. Anthony Kelez.
4. Shirley.

VIII. **Horace E. Varney** (Amasa,⁷ Nathaniel,⁶ Silas,⁵ Nathaniel,⁴ Ebenezer,³ Humphrey,² William¹), m. Etta Carson; one child: Floyd Varney.

VIII. **Frank A. Varney** (Amasa,⁷ Nathaniel,⁶ Silas,⁵ Nathaniel,⁴ Ebenezer,³ Humphrey,² William¹), b. Nov. 8, 1874; m. Feb. 12, 1896 Philona Parkman, twin daughter of Philander and Clara (Farrer) Parkman; Children:

1. Pearl, b. Feb. 24, 1897; m. Verne Merrill, son of George and Lena Hanson Merrill (See Merrill family)
2. Enzer, b. June 6, 1909; m. Preston Lewis.
3. Esther, b. June 6, 1909; m. (1st) Roy Chase; (2nd) Ivan Chambers.
4. Amasa Stewart, b. Sept. 6, 1912; m. Irma Johnson, daughter of Lewis and Stella (Bean) Johnson. One son, Erlon.

# VINING

The first record we have of the Vining family in St. Albans is Josiah and Esther Vining who came from Litchfield, Maine.

I. **Josiah Vining**, b. April 10, 1784 and d. 1859; m. Esther, b. October 10, 1787. Children:
1. Isreal, b. 1808 was probably born in Litchfield (Others all recorded in St. Albans).
2. Sarah C., b. March 28, 1838; m. Hiram Hawes.
3. Louisa.
4. Jacob H., b. November 20, 1815.
5. Abigail, b. 1817.
6. Esther, b. 1820.
7. Josiah, b. 1822.
8. Ruth, b. 1824 - an early teacher in St. Albans.
9. John, b. May 19, 1827.
10. William Francis, b. Dec. 22, 1831.

There may also have been other children born in Litchfield.

II. **Isreal Vining** (Josiah$^1$), b. 1808; d. 1860; m. Dec. 1, 1835 Rebecca Norton; m. second Nov. 17, 1837 Joanna Bigelow Hawes, b. 1808, d. 1876. (List of children unknown).

III. **Nathaniel Vining** (Isreal$^2$, Josiah$^1$), b. 1838 and d. 1899; m. 1864 Anna L. Stone, daughter of Cyrus and Maria Prescott Stone. Children:
1. Seldon.
2. Carrie, 1866-1887.
3. Florence, 1876-1937.
4. Clifford.
5. Frank, 1872-1919.

IV. **Florence Vining** (Nathaniel$^3$, Isreal$^2$, Josiah$^1$), b. 1876; m. Hugh Chisholm. Children:
1. Clifford Chisholm, m. (1st) Vaughnie Coombs; m. (2nd) Marjorie Martin.

IV. **Frank Vining** (Nathaniel$^3$, Isreal$^2$, Josiah$^1$), b. 1872; m. Carrie Hanson. One son, Nathaniel, b. 1909 and d. 1971; m. Elsie Baird. Children:
1. Anna, m. Clayton Merrill.
2. Jacqueline.

3. Clifford, m.
4. Helen, m. Lawrence Springer.

(A George Vining married March 12, 1878 - Edna Lucus.)


# WYKE - WEEKS

I.  **Leonard Wykes**, b. 1635 in England; m. 1667 Mary Haines, daughter of Samuel Haines. He received a grant of 8 acres of land in Greenfield, N.H. 8 children:

1
II.  **Capt. Samuel Weeks** (Leonard), b. Dec. 14, 1670; d. Mar. 26, 1746; m. Aug. 1675 Eleanor Haines, daughter of Samuel Haines, Jr. Samuel Weeks was a farmer, a man of influence in the church and town. 7 children:

2        1
III.  **Walter Weeks** (Samuel, Leonard), b. 1706; d. 1774; m. Comfort Weeks, daughter of Capt. Joshua Weeks and Comfort Hubbard. 11 children:

3        2        1
IV.  **Samuel Weeks** (Walter, Samuel, Leonard), bapt. 1728; m. Martha Haines. He left her when their only son was eight years old. She later married a Morrison and was buried in an unmarked grave in Danville, Vermont.

4        3        2        1
V.  **Samuel Weeks** (Samuel, Walter, Samuel, Leonard), b. 1767; d. May 7, 1834; m. Ruth Eastman b. April 7, 1772, daughter of Stilson and Mehitable Hutchins Eastman at Enfield, N.H. 14 children:

5        4        3        2        1
VI.  **Dr. Abram Weeks** (Samuel, Samuel, Walter, Samuel, Leonard), b. April 22, 1810 at Danville, Vermont; d. July 20, 1888. Buried in Hartland. Married first Melessa Randall - 3 children; married second Analine Duntly of London, Vermont; married third Hannah Osborn, daughter of Eunice Ann Seavey and John Osborn (Eunice, daughter of Hiram and Eunice Brown Seavey) (John, the son of John and Sarah Wing Osborn) 4 children to Abram and Hannah:
1. Samuel, b. Nov. 1877.
2. John M., b. May 30, 1880.
3. Charles H., b. Dec. 11, 1882.

4. Earle, b. Dec. 24, 1885.

All born in Palmyra. Hannah Weeks later married James Atwood and had one son, Nelson Atwood, born July 5, 1896.

VII. **Samuel H. Weeks** (Abram,⁶ Samuel,⁵ Samuel,⁴ Walter,³ Samuel,² Leonard¹), b. Nov. 27, 1877; d. Feb. 7, 1960; California; m. Grace Scott.

VII. **John Milton Weeks** (Abram,⁶ Samuel,⁵ Samuel,⁴ Walter,³ Samuel,² Leonard¹), b. May 30, 1880; d. Sept. 4, 1945; m. Ethel Wilkins.

VII. **Charles Harrison Weeks** (Abram,⁶ Samuel,⁵ Samuel,⁴ Walter,³ Samuel,² Leonard¹), b. Dec. 11, 1882; m. Mabel Wheeler.

VII. **Earle Osborn Weeks** (Abram,⁶ Samuel,⁵ Samuel,⁴ Walter,³ Samuel,² Leonard¹), b. Dec. 24, 1885; m. first Etta Leola Farrer June 17, 1905; m. second Lillian Thomas. Children (by 1st wife):

1. Gladys Merle Weeks, b. Sept. 6, 1909; m. Frederick Richards Jones, June 28, 1924.
2. John Weeks, b. May 31, 1915; m. Genevieve Clifford, Nov. 16, 1935.


# WEYMOUTH

I. **Edward Weymouth**, b. 1639 in England or maybe on a ship; married Esther Hodsdon b. Sept. 20, 1640; Edward was a tailor and owned land in Kittery. He was also a town constable.

II. **Timothy Weymouth** (Edward¹), b. 1675; m. Patience Stone b. March 23, 1683. He was thrown from his horse and killed.

III. **Ichabod Weymouth** (Timothy,² Edward¹), b. May 10, 1707; d. Berwick Dec. 8, 1760; m. Mary Knight, daughter of Grindall and Mary (Harris) Knight.

IV. **Jonathan Weymouth** (Ichabod,³ Timothy,² Edward¹), b. 1747; d. 1819; m. Molly (surname unknown) b. in 1759.

251

$$\overset{4}{\phantom{x}}\quad\overset{3}{\phantom{x}}\quad\overset{2}{\phantom{x}}\quad\overset{1}{\phantom{x}}$$

V. **Walter Weymouth** (Jonathan, Ichabod, Timothy, Edward), b. Oct. 15, 1777 probably in Webster; m. Mary Labree, b. June 18, 1783, daughter of James and Mercy (Austin) Labree. He moved to Corinna.

$$\overset{5}{\phantom{x}}\quad\overset{4}{\phantom{x}}\quad\overset{3}{\phantom{x}}\quad\overset{2}{\phantom{x}}$$

VI. **Jonathan Weymouth** (Walter, Jonathan, Ichabod, Timothy,

$$\overset{1}{\phantom{x}}$$

Edward), b. April 9, 1816; d. Oct. 4, 1855 in St. Albans; m. Jane Bates, daughter of Alexander and Nancy Robertson Bates.

$$\overset{6}{\phantom{x}}\quad\overset{5}{\phantom{x}}\quad\overset{4}{\phantom{x}}\quad\overset{3}{\phantom{x}}$$

VII. **Hiram Weymouth** (Jonathan, Walter, Jonathan, Ichabod,

$$\overset{2}{\phantom{x}}\quad\overset{1}{\phantom{x}}$$

Timothy, Edward), b. 1844; m. Hannah E. Cyphers.

$$\overset{7}{\phantom{x}}\quad\overset{6}{\phantom{x}}\quad\overset{5}{\phantom{x}}\quad\overset{4}{\phantom{x}}$$

VIII. **Guy Carlton Weymouth** (Hiram, Jonathan, Walter, Jonathan,

$$\overset{3}{\phantom{x}}\quad\overset{2}{\phantom{x}}\quad\overset{1}{\phantom{x}}$$

Ichabod, Timothy, Edward), b. 1872; m. Jan. 30, 1890 Etta May Cole, daughter of Dow L. and Melissa (Boston) Cole. Children:
1. Bernard Colby, b. June 13, 1894; m. 1915 Athens, Me. Lottie May Gardiner, b. in Cornville, daughter of Charles and Caddy (Berry) Gardiner.
2. Harold, b. Feb. 19, 1899 St. Albans; m. (1st) Feb. 3, 1918 Edith Jennett Hollis b. 1900; m. (2nd) at Hartland 1931 Grace Louise Griffith b. Nov. 9, 1909, daughter of Frank and Mae Bell (Pickard) Griffith. Children:
    1. Kendrick Gordon, b. April 8, 1922.
    2. Hiram Bates, b. Aug. 17, 1943.
    3. David C.
    4. Richard L., b. Sept. 11, 1946.
    5. Ira.
    6. Barbara.

# WING

I. **John Wing** , m. Deborah Batchelder, daughter of Rev. Stephen Batchelder, the fourth great-grandfather of Daniel Webster. Four sons and three daughters. (Rev. Stephen Batchelder came in the ship Arabella.)

$$\overset{1}{\phantom{x}}$$

II. **Stephen Wing** (John), married first Aseah Dillingham, daughter of Edward Dillingham; married second Sarah Briggs, daughter of John Briggs.

**III.** **Nathaniel Wing** (Stephen,² John¹), b. 1647; three sons.

**IV.** **Ebenezer Wing** (Nathaniel,³ Stephen,² John¹), three sons.

**V.** **Simon Wing** (Ebenezer,⁴ Nathaniel,³ Stephen,² John¹), b. Nov. 17, 1722 in Sandwich, Mass. Married Mary Allen, b. Sandwich. Mr. Wing was exceedingly prominent in town affairs. Children listed:

1. Elizabeth, b. Aug. 6, 1746; married Job Fuller.
2. Abisha, b. Aug. 26, 1749.
3. William, b. Aug. 20, 1751; married Deborah Besse; married second to Lucy Blackstone; 11 children.
4. Simon, b. Dec. 29, 1752; married Elizabeth Atkinson; 6 children.
5. Thomas, b. Oct. 26, 1754.
6. Sarah, b. July 22, 1756.
7. Ebenezer, b. Dec. 22, 1759; married Mrs. Lucy Bonney whose maiden name was Chandler.
8. Moses, b. Apr. 25, 1760; married first Molly (Taylor) Chandler; second, Martha Polly Maxium; five children. Dr. Moses Wing was a most able and efficient physician, a Christian gentleman. At the age of 26, he represented The District of Maine in the legislature in Boston.
9. Aaron, b. Mar. 23, 1761; m. Sylvina Perry; 12 children.
10. Allen, b. Mar. 22, 1763; m. first Teniphanee Perry; m. second Cynthia Burgess; 10 children.
11. Thomas.
12. Mary.

Simon Wing's oldest daughter, Elizabeth, who married Job Fuller, gave such a glowing account of the new country in Maine, the whole family decided to emigrate to it. It was agreed that the youngest son, William, should remain for a time with the parents, and that the other brothers should take up a tract of land and make a clearing of so many acres, build a house and barn, and when done, William was to have it, together with what the parents should give him, and he should care for his parents in their old age. The brothers chartered a coasting vessel to take them to the Kennebec River. After the vessel had proceeded too far to return, great was their surprise to see William emerge from a hiding place among the freight. This family settled in the Wayne area. William lived in Winthrop.

VI. **Ebenezer Wing** (Simon,⁵ Ebenezer,⁴ Nathaniel,³ Stephen,² John¹), b. Dec. 22, 1759; m. Mrs Lucy (Chandler) Bonney.

VII. **William Wing** (Ebenezer,⁶ Simon,⁵ Ebenezer,⁴ Nathaniel,³ Stephen,² John¹), b. August 25, 1789; m. first Oct. 23, 1812; Lois Raymond. In 1845 the family suffered an epedemic of typhoid fever. The mother and four children died. William removed from Wayne to Ripley.

VIII. **William Allen Wing** (William,⁷ Ebenezer,⁶ Simon,⁵ Ebenezer,⁴ Nathaniel,³ Stephen,² John¹), b. 1815; m. Sarah Frost, daughter of Jacob and Sarah (Sylvester) Frost. They were the parents of 13 children. Several will be listed:

IX. **Jacob Wing** (William,⁸ William,⁷ Ebenezer,⁶ Simon,⁵ Ebenezer,⁴ Nathaniel,³ Stephen,² John¹), m. first Etta Grant; two daughters, Clara and Leora E.; m. second Mary Moorse; son Harold married Jessie Wing.

IX. **Lois Ann Wing** (William,⁸ William,⁷ Ebenezer,⁶ Simon,⁵ Ebenezer,⁴ Nathaniel,³ Stephen,² John¹), d. 1931 age 84; m. second Theodore Woodcock. Theodore Woodcock by his first marriage had a daughter Deborah, who married (1st) John Bowman. (See Bowman family). The children of Lois Wing and Theodore Woodcock:
 1. William Woodcock, m. Lula Avery; daughter Agnas m. Clyde Cook.
 2. Milton Woodcock, m. Lois Peakes; their children:
  1. Dorothy.
  2. John, m. Lura Read.

IX. **William Wing** (William,⁸ William,⁷ Ebenezer,⁶ Simon,⁵ Ebenezer,⁴ Nathaniel,³ Stephen,² John¹), m. Lanzarah Cooley, daughter of Isaac Cooley. Children:
 1. Carrie, m. Leslie Leavitt.
 2. Effie, m. Nelson Corey; m. second William Snowman.
 3. Belina, m. Lery Nichols; daughters, Virginia and Dorothy.

4. Sarah, m. Tompkins m. 2nd Reed.
5. Pearl, m. Jerry York.
6. Mary, m. first Judson; second, Straight.

IX. **Henry Wing** (William[8], William[7], Ebenezer[6], Simon[5], Ebenezer[4], Nathaniel[3], Stephen[2], John[1]), m. Hattie Goodale, daughter of Wm. Goodale.

IX. **Albert Wing** (William[8], William[7], Ebenezer[6], Simon[5], Ebenezer[4], Nathaniel[3], Stephen[2], John[1]), m. Anna Page; children:
1. Bessie, m. Lee Brown.
2. Jessie, m. Harold Wing.

IX. **Mary Ellen Wing** (William[8], William[7], Ebenezer[6], Simon[5], Ebenezer[4], Nathaniel[3], Stephen[2], John[1]), m. Walter Wilkins; 8 children:
1. Vesta M., m. Harry J. Hilton; no children.
2. Harland, m. Jennie Hersom.
3. Elden.
4. Alma.
5. Wilma, m. Bouton.
6. Clifford, m. first Clara Stevens; 1 son; m. second Gladys Grant Avery.
7. Lois, m. Dana Worthen; 1 daughter Mary Ellen Worthen who married Fred Cooper.

IX. **Eldon Wing** (William[8], William[7], Ebenezer[6], Simon[5], Ebenezer[4], Nathaniel[3], Stephen[2], John[1]), m. Nov. 29, 1899 Mrs Ella J. Ellsmore, the second wife of David Knowles; two children:
1. Bernice Wing, m. Harry Nelson.
2. Casimir Wing, m. first Eleanor Springer, daughter of Wesley and Eva Springer; m. second Arlene Osborn.

# INDEX - SURNAMES

**Avery -Averill family.**
Jackson, Brown, Kinney, Hilton, Clark, Dow, Southard, Raymond, Russell, Lock, Adams, Anderson, Hight, Wippich, Ross, Page, Woodcock, Philbrick, Nelson, Mathews, Warner, Lord, Merrow, Lewis, Lary, Cranshaw, Killam, Jones, Gallant.

**Buker family.**
Butler, Stevens, Goodridge, Seekins, Cook, Worth, Shaw, Page, Bickford, Folsom, Holt, Serencha, Dyer, Worster, Turner, Worthen, Moody, Cooley, Phinney, Bigelow, Libby, Tilton, Hughes, Whitney, Hazelton, Worster, Mererik.

**Bates family.**
Lapham, Gibbs, Bailey, Herrick, Robinson, Cushman, Daggett, Stevens, Leavitt, Albee, Mower, Jones, Smith, Crocker, Weymouth, Parker, Daggett.

**Bagaley - Bigelow family.**
Warren, Flagg, Bemis, Sawyer, Davis, Emery, Monroe, Bowden, Merrill, Wing, Lothrop, Maxwell, Ford, Webster, Abbey, Butler, Douglas, Marble, Buker, Frost, Smith, Osborn, Howes, Vining, Knowles, Jones, Worthen, Stevens, Foss, Browning, Coolidge, King, Mills, Wilkens, Fairbrother, Atwood.

**Bowman family.**
Richards, Adams, Hawks, Burton, Woodcock, Fields, Beatty, Purman, Gifford, Whitney, Leach, Folsom, Gilman, Nichols, Ross, Dearborn, Springer, Littlefield.

**Braley family.**
Raymond, Smart, Reze, Frost, Willard, Hatch, Sawyer, Hanson, Plummer, Chase.

**Cooley family.**
White, Thompson, Holbrook, Lunt, Pingree, Johnson, Schoff, Bryant, Hanson, Smith, Ellis, Bailey, Magoon, Ross, Wing, Nickerson, Munn.

**Crocker family.**
Bodfish, Parker, Blish, Taylor, Walley, Hinckley, Chipman, Phinney, Bursley, Bates, Braley, Sprague, Ransom, Gray,

Robertson, Mower, Keene, Leavitt, Cole, Libby, Varney, Rines, Patterson, Nelson, Dickey, Martin, Tibbetts, Thomas, Nickerson, Davis.

**Emery family.**

Ridge, Newcomb, Goodwin, Reddington, Foster, Stevens, Ireland, Bigelow, Steward, Flagg, Fowler, Cole, Moor, Ryerson, Winner, Given, Jackson, Prescott, Seekins, Neal, Libby, Sinclair, Fuller, Springer, Waldron, Dickey, Ballard, Monroe, Preston, Davis, Hutchins, Wheeler, Boston, Butler, Davenport, Leavitt, Allen, Greeley, Bassett, Stafford, Knowles, Ramsdell, Haskell, Trafton, Howes, Hartwell, Richards, Denning.

**2nd Emery family cont.**

Webster, Woodman, Watson, Barron, Goodwin, Nedeau, Plourde, Knowles, Ginn, Cummings, Bishop, Ross, Bane, Dearborn, Burpee.

**3rd Emery family cont.**

Farrer, Cook, Wheeler, Hatch, Braley.

**Finson family.**

Lane, Thurston, Dressor, Jordan, Rand, Homer, Chase, Robertson, Sherbourne, Cuddy, Bubar, Baird.

**Frost family.**

Cole, Miller, Dunton, Ware, Adams, Clark, Curtis, Ellis, Osborn, Bigelow, Boston, Pomery, Luce, Ellis, Marsh, Lowell, Sally, Clark, White, Nichols.

**Hilton family.**

Dudley, Moulton, Watson, Stoddard, Osborn, Brown, Dunlap, Smith, Merrick, Sawyer, Philbrick, Hanson, Howes, Avery, Wilkins, Lambert, Ramsdell, Whitney, Knowles, Gusha, Robertson.

**Libby family.**

Brown, Furber, Plummer, Boynton, Sampson, Winslow, Magoon, Prescott, Webb, Parkman, Lancaster, Welch, Philbrick, Jordon, Knight, Nye, Varney, Crocker, Babb, Stone, Mower, Thomas, Moor, Norcross, Wing, Mayo, Harvey, Varcruise, Smith, Schmitz, Murphy, Pease, Ward, Leavitt.

**Lucus family.**

Lyford, Osborn, Jones, Libby, Watson, Lewis, Durgen,

Ramsdell, Hopkins, Jackson, Frost, Bigelow, Goodwin, Martin, Reed, Marden, Seavey, Ross, Berry, Merrill, Cooper, Dumont, Carson, Deering.

**Lyford family.**
Dudley, Leavitt, Follett, Hardy, Folsom, Gilman, Wilson, Pike, Oliver, Kinsley, Wiggin, Robinson, Sanborn, Thing, Lampney, Hilton, Dearborn, Lucus, Osborn, Blake, Fogg, Worthen, Rowe, Lane, Batchelder, Webster, Dow, Snow, Bates, Skinner, Ellis, King, Rollins, Knowles, Judkins, Given, Costello, Bigger, Buck, Anderson, Leighton, Maguire, Clement, Brooker, Rines, McGowan, Bovat, Spaulding, Holt.

**Merrill family.**
Willshire, Sawyer, Steward, Sevey, Weston, Bigelow, Bullen, Bowden, Hayes, Walker, George, Soule, Chandler, Hunt, Turner, Bickford, Palmer, Chabbuck, Reidhead, Eastman, Downing.

**2nd Merrill family**
Downing, Hanson, Bates, Plummer, Patterson, Varney, Warren, Vining, Powers.

**Mower family.**
Marshall, Greene, Sprague, Bemis, Robinson, Ward, Davis, Adams, Harlow, Conners, Farrer, Hazelton, Bates, Turner, Kimball, Higgins, Parker, Gould, Ellms, Horn, Buxton, Katon, Morse, Brown, Gilman, Coburn, Crocker, Gray, Libby, Mills, Smith, Fisher, Dickenson, Anderson, Heath, Berry, Dunn, Russell, Philbrick, Brawn, Brooks, Hanford.

**Osborn - Osbourne family.**
Love, Wyman, Jackson, Littlefield, Saliner, Burrill, Wing, Burgess, Haskell, Holway, Hilton, Lucus, Grafton, Crinsley, Benton, Frost, Reade, Goodwin, Martin, Randall, Matthews, Lombard, McClowd, Ellis.

**Parkman family.**
Vining, Merrill, House, Weston, Lathram, Gardiner, Pratt, Higgins, Berry, McLuer, Tracy, Goodwin, Wheeler, Lary, Church, Springer, Ames, Lord, Allen, Wood, Farnsworth, Niles, Laughton, Osbourne, Wells, Steward, Crocker, Sevey, Farrer, Collins, Varney, Libby, Hanson, Merrill, Johnson, Chase,

Chambers, Lewis, Martin, Greene, Bickmore, Lombard, Patten, Chadbourne, Cole.

**Philbrick family.**
Pierce, Morrill, Hurd, Buxton, Dore, Hilton, Greene, Powers, Mower, Goodwin, Libby, Wiers, Fox, Merrill, Maxim, Whittier.

**Ross family.**
Dyer, Smith, Goulette, Sturdevant, French, Avery, Nichols, Cooley, Nickerson, Bowman, Fellows, Parker, Wood, Dickey, Emery, Bane, Mann, Grant, Atwater, Cain, Bartlett, Hanson, Burns.

**Richards family.**
Goodrich, Chiney, Staples, Bradley, Kent, Adams, Wiggin, Hodgdon, Bowman, Nudd, Whitelaw, Dondero, Johnson, Butler, McGregor, Jones, Turner, Weeks.

**Stinchfield family.**
Burns, Farmer, Smith, Moore, Briggs, Knowles, Steward, Lyford, Morrill, Baird, Finson, Vining.

**Steward family.**
Farrington, Taylor, Sawyer, Russell, Bigelow, Jewett, Hartwell, Weston, Emery, Turner, Wyman, Snow, McKenzie, Moore, Cleveland, Parker, Baker, Densmore, Wyman, White, Goodrich, Springer, Lambert, Whitcomb, Ireland, Varney, Wardwell, Tuttle, Spaulding, Patten, Smith, Estes, Tobey, Allen, Richardson, Jackson, Mathews, Pooler, Hood, Pattee, Niles, Merrick, Winchester, Hilliker, Hanson, Knowles, Chaplin.

**Turner family.**
Bullen, Gould, French, Longley, Hanson, Haines, Goodwin, Emery, Libby, Greenwood, Worthen, Buker, Davis, Lincoln, Brackett, Whittier, Webb, Goodwin.

**Varney family.**
Knight, Parsons, Starbuck, Austin, Pitman, Otis, Gaskell, Stinson, Dunlap, Robertson, Fuller, Flint, Badger, Prescott, Finson, Chase, Sherbourne, Cuddy, Babb, Nutter, Stone, Libby, Mower, Mills, Fisher, Norcross, Thomas, Moor, Crocker, Ireland, Newcomb, Kelez, Parkman, Farrer, Merrill, Lewis, Chase, Chambers, Johnson, Bean.

**Vining family.**

Howes, Stone, Prescott, Chisholm, Coombs, Martin, Hanson, Baird, Merrill, Springer.

**Weeks family.**

Haines, Hubbard, Eastman, Hutchins, Randall, Duntley, Osborn, Seavy, Brown, Wing, Atwood, Scott, Wilkins, Wheeler, Farrer, Thomas, Jones, Clifford.

**Weymouth family.**

Hodsdon, Stone, Knight, Labree, Austin, Bates, Cyphers, Cole, Boston, Gardiner, Berry, Griffith, Packard.

**Wing family.**

Batchelder, Webster, Dillingham, Briggs, Allen, Fuller, Besse, Blackstone, Atkinson, Bonney, Chandler, Taylor, Maxim, Perry, Burgess, Raymond, Sylvester, Frost, Morse, Woodcock, Bowman, Bessey, Avery, Cook, Peaks, Read, Cooley, Leavitt, Snowman, Tompkins, York, Judson, Straight, Goodale, Page, Wilkins, Hilton, Hersom, Bouton, Stevens, Worthen, Cooper, Ellsmore, Nelson, Springer, Osborn, Knowles.

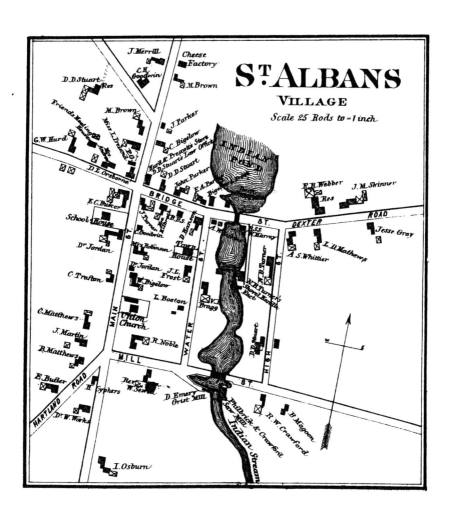

St. ALBANS
VILLAGE
Scale 25 Rods to = 1 inch

# REFERENCES

"We Walk on Jewels" by Jean Blakemore, Copyright 1976. Page 147, 2nd Paragraph. St. Albans Mines Chapter 7, Page 67.

"Gold Hunters Field Book" by Jay, Ellis, Ransom, Copyright 1975, Harper-Row, St. Albans Mines Chapter.

## MARRIAGES AND INTENTIONS
## 1813 - 1920

### Marriages - 1813

| | | |
|---|---|---|
| Moor, Daniel | Fairhaven | Jan. 21 |
| Smith, Polly | Fairhaven | |
| | | |
| Manering, John | Sebasticook | Sep. 13 |
| Bennett, Polly | Sebasticook | |

### Marriages - 1814

| | | |
|---|---|---|
| Webb, Christoper | Canaan | Jan. 6 |
| Palmer, Mary | St. Albans | |
| | | |
| Chase, Mark | No. 3 | Apr. 7 |
| Speaving, Sally | No. 3 | |
| | | |
| Farrar, Nathan | St. Albans | Oct. 15 |
| Quimby, Lydia | St. Albans | |

### Intentions - 1815

| | | |
|---|---|---|
| Eliot, Daniel Eli | No. 4 | Jan. 26 |
| Haydon, Edith | Madison | |
| | | |
| Stanchfield, John | St. Albans | July 2 |
| Moore, Mary | St. Albans | |

### Marriages - 1815

| | | |
|---|---|---|
| Richards, David | St. Albans | Dec. 31 |
| Wiggin, Abigail | St. Albans | |
| | | |
| Smith, Thomas | No. 3 | Sep. 24 |
| Stewert, Lydia | No. 3 | |

# Marriages - 1816

| | | |
|---|---|---|
| Morrill, James | Canaan Gore | June 2 |
| Hayden, Olive | Canaan Gore | |
| | | |
| Bennett, Samuel | Sebasticook | Nov. 5 |
| Getchell, Nancy | Sebasticook | |
| | | |
| Steward, John | Canaan | Nov. 28 |
| Moore, Nancy | St. Albans | |

# Marriages - 1817

| | | |
|---|---|---|
| Elliot, John | No. 4 | Jan. 5 |
| Steward, Lucy | No. 4 | |
| | | |
| Lyford, John | St. Albans | Feb. 15 |
| Bean, Abigail | Cornville | |
| | | |
| Martin, Avon | Sebasticook | June 26 |
| Mason, May | Sebasticook | |
| | | |
| Church, George | St. Albans | Nov. |
| Vipen, Elizabeth | Madison | |
| | | |
| Davis, John | No. 3 | Nov. 14 |
| Fairbrother, Mary | No. 3 | |
| | | |
| Rowe, David | St. Albans | Nov. |
| Melone, Betsey | Palmyra | |
| | | |
| Stanchfield, Thomas | St. Albans | Dec. 25 |
| Moore, Alphia | St. Albans | |

# Marriages - 1818

| | | |
|---|---|---|
| Spearing, Heziah | St. Albans | April |
| Pushaw, Peggy | North Canaan | |

| | | |
|---|---|---|
| Sibley, David | Canaan Gore | Sep. 24 |
| Church, Polly | Canaan Gore | |

## Marriages - 1819

| | | |
|---|---|---|
| Veasey, Daniel | Plantation 5 | Jan. 3 |
| Austin, Hannah | Jay | |
| | | |
| Sampson, Hiram | St. Albans | May 10 |
| Dunlap, Martha | Ripley | |
| | | |
| Haskell, Stephen | St. Albans | May 1 |
| Dearborn, Polly | St. Albans | |

## Marriages - 1820

| | | |
|---|---|---|
| Withee, Ezra | Hartland | Mar. 30 |
| Gonto, Rebecca | Harmony | |
| | | |
| Hinman, Rev. William | St. Albans | Aug. 7 |
| Stanchfield, Susan | St. Albans | |
| | | |
| Lancey, John | Palmyra | Nov. 30 |
| Steward, Electa | Hartland | |

## Marriages - 1821

| | | |
|---|---|---|
| Darling, Joseph | Hartland | Feb. 22 |
| Coffin, Meriam | Hartland | |
| | | |
| Booker, Joseph | Hartland | Mar. 15 |
| Phelps, Elizabeth | Hartland | |
| | | |
| McKenney, William | Corinna | Mar. 29 |
| Adams, Anna | Corinna | |
| | | |
| Dearborn, Joseph | St. Albans | Apr. 3 |
| Sampson, Mary | Norridgewock | |

| | | |
|---|---|---|
| Deveraux, James | St. Albans | Apr 18 |
| Marsh, Sally | Palmyra | |
| | | |
| Boutton, Adna | Township 5 | Aug. 2 |
| Pushor, Eunice | Township 5 | |
| | | |
| Moor, James | St. Albans | Aug. 12 |
| Wiggin, Dorothy | St. Albans | |
| | | |
| Church, James | | Dec. 2 |
| McCuslin, Hannah | | |
| | | |
| Witham, Ichabod L. | St. Albans | Dec. 27 |
| Braley, Pauline | St. Albans | |

## Marriages - 1822

| | | |
|---|---|---|
| Smith, Wm. Jarvis | St. Albans | Jan. 7 |
| Stewart, Sarah | St. Albans | |
| | | |
| Sanborn, Samuel | St. Albans | June 24 |
| Mellows, Sally | St. Albans | |
| | | |
| Remmick, Samuel | Clinton | Oct. 17 |
| Dearborn, Abigail | St. Albans | |
| | | |
| Braley, Ephraim | St. Albans | Dec. 23 |
| Raymond, Clarissa | St. Albans | |
| | | |
| Shaw, John | Exeter | Dec. 29 |
| French, Frances | St. Albans | |

## Marriages - 1823

| | | |
|---|---|---|
| Richard, Amos | St. Albans | Jan. 6 |
| Witherall, Elizabeth | Norridgewock | |
| | | |
| Hodgdon, Rufus | St. Albans | Feb. 22 |
| Richard, Aline | St. Albans | |

| | | |
|---|---|---|
| Judkins, Benjamin Shepherd | Palmyra | Mar. 27 |
| Palmer, Elizabeth | St. Albans | |
| | | |
| Tinney, Thomas V. | St. Albans | Mar. 30 |
| Lyford, Dolly | St. Albans | |
| | | |
| Starbird, Jr., John | Hartland | Apr. 10 |
| Littlefield, Catherine | Hartland | |
| | | |
| Jackson, Peltiah | St. Albans | Sep. 12 |
| Trafton, Harriet | Waterville | |
| | | |
| Ellis, Atkins | St. Albans | Nov. 11 |
| Braley, Elizabeth | St. Albans | |
| | | |
| Newils (?), George | St. Albans | Nov. 20 |
| Church, Miriam | Ripley | |
| | | |
| Frost, Daniel | St. Albans | Dec. 25 |
| Ellis, Patience | St. Albans | |

## Marriages - 1824

| | | |
|---|---|---|
| Rogers, Jr., Richard | Ripley | Nov. 20 |
| Watson, Mary | St. Albans | |
| | | |
| Dunlap, William | Ripley | Nov. 29 |
| Sampson, Silvia | St. Albans | |

## Marriages - 1825

| | | |
|---|---|---|
| Matthews, Joshua | St. Albans | Mar. 29 |
| Meloon, Mary Ann | St. Albans | |
| | | |
| Williams, Joseph | Dexter | Apr. 12 |
| Leech, Nancy | St. Albans | |

| | | |
|---|---|---|
| Hoyt, George W. | Ripley | May 26 |
| Jones, Mariam I. | Ripley | |
| | | |
| Hopkins, Richard | St. Albans | July 27 |
| Cass, Maria A. | Cornville | |
| | | |
| Blake, Dr. Calvin | St. Albans | Dec. 4 |
| Haskell, Louise | New Gloucester | |
| | | |
| Rogers, Richard | Ripley | Dec. 6 |
| Watson, Mary | St. Albans | |

## Marriages - 1826

| | | |
|---|---|---|
| Starbird, John | St. Albans | Jan. 25 |
| Miles, Susan | St. Albans | |
| | | |
| Merriman, Thomas | St. Albans | Feb. 2 |
| Melcher, Martha | Brunswick | |
| | | |
| Starbird, John | St. Albans | Mar. 4 |
| Bates, Mary | Norridgewock | |
| | | |
| Ellis, Elijah | St. Albans | Apr. 4 |
| Ellis, Mary | St. Albans | |
| | | |
| Wing, Joshua | St. Albans | May 26 |
| Osborn, Anna | St. Albans | |
| | | |
| Bopey, Ebenezer | Norridgewock | Aug. 21 |
| Moore, Esther | Norridgewock | |
| | | |
| Church, Hanson | St. Albans | Nov. 30 |
| Bowley, Fanny | St. Albans | |
| | | |
| Quimby, Aaron | St. Albans | Dec. 21 |
| Crocker, Anna | Parkman | |

# Marriages - 1827

| | | |
|---|---|---|
| Johnson, Charles | Orono | Jan. 24 |
| Wiggin, Betsy | St. Albans | |
| | | |
| Horsham, Thomas | St. Albans | Jan. 27 |
| Folsom, Mary | Palmyra | |
| | | |
| Merrill, Joseph | St. Albans | Feb. 10 |
| Bigelow, Mary | Bloomfield | |
| | | |
| Libby, Wentworth | St. Albans | Feb. 19 |
| Parsons, Charlotte | Harmony | |
| | | |
| Braley, David | St. Albans | Mar. 19 |
| Raymond, Jemima | St. Albans | |
| | | |
| Gray, Morrill | Harmony | Apr. 23 |
| Magoon, Abigail | St. Albans | |
| | | |
| Frost, Thomas | St. Albans | Apr. 26 |
| Ellis, Lydia | St. Albans | |
| | | |
| Greeley, Rufus | St. Albans | Apr. 27 |
| Emery, Mary | Ripley | |
| | | |
| Gordon, Alexander | Winthrop | July 4 |
| Leech, Dorcas | St. Albans | |
| | | |
| Kittridge, Benjamin | St. Albans | Aug. 12 |
| Dearborn, Susanna | St. Albans | |
| | | |
| Farnham, Thomas | St. Albans | ? |
| Folsom, Mary | Palmyra | |
| | | |
| Page, William | ?? | Nov. 19 |
| Sampson, Mary | St. Albans | |

# Marriages - 1828

| | | |
|---|---|---|
| Mitchell, James | Hartland | Jan. 13 |
| Hanson, Mary | Hartland | |
| Willey, Hiram | Mattanaighock | Mar. 16 |
| Mellows, Betsy | St. Albans | |
| Prescott, Sewell | Dexter | Apr. 20 |
| Wood, Mary | Winthrop | |
| Clay, Henry | Palmyra | Apr. 27 |
| Gardiner, Polly | Palmyra | |
| Roberts, Ira | Athens | June 16 |
| Libby, Jane | St. Albans | |
| Mellows, Shedrach | St. Albans | July 26 |
| Wiggin, Dolly | St. Albans | |
| House, Elijah | Palmyra | Aug. 3 |
| Cole, Betsey | Palmyra | |
| Thompson, William | | Oct. 2 |
| Childs, Lucinda | Hartland | |
| Hayden, David | Hartland | Oct. 21 |
| Withee, Betsey | Hartland | |

# Marriages - 1829

| | | |
|---|---|---|
| Whitney, Leonard | Hartland | Jan. 4 |
| Dyer, Mary | Hartland | |
| Dormon, Hiram | St. Albans | Jan. 10 |
| Potter, Laura | St. Albans | |
| Haydon, David | Hartland | Feb. 15 |
| Withee, Betsey | Hartland | |
| Mower, Dan | St. Albans | Apr. 18 |
| Horn, Mary | Ripley | |

| | | |
|---|---|---|
| Perley, Jacob | Orono | Apr. 18 |
| French, Mary Ann | St. Albans | |
| Skinner, Thomas | St. Albans | June 7 |
| Hackett, Sarah | St. Albans | |
| Clark, Frederick | Boston | June 7 |
| Stafford, Jane | St. Albans | |
| Leech, Isaiah | St. Albans | Oct. 16 |
| Webber, Elizabeth | St. Albans | |
| Wadleigh, Daniel | New Portland | Nov. 12 |
| Footman, Elizabeth | Newport | |

## Intentions - 1830

| | | |
|---|---|---|
| Wiggin, Chase | St. Albans | Jan. 22 |
| Burpee (?), Ann | Fayette | |
| Merrill, James | St. Albans | Feb. 6 |
| Weston, Pauline | Bloomfield | |
| Welch, Converse | | Feb. 9 |
| French, Emily | St. Albans | |
| Nason, Henry | St. Albans | Mar. 10 |
| Miles, Polly | Newport | |
| Bowman, Isaac | St. Albans | June 5 |
| Richard, Phebe | St. Albans | |
| Lyford, Billy | St. Albans | Nov. 21 |
| Dow, Catherine | St. Albans | |
| Rice, Sanford | Hartland | Nov. 29 |
| Wiggin, Mary | Hartland | |
| Bates, William | St. Albans | Dec. 23 |
| Smith, Milanda | Corinna | |

Gould, Elijah                                    Dec. 29
Cook, Lydia            Hartland


                   Intentions - 1831

Merrill, Joseph       St. Albans         Jan. 3
Bullen, Sarah Ann     St. Albans

Holway, Xenophen      St. Albans         Jan. 28
Meloon, Adaline       St. Albans

Steve, James          St. Albans         Mar. 5
Johnson, Eliza        St. Albans

Leathers, Levi                           Mar. 11
Elder, Joann          Corinna

Withee, Walton        Hartland           Apr. 28
Priest, Parthene      Pittsfield

Dunlap, John          St. Albans         May 25
Simpson, Loriamah     St. Albans

Stevens, William      Dixmont            June 9
Lang, Mary Ann        Palmyra

Sevey, Ancil          Bangor             July 8
Ireland, Mary         St. Albans

Smith, John           Corinna            Aug. 14
Bates, Elizabeth      St. Albans

Jordon, Jerome        St. Albans         Aug. 20
Dolin, Elizabeth      Cape
                      Elizabeth

Frost, Elias          St. Albans         Sept. 1
Ellis, Betsey         St. Albans

Mosman, Moses         Prospect           Nov. 10
Ridley, Susan         St. Albans


                          272

| | | |
|---|---|---|
| Bullen, Ancil | | Nov. 10 |
| Lambert, Harriett | Readfield | |
| | | |
| Day, Hersey | St. Albans | Nov. 20 |
| Bailey, Eunice | Greene | |

## Intentions - 1832

| | | |
|---|---|---|
| Pray, Edward | Augusta | Mar. 8 |
| Willey, Abigail | Augusta | |
| | | |
| Luce, George | St. Albans | May 9 |
| Pooler, Mary B. | Hartland | |
| | | |
| Towle, John | Hartland | May 12 |
| Smith, Elvira | St. Albans | |
| | | |
| Webb, Hanson | St. Albans | Sep. 11 |
| Patterson, Emily | Hampden | |
| | | |
| Stewert, Alonzo | St. Albans | Sep. 20 |
| Ireland, Isabel | St. Albans | |
| | | |
| Carson, Elijah | St. Albans | Oct. 12 |
| Bates, Hannah | St. Albans | |
| | | |
| Crocker, Lowell J.R. | St. Albans | Oct. 19 |
| Small, Hannah | Dexter | |
| | | |
| Lyford, Albert | St. Albans | Nov. 19 |
| Bates, Phebe | Fairfield | |
| | | |
| Magoon, Woodman | St. Albans | Dec. 1 |
| Stinchfield, Sarah | St. Albans | |
| | | |
| Holway, Daniel | St. Albans | Dec. 27 |
| Meloon, Harriett | St. Albans | |

## Intentions - 1833

| | | |
|---|---|---|
| Dow, Parker | St. Albans | Jan. 21 |
| Sanborn, Clarissa | St. Albans | |
| | | |
| Wood, Moses | Ripley | Jan. 29 |
| Todd, Pamela | Ripley | |
| | | |
| Ray, Frederick | Newport | Feb. 4 |
| Beane (Bane), Elizabeth | St. Albans | |
| | | |
| Perry, Stephen | St. Albans | May 12 |
| Merrill, Martha | St. Albans | |
| | | |
| Roberts, Joseph | St. Albans | May 24 |
| Sewell, Lydia | Pittsfield | |
| | | |
| Robinson, David G. | St. Albans | June 13 |
| Keith, Sarah B. | Vassalboro | |
| | | |
| Devereaux, Dennis | St. Albans | July 5 |
| Parker, Rhoda | Palmyra | |
| | | |
| Mansfield, Thomas | St. Albans | July 28 |
| Jones, Polly | Dexter | |
| | | |
| White, Isaac | St. Albans | Aug. 14 |
| Page, Mary | St. Albans | |
| | | |
| Jewett, Samuel | St. Albans | Oct. 24 |
| Kennedy, Hannah | Orono | |
| | | |
| Folsom, David | Palmyra | Nov. 10 |
| Roberts, Sarah | St. Albans | |
| | | |
| Goodwin, William | St. Albans | Nov. 10 |
| Rupell, Hannah | St. Albans | |

## Marriages - 1833

| | | |
|---|---|---|
| Holway, Daniel | St. Albans | Feb. 7 |
| Melon, Harriet | St. Albans | |

| | | |
|---|---|---|
| Perry, Stephen | St. Albans | May 20 |
| Merrill, Martha | St. Albans | |
| | | |
| Roberts, Joseph | St. Albans | June 18 |
| Sewell, Lydia | Pittsfield | |
| | | |
| Adams, Herman | Palmyra | Oct. 31 |
| Ward, Elmira | Palmyra | |
| | | |
| Boardman, Charles | Bloomfield | Nov. 20 |
| Rupell, Philena S. | Norridgewalk | |
| | | |
| Boston, Jesse | St. Albans | Nov. 20 |
| Cyphers, Sally | Ripley | |
| | | |
| Prescott, Gorham | St. Albans | Dec. 10 |
| Moore, Mary | St. Albans | |

## Intentions - 1834

| | | |
|---|---|---|
| Batchelder, Ephraim | St. Albans | Jan. 28 |
| Shean, Mrs. Elizabeth | St. Albans | |
| | | |
| Bonney, Gardiner | Palermo | Feb. 14 |
| Moore, Eunice | St. Albans | |
| | | |
| Turner, John | St. Albans | Mar. 11 |
| Bullen, Belinda | St. Albans | |
| | | |
| Rider, Andrew | Albion | Mar. 17 |
| Webber, Mary Ann | St. Albans | |
| | | |
| Eaton, Joseph W. | Plymouth | Mar. 19 |
| Ireland, Samantha R. | St. Albans | |
| | | |
| Stewart, James | St. Albans | Apr. 22 |
| Wilson, Deborah | St. Albans | |

| | | |
|---|---|---|
| Prescott, Gorham | Hartland | Apr. 18 |
| Moor, Mary | Hartland | |
| | | |
| Day, John | St. Albans | July 3 |
| Gordon, Mary | St. Albans | |
| | | |
| Crockett, Daniel | Parkman | Sep. 2 |
| Tozier, Catherine | St. Albans | |
| | | |
| Pierce, Hermon B. | Moscow | Oct. 14 |
| Holman, Achsa | Canaan | |
| | | |
| Clark, Herman | St. Albans | Nov. 21 |
| Goodwin, Matilda S | St. Albans | |

## Marriages - 1834

| | | |
|---|---|---|
| Bachelor, Ephraim | St. Albans | Feb. 18 |
| Shean, Elizabeth | St. Albans | |
| | | |
| Bonney, Gardiner | Palermo | Mar. 23 |
| Moor, Eunice | St. Albans | |
| | | |
| Day, John | St. Albans | July 3 |
| Gordon, Mary | St. Albans | |
| | | |
| Goodwin, William | St. Albans | Dec. 5 |
| Rupell, Hannah | St. Albans | |

## Intentions - 1835

| | | |
|---|---|---|
| Rand, John | St. Albans | Jan. 3 |
| Jumper, Laura | Dexter | |
| | | |
| Webb, John C. | St. Albans | Jan. 14 |
| Nay, Clarisa A. | Palmyra | |
| | | |
| Matthews, Amox | St. Albans | Jan. 24 |
| Collins, Melinda | Winslow | |

| | | |
|---|---|---|
| Southards, John | St. Albans | Jan. 28 |
| Sampson, Lois | St. Albans | |
| | | |
| Deavereaux, Elisha | St. Albans | Feb. 17 |
| York, Eleanor | Newport | |
| | | |
| Foss, Tabor | St. Albans | Mar. 21 |
| Bigelow, Betsey | Bloomfield | |
| | | |
| Mower, John R. | St. Albans | Apr. 15 |
| Buxton, Eileen | Corinna | |
| | | |
| White, James | St. Albans | Apr. 25 |
| Brown, Mary | St. Albans | |
| | | |
| White, Amerst | St. Albans | May 9 |
| Dunlap, Hannah | St. Albans | |
| | | |
| Snow, John | Exeter | Oct. 12 |
| Lyford, Mary | St. Albans | |
| | | |
| Eddy, Sylvester | East Corinth | Nov. 4 |
| Goodwin, Elmyra | St. Albans | |
| | | |
| Dearborn, Joseph | St. Albans | Dec. 4 |
| Southards, Fanny | St. Albans | |
| | | |
| Vining, Israel | St. Albans | Dec. 5 |
| Norton, Rebecca | Pittsfield | |
| | | |
| Moore, Samuel | St. Albans | Dec. 6 |
| Evans, Zepporah | St. Albans | |
| | | |
| Evans, Samuel | St. Albans | Dec. 21 |
| Rideout, Charity | Clinton | |
| | | |
| Moody, William | Corinna | Dec. 24 |
| Maines, Jane | St. Albans | |

Marriages - 1835

| | | |
|---|---|---|
| Day, John | St. Albans | July 3 |
| Gordon, Mary | St. Albans | |

| | | |
|---|---|---|
| Merrill, Ebenezer | St. Albans | Jan. 23 |
| Haynes, Olive W. | Norridgewock | |
| | | |
| Powers, Arba | St. Albans | Mar. 5 |
| Matthews, Naomi | St. Albans | |
| | | |
| Frost, Jacob | St. Albans | Mar. 19 |
| Tozier, Catherine | St. Albans | |
| | | |
| Humphrey, Moses | St. Albans | Apr. 2 |
| Batchelder, Harriett | Hermon | |
| | | |
| Evans, Ephraim | | May 9 |
| Emery, Sylvia | Canaan | |
| | | |
| Johnson, William | St. Albans | June 2 |
| Goodwin, Betsey | St. Albans | |
| | | |
| Russell, Seth | St. Albans | June 30 |
| Walker, Martha | Canaan | |
| | | |
| Jackson, John | Palmyra | July 10 |
| Lecoe, Rachel | | |
| | | |
| Parker, Moses | St. Albans | July 10 |
| Bates, Sally | St. Albans | |
| | | |
| Steward, James | Sangerville | July 23 |
| Longfellow, Rebecca | St. Albans | |
| | | |
| Corson, Jr., John | St. Albans | Aug. 20 |
| Cooley, Nancy | St. Albans | |
| | | |
| Day, Henry | St. Albans | Aug. 22 |
| Copp, Hester A. | Winthrop | |
| | | |
| Dore, True | Harmony | Sept. 5 |
| Grover, Mariam | St. Albans | |

## Marriages - 1836

| | | |
|---|---|---|
| Humphrey, Moses | St. Albans | Aug. 2 |
| Batchelder, Harriet | Herman | |
| | | |
| Davis, John | Palmyra | Nov. 3 |
| Sampson, Olive | Palmyra | |
| | | |
| Grant, John | St. Albans | Dec. 8 |
| Maloon, Elsie | St. Albans | |
| | | |
| Bosworth, Jonathan | St. Albans | Dec. 12 |
| Noble, Caroline | St. Albans | |
| | | |
| Snell, William | St. Albans | Dec. 12 |
| Snell, Charlotte | St. Albans | |

## Marriages - 1837

| | | |
|---|---|---|
| Dingley, William | Lewiston | Jan. 18 |
| Dingley, Mrs. Mary | St. Albans | |
| | | |
| Frost, Elijah | St. Albans | Feb. 13 |
| Ellis, Cynthia | St. Albans | |
| | | |
| Shorey, Richard | Palmyra | Mar. 9 |
| McNire, Caroline | Hartland | |
| | | |
| Holway, Watson | Fairfield | Mar. 29 |
| Yarney, Treasa | St. Albans | |
| | | |
| Dyer, Charles | Orono | Mar. 10 |
| Cristy, Abigail | St. Albans | |
| | | |
| Stewart, Horace M. | Orono | Mar. 2 |
| Wilson, Hannah June | St. Albans | |
| | | |
| Smith, Samuel | St. Albans | Apr. 6 |
| Sleeper, Jane | St. Albans | |

| | | |
|---|---|---|
| Evans, Benjamin | St. Albans | Apr. 11 |
| Goodwin, Sarah | St. Albans | |
| | | |
| Hall, Abner | Athens | Apr. 10 |
| Morse, Christina | St. Albans | |
| | | |
| Jackson, John | Palmyra | July 10 |
| Lecoe, Rachael | | |
| | | |
| Farris, Elbridge | Bangor | July 2 |
| Collins, Harriett | St. Albans | |
| | | |
| Hartwell, Lysander | St. Albans | July 2 |
| Collins, Elizabeth | St. Albans | |
| | | |
| Dudley, Horace | Carmel | Aug. 1 |
| Wilson, Lydia | Palmyra | |
| | | |
| Hoyt, Nathan | St. Albans | Oct. 1 |
| Maines, Olive | St. Albans | |
| | | |
| Weymouth, Benjamin | Corinna | Oct. 3 |
| Lyford, Aurilia | St. Albans | |
| | | |
| Robinson, Stephen | Palmyra | Oct. 12 |
| Palmer, Dorothy | Palmyra | |
| | | |
| Vining, Israel | St. Albans | Nov. 19 |
| Hawes, Joanna | St. Albans | |
| | | |
| Hanson, Meshark | Palmyra | Nov. 30 |
| Tibbetts, Nancy | Palmyra | |
| | | |
| Ireland, Fareesell | St. Albans | Nov. 30 |
| Gordon, Minera | St. Albans | |
| | | |
| Bailey, Ebenezer | Pittsfield | Dec. 18 |
| Magoon, Phebe | St. Albans | |

Marriages - 1838

| | | |
|---|---|---|
| Miles, William | Newport | Jan. 14 |
| Stinson, Lydia G. | Palmyra | |

| | | |
|---|---|---|
| Hanson, Nathan | Palmyra | Jan. 17 |
| Hanson, Eliza | Palmyra | |
| | | |
| Wilson, Joseph | Palmyra | Feb. 12 |
| Wood, Mehitable | Palmyra | |
| | | |
| Bates, Seth | St. Albans | Feb. 20 |
| Douglas, Elizabeth Ann | St. Albans | |
| | | |
| Hilton, Stephen | St. Albans | Feb. 27 |
| Osborn, Eliza | St. Albans | |
| | | |
| Wood, Moses | Ripley | Mar. 8 |
| Allen, Esther S. | Cambridge | |
| | | |
| Wiggin, Jr., Asa | St. Albans | Apr. 12 |
| Mellows, Jane | St. Albans | |
| | | |
| Frost, Harrison | St. Albans | June 24 |
| Wing, Elizabeth | St. Albans | |
| | | |
| Ham, Jr., Samuel | Cambridge | Aug. 26 |
| Davis, Naomi | Cambridge | |
| | | |
| Robinson, John | St. Albans | Oct. 7 |
| Nutter, Mary | St. Albans | |
| | | |
| Herrick, Orvil | Cambridge | Nov. 11 |
| Davis, Martha Ann | Cambridge | |
| | | |
| Foster, David | Canterbury, NH | Nov. 18 |
| Robertson, Sarah B. | St. Albans | |

## Marriages - 1839

| | | |
|---|---|---|
| Cook, Robert | St. Albans | Jan. 12 |
| Smith, Mariam | Orrington | |

| | | |
|---|---|---|
| Harvey, Jr. | St. Albans | Feb. 11 |
|     William | St. Albans | |
| Huff, Lucinda | | |
| | | |
| Cooley, John | St. Albans | Mar. 17 |
| Johnson, Mary Ann | St. Albans | |
| | | |
| Hawes, Hiram | St. Albans | Mar. 28 |
| Vining, Sarah | St. Albans | |
| | | |
| Jones, Thomas | Corinna | Mar. 29 |
| Snell, Charlotte | Corinna | |
| | | |
| Cook, Noah | Hartland | Apr. 12 |
| Huff, Lovina | Hartland | |
| | | |
| Jackson, Myrick S. | St. Albans | Apr. 12 |
| Batchelder, | Bangor | |
|     Lydia Ann | | |
| | | |
| Miller, Samuel | Palmyra | June 30 |
| Brown, Sarah | Palmyra | |
| | | |
| Ellis, Jr., Atkins | Ripley | July 7 |
| Church, Esther Ann | Ripley | |
| | | |
| Buzzell, Dea. Mark | St. Albans | July 8 |
| Davis, Lydia | Palmyra | |
| | | |
| Ellis, Asa | St. Albans | Aug. 11 |
| Steward, Elizabeth | St. Albans | |
| | | |
| Moody, Isaac | Corinna | Sep. 25 |
| Weymouth, Mercy | Corinna | |
| | | |
| Ridley, Loring B. | St. Albans | Oct. 17 |
| Safford, Margaret | St. Albans | |
| | | |
| Ridley, Daniel B. | St. Albans | Oct. 18 |
| Steward, Sarah | St. Albans | |

| | | |
|---|---|---|
| Brown, William | St. Albans | Nov. 12 |
| Handy, Philena | St. Albans | |
| | | |
| Mackie, George | Hartland | Dec. 20 |
| Brown, Jane | Hartland | |
| | | |
| York, Joseph | St. Albans | Dec. 22 |
| M.Buzzell, Lovina | St. Albans | |
| | | |
| Matthews, Joel | St. Albans | Dec. 25 |
| Noble, Elizabeth | St. Albans | |
| | | |
| Powers, Philip | St. Albans | Dec. |
| Matthews, Sophronia | St. Albans | |

## Marriages - 1840

| | | |
|---|---|---|
| Cook, Noah | Hartland | Jan. 14 |
| Huff, Lavinia | Hartland | |
| | | |
| Cooley, John | St. Albans | Mar. 17 |
| Johnson, Mary Ann | St. Albans | |
| | | |
| Miller, Samuel | Palmyra | June 30 |
| Brown, Sarah | Palmyra | |
| | | |
| Ellis, Asa | St. Albans | Aug. 11 |
| Steward, Eliza | St. Albans | |
| | | |
| Campbell, Alexander | Hartland | Sept. 5 |
| Jackson, Ursula | Hartland | |

## Marriages - 1841

| | | |
|---|---|---|
| Jones, Thomas | Corinna | Mar. 29 |
| Snell, Charlotte Ann | Palmyra | |

| | | |
|---|---|---|
| Lane, Daniel | St. Albans | Apr. 28 |
| Dickey, Mary | Ripley | |
| | | |
| Rollins, Enoch | St. Albans | May 9 |
| Lyford, Pamelia H. | St. Albans | |
| | | |
| Smith, Cyrus | Plymouth | May 27 |
| Matthews, Betsey | St. Albans | |
| | | |
| Osborn, Isaac | St. Albans | Aug. 30 |
| Lucus, Hannah | St. Albans | |
| | | |
| Burrill, Benjamin | Fairfield | Sep. 15 |
| Osborn, Rebecca | St. Albans | |
| | | |
| Osborn, Alfred | St. Albans | Sep. 16 |
| Holway, Mary | St. Albans | |
| | | |
| Goodwin, Henry H. | Garland | Sep. 21 |
| Brown, Mary T. | Newport | |
| | | |
| Bailey, Moody | Garland | Sep. 21 |
| Leach, Sarah Ann | St. Albans | |
| | | |
| Spaulding, James | St. Albans | Nov. 25 |
| Randall, Mary | St. Albans | |
| | | |
| Getchell, Asa | Litchfield | Dec. 5 |
| Fuller, Lucy Ann | St. Albans | |
| | | |
| Denning, Alonzo F. | St. Albans | Dec. 16 |
| Crocker, Deborah | St. Albans | |
| | | |
| Shean, Woodman M. | St. Albans | Dec. 30 |
| Dudley, Anstrop | St. Albans | |

## Marriages - 1842

| | | |
|---|---|---|
| Sleeper, William | St. Albans | Jan. 27 |
| , Elmira | St. Albans | |

| | | |
|---|---|---|
| Pratt, Noah | Skowhegan | Feb. 16 |
| Eaton (Estes) Lydia | St. Albans | |
| | | |
| Austin, Alpheas | St. Albans | Apr. 11 |
| Frost, Lovina | St. Albans | |
| | | |
| Smith, Charles B. | | May 1 |
| Tift, Mary B. | | |
| | | |
| Mitchell, Peter | Dexter | May 20 |
| Davis, Lovina | Dexter | |
| | | |
| Knowles, George W. | St. Albans | May 27 |
| Moody, Lucinda | St. Albans | |
| | | |
| Merryman, Thomas | St. Albans | June 23 |
| Rollins, Hannah Ann | St. Albans | |
| | | |
| Frost, Lewis | St. Albans | July 3 |
| Frost, Sarah L. | St. Albans | |
| | | |
| Burrill, Benjamin | Fairfield | Sep. 15 |
| Osbourne, Rebecca | St. Albans | |
| | | |
| Fields, Benjamin | Palmyra | Sep. 19 |
| Leach, Ruth Ann | St. Albans | |
| | | |
| Dickey, David | Ripley | Oct. 11 |
| Additon, Mary Eliza | Dexter | |
| | | |
| Doe, Welcome | Milford | Nov. 13 |
| Leach, Rebecca L. | St. Albans | |
| | | |
| Hanson, Edward W. | Palmyra | Nov. 17 |
| Douglas, Nancy | | |
| | | |
| Powers, Jonathan | St. Albans | Dec. 11 |
| Matthews, Belinda | St. Albans | |

# Marriages - 1843

| | | |
|---|---|---|
| Goodwin, Hiram | St. Albans | Jan. 1 |
| Hartwell, Emily | St. Albans | |
| | | |
| Emery, Jonathan | St. Albans | Jan. 1 |
| Leathers, Mary | St. Albans | |
| | | |
| Burnham, John | St. Albans | Jan. 4 |
| Goodwin, Olivia | St. Albans | |
| | | |
| Footman, James M. | St. Albans | Feb. 18 |
| Pease, Sarah | Exeter | |
| | | |
| Rackliff, John | Corinna | Feb. 18 |
| Mills, Lydia | Corinna | |
| | | |
| Southards, William | St. Albans | Feb. 28 |
| Avery, Julia A. | St. Albans | |
| | | |
| Allen, E. P. | Fairfield | Mar. 9 |
| Stewart, Clarinda A. | Fairfield | |
| | | |
| Abee, Claudius P. | St. Albans | Mar. 21 |
| Bates, Florintine | St. Albans | |
| | | |
| French, Enoch | St. Albans | Mar. 21 |
| Turner, Sarah Ann | St. Albans | |
| | | |
| Martin, Jacob | St. Albans | Mar. 22 |
| Gordon, Charlotte | St. Albans | |
| | | |
| Leathers, Loring | St. Albans | Mar. 26 |
| Bates, Marilla M. | St. Albans | |
| | | |
| Wiggins, John G. | St. Albans | Apr. 12 |
| Morrill, Ann H. | Williamsburg | |
| | | |
| Blaisdell, David | Plymouth | May 25 |
| Wedgewood, Sarah | Newport | |

| | | |
|---|---|---|
| Bigelow, Charles | Corinna | July 30 |
| Mathews, Mary Ann | St. Albans | |
| | | |
| Ashford, Jr. Robert | Litchfield | Aug. 27 |
| Hilton, Sarah | | |
| | | |
| Smith, Andrew | St. Albans | Nov. 14 |
| Bates, Sarah | St. Albans | |
| | | |
| Wood, John | St. Albans | Nov. 23 |
| Gordon, Alma Jane | St. Albans | |
| | | |
| Hanson, Jess | Palmyra | Dec. 7 |
| Stimpson, Mary P. | Palmyra | |
| | | |
| Robinson, Richard | Newport | Dec. 7 |
| Stimpson, Selina | | |

## Marriages - 1844

| | | |
|---|---|---|
| Bragg, Nicholas F. | Unity | Jan. 3 |
| Holton, Mary | St. Albans | |
| | | |
| Davis Jr., Samuel | | Jan. 9 |
| Hanson, Ruth | Palmyra | |
| | | |
| Sanborn, Jr., Samuel | St. Albans | Jan. 21 |
| Douglas, Elizabeth | St. Albans | |
| | | |
| Weymouth, Jonathan | St. Albans | Jan. 21 |
| Bates, Jane | St. Albans | |
| | | |
| Lyford, John | St. Albans | Feb. 8 |
| Rowe, Farinea | St. Albans | |
| | | |
| Sampson, James | St. Albans | Apr. 27 |
| Rupell, Hannah | Palmyra | |
| | | |
| Ellis, William | St. Albans | June 23 |
| Sole, Celia Jane | Dexter | |

| | | |
|---|---|---|
| Carle, Asa | Stetson | Sep. 15 |
| Ellis, Mary | St. Albans | |
| | | |
| Turner, Israel P. | St. Albans | Oct. 6 |
| Gould, Sarah | St. Albans | |
| | | |
| Gardner, Thomas | Troy | Oct. 14 |
| Smith, Lucinda F. | St. Albans | |
| | | |
| Lincoln, Matthew | Corinna | Oct. 24 |
| Hanson, Elizabeth | Palmyra | |
| | | |
| Merrill, William L | Newport | Oct. 27 |
| Simpson, Martha | Palmyra | |
| | | |
| Lewis, James B. | Wayne | Nov. 21 |
| Lucas, Mary J. | St. Albans | |
| | | |
| Smith, Albert | St. Albans | Dec. 1 |
| Steward, Sarah | St. Albans | |

## Marriages - 1845

| | | |
|---|---|---|
| Holway, Olin | St. Albans | Jan. 8 |
| Smith, Prudence S. | St. Albans | |
| | | |
| Hartwell,<br>    Lysander W. | St. Albans | Jan. 30 |
| Rollins, Lucy Ann | St. Albans | |
| | | |
| Cook, William | Hartland | Mar. 6 |
| Austin, Dorothy | Hartland | |
| | | |
| Fops, Charles | Wales | Mar. 17 |
| Ransom, Frances | St. Albans | |
| | | |
| Dovey, Calvin S. | Sangerville | Apr. 12 |
| Bailey, Emily C. | Sangerville | |

288

| | | |
|---|---|---|
| Tripp, Lewis | St. Albans | June 2 |
| Sanborn, Caroline A. | St. Albans | |
| | | |
| Smith, Theodore C. | Corinna | July 10 |
| Lancaster, Sarah C. | Corinna | |
| | | |
| Soule, Norman | Dexter | July 26 |
| White, Nancy J. | Palmyra | |
| | | |
| Jewett, Caleb | St. Albans | Sep. 7 |
| Stewart, Nancy | St. Albans | |
| | | |
| Harding, Thomas | Unity | Sep. 18 |
| Hopkins, Sarah | St. Albans | |
| | | |
| Larabee, Jacob | Parkman | Sep. 28 |
| Philbrick, Mary | St. Albans | |
| | | |
| Moor, Ebenezer | St. Albans | Oct. 7 |
| Carlton, Ann | St. Albans | |
| | | |
| Monahan, John B. | Newport | Oct. 15 |
| Mackie, Emily Jane | Palmyra | |
| | | |
| Prescott, Daniel | Palmyra | Oct. 23 |
| Brown, Margaret | Palmyra | |
| | | |
| Bates, John S. | St. Albans | Nov. 2 |
| Hoit, Mercy R. | St. Albans | |
| | | |
| Christie, Thomas W. | St. Albans | Nov. 10 |
| Bryant, Catherine | St. Albans | |
| | | |
| Bragg, Holman | St. Albans | Dec. 15 |
| Eldridge, Julia | Clinton | |
| | | |
| Bates, Asa S. | Fairfield | Dec. 31 |
| Lyford, Abigail | St. Albans | |

# Marriages - 1846

| | | |
|---|---|---|
| Robertson, Rufus | St. Albans | Jan. 6 |
| Fuller, Juliett | St. Albans | |
| | | |
| Estes, Valentine | St. Albans | Apr. 27 |
| Ridley, Sarah S. | St. Albans | |
| | | |
| Martin, Alfred | St. Albans | June 2 |
| Carr, Almedia M. | St. Albans | |
| | | |
| Morrill, Americus | Palmyra | June 2 |
| Philbrick, Sarah | St. Albans | |
| | | |
| Moon, Abnam | | June 3 |
| Clement, Julia | Newport | |
| | | |
| Fish, William | Fairfield | |
| Records, | | |
| Lydia Lane | St. Albans | |
| | | |
| Matthews, Cyrus | St. Albans | Sep. 2 |
| Steward, Loantha A | St. Albans | |
| | | |
| Christie, Wesley | St. Albans | Dec. 3 |
| Avery, Martha | St. Albans | |
| | | |
| Dodge, Arnold | St. Albans | Dec. 3 |
| Trafton, Drucilla | St. Albans | |

# Marriages - 1847

| | | |
|---|---|---|
| Burrill, William | St. Albans | Jan. 1 |
| Osborne, Eunice | St. Albans | |
| | | |
| Prince, Darius | St. Albans | Feb. 7 |
| Finson, Caroline | St. Albans | |
| | | |
| Wells, Amos | St. Albans | Feb. 14 |
| Frost, Pamela | St. Albans | |

| | | |
|---|---|---|
| Crummett, Nathaniel | Sebec | Feb. 14 |
| Glidden, Emily | St. Albans | |
| | | |
| Smith, Henry | St. Albans | Mar. 23 |
| Lancaster, Hannah | St. Albans | |
| | | |
| Watson, William | St. Albans | Mar. 28 |
| Lucus, Sarah | St. Albans | |
| | | |
| Ellis, Hiram | St. Albans | Mar. 31 |
| Whitcomb, Sophia | St. Albans | |
| | | |
| Smith, Alfred | St. Albans | July 5 |
| Johnson, Sarah | St. Albans | |
| | | |
| Page, Snow B. | Dexter | Nov. 25 |
| Tozier, Lovina | St. Albans | |

## Marriages - 1848

| | | |
|---|---|---|
| Plummer, Abram W. | Troy | Jan. 16 |
| Plummer, Clarissa | St. Albans | |
| | | |
| Tripp, Phineus | Lincoln | Jan. 26 |
| Bradford, Abbie L. | St. Albans | |
| | | |
| Davis, William | St. Albans | Apr. 20 |
| Matthews, Nancy | St. Albans | |
| | | |
| Farnham, Simon | St. Albans | Apr. 20 |
| Cook, Lovina | St. Albans | |
| | | |
| Goodale, William | St. Albans | May 7 |
| Hersom, Lydia Ann | St. Albans | |
| | | |
| Blasdell, James A. | St. Albans | July 2 |
| Douglas, Angeline | St. Albans | |
| | | |
| Smith, Alfred | St. Albans | July 5 |
| Johnson, Sarah | St. Albans | |

| | | |
|---|---|---|
| Spaulding, Albert | Palmyra | Aug. 27 |
| Whitney, Caroline | Palmyra | |
| | | |
| Douglas, Nathan B. | St. Albans | Sep. 12 |
| Andrews, Belinda | St. Albans | |
| | | |
| Whitsom, Henry | Freedom | Sep. 16 |
| Berry, Thankful | Pittsfield | |
| | | |
| Leech, William | Sangerville | Sep. 21 |
| Gordon, Sophronia | St. Albans | |
| | | |
| Keen, Moses | St. Albans | Oct. 24 |
| Turner, Augusta | | |
| | | |
| Davis, John | Cambridge | Nov. 26 |
| Wing, Maria | Ripley | |

## Marriages - 1849

| | | |
|---|---|---|
| Austin, Jr., Daniel | Parkman | June 3 |
| Philbrick, Hannah | St. Albans | |
| | | |
| Goodwin, Charles L | St. Albans | July 18 |
| Johnson, Eliza H. | St. Albans | |
| | | |
| Stinson, George | Palmyra | July 26 |
| Philsbury, Elvira | Palmyra | |
| | | |
| Waldron, John D. | St. Albans | Aug. 17 |
| Plummer, Jane | St. Albans | |
| | | |
| Morse, George W. | St. Albans | Aug. 26 |
| Hilton, Jane | St. Albans | |
| | | |
| Mitchell, Francis | Hartland | Aug. 26 |
| Wheeler, Betsey | Hartland | |
| | | |
| Smith, John M. | Barnet, Ver. | Oct. 23 |
| Hopkins, Amanda | St. Albans | |

| | | |
|---|---|---|
| Smith, Greenwood C. | St. Albans | Nov. 4 |
| Tripp, Rebecca | St. Albans | |
| Washburn, Daniel | Hartland | Nov. 26 |
| Cook, Elvira | | |

## Marriages - 1850

| | | |
|---|---|---|
| Russell, Charles | St. Albans | Jan. 21 |
| Small, Mary | Exeter | |
| Wilbur, Alonzo | Sidney | Apr. 3 |
| Farnham, Mary | St. Albans | |
| Burgess, Francis | St. Albans | Apr. 9 |
| Tuttle, Dianna | Athens | |
| Cross, William | Hampden | July 10 |
| Morse, Sarah Jane | St. Albans | |
| Packard, Philip C. | St. Albans | July 25 |
| Witham, Harriett | St. Albans | |
| Andrews, John | Corinna | Aug. 13 |
| Douglas, Isabella | St. Albans | |
| Brown, Sewell | St. Albans | Aug. 15 |
| Parker, Loantha | St. Albans | |
| Stafford, Johnson S. | Hartland | Aug. 19 |
| Brand, Mary | Hartland | |
| Bradford, Charles | St. Albans | Oct. 15 |
| Prentis, Mary | St. Albans | |
| Grant, Samuel | St. Albans | Oct. 30 |
| Huff, Mary P. | St. Albans | |
| Jackson, Benjamin | St. Albans | Nov. 26 |
| Sleeper, Sarah | St. Albans | |

| | | |
|---|---|---|
| Boston, Jason | St. Albans | Dec. 19 |
| Batchelder, Emily | St. Albans | |
| | | |
| Woodbury, Charles | St. Albans | Dec. 31 |
| Tripp, Sarah | St. Albans | |

## Marriages - 1851

| | | |
|---|---|---|
| Sargent, Theophilus | St. Albans | Jan. 1 |
| Rollins, Abigail | St. Albans | |
| | | |
| Tenny, J. Lyford | St. Albans | Jan. 5 |
| Leach, E. Ann | St. Albans | |
| | | |
| Leach, Sewell | St. Albans | Jan. 5 |
| Day, Sarah | St. Albans | |
| | | |
| Rowe, Jeremiah B. | St. Albans | Feb. 15 |
| Libby, Mary | Exeter | |
| | | |
| Rowe, Samuel W. | St. Albans | Feb. 26 |
| Tuttle, R. Sylvia | St. Albans | |
| | | |
| Fisher, Enoch | St. Albans | Mar. 25 |
| Austin, Lovina | St. Albans | |
| | | |
| Adams, Joseph | St. Albans | Apr. 2 |
| Avery, Clarisa | St. Albans | |
| | | |
| Rogers, James | St. Albans | Apr. 6 |
| Nutter, Lovina | St. Albans | |
| | | |
| Hawks, Isaiah P. | St. Albans | Apr. 14 |
| Thurston, Huldah | St. Albans | |
| | | |
| Pratt, Turner | Corinna | May 10 |
| Fop, Sarah J. | St. Albans | |
| | | |
| Whitney, Calvin H. | Newburgh | June 6 |
| Steward, Rebecca C. | St. Albans | |

| | | |
|---|---|---|
| Tripp, Horatio | St. Albans | July 6 |
| Bates, Lorana | St. Albans | |
| | | |
| Rupell, Stephen | St. Albans | July 21 |
| Johnston, Lucinda H. | St. Albans | |
| | | |
| Hawkes, Nathaniel | St. Albans | July 28 |
| Handy, Deborah P. | St. Albans | |
| | | |
| Frost, John | Bangor | Sep. 7 |
| Frost, Huldah | St. Albans | |
| | | |
| Laughton, Josiah N | St. Albans | Dec. 7 |
| Smith, Nancy | St. Albans | |
| | | |
| Bigelow, James | St. Albans | Dec. 28 |
| Ricker, Abba | St. Albans | |

## Marriages - 1852

| | | |
|---|---|---|
| Buxton, David H. | Corinna | Feb. 9 |
| Merrill, Sarah E. | St. Albans | |
| | | |
| Sands, Nicholas | Dexter | Mar. 7 |
| Grover, Abby | St. Albans | |
| | | |
| Rollins, Eben | St. Albans | Mar. 27 |
| Nelson, Lois, Mrs. | Sebec | |
| | | |
| Morse, George W. | St. Albans | Apr. 15 |
| Avery, Adelia | St. Albans | |
| | | |
| Wing, Joshua | St. Albans | July 29 |
| White, Cynthia B. | Exeter | |
| | | |
| White, John | Hartland | Aug. 11 |
| Hunbiens, Susan | Hartland | |
| | | |
| Frost, Grafton | St. Albans | Aug. 22 |
| Wheeler, Nancy | Ripley | |

| | | |
|---|---|---|
| Glidden, John | Ripley | Sep. 7 |
| Clark, Betsy | St. Albans | |
| | | |
| Maxwell, William | St. Albans | Sep. 29 |
| Lothrop, Mary B. | St. Albans | |
| | | |
| Whittemore, Franklin | Dexter | Oct. 19 |
| Sleeper, Christina B. | St. Albans | |
| | | |
| Wing, Simon | St. Albans | Nov. 25 |
| Merrill, Mary | St. Albans | |
| | | |
| Mellows, Job | St. Albans | Nov. 28 |
| Snell, Georgiana | St. Albans | |
| | | |
| Mower, Jesse C. | St. Albans | Dec. 21 |
| Brown, Angeline L. | St. Albans | |
| | | |
| Hanson, Turner | St. Albans | Dec. 29 |
| Wheeler, Ruth Mrs. | St. Albans | |
| | | |
| Mower, Sterling | St. Albans | Dec. 29 |
| Laughton, Betsy | St. Albans | |

## Marriages - 1853

| | | |
|---|---|---|
| Church, Hiram | Levant | May 30 |
| Merryman, Nancy A. | St. Albans | |
| | | |
| Greely, Cyrus S. | St. Albans | July 31 |
| Parker, Elizabeth | St. Albans | |
| | | |
| Smith, Andrew H. | St. Albans | Aug. 1 |
| Hoyt, Mary | St. Albans | |
| | | |
| Bangs, Robert | St. Albans | Aug. 6 |
| Smith, Sarah G. | St. Albans | |
| | | |
| White, John | St. Albans | Aug. 11 |
| Thurston, Susan | St. Albans | |

| Briggs, John H. | St. Albans | Oct. 15 |
|---|---|---|
| Tripp, Eliza F. | St. Albans | |

## Marriages - 1854

| Stewart, Esq., David | St. Albans | Mar. 16 |
|---|---|---|
| Merrick, Ariminta | Pittsfield | |

| Judkins, Henry | Parkman | Mar. 26 |
|---|---|---|
| Steward, Elizabeth | Pittsfield | |

| Brown, William | St. Albans | Nov. 19 |
|---|---|---|
| Greely, Mary | St. Albans | |

| Hilton, Goodwin | St. Albans | Nov. 27 |
|---|---|---|
| Gordon, Rosella | St. Albans | |

| Withee, John O. | St. Albans | Dec. 25 |
|---|---|---|
| Tripp, Deborah | St. Albans | |

| Fairbanks, John | St. Albans | Dec. 30 |
|---|---|---|
| Hilton, Mary Jane | St. Albans | |

## Marriages - 1855

| Gifford, James E. | Falmouth | Jan. 21 |
|---|---|---|
| Bowman, Eliza A. | St. Albans | |

| Prentiss, Jessie | Milford | Mar. 28 |
|---|---|---|
| Devereux, Sarah E. | St. Albans | |

| Pettigrove, Allen | St. Albans | Sep. 30 |
|---|---|---|
| Warmwood, Mary | Cambridge | |

| Wright, John | Palmyra | Sep. 3 |
|---|---|---|
| Pettigrove, Mary Ann | St. Albans | |

Whitney, George W.   Newport        Dec. 17
Skinner, Mary F.     St. Albans


## Marriages - 1856

Gifford, James E.    St. Albans     Jan. 1
Bowman,           St. Albans
    Elizabeth A.

Litchfield, Ensign  St. Albans     Mar. 20
    Sanforth
McGray, Elizabeth   St. Albans

Bradford, William   St. Albans     Apr. 16
Marsh, Sylvia A.    Bangor

Frost, Curtis       St. Albans     May 4
Brown, Sarah        St. Albans

Frost, Curtis       St. Albans     May 25
Boston, Sarah M.    St. Albans

Douglas, Robert W.  St. Albans     May 27
Gifford,          Palmyra
    Margaret A.

Tracy, Jeremiah    Pittsfield    June 5
Moor, Lydia        St. Albans

Crocker,          St. Albans    June 23
    S. Greenville
Leathers,        St. Albans
    Amanda D.

Holway, Daniel     St. Albans    July 9
McIlroy, Charity D  St. Albans

Stafford,         St. Albans    Aug. 19
    Frederick
Braley, Hester A.   St. Albans

| | | |
|---|---|---|
| Braley, John | St. Albans | Aug. 31 |
| Frost, Caroline | Ripley | |
| | | |
| Golding, Absalom | St. Albans | Sep. 25 |
| Buzzell, Nancy | St. Albans | |
| | | |
| Page, Hiram W. | Dexter | Oct. 3 |
| Bradbury, Louise | Exeter | |
| | | |
| Bean, Calvin M. | Ripley | Oct. 18 |
| Braley, Jane | St. Albans | |
| | | |
| Rollins, Enoch W. | St. Albans | Nov. 20 |
| Knowles, Savilla | St. Albans | |
| | | |
| Webber, Franklin R. | St. Albans | Dec. 17 |
| Skinner, Sarah | St. Albans | |
| | | |
| Whitney, George N. | Newport | Dec. 17 |
| Skinner, Mary | St. Albans | |
| | | |
| Whitman, William | Bangor | Dec. 25 |
| Higgins, Mary | St. Albans | |
| | | |
| Chandler, Alonzo D. | St. Albans | Dec. 28 |
| Smith, Sarah | St. Albans | |
| | | |
| Webb, Benjamin | | Dec. 29 |
| Robinson, Olive D. | Palmyra | |

## Intentions - 1857

| | | |
|---|---|---|
| Tripp, Lewis | St. Albans | Aug. 22 |
| Peterson, Mary Jane | Palmyra | |
| | | |
| Foss, William | Palmyra | Sep. 13 |
| Ireland, Isabella | Palmyra | |

| | | |
|---|---|---|
| Millett, Thomas | Palmyra | Sep. 26 |
| Gordon, Fannie | St. Albans | |
| | | |
| Rowe, David M. | St. Albans | Oct. 10 |
| Smith, Elizabeth | St. Albans | |
| | | |
| Norton, Edwin | Troy | Oct. 17 |
| Gage, Olive | St. Albans | |
| | | |
| Cole, Ivory H. | St. Albans | Nov. 6 |
| Davis, Anna M. | St. Albans | |
| | | |
| Varney, Amasa S. | St. Albans | Nov. 26 |
| Dunlap, Hannah | Ripley | |
| | | |
| Bradford, Andrew | St. Albans | Dec. 31 |
| Sanborn, Lovina M. | St. Albans | |

## Marriages - 1857

| | | |
|---|---|---|
| Estes, Melsar D. | St. Albans | Jan. |
| Johnson, Augusta E. | St. Albans | |
| | | |
| Fuller, Henry | St. Albans | Jan. 15 |
| Tinney, Caroline | St. Albans | |
| | | |
| Goding, Absalom | St. Albans | Apr. 27 |
| Buzzell, Nancy | St. Albans | |
| | | |
| Buker, Abel | Bowdoin | May 4 |
| Hawkes, Mary | St. Albans | |
| | | |
| Foss, William | St. Albans | May 5 |
| Ireland, Isabelle | St. Albans | |
| | | |
| Packard, Leonard | St. Albans | July 4 |
| Parker, Mary | St. Albans | |

| | | |
|---|---|---|
| Maxwell, Thomas L. | Canaan | July 12 |
| Bailey, Meribah D. | Canaan | |
| | | |
| Frost, Gilman | St. Albans | Aug. 7 |
| Frost, Betsey | St. Albans | |

Intentions - 1858

| | | |
|---|---|---|
| Hayes, Loring D. | Dexter | Jan. 24 |
| Higgins, Lizzie S. | St. Albans | |
| | | |
| Philbrick, Fifield | St. Albans | Feb. 27 |
| Bates, Clarenda L. | St. Albans | |
| | | |
| Frost, Aaron | St. Albans | Apr. 12 |
| Moulton, Mrs. Emeline | St. Albans | |
| | | |
| Brown, Sewell | St. Albans | Apr. 22 |
| Frost, Sarah | St. Albans | |
| | | |
| Cooley, Greenlief | St. Albans | May 6 |
| Hutchins, Olive | St. Albans | |
| | | |
| Leach, Phineaus | St. Albans | May 6 |
| Perkins, Mary | | |
| | | |
| Higgins, Edwin | St. Albans | May 16 |
| Jackson, Miranda E. | Hartland | |
| | | |
| Packard, Lorenzo D. | St. Albans | May 8 |
| Grant, Relience N. | Frankfort | |
| | | |
| Hinkley, Thomas M. | LaGrange | July 13 |
| Moor, Adaline | St. Albans | |
| | | |
| Clough, Ira | St. Albans | Aug. 8 |
| French, Caroline | St. Albans | |

| | | |
|---|---|---|
| Brown, William | St. Albans | Aug. 23 |
| Johnson, Julia Ann | Parkman | |
| | | |
| Frost, Horace | St. Albans | Aug. 28 |
| Jewett, Mary | St. Albans | |
| | | |
| Merrill, Phinias | St. Albans | Oct. 11 |
| George, Mary E. | Newport | |
| | | |
| Hawkes, Albert | St. Albans | Oct. 18 |
| Buker, Eunice E. | Bowdoin | |
| | | |
| Searborn, Charles | Newport | Nov. 23 |
| McClues, Mary | St. Albans | |
| | | |
| Goodwin, William H. | St. Albans | Nov. 28 |
| Church, Betsey | St. Albans | |
| | | |
| Goodwin, William | St. Albans | Dec. 4 |
| Church, Betsey | | |
| | | |
| Foss, Daniel | St. Albans | Dec. 11 |
| White, Betsey | Skowhegan | |
| | | |
| Miller, William G. | Palmyra | Dec. 20 |
| Chandler, Mary Abby | St. Albans | |

## Marriages - 1858

| | | |
|---|---|---|
| Frost, William S. | St. Albans | Aug. 28 |
| Pomroy, Corisinda | Carmel | |

## Intentions - 1859

| | | |
|---|---|---|
| Crocker, Solomon | St. Albans | Jan. 31 |
| Keene, Sarah | Dexter | |

| | | |
|---|---|---|
| Parker, John | St. Albans | Mar. 21 |
| Bigelow, Sarah Goodwin | St. Albans | |
| | | |
| Frost, Aaron | St. Albans | Apr. 2 |
| Moulton, Eveline | St. Albans | |
| | | |
| Bates, Constantine | St. Albans | Apr. 14 |
| Hawes, Sarah | St. Albans | |
| | | |
| Gordon, Stephen L. | St. Albans | Apr. 14 |
| Cook, Nancy | St. Albans | |
| | | |
| Fisher, Augustus | Hartland | May 20 |
| Graves, Mary S. | Hartland | |
| | | |
| Mayo, Stephen | Newburgh | May 15 |
| Steward, Josephine | St. Albans | |
| | | |
| Boynton, John E. | St. Albans | June 28 |
| Cook, Mary A. | St. Albans | |
| | | |
| Salley, Hiram | Palmyra | July 23 |
| Tuttle, Elizabeth | St. Albans | |
| | | |
| Withee, William | Hartland | Aug. 1 |
| Huff, Clara | Hartland | |
| | | |
| Frost, Orrin M. | St. Albans | Aug. 10 |
| Nutter, Hannah | St. Albans | |
| | | |
| Frost, Gilman | St. Albans | Aug. 23 |
| Frost, Betsey | St. Albans | |
| | | |
| Bigelow, Alfred | St. Albans | Sep. 24 |
| Butler, Caroline | Ripley | |
| | | |
| Webb, Ruel | | Sep. 18 |
| Pattridge, Mary | Houlton?? | |
| | | |
| Rowe, David M. | St. Albans | Sep. 29 |
| Jeffery, Mrs. Mary M. | St. Albans | |

| | | |
|---|---|---|
| Braley, Seth | St. Albans | Nov. 29 |
| Smart, Francis D. | St. Albans | |
| | | |
| Lyford, Samuel | St. Albans | Nov. 12 |
| Robinson,<br>    Almeda A. | Palmyra | |
| | | |
| Spaulding,<br>    Llewellyn F. | Belgrade | Dec. 16 |
| Church, Sylvia A. | St. Albans | |
| | | |
| Goodwin,<br>    Charles H. | Stetson | Dec. 17 |
| Fuller, Nancy | St. Albans | |
| | | |
| Matthews,<br>    Joshua V. | St. Albans | Dec. 30 |
| Wing, Sarah | Readfield | |

## Intentions - 1860

| | | |
|---|---|---|
| Braley, William H. | St. Albans | Jan. 16 |
| Frost, Sarah | St. Albans | |
| | | |
| Morton, Henry | Palmyra | Feb. 6 |
| Hubbard, Mary F. | Palmyra | |
| | | |
| Ireland, Condon G. | St. Albans | Mar. 8 |
| Roberts, Abbie S. | Lewiston | |
| | | |
| Nelson, George L. | Cambridge | Mar. 4 |
| Matthews, Mary J. | St. Albans | |
| | | |
| Bowdoin,<br>    Gustavus M. | St. Albans | Apr. 29 |
| Bowdoin,<br>    Lucinda E. | St. Albans | |
| | | |
| Fairbrother,<br>    Browning G. | St. Albans | May 12 |
| Foss, Mary | St. Albans | |

| | | |
|---|---|---|
| Ramsdell, Henry | Ripley | May 21 |
| Andrews, Mary | St. Albans | |
| | | |
| Coston, Joshua | Athens | July 6 |
| Stafford, ?? | Hartland | |
| (Starbird) Aurillia | | |
| | | |
| Frost, Aaron | St. Albans | July 26 |
| Morse, Sophia | St. Albans | |
| | | |
| Gordon, Samuel | St. Albans | Aug. 20 |
| Leech, Mary G. | Levant | |
| | | |
| Hopkins, Chandler | | Aug. 23 |
| Johnson, Mrs. | Newport | |
| Betsey | | |
| | | |
| Sanborn, Charles | Corinna | Oct. 7 |
| Chase, Emily | Corinna | |
| | | |
| Knowles, George W. | Corinna | Nov. 26 |
| Stinchfield, | St. Albans | |
| Henrietta | | |
| | | |
| Woodbury, | Harmony | Nov. 28 |
| Abraham P. | | |
| Avery, Fanny A. | St. Albans | |
| | | |
| Marr, Jordon | Webster | Dec. 1 |
| Hoyt, Lydia | St. Albans | |

Marriages - 1860

| | | |
|---|---|---|
| Matthews, J. D. | St. Albans | Jan. 7 |
| Wing, Sarah E. | Readfield | |
| | | |
| Braley, Seth | St. Albans | Jan. 7 |
| Smart, Francis | St. Albans | |

| Ham, A. H. P. | Wales, Maine | Jan. 26 |
| Ransom, Abby A. | St. Albans | |

| Richards, | St. Albans | Mar. 2 |
| Frederick | | |
| Whitelaw, Margaret | Dexter | |

| Philbrick, Charles | St. Albans | Apr. 8 |
| Maxim, Harriett A. | Biddeford | |

| Goodwin, George | St. Albans | Apr. 11 |
| Haws, Abby | St. Albans | |

| Hurd, Charles | Harmony | Apr. 18 |
| Bigelow, Clarissa | St. Albans | |

| Mumfurd, Edward L. | Newport, R.I. | Apr. 25 |
| Cooley, Mary | St. Albans | |

| Smith, John | St. Albans | May 8 |
| Dunlap, Lydia Ann | Ripley | |

| Bonney, Andrew J. | St. Albans | May 13 |
| Getchell, Mary | St. Albans | |

| Webb, Nathan M. | St. Albans | June 27 |
| Moor, Almedia | Hartland | |

| Rideout, Nelson R. | St. Albans | June 29 |
| Robbins, Mary E. | St. Albans | |

| Smith, S. Wilson | St. Albans | July 6 |
| Richards, Nellie | St. Albans | |

| Hersom, John W. | St. Albans | July 11 |
| Ross, Elizabeth F. | | |

| Pettegrove, Lyman | Newport | July 24 |
| Keene, Rasane M. | Palmyra | |

| | | |
|---|---|---|
| Ireland, Addison O. | Newport | Sep. 19 |
| McGray, Jane C. | St. Albans | |
| Webb, Luther H. | St. Albans | Oct. 2 |
| Page, Emily | Hartland | |
| Haskell, Plummer T. | Hartland | Oct. 2 |
| Webb, Clara A. | St. Albans | |
| Moor, Samuel | St. Albans | Oct. 7 |
| Pratt, Betsey | | |
| Webber, Charles M. | Hartland | Oct. 15 |
| Tripp, Elizabeth S. | Hartland | |
| Batchelder, Horatio G. | St. Albans | Nov. 26 |
| Getchell, Elvira | St. Albans | |
| Shorey, Isaac | Corinna | Dec. 6 |
| Grant, Diana | St. Albans | |
| Farnham, Ruel | St. Albans | Dec. 16 |
| Hawes, Ellen L. | St. Albans | |
| Hilton, Jonathan | St. Albans | Dec. 21 |
| Brown, Ann A. | St. Albans | |
| Ross, Charles H. | St. Albans | Dec. 23 |
| Dyer, Lydia E. | St. Albans | |
| Merrill, Harlan P. | St. Albans | Dec. 25 |
| White, Maria | St. Albans | |
| Smart, Marquis O. | St. Albans | Dec. 27 |
| Bonney, Eliza A. | St. Albans | |
| Tuttle, Frederick | Athens | |
| Coston, Mary | Hartland | |

# Intentions - 1862

| | | |
|---|---|---|
| Whitney, Thomas | St. Albans | Jan. 11 |
| Hilton, Nancy | St. Albans | |
| | | |
| Lyford, Daniel | St. Albans | Feb. 7 |
| Fletcher, Lodoski M. | Corinna | |
| | | |
| Frost, Abel U. | Ripley | Mar. 2 |
| Emery, Ann L. | St. Albans | |
| | | |
| Clark, George W. | St. Albans | Mar. 14 |
| Fairfield, Margaret | Vassalboro | |
| | | |
| Skinner, Charles | St. Albans | Mar. 16 |
| Hilton, Emma | Dixmont | |
| | | |
| Stevens, Jeremiah | St. Albans | Apr.7 |
| Jacobs, Olive J. | Skowhegan | |
| | | |
| Parker, Simon S. | St. Albans | Apr. 8 |
| Frost, Maria | St. Albans | |
| | | |
| Huff, Elbridge | Hartland | May 3 |
| Ricker, Susan A. | Hartland | |
| | | |
| Dearborn, William | Corinna | June 14 |
| Bates, Melissa | St. Albans | |
| | | |
| Frost, Daniel | St. Albans | July 12 |
| Osborn, Henrietta | St. Albans | |
| | | |
| Tucker, Timothy | Harmony | July 27 |
| Stewart, Irena | St. Albans | |
| | | |
| Parker, Edwin A. | St. Albans | Aug. 8 |
| Bonney, Maria A. | St. Albans | |
| | | |
| White, James S. | St. Albans | Aug. 24 |
| Grant, Margaret A. | St. Albans | |

| | | |
|---|---|---|
| Homstead, Charles | Palmyra | Sep. 14 |
| Holway, Della | St. Albans | |

| | | |
|---|---|---|
| Loomis, Warren | Skowhegan | Sep. 22 |
| Judkins, Elizabeth A. | St. Albans | |

| | | |
|---|---|---|
| White, Harrison W. | St. Albans | Oct. 18 |
| Kendall, Olive | Newport | |

| | | |
|---|---|---|
| Mower, Isaac | Dexter | Nov. 23 |
| Robinson, Rebecca J. | St. Albans | |

| | | |
|---|---|---|
| Braley, William | St. Albans | Dec. 18 |
| Hatch, Lucy | Cambridge | |

## Marriages - 1862

| | | |
|---|---|---|
| Tucker, Timothy | Harmony | Jul. 27 |
| Stewert, Irene | St. Albans | |

## Marriages - 1863

| | | |
|---|---|---|
| Luce, Fanlin (?) B. | Hartland | Jan. 16 |
| Frost, Lydia | St. Albans | |

| | | |
|---|---|---|
| Fuller, Alonzo E. | St. Albans | Feb. 19 |
| Tenney, Mary E. | St. Albans | |

| | | |
|---|---|---|
| Butterfield, Joseph | St. Albans | Feb. 9 |
| Jones, Roxanna | St. Albans | |

| | | |
|---|---|---|
| White, John | St. Albans | Feb. 18 |
| Smith, Philinda A. | St. Albans | |

| | | |
|---|---|---|
| Webb, John R. | St. Albans | Mar. 9 |
| Weston, Henrietta L. | Skowhegan | |

| | | |
|---|---|---|
| Pushor, Albert | Hartland | Mar. 19 |
| Ricker, Sarah E. | Hartland | |
| | | |
| Grant, David H. | St. Albans | Apr. 6 |
| Nelson, Mary S. | Cambridge | |
| | | |
| Frost, Grafton H. | St. Albans | May 1 |
| Frost, Nancy | St. Albans | |
| | | |
| Weeks, William F. | St. Albans | May 23 |
| Lane, Velona A. | St. Albans | |
| | | |
| Polland, Alfred G. | St. Albans | May 31 |
| Davis, Lizzie | St. Albans | |
| | | |
| Batchelder, Albert S. | Garland | June 27 |
| Rand, Mary E. | St. Albans | |
| | | |
| Downs, Eben | Harmony | June 27 |
| Braley, Mrs. Martha | St. Albans | |
| | | |
| Rowe, John F. | St. Albans | July 5 |
| Hoyt, Mary E. | St. Albans | |
| | | |
| Brown, Frederick L. | St. Albans | Aug. 2 |
| Johnson, Alvira F. | St. Albans | |
| | | |
| Thompson, Charles E. | Corinna | Aug. 12 |
| Cooley, Caroline | St. Albans | |
| | | |
| Bennett, Ansil | Plymouth | Aug. 24 |
| Gray, Melissa A. | St. Albans | |
| | | |
| Robinson, Orlando M. | St. Albans | Aug. 30 |
| Magoon, Laura F. | Harmony | |
| | | |
| Collins, James F. | St. Albans | Sep. 6 |
| Stafford, Flora | St. Albans | |

| | | |
|---|---|---|
| Adkins, John F. | St. Albans | Oct. 26 |
| Boston, Lydia | Mayfield | |
| | | |
| Matthews, Jr., John | Harmony | Nov. 11 |
| Thayer, Eliza W. | St. Albans | |
| | | |
| Snell, Charles | St. Albans | Nov. 12 |
| Denning, Mrs. Florence | St. Albans | |
| | | |
| Weeks, Daniel | St. Albans | Dec. 26 |
| Daggett, Carrie | Palmyra | |
| | | |
| Parkman, O.A. | Palmyra | Dec. 30 |
| McLure, Esther | St. Albans | |

## Marriages - 1864

| | | |
|---|---|---|
| Smith, Charles H. | St. Albans | Jan. 12 |
| Butler, Mehilable H. | St. Albans | |
| | | |
| Ransom, Thomas B. | St. Albans | Jan. 30 |
| Austin, Laura F. | St. Albans | |
| | | |
| Nickerson, Henry | St. Albans | Mar. 24 |
| White, Thankful | St. Albans | |
| | | |
| Bowman, Daniel | St. Albans | Apr. 18 |
| Wilkins, Lucretia | St. Albans | |
| | | |
| Lord, Henry K. | St. Albans | Apr. 20 |
| Wyman, Mary J. | St. Albans | |
| | | |
| Smith, Joseph | Corinna | May 3 |
| Devereaux, Arminder H. | St. Albans | |
| | | |
| Howard, Daniel H. | Dexter | June 11 |
| Merrill, Ann M. | St. Albans | |

| | | |
|---|---|---|
| Williams, Albert | Hartland | Aug. 16 |
| Prescott, Elizabeth | Hartland | |
| | | |
| Vining, Nathaniel | St. Albans | Sep. 17 |
| Stone, Anna L. | Ripley | |
| | | |
| Wright, George | Hartland | Sep. 18 |
| Holt, Lucinda | Hartland | |
| | | |
| Robinson, Henry J. | Hartland | Sep. 21 |
| Webb, Mary P. | St. Albans | |
| | | |
| Chase, Stephen | Lowell | Sep. 28 |
| Lothrop, Aritta | St. Albans | |
| | | |
| Parkman, John W. | St. Albans | Oct. 14 |
| Steward, Lucy A. | St. Albans | |
| | | |
| Holt, Augustus | Bingham | Oct. 14 |
| Holbrook, Mary | St. Albans | |
| | | |
| Webb, C. L. | St. Albans | Oct. 20 |
| Cummings, Ceyuna C. | Dexter | |
| | | |
| Parkman, John | St. Albans | Oct. 27 |
| Sewell, Lucy | St. Albans | |
| | | |
| Gerrish, James | Ripley | Oct. |
| Jones, Clara | Ripley | |
| | | |
| Southard, Charles | St. Albans | Nov. 2 |
| Goodwin, Abbie | St. Albans | |
| | | |
| Prince, Henry W. | Pittsfield | Nov. 6 |
| Richardson, Sylvia E. | Pittsfield | |

| | | |
|---|---|---|
| Skinner, John M. | St. Albans | Jan. 2 |
| Leathers, Annie E. | St. Albans | |
| | | |
| Foss, Mayhew E. | St. Albans | Jan. 4 |
| Grant, Hattie | St. Albans | |
| | | |
| Osborne, Isaac | St. Albans | Feb. 10 |
| Trafton, Laura D. | St. Albans | |
| | | |
| Davis, Joseph | Palmyra | Feb. 23 |
| Wing, Addie | Palmyra | |
| | | |
| Snell, William H. | St. Albans | Mar. 5 |
| Harvey, Mary F. | Corinna | |
| | | |
| Cooley, Melvin | St. Albans | Mar. 16 |
| Holbrook, Dora | Newport | |
| | | |
| Fox, John T. | Palmyra | Mar. 27 |
| Footmand, Mary | St. Albans | |
| | | |
| Frost, Joseph | St. Albans | Mar. 30 |
| Booker, Olive | Dover | |
| | | |
| Everson, Albert | St. Albans | Apr. 20 |
| Smith, Hannah | St. Albans | |
| | | |
| Lewis, John P. | Corinna | May 25 |
| Wyman, Eliza | St. Albans | |
| | | |
| Foss, Phineas | Mattawamkeag | June 16 |
| Bradford, Emily | St. Albans | |
| | | |
| Frost, Charles W. | St. Albans | June 30 |
| Wheeler, Louisa L. | St. Albans | |
| | | |
| Withee, Jr. Ezra | Hartland | July 7 |
| Woodbury, Jennie | St. Albans | |

| | | |
|---|---|---|
| Stevens, Jeremiah L. | St. Albans | July 20 |
| Whitney, Loantha | Hartland | |
| | | |
| Taylor, Abiathar B. | St. Albans | July 21 |
| Wilkins, Lucretia | St. Albans | |
| | | |
| Chase, Charles H. | St. Albans | July 31 |
| Smith, Jennie C. | St. Albans | |
| | | |
| Frost, Edmond O. | St. Albans | July 31 |
| Grant, Ellen | St. Albans | |
| | | |
| Madin, George W. | St. Albans | Sep. 2 |
| Goodwin, Phoebe | St. Albans | |
| | | |
| Woodbury, Abram P. | St. Albans | Sep. 4 |
| Hart, Jennie S. | St. Albans | |
| | | |
| Goodwin, Oliver | Detroit | Oct. 12 |
| Smiley, Emma L. | St. Albans | |
| | | |
| Burrill, Albert H. | Newport | Oct. 16 |
| Snell, Sarah | St. Albans | |
| | | |
| Dillingham, Lloyd | St. Albans | Oct. 20 |
| White, Angelle C. | St. Albans | |
| | | |
| Pettigrew, William T. | St. Albans | Oct. 21 |
| Tilton, Pamelia C. | Canaan | |
| | | |
| Frost, Albert W. | St. Albans | Oct. 30 |
| Smith, Martha | Smithfield | |
| | | |
| Goodwin, Daniel | St. Albans | Nov. 3 |
| Hatfield, Mary | Poughkeepsie, N.Y. | |

| Leech, Isaiah | St. Albans | Nov. 3 |
| Smith, Mrs. Charity | St. Albans | |
| | | |
| Snell, Hosea B. | St. Albans | Nov. 25 |
| Harvey, Anna E. | Corinna | |
| | | |
| Boston, Gorham | St. Albans | Dec. 3 |
| Reynolds, Sabrina E. | Acton | |
| | | |
| Adkins, John H.D. | St. Albans | Dec. 26 |
| Shorey, Mary J. | St. Albans | |

## Marriages - 1865

| Davis, Joseph | Palmyra | Mar. 2 |
| Wing, Addis | Palmyra | |
| | | |
| McCrillis, Nathaniel L. | Moscow | June 14 |
| Towle, Ann E. | St. Albans | |
| | | |
| Wing, Gorham A. | Winthrop | Oct. 26 |
| Martin, Mary L. | St. Albans | |
| | | |
| Stevens, Arland | Corinth | Nov. 15 |
| Towle, Eunice | Hartland | |
| | | |
| Taylor, John F. | Waterville | Dec. |
| Mosher, Eleanor | Waterville | |
| | | |
| Dunlap, Horace | St. Albans | Dec. 18 |
| Stone, Harriett A. | St. Albans | |

## Intentions - 1866

| Badger, Rufus | St. Albans | Jan. 11 |
| Brazier, Mary E. | St. Albans | |

| | | |
|---|---|---|
| Bowman, John H. | St. Albans | Jan. 11 |
| Woodcock,<br>    Deborah E. | Ripley | |
| Given, Isaac C. | St. Albans | Feb. 6 |
| Emery, Ellen C. | St. Albans | |
| Ireland, Cullen L. | St. Albans | Feb. 9 |
| Parker, Ann H. | St. Albans | |
| Rowe, Alonzo T. | Harmony | Feb. 9 |
| Frost, A. | St. Albans | |
| Crockett, Daniel | Hartland | Feb. 13 |
| Crockett, Mary E. | St. Albans | |
| Grover, Leonard | St. Albans | Feb. 28 |
| Hanscom, Rebecca | Wellington | |
| Whitney, Thomas | St. Albans | Mar. 13 |
| Elder, Clara R. | Lewiston | |
| Noyes, Isaac D. | St. Albans | Mar. 27 |
| White, Elizabeth | St. Albans | |
| Gray, Andrew | Palmyra | Mar. 30 |
| Snell, Abby R. | St. Albans | |
| Woodcock, Theodore | Ripley | Apr. 3 |
| Wing, Ann | St. Albans | |
| Gordon, Frank | St. Albans | Apr. 4 |
| Leech, Sarah E. | St. Albans | |
| Rand, George H. | St. Albans | Apr. 9 |
| Stone, Frederia | Ripley | |
| Hanson, Daniel | St. Albans | Apr. 9 |
| French, Henrietta | St. Albans | |
| Russell, Charles | St. Albans | May 11 |
| Spaulding,<br>    Mrs. Sylvia | St. Albans | |

| | | |
|---|---|---|
| Magoon, James F. | St. Albans | May 12 |
| Brown, Mary A. | Parkman | |
| | | |
| Lane, Reuben W. | Ripley | May 12 |
| Hopkins, Martha | St. Albans | |
| | | |
| Sherburn, Andrew | St. Albans | May 21 |
| Dow, Emma | Plymouth | |
| | | |
| Marble, Isaac J. | Brownville | June 14 |
| Bigelow, Joanna | St. Albans | |
| | | |
| Libby, Joseph | Hartland | June 18 |
| Hopkins, Sarah F. | Hartland | |
| | | |
| Fisher, James L. | St. Albans | June 26 |
| Sprague, Maria A. | St. Albans | |
| | | |
| Stevens, Jerry | St. Albans | June 28 |
| Wyman, Olive | St. Albans | |
| | | |
| Footman, Arrin | St. Albans | July 1 |
| Dearborn, Sarah | Corinna | |
| | | |
| Bigelow, Jonathan G. | St.Albans | Aug. 7 |
| Given, Lydia A. | St. Albans | |
| | | |
| Johnson, Sullivan | St. Albans | Aug. 8 |
| Bonney, Clara J. | St. Albans | |
| | | |
| Dyson (or Ditson), Mark | St. Albans | Aug. 14 |
| Wilbur, Clara A. | St. Albans | |
| | | |
| Moore, William H. | St. Albans | Aug. 18 |
| Morrill, Eliza M. | St. Albans | |
| | | |
| Southards, Beldon | St. Albans | Aug. 22 |
| Martin, Almyra | St. Albans | |
| | | |
| Weeks, John H. | St. Albans | Aug. 23 |
| Cox, Elvira F. | Cambridge | |

317

| | | |
|---|---|---|
| Hutchins, Benjamin F. | Brighton | Sep. 1 |
| Abbie, Sarah S. | St. Albans | |
| | | |
| Grant, William | St. Albans | Sep. 1 |
| Cook, Occina J. | St. Albans | |
| | | |
| Works, William | St. Albans | Sep. 2 |
| White, Clara | St. Albans | |
| | | |
| Robertson, John F. | St. Albans | Sep. 6 |
| Hartwell, Jennie E. | St. Albans | |
| | | |
| Southards, Daniel H. | St. Albans | Sep. 10 |
| Leech, Frances E. | St. Albans | |
| | | |
| Douglas, Elbridge F. | Dover | Sep. 12 |
| Bigelow, Louisa | St. Albans | |
| | | |
| Johnson, Joseph T. | St. Albans | Sep. 14 |
| Wiggin, Abby W. | St. Albans | |
| | | |
| Stafford, Leonard | Dexter | Sep. 16 |
| Cook, Rose | St. Albans | |
| | | |
| Bigelow, Wilson | St. Albans | Sep. 22 |
| Lothrop, Esther E. | St. Albans | |
| | | |
| Bigelow, Calvin | St. Albans | Oct. 12 |
| Douglas, Nellie | Dover | |
| | | |
| Hall, Eben K. | Lowell, Mass. | Oct. 20 |
| Mellows, Elizabeth | St. Albans | |
| | | |
| Austin, Daniel | St. Albans | Oct. 23 |
| Chase, Sarah F. | Corinna | |
| | | |
| Grant, Samuel F. | St. Albans | Oct. 31 |
| Clark, Mary | St. Albans | |

318

| | | |
|---|---|---|
| Osborn, Daniel L. | St. Albans | Nov. 3 |
| Randall, Roxanna | St. Albans | |
| | | |
| Parker, Richard | St. Albans | Nov. 12 |
| Goodwin, Emma | St. Albans | |
| | | |
| Hoyt, John | St. Albans | Nov. 14 |
| Bates, Sarah R. | St. Albans | |
| | | |
| Grant, Charles | St. Albans | Nov. 20 |
| Bates, Addie V. | St. Albans | |
| | | |
| Abby, William | St Albans | Dec. 17 |
| Hutchins, Tryphena E. | Brighton | |
| | | |
| Willey, John M. | St. Albans | Dec. 23 |
| Hill, Sarah C. | Corinna | |

## Marriages - 1866

| | | |
|---|---|---|
| Atkins, John | St. Albans | Jan. 1 |
| Shorey, Mary | St. Albans | |
| | | |
| Foss, Jr., John | Brighton | May 13 |
| Hurd, Martha E. | Harmony | |
| | | |
| Grant, William | St. Albans | Sep. 14 |
| Cook, Occena J. | St. Albans | |
| | | |
| Morton, Charles C. | Corinna | Oct. 12 |
| Nickerson, Anna | St. Albans | |
| | | |
| Hoyt, John | St. Albans | Nov. 20 |
| Bates, Sarah | St. Albans | |
| | | |
| Stevens, Arland | Corinth | |
| Towle, Eunice | Hartland | |
| | | |
| Grant, Samuel | St. Albans | Dec. 2 |
| Clark, Mary | St. Albans | |

## Marriages - 1867

| | | |
|---|---|---|
| Bowman, John H.<br>Woodcock,<br>    Deborah E. | St. Albans<br>Ripley | Feb. 17 |
| Whitney, Thomas O.<br>Eliam, Clara R. | St. Albans<br>Lewiston | Mar. 21 |
| Johnson, Joseph G.<br>Case, Angie E. | St. Albans<br>St. Albans | Mar. 29 |
| Gordon, Frank<br>Leech, Sarah | St. Albans<br>St. Albans | Apr. 10 |
| Estes, Valentine<br>Ridley, Sarah | St. Albans<br>St. Albans | Apr. 27 |
| Harris, George<br>Parker, Lottie | Dexter<br>Dexter | July 17 |
| Osborne, Peter<br>Manson, Adalaide | Pittsfield<br>Hartland | Aug. 4 |
| Wheeler, George<br>Cook, Lydia | Hartland<br>Hartland | Oct. 6 |
| Blake, Charles<br>Taylor, Etta | Hartland<br>Hartland | Dec. 2 |
| Blaisdell,<br>    Horace G.<br>Badger,<br>    Mrs. Frank A. | Palmyra<br><br>St. Albans | Dec. 24 |

## Intentions - 1868

| | | |
|---|---|---|
| Parkman,<br>    Richard C.<br>Libby, Flora A. | St. Albans<br><br>St. Albans | Jan. 17 |

| | | |
|---|---|---|
| McDonald, William P. | St. Albans | Jan. 23 |
| Cooley, Melvina | St. Albans | |
| | | |
| Higgins, Henry B. | Benton | Feb. 14 |
| Bates, Sarah A. | St. Albans | |
| | | |
| Turner, William W. | St. Albans | Feb. 18 |
| Webb, Clara | Palmyra | |
| | | |
| Dearborn, Simon S. | Solon | Mar. 19 |
| Adams, Pamella P. | St. Albans | |
| | | |
| Smith, G.W. | Levant | Mar. 13 |
| Hopkins, Lavina | St. Albans | |
| | | |
| Johnson, Joseph C. | St. Albans | Mar. 21 |
| Cass, Angie E. | St. Albans | |
| | | |
| Stevens, Matthew B. | St. Albans | Apr. 1 |
| Taylor, Cynthia B. | Hartland | |
| | | |
| Cooley, George | St. Albans | Apr. 5 |
| Maxim, Mrs. Harriett | | |
| | | |
| Stafford, Alfred | Hartland | Apr. 29 |
| Woodbury, Jennie | St. Albans | |
| | | |
| Wilkins, Francis M. | St. Albans | May 25 |
| Knight, Emily C. | Gray | |
| | | |
| Spaulding, Albert P. | St. Albans | Aug. 7 |
| Field, Mary E. | Millbridge | |
| | | |
| Woodbury, Charles | Hartland | Sep. 7 |
| Boston, Mrs. Emily F. | St. Albans | |

| | | |
|---|---|---|
| Steward, Pembrook S. | St. Albans | Sep. 28 |
| Bennett, Lenora | Searsmont | |
| | | |
| Chase, William | St. Albans | Oct. 12 |
| Webb, Ella | St. Albans | |
| | | |
| Stanchfield, Earl G. | St. Albans | Oct. 14 |
| Goff, Christinna L. | Hartland | |
| | | |
| Wood, Henry P. | St. Albans | Nov. 13 |
| Hubbard, Ellen F. | Palmyra | |
| | | |
| Long, William H. | St. Albans | Nov. 12 |
| Goodale, Lydia | Ripley | |
| | | |
| Mason, Charles | St. Albans | Dec. 5 |
| Mellows, Aramilla | St. Albans | |

Intentions - 1869

| | | |
|---|---|---|
| Snell, William | St. Albans | Jan. 4 |
| Butters, Mary A. | Exeter | |
| | | |
| Badger, Joseph S. | St. Albans | Jan. 14 |
| Blaisdell, Frances E. | Palmyra | |
| | | |
| Stevens, Joseph B. | Sebec | Jan 30 |
| Davis, Mrs. Abbie E. | St. Albans | |
| | | |
| Snell, William | St. Albans | Feb. 17 |
| Morrill, Diana | Milford | |
| | | |
| Austin, Daniel | St. Albans | Mar. 5 |
| Beal, Lydia | Lewiston | |

| | | |
|---|---|---|
| Fish, Lewis | Somerset Co. | Mar. 13 |
| Crocker, Sarah Maria | Somerset Co. | |
| Maxim, Sullivan | St. Albans | Mar. 29 |
| Cook, Abigail | St. Albans | |
| Steward, Palmer | St. Albans | Apr. 5 |
| Moore, Eliza A. | St. Albans | |
| Butterfield, John W. | Hartland | Apr. 13 |
| Phelan, Lenna | St. Albans | |
| Watson, Henry | St. Albans | Apr. 21 |
| Russell, Jennie S. | Cambridge | |
| Batchelder, Abram | Waterville | June 12 |
| Farnham, Laura | St. Albans | |
| Horn, William H. | West Gardiner | July 12 |
| Fuller, Sylvia K. | St. Albans | |
| Mitchell, Joseph | Shirley | Aug. 20 |
| Withee, Mary | St. Albans | |
| Maddock, Edison | Farmington | Sep. 13 |
| Smith, Verona V. | St. Albans | |
| Brown, William | Newport | Sep. 18 |
| Bane, Hannah | Newport | |
| Ryerson, Richard D. | St. Albans | Sep. 26 |
| Stevens, Etta | Guilford | |
| Bates, Joseph | St. Albans | Dec. 16 |
| Hale, Georgianna | Vienna | |

# Marriages - 1869

| | | |
|---|---|---|
| Stanchfield, William | Skowhegan | Jan. 23 |
| Stanchfield, Ann | Skowhegan | |
| | | |
| Gould, Ebenezer | Vassalboro | Jan. 28 |
| Swift, Alvira | Vassalboro | |
| | | |
| Dearborn, Simon | St. Albans | Mar. 19 |
| Adams, Pamelia | St. Albans | |
| | | |
| Smith, G.W. | St. Albans | Apr. 8 |
| Hopkins, Sabrina | St. Albans | |
| | | |
| Clough, Charles O. | West Gardiner | July 4 |
| Farnham, A. | St. Albans | |
| | | |
| Irving, Joseph | Hartland | July 20 |
| Sanborn, Etta | Hartland | |
| | | |
| Annis, Morrill | Pittsfield | Aug. 21 |
| Woodbury, Susan | Pittsfield | |
| | | |
| White, Sylvanes R. | St. Albans | Nov. 4 |
| Rines, Julia A. | St. Albans | |
| | | |
| Frost, Ephraim | Palmyra | Nov. 9 |
| Grant, Emily F. | Palmyra | |
| | | |
| Mason, Charles | St. Albans | Dec. 5 |
| Mellows, Aramilla | St. Albans | |

# Intentions - 1870

| | | |
|---|---|---|
| Davis, Samuel | Corinna | Mar. |
| Jackson, Sarah E. | St. Albans | |
| | | |
| Richardson, Stephen F. | Hartland | May 1 |
| Burrill, Loilla | Canaan | |

324

| | | |
|---|---|---|
| Stedman, Vialle | Hartland | June 19 |
| McCauseland, Orilla A. | Hartland | |
| | | |
| Merrill, Jesse | Harmony | July 9 |
| Berry, Ruth | Hartland | |
| | | |
| Gardiner, Hiram | Pittsfield | Aug. 19 |
| Sally, Martha | Palmyra | |
| | | |
| Soule, Charles | Boston | Sep. 21 |
| Merrill, Francis | St. Albans | |
| | | |
| Matthews, J.O. | St. Albans | Oct. 4 |
| Fields, Monica | St. Albans | |
| | | |
| Trafton, Charles C. | St. Albans | Oct. 10 |
| Marston, Franny S. | Skowhegan | |
| | | |
| Forsythe, William | St. Albans | Oct. 11 |
| Steward, Frances E. | St. Albans | |
| | | |
| York, Frank | St. Albans | Oct. 26 |
| Spencer, Ellen | St. Albans | |
| | | |
| Bragg, Volney H. | St. Albans | Dec. 28 |
| Boston, Lydia M. | St. Albans | |
| | | |
| Martin, Charles G. | St. Albans | Dec. 27 |
| Collins, Jennie A. | Bridgewater | |

Intentions - 1871

| | | |
|---|---|---|
| Frost, Aaron | St. Albans | Jan. 10 |
| Boston, Sarah | St. Albans | |
| | | |
| Hubbard, Freeman | St. Albans | Jan. 30 |
| Tripp, Ellen | St. Albans | |

| | | |
|---|---|---|
| Christie, George S. | St. Albans | Feb. 4 |
| Bradford, Jennie S. | St. Albans | |
| | | |
| Lane, Alonzo | St. Albans | Feb. 27 |
| Nevins, R. Bell | Exeter | |
| | | |
| Marsh, Henry E. | St. Albans | Mar. 4 |
| Emerson, Mary O. | Dexter | |
| | | |
| Hines, William S. | St. Albans | Mar. 17 |
| Welch, Maria F. | St. Albans | |
| | | |
| Braley, Edwin | St. Albans | Apr. 22 |
| Foss, Elizabeth | Harmony | |
| | | |
| Buker, Henry E. | St. Albans | Apr. 22 |
| Stevens, Lizzie E. | St. Albans | |
| | | |
| Welch, Delbert G. | | Apr. 24 |
| Hines, Anna | Hartland | |
| | | |
| Chambers, Thomas W. | St. Albans | May 2 |
| Ditson, Ella M. | St. Albans | |
| | | |
| Withee, Llewellyn | St. Albans | May 8 |
| Welch, Flora | St. Albans | |
| | | |
| Emery, Zerah | Ripley | May 15 |
| Cook, Hannah | St. Albans | |
| | | |
| Hunt, Nathan W. | Hartland | May 15 |
| Sleeper, Catherine W. | St. Albans | |
| | | |
| Larrabee, Alonzo H. | St. Albans | May 16 |
| Woodbury, Belle F. | St. Albans | |
| | | |
| Spaulding, Ephraim | Anson | May 20 |
| Mower, Emily | St. Albans | |

326

| | | |
|---|---|---|
| Packard, Edwin S. | St. Albans | June 5 |
| Fowler, Ida | St. Albans | |
| Libby, Edward | St. Albans | June 8 |
| Sampson, Alvina | St. Albans | |
| Stedman, Violla | Hartland | June 19 |
| McCausland, Arilla | Hartland | |
| Magoon, Lindsay H. | St. Albans | June 28 |
| Bates, Elizabeth | St. Albans | |
| Frost, Thomas | St. Albans | |
| Fairbrother, Emma | Palmyra | |
| Gifford, William H. | St. Albans | July 15 |
| McKenney, Susan | St. Albans | |
| Adams, Joseph | St. Albans | July 31 |
| Bradbury, Laura | Philips | |
| Boynton, Charles | St. Albans | Oct. 18 |
| Weymouth, Roxi | St. Albans | |
| Bussell, Melvin | St. Albans | Nov. 13 |
| Sinclair, Hattie | Palmyra | |
| Tuttle, David | Palmyra | Nov. 21 |
| Wing, Mary | St. Albans | |
| Southards, Beldon | St. Albans | Nov. 21 |
| Hartwell, Eliza | St. Albans | |

## Marriages - 1871

| | | |
|---|---|---|
| Richardson, Stephen | Hartland | May 1 |
| Burrell, Loella | Canaan | |
| Goodale, Perley | St. Albans | May 1 |
| Cooley, Hannah | Corinna | |

327

| | | |
|---|---|---|
| Emerson, Elisha | St. Albans | May 27 |
| Tripp, Maria | St. Albans | |
| | | |
| Wood, Cyrus | Stetson | May 27 |
| Cole, Pamelia | St. Albans | |
| | | |
| Merrill, Jessie | Harmony | July 9 |
| Perry, Ruth | Hartland | |

Intentions - 1872

| | | |
|---|---|---|
| Batchelder, George | St. Albans | Jan. 15 |
| Stewert, Jane | St. Albans | |
| | | |
| Bickford, Charles | Greenfield, Mass. | Feb. 19 |
| Magoon, Mary W. | St. Albans | |
| | | |
| Turner, Elmer E. | St. Albans | Apr. 6 |
| Davis, M. E. | St. Albans | |
| | | |
| Cooley, Chalma A. | St. Albans | Apr. 16 |
| Smith, Eva | St. Albans | |
| | | |
| Furber, A. Wilson | St. Albans | May 27 |
| Pettigrove, Ella F. | St. Albans | |
| | | |
| Southards, C.B. | St. Albans | June 3 |
| Marble, Melissa | Brighton | |
| | | |
| Farrar, George | Ripley | June 7 |
| Bigelow, Pamelia | St. Albans | |
| | | |
| Prince, Henry R. | Auburn | June 11 |
| Merrill, Emma | St. Albans | |
| | | |
| Steward, John F. | St. Albans | June 12 |
| Thompson, Sarah | Pittsfield | |
| | | |
| Dore, E. | St. Albans | June 15 |
| Rowe, Hattie | Harmony | |

| | | |
|---|---|---|
| Snell, Ansell | St. Albans | July 14 |
| Cook, Nellie | Palmyra | |
| | | |
| Ellis, Charles O. | St. Albans | Aug. 6 |
| McDonald, Melvina | St. Albans | |
| | | |
| Getchell, Charles B. | St. Albans | Aug. 24 |
| Bigelow, Betsy A. | St. Albans | |
| | | |
| Wing, William | St. Albans | Sep. 23 |
| Cooley, Lanzarah | St. Albans | |
| | | |
| Robinson, Alfred | St. Albans | Oct. 18 |
| Tracy, Mary A. | Lewiston | |
| | | |
| Robinson, Everett | St. Albans | Oct. 21 |
| Frost, Nellie | Hartland | |
| | | |
| Seekins, Charles F. | St. Albans | Nov. 3 |
| Seekins, Lilla D. | Pittsfield | |
| | | |
| Atwood, James B. | St. Albans | Nov. 21 |
| Lord, Abbie F. | Skowhegan | |
| | | |
| Bowman, John | St. Albans | Nov. 28 |
| Fields, Lydia E. | St. Albans | |
| | | |
| Snell, William H. | St. Albans | Dec. 13 |
| Barnum, Amelia A. | St. Albans | |
| | | |
| Boston, Jessie | St. Albans | Dec. 19 |
| Rollins, Julia A. | Abbott | |

## Marriages - 1872

| | | |
|---|---|---|
| Veazie, Labon | Corinna | Jan. 23 |
| Field, Jennie | St. Albans | |
| | | |
| Tracey, Elmore | Pittsfield | Mar. 21 |
| Robertson, Abby | St. Albans | |

| | | |
|---|---|---|
| Buker, Henry | St. Albans | Apr. 27 |
| Stevens, Elizabeth | | |
| | | |
| Wyman, Charles | St. Albans | Oct. 30 |
| Labree, Mary | St. Albans | |
| | | |
| Bowman, John | St. Albans | Dec. 8 |
| Fields, Lydia | St. Albans | |

Intentions - 1873

| | | |
|---|---|---|
| White, Addison | St. Albans | Jan. 2 |
| Goodale, Hannah E. | St. Albans | |
| | | |
| Dyer, Ruel H. | Brighton | Jan. 11 |
| Abbee, Louise M. | St. Albans | |
| | | |
| Lyford, F.O. | St. Albans | Jan. 16 |
| Skinner, E.S. | St. Albans | |
| | | |
| Frost, Nathan | St. Albans | Feb. 26 |
| Grover, Mary A. | St. Albans | |
| | | |
| Ellis, Sidney | St. Albans | Mar. 27 |
| Welch, Paulina | Wellington | |
| | | |
| McFarland, Asa | Cornville | Mar. 31 |
| Abbie, Gracie | St. Albans | |
| | | |
| Ireland, Benjamin | St. Albans | Apr. 14 |
| Maxfield, Sarah | St. Albans | |
| | | |
| Richards, | Ripley | May 12 |
|     Alonzo S. | | |
| Packard, Addie S. | St. Albans | |
| | | |
| Hopkins, George A. | St. Albans | May 16 |
| Jacobs, Ellen | Palmyra | |
| | | |
| Russell, Asa | St. Albans | May 18 |
| Frost, Lizzie | St. Albans | |

| | | |
|---|---|---|
| Powell, Cyrus | St. Albans | July 8 |
| Morrill, Mary | St. Albans | |
| | | |
| Emery, J.D. | St. Albans | June 25 |
| Ryerson, Hattie B. | Palmyra | |
| | | |
| Howes, Charles H. | St. Albans | July 21 |
| Miller, Mary S. | Palmyra | |
| | | |
| Rowe, Sanford | St. Albans | Aug. 12 |
| Youngman, Mary | St. Albans | |
| | | |
| Coffin, Cyrus S. | Stetson | Aug. 29 |
| Braley, Frances D. | St. Albans | |
| | | |
| Millett, Abner | Garland | Sep. 7 |
| Brown, Olive | Sangerville | |
| | | |
| Tracey, Simeon | St. Albans | Oct. 13 |
| Dakin, Abbie W. | Cincinnati, Ohio | |
| | | |
| Rand, William | St. Albans | Oct. 11 |
| Boynton, Vestie J. | St. Albans | |
| | | |
| Turner, Napoleon B | ? | Oct. 28 |
| Henderson, Mary C. | Readfield | |
| | | |
| Parkman, A.B. | St. Albans | Nov. 10 |
| Libby, Betsy E. | St. Albans | |
| | | |
| Turner, John O. | St. Albans | Nov. 24 |
| Goddard, Naomi B. | Winslow | |
| | | |
| Philbrick, H.E. | St. Albans | Nov. 28 |
| Burton, Parintha | Hartland | |
| | | |
| Grant, David N. | St. Albans | Dec. 12 |
| Doe, Sarah E. | St. Albans | |
| | | |
| Field, Llewellyn C | St. Albans | Dec. 18 |
| Page, Cora E. | Corinna | |

| | | |
|---|---|---|
| Reed, Theodore | Wellington | Dec. 25 |
| Frost, Emily | St. Albans | |
| | | |
| Grant, David | St. Albans | Dec. 25 |
| Doe, Sarah | St. Albans | |

## Intentions - 1874

| | | |
|---|---|---|
| Lyford, H.H. | St. Albans | Jan. 29 |
| Rollins, Violette | Dexter | |
| | | |
| Bragg, Anthony | St. Albans | Feb. 18 |
| Smith, Eliza M. | St. Albans | |
| | | |
| Damon, William P. | St. Albans | Mar. 11 |
| Cox, Amanda B. | St. Albans | |
| | | |
| Wilkins, Walter | St. Albans | Apr. 8 |
| Wing, Mary E. | St. Albans | |
| | | |
| Richards, Greenlief | Oregon | Apr. 18 |
| Southards, Caroline | St. Albans | |
| | | |
| Melvin, Amos | Fitchburg, Mass. | Apr. 23 |
| Bradford, Mary S. | St. Albans | |
| | | |
| Maguire, A. | Bridgton | Apr. 23 |
| Pettigrove, Sarah J. | St. Albans | |
| | | |
| Folsom, Joseph P. | Palmyra | May 12 |
| Gifford, Emma H. | St. Albans | |
| | | |
| Parker, Horace N. | Ripley | June 1 |
| Grant, Annie S. | St. Albans | |
| | | |
| Hilton, John | St. Albans | June 24 |
| Spencer, Hannah | St. Albans | |

| | | |
|---|---|---|
| Fisher, Fred W. | Dexter | June 30 |
| Moody, Percia | St. Albans | |
| | | |
| Moore, John | St. Albans | July 25 |
| McNally, Lizzie | Baring | |
| | | |
| Woodbury, Henry S. | Skowhegan | Aug. 24 |
| Hanson, Sarah E. | St. Albans | |
| | | |
| Gray, James H. | Barrington, NH | Sep. 10 |
| Jones, Ida M. | St. Albans | |
| | | |
| Burrill, J.S. | Corinna | Nov. 30 |
| Rowe, Mary M. | St. Albans | |

## Intentions - 1875

| | | |
|---|---|---|
| Mitchell, Benson | Shirley | Jan. 3 |
| Withee, Mira | St. Albans | |
| | | |
| Holway, Charles F. | Palmyra | Mar. 24 |
| Berry, Mary E. | St. Albans | |
| | | |
| Leadbetter, James W. | St. Albans | Apr. 19 |
| Martin, Flora | St. Albans | |
| | | |
| Pennell, Frank P. | St. Albans | Apr. 24 |
| Hurd, Emma | Harmony | |
| | | |
| Small, James W. | Bath | Apr. 28 |
| Cyphers, Maria E. | St. Albans | |
| | | |
| Holway, Anson C. | St. Albans | Apr. 30 |
| Haskell, Martha E. | Garland | |
| | | |
| Bell, William | Portland | May 5 |
| Lothrop, Aretta | St. Albans | |
| | | |
| Shean, Lester W. | St. Albans | May 12 |
| Davis, Eva | Palmyra | |

| | | |
|---|---|---|
| Goodwin, G.H. | St. Albans | May 29 |
| Turner, Myrtie S. | St. Albans | |
| | | |
| Ellis, Charles O. | St. Albans | June 16 |
| Morgan, Mary | Dexter | |
| | | |
| Cooley, Charles F. | St. Albans | June 17 |
| Holbrook, Carrie E. | Newport | |
| | | |
| Goodell, Joseph E. | Monson | Aug. 5 |
| Weeks, Martha J. | St. Albans | |
| | | |
| Lincoln, Israel W. | Harmony | Aug. 19 |
| Chase, Mary E. | St. Albans | |
| | | |
| Goodwin, George F. | St. Albans | Sep. 6 |
| Murray, Mary | St. Albans | |
| | | |
| Southards, Frank E. | Charleston, Massachusetts | Sep. 8 |
| Morse, Abbie | St. Albans | |
| | | |
| Hurd, Iva | Harmony | Oct. 4 |
| Merriman, Hannah | St. Albans | |
| | | |
| Litchfield, Vinson | Hartland | Oct. 6 |
| Rogers, Rosena | St. Albans | |
| | | |
| Moody, Freeman | St. Albans | Oct 13 |
| Maxfield, Laura | St. Albans | |
| | | |
| Genthner, Daniel E. | Dover | Oct. 16 |
| Robinson, Lorinda S. | St. Albans | |
| | | |
| Peakes, Alfred W. | St. Albans | Oct. 22 |
| Merryman, Martha M. | St. Albans | |
| | | |
| Bigelow, James E. | St. Albans | Nov. 22 |
| Maxwell, Ella | St. Albans | |

| | | |
|---|---|---|
| Gifford, Walter | St. Albans | Dec. 5 |
| Prescott,<br>    Mrs. Eliza | Skowhegan | |
| | | |
| Parkman, Noah | Dexter | Dec. 22 |
| Parkman, Nancy A. | St. Albans | |

Marriages - 1875

| | | |
|---|---|---|
| Mitchell,<br>    Benson J. | Shirley | Jan. 3 |
| Withee, Marie E. | St. Albans | |
| Hilton, John | St. Albans | Jan. 13 |
| Skinner, Hannah | St. Albans | |
| Vining, J. Cushman | St. Albans | Jan. 31 |
| Whittemore, Ella | Dexter | |
| Frost, Holman J. | St. Albans | Mar. 4 |
| Welch, Lydia A. | St. Albans | |
| Currier, Judson | Garland | Mar. 11 |
| Woodbury,<br>    Nellie A. | St. Albans | |
| Hamilton, Mark | Corinna | Mar. 15 |
| Titcomb, Genie E. | Corinna | |
| Holway, Charles | Palmyra | Apr. 5 |
| Berry, May | St. Albans | |
| Small, James W. | Bath | Apr. 24 |
| Cyphers, Maria | St. Albans | |
| Leadbetter, James | St. Albans | Apr. 25 |
| Martin, Flora | Hartland | |
| Bell, William | Cape<br>Elizabeth | May 13 |
| Chase, Mrs. Aretta<br>    Lothrop | St. Albans | |

335

| | | |
|---|---|---|
| Goodwin, Charles | St. Albans | June 5 |
| Turner, Myrtie L. | St. Albans | |
| | | |
| Southards, Leander | St. Albans | June 8 |
| Packard, Hattie F. | St. Albans | |
| | | |
| Nichols, Julian | St. Albans | June 12 |
| Ellis, Melvina | St. Albans | |
| | | |
| Southards, Warren A. | St. Albans | June 12 |
| Rogers, Roxy E. | Ripley | |
| | | |
| Kimball, William H. | St. Albans | June 16 |
| Hines, Lucinda | Hartland | |
| | | |
| Taylor, Abeline | St. Albans | June 19 |
| Spooner, Ellen | St. Albans | |
| | | |
| Larrabee, Joseph | Augusta | July 1 |
| Frost, Annie M. | Augusta | |
| | | |
| Smith, Joseph D. | St. Albans | July 20 |
| Jewett, Lydia J. | Ripley | |
| | | |
| Ellis, Nathan | St. Albans | Aug. 9 |
| Frost, Priscilla | Monson | |
| | | |
| Boston, Jesse S. | | Aug. 22 |
| Frost, Lydia | St. Albans | |
| | | |
| Trafton, William | St. Albans | Aug. 28 |
| Marston, Evelyn B. | Skowhegan | |
| | | |
| Goodwin, George | St. Albans | Sep. 12 |
| Murray, Mary | St. Albans | |
| | | |
| Spencer, Charles | Lewiston | Sep. 16 |
| Dearborn, Rosanna | Corinna | |

| | | |
|---|---|---|
| Blanchard,<br>    R. Albert<br>Abbie, Flora O. | Corinna<br><br>St. Albans | Sep. 22 |
| Pettigrove,<br>    William<br>Tilton, Pamela | St. Albans<br><br>Canaan | Oct. 21 |
| Seekins,<br>    Herbert L.<br>Brown, Julia | Hartland<br><br>St. Albans | Oct. 30 |
| Bigelow, John G.<br>Smith, Lucy | St. Albans<br>Hollis | Nov. |
| Nichols, George F.<br>Remick, Ann | St. Albans<br>St. Albans | Nov. 13 |
| Litchfield, Vinson<br>Rogers, Rosena | Hartland | Nov. 19 |
| Bradford,<br>    Albert S.<br>Murray, Fannie S. | St. Albans<br><br>St. Albans | Dec. 4 |
| Bigelow, W.A.<br>Thompson, A.L. | St. Albans<br>St. Albans | Dec. 8 |
| Parkman, Rev. Noah<br>Parkman, Nancy | Dexter<br>St. Albans | Dec. 25 |

Intentions - 1876

| | | |
|---|---|---|
| Vining, J. Cushman<br>Whittemore, Ella | St. Albans<br>Dexter | Jan. 31 |
| Currier, Judson W.<br>Woodbury, Nellie | Garland<br>St. Albans | Mar. 11 |
| Kimball,<br>    William H.<br>Hines, Lucinda | St. Albans<br><br>Hartland | June 16 |

| | | |
|---|---|---|
| Nichols, Julian | St. Albans | June 12 |
| Ellis, Melvira | St. Albans | |
| | | |
| Southards, Warren A. | St. Albans | June 12 |
| Rogers, Roxy E. | Ripley | |
| | | |
| Smith, Joseph | St. Albans | July 20 |
| Jewett, Lydia | Ripley | |
| | | |
| Ellis, Nathan | St. Albans | Aug. 9 |
| Frost, Pricilla | Monson | |
| | | |
| Boston, Jessie S. | St. Albans | Aug. 22 |
| Frost, Lydia | St. Albans | |
| | | |
| Blanchard, R. Albert | Corinna | Sep. 22 |
| Abbie, Flora | St. Albans | |
| | | |
| Nichols, George | St. Albans | Nov. 13 |
| Remick, Ann | St. Albans | |
| | | |
| Bigelow, George | St. Albans | Nov. 18 |
| Smith, Lucy | St. Albans | |

## Marriages - 1876

| | | |
|---|---|---|
| Frost, Holman | St. Albans | Mar. 13 |
| Welch, Lydia | St. Albans | |
| | | |
| Litchfield, Vinson | St. Albans | Mar. 31 |
| Rogers, Rosanna | St. Albans | |
| | | |
| Spofford, Warren | Bingham | Apr. 12 |
| Freeborn, Eldora | St. Albans | |
| | | |
| Nutter, Eben | Dexter | May 4 |
| Treat, Myra | Frankfort County | |

| | | |
|---|---|---|
| Seekins, Stephen | Pittsfield | May 25 |
| Chase, Susie W. | St. Albans | |
| | | |
| Lucus, Charles | Palmyra | May 27 |
| Ross, Eva | Levant | |
| | | |
| Southards, Leander | Pittsfield | June 16 |
| Packard, Hattie | Hartland | |
| | | |
| Burton, Laforest | Pittsfield | July 8 |
| Woobury, Crissie | Woodbury | |
| | | |
| Spencer, Charles | Lewiston | Sep. 16 |
| Dearborn, Rosanna | Corinna | |
| | | |
| Seekins, Herbert | Hartland | Nov. 4 |
| Brown, Julia | St. Albans | |
| | | |
| Hanson, Frank | Ripley | Dec. 20 |
| Adams, Nancy | | |
| | | |
| Bigelow, W.A. | St. Albans | Dec. 8 |
| Thompson, P.L. | St. Albans | |
| | | |
| Bradford, Albert | St. Albans | Dec. 24 |
| Murray, Fannie | St. Albans | |
| | | |
| Nichols, Theodore | St. Albans | Dec. 25 |
| Goodale, Etta | St. Albans | |

## Marriages - 1877

| | | |
|---|---|---|
| Briggs, Mellen T. | Hartland | Jan. 1 |
| Starbird, Isadora S. | Hartland | |
| | | |
| Libby, Preston | St. Albans | Jan. 11 |
| Knights, Violette E. | St. Albans | |
| | | |
| Corson, Ansel Y. | Brighton | Jan. 12 |
| Tuttle, Julia | Brighton | |

| | | |
|---|---|---|
| White, Sylvanus R. | St. Albans | Jan. 26 |
| Debeck, Lucy | Clifton | |
| | | |
| Buker, Albion | St. Albans | Feb. 3 |
| Turner, Alice | St. Albans | |
| | | |
| White, Frank | St. Albans | Feb. 28 |
| Palmer, Flora | St. Albans | |
| | | |
| Daggett, Nathan | Dexter | Mar. 31 |
| Welch, Charlotte | St. Albans | |
| | | |
| Locke, A.F. | Hartland | Apr. 5 |
| Webb, Lizzie | Hartland | |
| | | |
| Boothby, I. | Athens | Apr. 19 |
| Spooner, Ida | St. Albans | |
| | | |
| Footman, James | St. Albans | Apr. 23 |
| Walker, Jennie | Newport | |
| | | |
| Welch, Joseph | St. Albans | May 1 |
| Braley, Clara | St. Albans | |
| | | |
| Cook, Sprague H. | St. Albans | June 26 |
| Berry, Arlene | St. Albans | |
| | | |
| Spencer, George E. | St. Albans | July 3 |
| Footman, Mrs. Sarah | St. Albans | |
| | | |
| Mitchell, Henry W. | Shirley | July 24 |
| Shorey, Olive | | |
| | | |
| Judkins, L.W. | St. Albans | Aug. 23 |
| Packard, Alice | St. Albans | |
| | | |
| Hanson, Charles | St. Albans | Sep. 19 |
| Frost, Mrs. Patience | St. Albans | |
| | | |
| Ham, Sylvester | Hartland | Sep. 22 |
| Jones, Ida E. | St. Albans | |

| | | |
|---|---|---|
| Batchelder, Frank | St. Albans | Oct. 10 |
| Webber, Lydia | St. Albans | |
| | | |
| Cypher, George | Ripley | Oct. 12 |
| Marsh, Eva | Ripley | |

## Marriages - 1878

| | | |
|---|---|---|
| York, Charles | Athens | Feb. 27 |
| Starbird, Alice | Harmony | |
| | | |
| Vining, George W. | St. Albans | Mar. 16 |
| Lucas, Mary | St. Albans | |
| | | |
| Martin, George L. | St. Albans | Apr. 13 |
| Miller, Annette D. | St. Albans | |
| | | |
| Spaulding, John | Madison | Apr. 19 |
| Clark, Eunice | St. Albans | |
| | | |
| Sampson, Alden | Hartland | June 26 |
| Leathers, Sarah R. | Hartland | |
| | | |
| Parkman, Seldon A. | Palmyra | July 4 |
| Jones, Nellie F. | St. Albans | |
| | | |
| Parker, John | St. Albans | Sep. 2 |
| Hanson, Ruth | St. Albans | |
| | | |
| Whitney, George | Lewiston | Sep. 4 |
| Maxim, Florilla E. | Lewiston | |
| | | |
| Dorr, Thomas | St. Albans | Sep. 17 |
| Packard, Dora E. | St. Albans | |
| | | |
| Buker, E.A. | St. Albans | Sep. 18 |
| Pooler, Lena E. | Palmyra | |
| | | |
| Libby, Albion R. | St. Albans | Sep. 13 |
| Lancaster, Estelle | St. Albans | |

| | | |
|---|---|---|
| Parker, John | St. Albans | Sep. 7 |
| Hanson, Ruth | St. Albans | |
| | | |
| Wing, Henry | St. Albans | Oct. 14 |
| Goodale, Hattie | St. Albans | |
| | | |
| Nutter, Fred | St. Albans | Nov. 21 |
| Sampson, Cora | Ripley | |
| | | |
| Stickney,<br>    Sylvanus G. | Newport | Nov. 21 |
| Lancaster, Susie | St. Albans | |
| | | |
| Whitman, Orson | Palmyra | Dec. 28 |
| Wright, Hattie | Palmyra | |

## Marriages - 1879

| | | |
|---|---|---|
| Colby, George | Vassalboro | Jan. 6 |
| Damon, Bina | St. Albans | |
| | | |
| Jones, Charles | Ripley | Jan. 28 |
| Lucas, Hannah | St. Albans | |
| | | |
| Bartlett, Frank | Harmony | Mar. 9 |
| Chase, Ada B. | St. Albans | |
| | | |
| Lincoln, Israel W. | Harmony | Mar. 9 |
| Brown, Alice | St. Albans | |
| | | |
| Brown, Charles S. | St. Albans | Apr. 17 |
| Blaisdell, Estella | Palmyra | |
| | | |
| Foster, Charles | St. Albans | June 2 |
| Moore, Ardella A. | St. Albans | |
| | | |
| Avery, Wilbra | St. Albans | June 12 |
| Hight, Lizzie F. | Harmony | |
| | | |
| Steward, Asa | St. Albans | July 3 |
| Wood, Anna J. | St. Albans | |

| | | |
|---|---|---|
| Holmes, Winslow B. | St. Albans | June 25 |
| Crocker, Amanda D. | St. Albans | |
| | | |
| Libby, Albion K. | St. Albans | Aug. 28 |
| Lancaster, Estella M. | St. Albans | |
| | | |
| Ayers, Frank W. | Montville | Nov. 8 |
| Bradford, Nettie | St. Albans | |
| | | |
| Bradford, George W. | St. Albans | Nov. 8 |
| Libby, Geneva M. | Newport | |
| | | |
| Devereaux, James | St. Albans | Dec. 20 |
| Tripp, Mary | St. Albans | |
| | | |
| Bigelow, William A. | St. Albans | Dec. 25 |
| Thompson, Mrs. A.L. | New York City New York | |

## Marriages- 1880

| | | |
|---|---|---|
| Turner, Gilbert | St. Albans | Aug. 2 |
| Goodwin, Emma | St. Albans | |
| | | |
| Buker, E.A. | St. Albans | Sep. 8 |
| Moody, Ella L. | St. Albans | |
| | | |
| Fields, George W. | Dexter | Sep 12 |
| Hovey, Emma | Dexter | |
| | | |
| Rogers, Lewellyn | St. Albans | Sep. 19 |
| Luce, Florilla | St. Albans | |
| | | |
| Gilpatrick, Thomas | Weston | Sep. 26 |
| Merrick, S. | St. Albans | |
| | | |
| Bates, George | St. Albans | Oct. 2 |
| Wiggins, Luella | St. Albans | |

# Marriages - 1881

| | | |
|---|---|---|
| Grant, John W. | St. Albans | Jan. 9 |
| Haskell, Mary E. | Dexter | |
| | | |
| Martin, James S. | St. Albans | Feb. 26 |
| Ryerson, Angie H. | St. Albans | |
| | | |
| Stanley, Orren E. | Winthrop | Mar. 23 |
| Rowe, Flora | St. Albans | |
| | | |
| Sanborn, O. | St. Albans | Mar. 23 |
| Rowe, Flora | St. Albans | |
| | | |
| Mower, Edwin E. | St. Albans | June 5 |
| Robertson, Nettie | St. Albans | |
| | | |
| Young, Charles Y. | Old Town | Nov. 29 |
| Nickerson, Nettie | Dexter | |
| | | |
| Dondero, Charles G. | Augusta | Dec. 18 |
| Richard, Jennette | St. Albans | |
| | | |
| Boynton, Charles S. | Ripley | Dec. 18 |
| Rand, Sarah R. | Ripley | |
| | | |
| Reynolds, Alonzo | St. Albans | Dec. 19 |
| Reynolds, Mary | St. Albans | |

# Marriages - 1882

| | | |
|---|---|---|
| Emery, Peter | St. Albans | Apr. 8 |
| Parker, Etta | St. Albans | |
| | | |
| Rowe, Perley | St. Albans | Apr. 20 |
| Damon, Myra | Carroll | |
| | | |
| Katon, Wilson W. | St. Albans | May 6 |
| Gee, Flora A. | St. Albans | |

344

| | | |
|---|---|---|
| Wright, George H. | St. Albans | July 9 |
| Parkhurst, Mary | St. Albans | |
| | | |
| Stewart, Asa | St. Albans | July 3 |
| Wood, Ann | Hartland | |
| | | |
| Campbell, Fred | St. Albans | Sep. 10 |
| Berry, Nettie E. | St. Albans | |
| | | |
| Fields, Nathaniel M. | St. Albans | Sep. 30 |
| Brown, Nettie M. | St. Albans | |
| | | |
| Bragg, Stephen | St. Albans | Oct. 18 |
| Ross, Carrie | St. Albans | |
| | | |
| Emery, Darius | St. Albans | Nov. 5 |
| LaBree, Ann M. | St. Albans | |
| | | |
| Thurston, George | Corinna | Dec. 4 |
| Winchester, Alice | Corinna | |
| | | |
| Smith, Robert S. | St. Albans | Dec. 25 |
| Spencer, Martha | St. Albans | |

## Marriages - 1883

| | | |
|---|---|---|
| Waldron, Charles | Corinna | Jan. 13 |
| Moore, Hattie | St. Albans | |
| | | |
| Bigelow, Melvin | St. Albans | Mar. 1 |
| Buker, Clara | St. Albans | |
| | | |
| Robertson, Osgood | St. Albans | Mar. 4 |
| Varney, Rose | St. Albans | |
| | | |
| Stedman, William A. | Waterville | Apr. 1 |
| McCrillis, Emma B. | Palmyra | |
| | | |
| Prescott, Henry C. | St. Albans | Apr. 15 |
| Emery, Anna E. | St. Albans | |

| | | |
|---|---|---|
| Parkman, George A. | St. Albans | Apr. 29 |
| Mills, Myra | Corinna | |
| | | |
| Thompson, Charles | St. Albans | May 9 |
| Berry, Lizzie | St. Albans | |
| | | |
| Leach, Charles A. | St. Albans | May 27 |
| Packard, Mabel | St. Albans | |
| | | |
| Ray, George W. | St. Albans | Aug. 4 |
| Gross, Anna A. | Hartland | |
| | | |
| Crawford, Ruel W. | St. Albans | Sep. 6 |
| Dority, A.H. | Skowhegan | |
| | | |
| Costello, Fred H. | Bangor | Sep. 13 |
| Lyford, Cora F. | St. Albans | |
| | | |
| Homestead, Timothy | Palmyra | Sep. 17 |
| Grant, Carrie | St. Albans | |
| | | |
| Crocker,Eleazor G. | St. Albans | Nov. 8 |
| Cole, Christina R. | St. Albans | |
| | | |
| Libby, John W. | St. Albans | Nov. 14 |
| Varney, Hannah H. | St. Albans | |

## Marriages - 1884

| | | |
|---|---|---|
| Smith, Theodore W. | St. Albans | Jan. 3 |
| Ross, Nina B. | St. Albans | |
| | | |
| Parker, John | St. Albans | Jan. 20 |
| Brown, Jennie | St. Albans | |
| | | |
| Powers, John C.F. | Pittsfield | Mar. 25 |
| Nelson, Blanche G. | Canaan | |
| | | |
| Prescott, Stephen | St. Albans | June 12 |
| Emery, Bessie | St. Albans | |

| | | |
|---|---|---|
| Snell, William H. | St. Albans | July 21 |
| Cooper, Mrs. Susan M. | Orrington | |
| | | |
| Wilson, Alphonso G. | Pittsfield | Aug. 25 |
| Brackett, Jennie | Hartland | |
| | | |
| Bartlett, Eddie C. | Winterport | Oct. 18 |
| Brown, Abbie T. | St. Albans | |
| | | |
| Folsom, Elmer G. | Cambridge | Dec. 31 |
| Watson, Abbie S. | Ripley | |

## Marriages - 1885

| | | |
|---|---|---|
| Grant, David | St. Albans | May 27 |
| Christie, Annie | | |
| | | |
| Abbott, George L. | East New Portland | June 6 |
| Spaulding, Anna B. | St. Albans | |
| | | |
| Buker, Frank E. | St. Albans | Oct. 10 |
| Bates, Lizzie R. | Harmony | |
| | | |
| Martin, Fred | St. Albans | Dec. 6 |
| Foss, Della | St. Albans | |

## Marriages - 1887

| | | |
|---|---|---|
| Hilton, Walter | St. Albans | Jan. 1 |
| Smith, Bertha | St. Albans | |
| | | |
| Soule, George | Hartland | May 4 |
| Nay, Natalie A. | St. Albans | |
| | | |
| Turner, Fred | Auburn | Sep. 22 |
| Chalmers, Mary F. | Auburn | |

| | | |
|---|---|---|
| Farnham, Simon | St. Albans | Nov. 3 |
| Lucas, Charlotte | St. Albans | |
| | | |
| Winchester, John Howard | Corinna | Dec. 4 |
| Dole, Sadie B. | Exeter | |
| | | |
| Thurston, George | Corinna | Dec. 4 |
| Winchester, Alice | Corinna | |
| | | |
| Hackett, John | Carmel | Dec. 9 |
| Gordon, Rose | St. Albans | |

## Marriages - 1888

| | | |
|---|---|---|
| Brown, James | Hartland | Mar. 9 |
| Hanson, Emma | St. Albans | |

## Marriages - 1896

Hussey, Fred E.
Martin, Melda J.

Worthen, Claradon
Burton,
    Mrs. Emma A.

Moore, William H.
Farnham, Mrs.
    Allen L.

Cyphers,
    Herbert E.
Laughton,
    Mrs. Myra B.

Emery, George
Braley, Evelyn

Kinney, Charles
Moore, Annie B.

Osborn, Wallace
Lombard, Ethel

Ross, Charles N.
Nichols, Nina

Martin, S.J.
Parkman, Nellie

Richards,
     Nathan W.
Johnson,
     Lillian V.

Knowles, Elbert
Lyford, Florence

Wheeler, George
Emery, Nina M.


Marriages - 1897

Day, Albert G.
Kincaid, Grace L.

Emery, Charles F.
Turner, Addie A.

Frost, W.J.
Marsh, Grace

Snell, William N.
Lyford, Vestie L.

Wood, Edward E.
Brown, Blance

Bane, Jepha J.
Ross, Mary A.

Whittier, H.L.
Quimby, Carrie E.

Rollins, Otis T.
Boston, Della


Marriages - 1898

Hope, Theodore P.
Robertson, Bertha

Hilton, Harry J.
Williams, Vesta M.

Russell,
     Charles W.
Pingree, Celia A.

Welch, Joseph N.
Gray, Bertha B.

Hatch, Elbridge C.
Emery, Lulu F.

Bryant, Frank E.
Cooley, Grace

Bigelow,
     William A.
Galerson, Mary E.

Bragg, Volney H.
Packard, Bertha


Marriages - 1899/1900

Brooks, Foster
Miller, Martha A.

Carle, A.A.
Miller, Lydia L.

Stevens, A.A.
Abbott, Mary R.

Frost, Leamond
Strickland,
      Lena M.

Parkman, Jeddie A.
Wheeler, Bertha S.

Merrill, Eugene
Faince, Annie L.

Holt, Albion A.
Philbrick, Effie

Seekins,
      Gilbert G.
Page, Alice

Brown, W.M.
Eldridge, Sadie

Steward,
      Charles A.
Tracy, Mary J.

Chandler, David A.
Wood, Betsy J.

Sedgwick, J.F.
Magoon, Lorena


Marriages - 1902/1903

Munn, James R.
Denning, Edith A.

Braley, Calvin
Perkins, Ida May

Schoff, Lee Forest
Cooley, Alma S.

Bragg, Theodore
Martin, Ada E.

Chisholm,
    Hugh Daniel
Vining,
    Florence R.

Clark, Clarence
Rowe, Myrtie

Clark, Vernie
Frost, Flora M.

Emerson,
    Densmore S.
Blaisdell,
    Harriett M.

Parkman, Frank L.
Rowe, Sarah Edith

Philbrick,
    William S.
Dore, Eva M.

Marriages - 1903/1904

Deveraux, James L.
Lawrence, Elsie

Field, Elmer E.
Farnham, Florence

Cooley, Wilbur A.
Chambers, Nora M.

Davis, Elmer
Eldridge, Lyllis

Nickerson, Almon
Nichols, Clara E.

Taylor,
     Albiatha B.
Matthews, Nina

Parker, Wallace E.
Taylor, Caddie E.

Brooks, Abner
Ricker, S. Melissa

Merrill, Henry
Dow, Camelia M.

Weeks, John M.
Wilkins, Ethel S.


              Marriages - 1904/1905

Dodge, Walter R.
Wilkins, Jessie

Martin, James S.
Furbush, Luella E.

Whitney,
     Herbert L.
Ames, Sarah E.

Field, Ernest L.
Herrin, Bessie A.

Stanley, B.F.
Atwood, Hannah A.


              Marriages - 1905/1906

Martin, Allen L.
Webber, Gertie
     Ireland

Webber, Perly
Wheeler, Else J.

Bragg, William A.
Woodward, Ethel

Weeks, Earle
Farrar, Etta

Jackson, Fred E.
Brooks, Bell H.

Cool, Charles F.
Hartwell, Burle

Fernald, Freeman
Henderson, Naoma

Abbott, Ernest L.
Brown, Ida M.

Snell, H.B.
Patterson, Lois E.

Elbridge, Allie
Southard, Frances

Worth, Willis
Matthews, Mabel M.

Dore, Joseph A.
Verrill, Alfreda


Marriages - 1906/1907

Field, Chester
Dearborn, Lois

Leo, Joseph
Nutter, Helen

Stevens, Ray
Porter,
     Bertha M.

Braley, Frank
Miller, Carrie S.

Emery, Carrol
Field, Inez

Webb, R. Weston
Willis, Iona May

Badger, Earle E.
Stevens, Hattie E.

Ray, Lester B.
Eldridge,
     Myrtle E.

Crocker,
     Wadsworth
Hadley, Emma M.

Tracey, Carol
Davis, Grace

Steen, Harold
Bragg, Annie

Berry, Wilber
Curtis, Katherine

Weeks, Wilbur M.
Brown, Carrie G.

Herrick, Samuel
Denning, Etta I.

Marriages - 1907/1908

Sanborn, Willie
Sanborn, Lena

355

Harris, Thomas J.
Hubbard, Emma E.

Crocker, Joseph E.
Leavitt, Edna L.

Mower, Charles E.
Libby, H. Ada

Jordon, Victor B.
Libby, Eva C.

Field, Oral C.
Frost, Alice F.

Libby, Chester E.
Emery, Susie E.

Philbrick,
     Ralph W.
Goodwin, Winifred

Prescott, Henry A.
Libby, Edna C.

Springer, Wesley
Stevens, Eva S.

Vining, Frank N.
Hanson, Carrie B.

Raymond, Ernest M.
Marsh, Ella M.

Herring,
     Oramandal L.
Cooley, Winnie M.

Hanson, Frank C.
Burdin, Hattie P.

Marriages - 1908/1909

Nichols, Jessie
Fields, Belle

Braley, David
Chase, Margaret E.

Fish, Albert
Foss, M.E.

Nutter, Harry M.
Ireland, Edna M.

Varney, Horace E.
Carson, Etta M.

Craig, Frederick
Wright, Eliza J.

Allen, Charles A.
Kimball, Lilian M.

Munn, Walter
Nichols, Vivian V.

Elliot, George F.
Ireland,
     Florence M.

Gray, Bennie
Pingree, Mary

Eldercan, Oscar
Parker, Ola B.

Buzzell, Harry E.
Pomroy, Blanche

Miller,
     Benjamin I.
Seekins, Ada M.

Mebane, William L.
Butler, Lena M.

Hanson, Arthur G.
Wilkins, Florence

Burrill,
     Charles S.
Carson, Bertha A.


Marriages - 1910/1911

Morrison, Allie E.
Brown, Lizzie

Ireland, Lyman D.
Nutter, Bertha G.

Burton, Edward T.
Goodwin,
     Caroline E.

Woodcock,
     Milton T.
Peakes, Lois

Bailey, William G.
Bragg, Helen L.

Curtis, Frank
Dow, Bessie

Blaisdell,
     William E.
Lucas, Flora M.

Coolidge, Paul
Thompson, Ina

Cole, Oreal C.
Stone, Lizzie M.

Buker, Earle
Page, Ethel

Frost, Wesley
Vicnarie, Vina

Craig, William
Badger, Flora


Marriages - 1911/1912

Givin, Alfonzo S.
Nichols, Ella

Emery, Alton Z.
Libby, Grace M.

Libby, Seldon
Wright, Gladys

Fellows, Samuel J.
Hilton, Sadie B.

Withee, Irvin S.
Hall, Mertie

McCrillis, Ivan W.
Leadbetter,
     Carrie A.

Merrow, Alton L.
Packard, Erma B.

Williams, Leo E.
Pratt, Eva

Seekins, Walter
Harding, Mollie M.

James, Warren W.
Laughton, Ethel V.

Robinson,
     Harold C.
Flint, Mary E.

Vicnaire, Peter
Dodge, Louisa


          Marriages - 1912/1913
             (From Feb. 20)

Wilkins, Walter H.
Hersom, Jennie
     Howe

Leavitt,
     Clarence W.
Barker, Daisy M.

Noble, Riley
Withee, Laura

Avery, Bernard
Grant, Gladys S.

Field, Oral C.
Spencer, Leah M.

Robertson,
     Clarence
Prescott,
     Alzada C.

Robinson,
     Adrain C.
Hoyt, Louise A.

Clukey, Henry
Parker, Ina May

Pratt, Ralph
Grant, Florence

Baird, Harold E.
Bennett, Etta

Libby, Alton L.
Stone, Marilla

Crocker, George C.
Libby, Laura Belle

McFarland, William
Ferguson, Etta

Grover,
     Eldridge W.
Phinney, Grace E.


Marriages - 1913/1914

Baird, Arthur A.
Carey, Alice B.

Robertson,
     Irvin O.
Badger, Mabel M.

Willey, John
Stewart, Gladys E.

Brown, Frank E.
Clark, Lenora M.

Parker, Erwin S.
McDonald,
     Eunice L.

Cook, W.B.
Spaulding, Lydia

Emery, Oral T.
Emery, Bernice N.

Bickford,
    Justin O.
Buker, Beryl W.

Libby, Joseph H.
Knight, Rose E.

McDonald, Charles
Parker, Una Maud

Merrow,
    Clifford L.
Emery, Stella May

Southard, Daniel
Buzzell, Cora


Marriages - Feb. 20, 1914/Feb. 20, 1915

Nichols, Ralph                    Mar. 21
Patterson,
    Jennie May

Merchant,                         May 2
    Oscar Ray
Millett, Annie C.

Whtiney, Halver H.                June 7
Linnell, Winnie

Parkman, Earle B.                 July 4
Hart, Violet

Sturtevant,                       July 5
    Leroy V.
Lewis, Grace May

Parker, Archie D.                 Oct. 3
Goundry,
    Phyllis H.

| | |
|---|---|
| Nichols, Robert E.<br>Ross, Elva Blanche | Oct. 5 |
| Parkman,<br>    Herbert L.<br>Deveraux, Ethel | Oct. 21 |
| Allen, Clarence E.<br>Holt, Addie R. | Oct. 28 |
| Tracy, Albert E.<br>Burgess, Rose L. | Nov. 26 |
| Lampher, Levi W.<br>Mitchell, Mattie | Nov. 26 |
| Waldron,<br>    Lawrence E.<br>Boynton, Ethel May | Dec. 20 |
| Carr, George F.<br>Newcomb, Iva Mary | Dec. 24 |
| Larrabee, Fred J.<br>Lawrence, Mabel | Jan. 27 |
| Smith, Theodore W.<br>Sturtevant,<br>    Hattie J. | Feb. 10 |

Marriages - Feb. 1915/Feb. 20, 1916

| | |
|---|---|
| Grant, Merle G.<br>Parker, Lida Mae | Apr. 24 |
| Hussey, Irving<br>Conroy, Beatrice | May 8 |
| Martin, Robert<br>Cottrill, Annie J. | June 6 |

| | |
|---|---|
| Foster, John<br>Cole, Letha Elvira | June 13 |
| Lancaster, Everett<br>Buzzell, Georgia | July 1 |
| Tobie, Walter<br>Nelson, Clara | Aug. 13 |
| Bell, Harold R.<br>Baird, Ethel May | Aug. 15 |
| Wilkins, Clifford<br>Stevens, Clara | Sep. 18 |
| Weymouth,<br>    Bernard C.<br>Gardiner, Lottie    Cornville | Oct. 12 |
| Mills, Wesley<br>    Horace<br>Batchelder, Zina<br>    Agnes | Nov. 6 |
| Hanson, Glen H.<br>Emery, Vera Mae | Nov. 24 |
| Hanson, Ralph<br>Parkman, Bessie E. | Nov. 24 |
| Nutter, Linwood G.<br>Sinclair, Victoria | Jan. 15 |

## Marriages - 1916/1917

| | |
|---|---|
| Piper, Ervin<br>Welch, Addie | Apr. 8 |
| Tracy, Lorin<br>Torsey, Sarah | Apr. 12 |

| | |
|---|---|
| Martin, Earl F.<br>Ireland, Gertrude<br>    Mae | May 3 |
| Robertson, Earl E.<br>Finson, Ruth Ellen | June 9 |
| Hanson, Stanley<br>Merchant, Dora G. | June 18 |
| Libby, Harry R.<br>Merrick, Leta H. | June 21 |
| Merrick, Frederick<br>Mitler, Josephine | Aug. 2 |
| Wing, Harold<br>Wing, Jessie | Sep. 18 |
| Parker, Erwin S.<br>Bragg, Lillian | Oct. 29 |
| Hamilton, Damon<br>Bryant, Velmar | Nov. 3 |
| Linnell, William<br>Butwell, L. | Nov. 29 |
| Emery, Charles F.<br>Beverage, Elsie | Nov. 30 |
| Emery, Ernest L.<br>Lufkin, Lillian | Nov. 20 |
| Bonney, Edwin A.<br>Fuller, Mabel | Jan. 24 |
| Sampson, Ralph<br>Bowker, Grace E. | Feb. 22 |

# Marriages - 1917

| | |
|---|---|
| Tracey, Alton<br>Witham, Carrie I. | Mar. 19 |
| Densmore, Harry<br>Reynolds, Audrey | Mar. 24 |
| Gross, Walter<br>Emery, Inez | June 4 |
| Bradford,<br>    William S.<br>Mitchell,<br>    Florence L. | June 20 |
| Thomas, Ford B.<br>Libby, Vira | July 11 |
| Marr, Albert A.<br>Buker, Doris | Aug. 17 |
| Wilcox, Stanley<br>Libby, Gladys | Aug. 29 |
| Baird, Elmer L.<br>Webb, Mildred L. | Sep. 1 |
| Clark, Wesley<br>Frost, Gladys | Sep. 8 |
| Page, Chellis M.<br>Nash, Emily V. | Oct. 3 |
| Varney, Horace E.<br>Given, Ella E. | Oct. 17 |
| Fellows, Frank<br>Ross, Doris M. | Nov. 7 |
| French, Barley H.<br>Smith, Ina Blanche | Nov. 19 |

# Marriages - 1918

| | |
|---|---|
| Cookson, Clyde<br>Merrick, Lida | Jan. 20 |
| Weymouth,<br>    Harold H.<br>Hollis, Jennett | Feb. 3 |
| Smith, Mark I.<br>Elderkin, Viola | May 15 |
| Parker, George W.<br>Bryant, Burnell | June 9 |
| Cook, W. Clyde<br>Woodcock, Agnes L. | June 9 |
| Campbell, George<br>Skillings, Ina | June 18 |
| Tracy, Scott<br>Cole, Florence May | June 22 |
| McDonald, Fred E.<br>Berry, Hattie M. | June 3 |
| Cooly, Eugene A.<br>Pearl, Hattie | Aug. 3 |
| Baird,<br>    Frederick T.<br>Hight, Ruth M. | Aug. 28 |
| Emery, Carroll C.<br>Ross, Emma M. | Oct. 24 |
| Brewer, Charles A.<br>Palmer, Marjorie | Nov. 28 |
| Cooley, Chester C.<br>Mountain,<br>    Hattie E. | Dec. 7 |

| | |
|---|---|
| Libby, George A. | Dec. 21 |
| Welch, Ethel M. | |

## Marriages - 1919

| | |
|---|---|
| Johnson, Merle E. | Jan. 23 |
| Parkman, Methel | |
| | |
| McCormack, | Feb. 1 |
|     M. Frank | |
| Bennett, Elsie G. | |
| | |
| Merrill, Verne A. | Feb. 12 |
| Varney, Pearle M. | |
| | |
| Cooley, William G. | Mar. 2 |
| Johnson, Celia | |
| | |
| Bragg, Nathan | Mar. 14 |
| Gifford, Estelle | |
| | |
| Martin, Robert E. | Apr. 6 |
| Woodman, | |
|     Florence E. | |
| | |
| Matthews, Floyd | Apr. 20 |
| Bonney, Gladys E. | |
| | |
| Welch, Delbert | Apr. 24 |
| Spencer, | |
|     Gertrude P. | |
| | |
| Ross, Arthur | Apr. 26 |
| Mills, C.J. | |
| | |
| Mills, George W. | June 7 |
| Worthen, Thelma G. | |
| | |
| Small, Harry W. | June 29 |
| Wing, Bernice | |

```
Parker, Horace                          Sep. 3
Coombs, Myrtle B.

Burns, David                            Oct. 11
Hunt, Mabel

Blake, Mellard J.                       Oct. 22
McPheters,
     Myrtle G.

Hilton, Alton E.                        Nov. 1
Berry, Erma L.

Brown, Lee Suel                         Nov. 7
Wing,
     Bessie Louise

Wheeler, Harold                         Nov. 9
Wood, Mabel M.

Knowles,                                Nov. 15
     Philander C.
Bigelow, Edna M.

Worthen, Dana R.                        Nov. 27
Wilkins, Mary L.

Fields, George S.                       Nov. 28
Estes, Laura

Mower, Philip E.                        Dec. 22
Heath, Marjorie

Johnson, George M.                      Dec. 25
Bragg, Harriett
```

## Marriages - 1920

```
Wright,Harry J.                         Jan. 1
Wood, Olive M.
```

| Neal, Gilbert | Feb. 25 |
| Seekins, Iva | |

Martin, Ervin W.                 Mar. 17
Cookson, Vivian

Baird, Carl A.                   Mar. 19
Robinson, Ella H.

Southard, Harry B.            Apr. 3
Whitney, Annie

Thomas, Leroy                   Sep. 19
Crocker, Grace H.

Goulette,                       Oct. 27
    Clifford T.
Smith, Bertha B.

Bradford,                      Nov. 6
    Philip A.
Davis, Laura M.

Magoon, William E.           Nov. 13
Nichols, Bessie

Kidder, Charles               Nov. 24
Newton, Mildred

Southard,                      Nov. 25
    Edward J.
Wheeler, Lottie C.

Source: Vertine Ellis, "Vital Records,"
Eastern Gazette, 1940's, Dexter Library,
Dexter, Maine. Marriages from 1884-1920.
St. Albans Town Reports. Spelling as it
appeared in the newspaper. Marriages and
Intentions were not always clear.

John Warren

## Our Warren Connection
## And Other Early History

The Warren name has been a distinguished name in both Great Britain and America for generations. Of all by the name of Warren, who served in the Revolutionary War, none has more connection with this area then Dr. John Warren of Boston, Massachusetts, who purchased the town of St. Albans on June 15, 1799.[1]

Dr. Warren's brother Joseph died in the Battle of Bunker Hill. The painting by John Trumbull with the dying Joseph is just one example of the prominence of the Warren family in colonial times.

John Warren's great-grandfather was Peter Warren, born 1628 in Boston. He is first mentioned in Suffolk deeds as purchasing land on Essex Street from Theodore Atkinson on March 4, 1659, and is there styled mariner. Dr. Warren's father was a substantial farmer and was the first who produced the species of russet apple with a red blush, called by the name of "Warren Russet" or "Roxbury Russet."[2]

Dr. Warren was not a bookish child, and did not learn to read until he was ten years old. He attended Roxbury, Latin, which prepared him for college in four years. He graduated from Harvard College in the class of 1771.

John met and fell in love with Abigail Collins, when he was stationed in Cambridge, Massachusetts. She was the daughter of Gov. John Collins of Rhode

---

[1]Deed of the town of St. Albans, Maine

[2]John C. Warren M.D., <u>Genealogy of Warren</u> (Boston, 1854)

Island. Abigail was very lovely with fine features and a good complexion. She was quiet and reserved, which was proper for a Quaker girl. She was sought after by many of the young officers. General George Washington thought of her as a proper young lady.

John Warren was neither dashing nor well to do. He lacked his brothers' radiance, and was smaller than Joseph. He had a high forehead with eyes which were deeply set and as blue as Joseph's were dark. John did possess a great deal of charm and won the heart of Abigail. On October 4, 1777, at the age of nineteen, in Boston she became the wife of Dr. John Warren.

After their marriage Abigail began to widen her interests. She drafted a petition for her husband to send to Congress. The petition concerned the horrible conditions which prevailed in the Continental Hospital.[3] [4]

A great deal of suffering was taking place in Boston during the winter of 1777-1778. Many paupers died from cold and hunger. Violence was everywhere, the residents did not venture out after dark. The thieves were, for the most part, ordinary citizens who had been demoralized when the British invaded Boston.

The following anthem was written at that time.

---

[3]Rhoda Troux, <u>The Doctors Warren of Boston</u>, (Houghton Mifflin Co., 1968)

[4]Clifford K. Shepton, <u>Sibley's Harvard Graduates</u>, Vol. XVII: <u>1768-1771</u>

"Lamentations Over Boston."

"By the rivers of Watertown
we sat down and wept
We wept, we wept, when we
remembered Boston
As for our friends, Lord God in Heaven
preserve them-
defend them, deliver them and restore
them unto us."[5]

The Collins's saw to it that the
newlyweds did not suffer as many of the
other families. Dr. Warren understood what
it was like to need help, and was often
seen throughout the city collecting food
for the needy.

Physicians were poorly paid for their
services, and on May 14, 1780 a group of
doctors, including Dr. John Warren met at
the Green Dragon to establish a set of
fees. Among the prominent doctors present
were Samuel Danforth, Thomas Kast and
Isaac Rand.

When word was received that the
French were going to fight the British
Bostonians feared that the British would
try to capture Boston so a expedition was
organized against Newport. John Warren
volunteered to go on this expedition,
commanded by Gen. John Sullivan, which
also included John Hancock, Lafayette,
Paul Revere, and the Massachusetts
Malitia.

The Revolutionary War was officially
ended in 1783 by the signing of the Treaty
of Paris between the United States and
Great Britain. Dr. John Warren was chosen

---

[5]"Pilgrim" Vol. II Old South Church of
Boston - Cropley Square, n. 53 - Mar. 1-15,
1986

by the town of Boston to pronounce the first oration in commemoration of our Independence on the Fourth of July.

Dr. Warren continued to work hard to support his family that was growing each year. After teaching all morning, he would visit soldiers in the hospital and make house calls.

Dr. Warren had a family pew in the Brattle Square Meeting House, conveniently near the door, in case of an emergency. He never joined the church, but insisted on strict Sabbath observance, and read family prayers each day from the Book of Common Prayer.

Dr. Warren did not join the French Revolution, partly because he considered it too aristocratic, but he also became conservative. He was constantly concerned about the senseless cruelty of the masses in France.[6][7]

More than any other man, Dr. John Warren changed the New England concept of a physician. Boys who had never dreamed of entering such a dirty trade were charmed and fascinated by his brilliant lectures, wholly done without notes.[8]

Dr. John Warren not only purchased the town of St. Albans, he purchased Corinna, Hartland, and Palmyra. It was in Palmyra that he chose to build the Warren Mansion, and in 1800 he sent his second son Joseph to Palmyra to supervise the

---

[6]Rhoda Troux, The Doctors Warren of Boston (Houghton Mifflin Co., 1968)

[7] Clifford K. Shepton, Sibley's Harvard Graduates Vol. VII: 1768-1771

[8] "Confessions of Worried Doctors," Yankee Magazine, Feb. 1986

clearing of land and the building of three Warren homes, perhaps more.

Joseph's wife's name was Abigail Whittier, not Whitten as recorded by past historians. She was the daughter of Clark Whittier and Deborah Clough.[9]

For several years the Warren influence was felt in Palmyra and the surrounding towns. They imported Durham cattle from England. Joseph was also growing hops on the farm, something his father and brother, Dr. John Collins Warren, would have frowned upon.[10]

When Dr. John Warren died Apr. 4, 1815, he left the Warren Estate, along with five hundred dollars, to Joseph. The remaining lands were under the administration of Dr. John Collins Warren of Boston.[11]

Joseph did not enjoy his inheritance very long. He died in 1820, leaving his wife Abigail and seven children. The eighth child was born after the death of the father.[12]

In 1823, Charles and Henry Warren arrived in Palmyra, they were brothers of Joseph. Henry was a graduate of Harvard College, and was practicing law in Boston in 1821. Henry was known as Squire Warren and held many town offices. In 1843 he

---

[9] Charles Whittier, <u>Whittier Genealogy</u> pg. 60

[10] Donald Hill, <u>History of Palmyra, Me.</u>

[11] Will of John Warren No. 24632

[12] Vital Records of Palmyra, Maine

moved to Bangor, Maine, where he practiced law.[13]

The Warren dynasty lasted only a few years in this area, but for over five generations the Warren family left their mark on the medical profession of America.

## TRIBUTE

The following tribute is found in The Warren Building of the Massachusetts General Hospital - Their Contributions to Medicine and Surgery of the World.

Dr. John Warren - 1753-1815. Leader in the establishment of the Medical Institution of Harvard College - First Professor of Anatomy and Surgery - A founder of the Massachusetts Medical Society, Director of a Military Hospital near this site during the Revolution.

Dr. Joseph Warren 1741-1775. Medical Practitioner and Patriot who gave his life on Bunker Hill as a General officer of the Revolutionary Army.

Dr. John Collins Warren 1778-1856 - Professor of Anatomy and Surgery at Harvard and Surgeon to the Massachusetts General Hospital joined with James Jackson in the founding of the hospital where he performed the historic operation under ether on Oct. 16, 1846.

Dr. Jonathan Mason Warren - 1811-1867. Visiting surgeon at the Massachusetts General Hospital who introduced the art Plastic Surgery from Europe to America and first performed free transplant of human skin.

Dr. John Collins Warren 1842-1927 - Professor of surgery at Harvard and

---

[13] Rhoda Troux, <u>The Doctors Warren of Boston</u>, (Houghton Mifflin Co., 1968)

visiting surgeon at the hospital pioneered
in bringing to America Lister's technique
of surgical healing without infection.
Performed on this site in 1889. The first
operation in a new surgical building
designed to protect patients from
operation infections.

The Warren mansion is presently owned
by Marion Furbush. It is still a
delightful specimen of a federal style
house, setting back some distance from the
highway.

There is some indication that the
hardware in this home was made by Paul
Revere. The author believes this could be
true for several reasons. A close friend
of Joseph Warren who died at the Battle of
Bunker Hill was burly Paul Revere. It was
Warren that brought Revere into the
exclusive Long Room Club, made up of
Harvard graduates, scholars and men of
wealth. He also belonged to the "Sons of
Liberty." These meetings were conducted
with great secrecy chiefly at the Green
Dragon Tavern in Boston. One day after the
Boston Tea Party their names were linked
in a street ballad.

> "Our Warrens there and Paul Revere
> With Hands to do and words to cheer
> For Liberty and Laws
> Our Country's brave and firm
> defenders
>> Shall ne'ir be left by true
>> North Enders
>> Fighting Freedom's call.
> Then rally boys and hasten in
> To meet our chiefs at the Green
> Dragon"[14]

---

[14] Esther Forbes, <u>Paul Revere and the
World He Lived In</u>

# DEED OF THE TOWN OF ST. ALBANS, MAINE TO DR. JOHN WARREN

Know all men by these Presents, that we whose names are undersigned and seals are hereunto affixed, appointed a committee by the General Court of the Commonwealth of Massachusetts, with full power to sell and convey the unappropriated lands of said Commonwealth lying within the district of Maine, in consideration of Seven thousand two hundred and sixty-four dollars to us in hand paid by John Warren of Boston, in the County of Suffolk, and State of Massachusetts, Physician, for the use of said commonwealth the receipt whereof we do hereby acknowledge, have given, granted, sold and conveyed, and by these present in behalf of said Commonwealth, do give, grant, sell and convey unto the said John Warren assignee of Moses Barnard & Joseph Hilton, both of Deerfield, & Isaac Thom & George Reid, both of Londonderry, and all of the State of New Hampshire Esquires, and their associates, a township of land, lying in the County of Lincoln, and containing about Twenty-six thousand, eight hundred and eighty acres (be the same more or less) the said Township being number five in the fourth range north of the Waldo Patent as the same was surveyed by Ephram Ballard and Samuel Weston, in the year Seventeen hundred & ninety-two, Bounded, Easterly by number four in the same range - Westerly by number three in the first range north of the Plymouth claim partly, & partly by number three in the second range north of said claim, and Northerly by number five in the fifth range north of the Waldo Patent, Excepting and reserving however, four lots of three hundred and twenty acres each, for the following uses, viz.,

One lot for the first settled minister, his Heirs or assigns, one lot for the use of the Ministry - One lot for the use of Schools, and one lot for the future disposition of the General Court the said Lots to average in situation and quality with the other lands in said township.

To have and to hold, the above granted premises, with the appurtenances thereof to the said, John Warren, his Heirs and assigns forever, on condition that the said John Warren, his Heirs or assigns, shall grant and convey to each settler in said township, who settled therein before the first day of Jan. seventeen hundred & eighty four, or in case of his decease without assignment, then to his Heirs, and in case of assignment, then to the assigns, One hundred acres to be so laid out as will best include the improvements of the settler, and be least injurious to the adjoining lands, so as that the settler, his Heirs or assigns, may hold the same in fee simple.

Provided, that the settler, his Heirs or assigns, shall within One year after notice and request, pay to the Grantees named in this Deed, their Heirs or assigns, Five dollars - And on this further condition, that the said John Warren, before the twentieth day of June, one thousand eight hundred, shall settle twenty families within said township, and before the twentieth day of June, one thousand eight hundred and four, shall settle twenty families more. And the said committee covenant with the said John Warren, that the said commonwealth, shall warrant and defend the above granted premises, to him the said John Warren, on these conditions and saving the reservations aforesaid, to him his Heirs and assigns forever, against the lawful claims and demands, of all Persons; the above granted township, having been contracted for by the said Moses Barnard, Joseph Hilton, Isaac Thom & George Reid, and their associates on the twenty-sixth day of Feb., one thousand seven hundred ninety-six.

In witness whereof, we have hereunto set our hands and seals, this fifteenth day of June, in the year of our Lord, seventeen hundred and ninety-nine.

Signed, Sealed, & Delivered in Presence of
John Vinall
John Read, Jr.
Nath.l Wells
Leo Jarvis

John Rea, Suffolk of Boston, June 15, 1799, Personally appeared Nath.l Wells - Leo Jarvis & John Read and acknowledged this instrument to be their free act and Deed - before - John Vinall, Jus. of Peace.

---

Two men whose names appear in the deed of St. Albans were from Deerfield, N.H. Joseph Hilton was a lieutenant in the Revolutionary War and was wounded at the Battle of Saratoga. His sons, Stephen and Daniel, and a daughter Hannah, moved to Cornville, Maine. Joseph Hilton's father was Theodore, who married Mary Sinclair of Stratham, N.H. His great grandfather was

Edward Hilton often referred to as the "Father of New Hampshire."[15]

Moses Barnard is listed on a gravestone in Deerfield, N.H. - "Col. Moses Barnard died Oct. 8, 1816 - age 66 - His name is also found on the deed of the town of Cornville, Maine. For many years, Cornville was known as Barnardstown in his honor.

One of the early surveyors of St. Albans was Samuel Weston. Some records indicate that Samuel Weston's mother was the first white woman to live in Somerset County, but on her gravestone it states she was the second woman who moved into the county. Her husband, Joseph Weston, and his brother-in-law, Peter Hayword, brought twenty head of cattle from their home in Massachusetts, stopping off in Sidney, Maine, - then called Vassalboro - at the home of Capt. Abiel Lovejoy. They then proceeded up the river on the ice to their new home in Canaan, Maine. Mrs. Weston brought along a window for her cabin.

Ephraim Ballard, the second surveyor came to Winslow, Maine in 1775 and subsequently lived in Augusta. His original home was in Oxford, Mass.[16] [17]

---

[15] Rev. Elliott C. Cogswell, <u>History of Nottingham, Duffield, Northwood, Cogswell</u>. 1878
    Letter dated      Mrs. Joanne Wason Town Clerk of Duffield, N.H.

[16] "Skowhegan on the Kennebec" by Louise Helen Coburn

[17] Clarence E. Lovejoy, <u>"Lovejoy Genealogy"</u>

## GILBERT LAFAYETTE TURNER

The great forests of Washington have made this state the leading one in the extent of its lumber industries in the entire country. Of this business Gilbert Lafayette Turner is a representative, being now the president of the Cascade Cedar Company of Snohomish. The enterprise of which he is at the head is an important one, not only to the individual stockholders, but to the community because it furnishes employment to a large number of workmen, and thus promotes the general prosperity.

Mr. Turner was born on the 12th of May, 1839, in St. Albans, Maine, and is a son of William Turner, who was also a native of that state. On the paternal side our subject comes of English and German lineage, and the Turner family was founded in America in early colonial days. Representatives of the name participated in the War of 1812. The father of our subject was a farmer by occupation, carrying on agricultural pursuits throughout his entire business career. He wedded Anne Bullen, also a native of Maine and a representative of an old American family of English origin, dating back in this country to a period prior to the Revolutionary war. Mr. and Mrs. Turner became the parents of five sons and eight daughters. The brothers and sisters of our subject are Israel Putnam, who is now deceased; Sarah and Napoleon Bonaparte, who have also passed away; Augusta, the wife of Moses Keen; John O. and Louisa, who have also departed this life; Elizabeth, the wife of William Lincoln; Hannah, who is the wife of John Bricket;

Susan, deceased; Harriet; Mary, the wife of Sewell Whittier; and William Wallace, who has also passed away.

When a little lad of but six years Gilbert Lafayette Turner began his education in the public schools of St. Albans, and later continued his studies in the high school there until eighteen years of age, when he put aside his textbooks and entered upon his business career. He has since been dependent upon his own resources for a living. He first worked in the lumber mills of Maine and at the age of twenty years made his way to California, attracted by the discovery of gold in that state. There he followed mining for a time and afterward again engaged in the lumber business. He remained in the Golden State for three years, or until 1862. In the following year he went to Nevada, where he was again connected with the lumber trade, spending a year in that state. On the expiration of that period he removed to Montana in the spring of 1864, and in company with his brother Wallace engaged in freighting between Helena, Montana, and Los Angeles, California. Subsequently he became connected with mercantile interests at what was known as Uncle Ben's Gulch, and there he also engaged in mining for two years. In the fall of 1866, however, he returned to the state of his nativity, where he remained for two years, going thence to Wisconsin, which continued to be his place of residence for about seventeen years, or until 1885. While residing in the Badger State he was identified with lumber interests and with the banking business, establishing the first bank at Phillips, Price county, Wisconsin, of which institution he became the president.

In the fall of 1885 Mr. Turner made his way to Las Vegas, New Mexico, where he remained until 1888 in the hope of benefiting his wife's health. He spent the succeeding winter at Salida, Colorado, and then went to Los Gatos, California, where he remained from 1889 until 1898, during which time he was engaged in the banking business as president of the Bank of Los Gatos. In the latter year Mr. Turner arrived in Snohomish, and here he became identified with business interests as proprietor of a ranch. He is now the president of the Cascade Cedar Company, manufacturers of all classes of fir and cedar lumber and shingles. The capacity of the mill is fifty thousand feet of lumber per day and one hundred and seventy-five thousand shingles daily. Employment is furnished to fifty men, and the industry is one of importance to the community. The plant is well equipped with the latest improved machinery, and pleasant business relations are maintained between employers and employees.

On the 6th of April, 1893, was celebrated the marriage of Mr. Turner and Mrs. Rose M. McMillan, a native of London, England, who came to America during her girlhood days with her parents, Edward F. and Sarah Norris, who settled in Iowa. To Mr. and Mrs. Turner have been born two children: Dorothy R., now nine years of age; and Gilbert N., a little lad of seven summers. Both Mr. and Mrs. Turner have a wide acquaintance and are held in the highest regard by their large circle of friends. He is a very prominent Mason, having attained to the thirty-second degree of the Scottish Rite, and he also belongs to the Independent Order of Odd Fellows. His political support is given to the Republican party, and his position in public regard is indicated by the fact that in 1899, 1900 and 1901 he served as mayor of Snohomish. His administration was business-like and progressive, his labors in behalf of the city being along lines of reform and improvement. Everything pertaining to the general welfare receives his endorsement, and to many movements for the good of the city he has given his active co-operation and substantial assistance. Throughout much of his life he has been identified with the lumber trade, which he thoroughly understands, and to-day he is in control of a business which is constantly growing in volume and importance. The company enjoys an enviable reputation in trade circles because of the honorable business policies it has ever pursued, and the success of the undertaking is attributable in very large measure to the enterprise and careful direction of Mr. Turner.[18]

---

[18] William Whitefield, <u>History of Puget Sound</u> (1900)

FRIENDS CHURCH, ST. ALBANS, ME.

COMMERCIAL ST., ST. ALBANS, ME.

## DR. FRANKLIN ORESTES LYFORD

Franklin Orestes Lyford (son of John Fogg and Fairrena B. (Rowe) Lyford), b. Jan. 21, 1847, at St, Albans, Maine; d. April 8, 1931, at Farmington, Maine; m. Jan. 22, 1873, at St. Albans, Ellen Susan Skinner (daughter of Thomas and Sarah (Hackett) Skinner), b. Jan. 5, 1848, at St. Albans, Maine; d. Aug. 11, 1930, at Farmington, Maine.

He attended the Corinna Union Academy, the Maine Central Institute, and the State Normal School at Farmington, Maine. After teaching for a year or more in Kansas he entered the Hahnemann Medical College in Philadelphia, from which he graduated (M.D.) in 1877.

Remembering the kind friends he had known while a student at Farmington, Dr. Lyford settled in that town and practiced there during the remainder of his life - a period of 54 years. His practice extended over a wide area, and in order to cover it (in the day before the advent of the motor car) he found it necessary to keep four horses. He retained his physical and mental vigor and continued in active practice up to the day of his decease, in his 85th year.

He was popular socially and prominent in several "fraternal orders", being a member of the K. of P. and the D.O.K.P., as well as a 32nd degree Free Mason. He had no desire for public office but was induced to serve on the Farmington School Board, and for a number of years was Secretary of the Board of Health. He and his wife were members of the First Congregational Church of Farmington.

Dr. Lyford had one son, Earle Howard Lyford, b. Dec. 22, 1873, at St. Albans, Maine; living (1939) in Berlin, New

Hampshire; m. Cora Sarah Burleigh, daughter of Gilman Burleigh. He graduated from Bowdoin (A.B.) in 1896, and from the Moss College of Pharmacy (Ph.C.) in 1901. He is the proprietor of a drug store in Berlin, New Hampshire.

## SAMUEL COPP WORTHEN

Samuel Copp Worthen (son of Joseph Henry and Amanda (Copp) Worthen), b. Apr. 10, 1871, at Corinna, Maine; living (1939) at East Orange, New Jersey; m. Aug. 28, 1909, Julia Regina McSwyny (daughter of Cornelius George and Elizabeth Boyce (Henderson) McSwyny), b. June 23, 1883, at New York, N.Y.; d. Oct. 31, 1918, at East Orange, N.J.

As a boy he attended the primary school and grammar school in Corinna Village. He then entered the Corinna Union Academy. There, as elsewhere, he manifested an interest in scholarship rather than sports or social affairs, but was a member of the Debating Society or "Lyceum" and was elected its president. He took the last part of his college preparatory work (about one and one third years) at the Maine Central Institute, Pittsfield, Maine, and graduated at the head of his class in 1891, being class poet and chief editor of "M. C. I.", the school periodical.

Not wishing to be dependent on others for the expenses of a college education, he then taught school for three years, being principal of the high school in Newport Village during the latter part of this period. In the fall of 1894 he took the examinations for entrance to Columbia College, in New York City and was admitted to the freshman class. Before his savings as a school teacher were exhausted, he had become self supporting as an unofficial tutor for the Department of Rhetoric and English Composition. Prof. George Rice Carpenter, head of this department, put practically all students who were deficient in the subject, under his care (as a private tutor) and even permitted some students to take one of the courses with him in the summer months instead of taking it the following autumn, with the regular instructor, - the department, however, conducted the examination.

The extra work as a tutor consumed much time, but he managed to maintain throughout his collegiate years the highest average rank of any student in his class. He was class poet, 1895-1897, and class president and salutatorian in 1898. He was elected president at the beginning of the senior year, which carried with it the office of salutatorian. He could not, of course, be valedictorian also, but would undoubtedly have received the appointment at the end of the year if he had refused the office of president at the beginning. He was one of two members of the class of 1898 elected to the Phi Beta Kappa Society in junior year and on graduation was awarded final honors in Rhetoric and English Composition. In 1900 he graduated (L. L. B.) from the Columbia Law School and also received from the University the degree of A. M. in Political Science.

He was admitted to the bar in 1900 and has since practiced in New York City. He is now (1939) a member of the firm of McLanahan, Marritt, Ingraham and Christy, 40 Wall Street, N. Y. City, having been associated with this firm and its predecessors for about 39 years. He has specialized in Wills and Surrogates Practice, drawing many important wills and settling many large estates. He drafted and procured the enactment by the Legislature of Maine, a statute for preservation of the ancient vital records of the State and has been active in promoting similar legislation in other states.

Mr. Worthen is a member of the New Jersey Society Sons of the American Revolution (Secretary of Orange Chapter 1918-1920, Historian, 1924 - 1928, and Genealogist of the State Society, 1920-1929); member of the Sons of the Revolution in the State of New York; member of the New York Genealogical and Biographical Society (serving on its Publication Committee since 1932); member of the New Jersey Historical Society; member of the New Hampshire Historical Society; life member of the Institute of American Genealogy; life member of the Genealogical Society of New Jersey (associate editor of its magazine - the Genealogical Magazine of New Jersey - and president of the society since 1925); member of the  Association of the Alumni of Columbia College; member of the Alumni Association of the Law School of Columbia University; member of the Metropolitan Museum of Art.

He is the author of many articles on historical and genealogical subjects and of several valuable unpublished manuscripts, including a history of Worthen-Worthing Family in America.


## BARTLETT TRIPP

In 1893 when the writer was teaching school in the old "Brick School House", in St. Albans, Maine (about three miles from the village), he received his first introdution to the striking story of the Hon. Bartlett Tripp, Minister Plenipotentiary and Envoy Extraordinary of the United States to the Austrian Empire, in those simpler days before our diplomatic representatives at the capitols of first class powers had received the more pretentious title of "Ambassador". Amusing stories were told about the experiences of Mr. Tripp at the time when he was merely the writer's predecessor as teacher in the "Brick School House".

Even then he seemed to have enjoyed some advantages over his successor, - for two of his fair pupils are said to have fallen deeply in love with him and to have been keen rivals for his favor. The competition had remained indecisive when he finished his school and left St. Albans. Thereafter he corresponded with both of them. According to the facetious Yankee version of the matter which came to the writer's ears, the more enterprising of the twain-named Ellen - followed him to Salt Lake City and married him. Then having in mind the peculiar marital customs of that locality - and fearing that he might send for the other "girl-friend", also - she could not rest content until she had succeeded in getting him out of Utah!

the Muse of History seems to have confirmed some of the more matter-of-fact details of this whimsical rural gossip, for upon investigation it appears the name of Mr. Tripp's first wife actually was Ellen; and that he <u>was</u> teaching school in Salt Lake City when he married her.

Mr. Tripp's formal record was as follows:- Bartlett Tripp (son of William and Narmah (Bartlett) Tripp), b. July 15, 1842, at Harmony, Maine [a small town adjoining St. Albans on the North West];

d. Dec. 8, 1911, at Yanktown, South Dakota; m. (1) in 1863, Ellen M. Jennings of Garland, Maine, who died in 1884, leaving one daughter, He m. (2) Nov. 6, 1887, Mrs. Maria Janet (Davis) Washburn.

He was associated with the Corinna Union Academy, not only as a student, but afterwards as a teacher. He was a resident of South Dakota when appointed United States minister to Austria (in 1893) by President Grover Cleveland. he held many other high offices, including that of Chief Justice of the Supreme Court of Dakota, president of the Bar Association of The Territory and president of the Bar Association of South Dakota after its admission as a state. He was president of the convention which framed the Constitution of South Dakota.

For an account of his life see Dictionary of American Biography, Vol. XVIII, pp. 643-644 and the authorities there cited.

## COURSE OF INSTRUCTION
### IN
## ST. ALBANS SCHOOLS

### RULES AND REGULATIONS
### ADOPTED IN 1894

## HIGH SCHOOL
### Course of Study

The High School is established to furnish those pupils who have finished the studies of the lower grades, and are possessed of the qualifications necessary to admit them, and desire to take an advanced course of study. It has two courses of study, a College Preparatory and English. It is now under the instruction of a Principal.

Parents or guardians shall determine what course of study shall be pursued by the pupil.

Pupils who complete either of the above courses of study and shall maintain an honorable rank in scholarship and deportment, shall receive a Diploma from the Board of Education.

### The Lower Grades

These grades are by far the most important since they form the basis on which to build. They shall be under the instruction of competent teachers and are subject to the same restrictions as to promotion and graduation as are laid down for the High School.

### Text Books

All text books used in the public schools of St. Albans are furnished by the town, and shall be regarded as property of

the town loaned to the pupil. All books
shall be labelled and numbered and a
record of them kept by the teacher and
returned to the Supervisor at the end of
each term.

Any pupil who shall lose or
unnecessarily injure any book or school
appliances furnished at the expense of the
town, their teacher shall report the same
to the Supervisor and to the parents or
guardians, and thereupon proceedings shall
be had according to Chapter Eleven,
Section Ten, of the Revised Statutes.

### Regulations for Pupils

Every pupil is expected to attend
school regularly and punctually, obey
promptly all directions of the teacher,
observe good order and behavior, to apply
themselves to their studies, be respectful
to their teachers, and kind and obliging
to their schoolmates, to refrain from all
profane language and bad habits, and be
neat and clean in person.

### Omitted Recitations

Absence from recitation shall be
regarded as a failure to recite, and be so
marked on the register, Omitted lessons
shall be subsequently recited, either in
or out of regular school hours, and such
pupil shall receive his rank thereon as in
regular work.

### Failure to Maintain Rank in Class

Pupils who have fallen behind their
classes by absence, indolence, inattention
or inability, may be placed in the next
lower grade at the discretion of the
teacher on consultation with the

Supervisor. If the parent or guardian be dissatisfied with the action they may apply to the Supervisor for a hearing in the matter.

## Tardiness

Tardiness not satisfactorily explained shall be subject to reasonable punishment. No pupil shall absent himself rom the regular school hours, for the purpose of receiving instruction elsewhere, except by permission of the teacher and the Supervisor. A pupil absent from school, on returning thereto, shall bring a written excuse from parent or guardian explaining such absence. If a pupil wishes to be excused before the close of the session he must give a satisfactory reason, and obtain the consent of the teacher. Habitual excuses and applications from the same pupil shall be investigated.

## System of Ranking

No scholar shall be deemed to have satisfactorily completed any term's work in High, Grammar, or Intermediate schools, who shall not have obtained a rank of seventy per cent. For the purpose of determining one's standing, daily recitations and examinations shall be ranked, but no scholar who has not ranked below eighty per cent, in daily work shall fall below the standard.

## List of Pupils for Promotion

Prior to the annual examinations the teachers of the several schools shall furnish to the Supervisor a list of those pupils who in their estimation are prepared to enter a higher grade. Such pupils at the close of the examinations if found as stated shall be promoted.

## COURSE OF STUDY
## Primary Schools

### Chart Class

Chart in course and lessons in script from chart and black board.

Sentence method should be employed. Primer may be used if teacher thinks it necessary as soon as children are able to read some, but the chart must not be neglected until every page is thoroughly mastered.

Teachers should spell all words be sound and pupils imitate slatework.

Numbers -- Counting from 1 to 12 with objects, then without them. Figures and signs taught as soon as the child has a clear idea of the "How many objects."

Oral instruction in color and form. Drawing, stick-laying, paper-folding, straight lines and simple combinations.

### Second Year

Reading - Sentence, word and phonic methods combined. Second half of chart reviewed, with vocabulary of words taken from First Reader, taught by use of blackboard, Reading book, No. 1, finished.

Special attention to position while reading, articulation and expression.

Spelling-- Simple words from vocabulary, taught by sound and letter. Words from reading lessons and from prepared lists. During last term, five words written each day and work kept.

Object lessons--Lessons in color and
form. Meaning of words descriptive of
place, size and prominent qualities, as
rough, smooth, etc.

Oral Lessons in Language--Correction
of common errors. Pupils to express
thoughts in complete sentences. Correct
use of the articles, singular and plural
forms.

Numbers--Counting from 1 to 100.
Additions, substraction, multiplication
and division of numbers from 1 to 12 by
means of numeral frame. Easy problems in
above processes by teacher and pupil.
Multiplication and division with objects
only. Roman numerals from 1 to 50.

Drawing--Right and left curves and
ovals taught to assist in writing script.
Review of first year's work.

Writing--On slates, practice paper
and in Tracing Book No. 1.

### Third Year

Reading--Second Reader, prepared
lessons. Supplementary reading at sight.
Attention to position, etc., as in first
and second years.

Spelling--Oral and written words from
reading lessons. Words studied from script
as much as possible.

Object lessons--Name and give use of
the principal parts of the body.
Description and habits of common domestic
animals. By means of chart or globe teach
cardinal points, position and distance. By
means of slate teach pupils right, left,
front, back, center, top, bottom, above,
below, beneath, on, under and vertical,
horizontal and parallel lines.

Oral lessons in Language--Correct use
of forms of verbs, with singular and
plural subjects. Writing of simple

sentences containing special words. Reproduction of simple stories. Teach use of capitals in beginning the sentence and in writing the pronoun I, and all proper names, and use of periods and interrogation marks.

Numbers--Review of previous work. Roman numerals from 1 to 500 written and read. Writing and reading numbers of six figures, Multiplication must be taught, using two figures, neither of which shall be larger than seven. Accuracy and rapidity are to be objective points.

Writing--Work of preceding year continued. Tracing book No. 2.

Drawing--Work of preceding year reviewed. White's Book No. 1. Work conducted according to White's Manual, using model sets 1 and 4.

Physiology--Pathfinder No. 1, read twice a week. Oral lessons on simple rules of health.

Memory Gems--Suitable selections memorized and recited.

Gymnastics--Exercise songs, light arm and foot movements throughout the course, when children become weary and restless. Ventilate the room during such exercise.

## Fourth Year

Third reader, read first half of term and reviewed. Prepared lessons. Sight reading daily. Vowels sounds and diacritical marks. Phonic drill on words frequently mispronounced.

Spelling--Difficult words in lessons. Begin natural speller taking definitions, phonic chart and rules, advancing to page 23.

Language--Previous work reviewed and continued. Special attention to correction of common errors.

399

Numbers--First term: Previous work carefully reviewed by practice exercise. Text book to subtraction. Second term: Principles already taken constantly reviewed by supplementary work. Text book to division. Third term: Work continued according to plan for other terms. Text book to fractions.

History--First term: Child's History to lesson ten and review. Teachers should make these lessons story work as much as possible, not requiring the pupil to remember too many dates. Second term: Text book to lesson twenty and review. Third term: Text book finished and reviewed.

Geography--Oral lessons. Idea of map developed. Plan of school room drawn, locating objects. Map of St. Albans village drawn by pupils. Locate mills, churches, and other important buildings. Charts, globes and maps constantly used.

Drawing--White's revise system continued according to Manual.

Writing--Copy Book No. 1 completed. Free hand movement, with exercises from chart.

Physiology--Oral lessons. Pathfinder No. 1, read twice a week until completed. Rules of health. Temperance in living.

Memory Gems--Suitable selections memorized and recited.

## INTERMEDIATE SCHOOLS,
### First Year

Reading--Fourth Reader to page 223 and reviewed. Reading cards. Sounds of letters. Phonics continued.

Spelling--Oral spelling reviewed. Eight words written daily.

Language--Text book, two lessons per week.

Numbers--First term: Fish's
Arithmetic No.2 to division. General
review of all preceding work. Second term:
Text book to fractions. Third term: Text
book to relation of numbers. Supplementary
work on all principles taken, with general
review of book.

Geography--First term: Text book to
page 35. Second term: Text book to page
63. Map drawing constantly taken. Third
term: Text book to page 90.

Drawing--White's revised system

Writing--Copy book No.2.

Physiology--Oral instruction to
comply with law.

Memory Gems--Memorized and recited.

## Second Year

Reading--Fourth Reader completed.
Special instruction of first year
continued. Supplementary reading twice a
week.

Spelling--Directions of first year
continued.

Numbers--First term: Text book to
accounts and bills, with much
supplementary work. Second term: Text book
to measurements. Third term: Text book to
percentage.

Language--Text book two lessons a
week.

Geography--First term: Text book
finish. Second term: Text book review to
page 90. Third term: Text book finish. Map
drawing, North America, New England and
Maine.

Drawing--White's system continued

Writing--Copy Book No. 3.

Physiology--Special reference to
diet, clothing, and cleanliness. Talk on
temperance monthly.

Memory Gems--Memorized and recited. These are carried though the course and are class exercises.

Gymnastics--Daily for the school

Morals and Manners--Familiar talks by the teacher.

### Third Year

Reading--Fourth Reader reviewed. Supplementary reading twice a week. Diacritical marks applied.

Spelling--Ten words written each day.

Language-Text book completed and reviewed during the year.

Numbers Review of text book to percentage. Supplementary work involving all principles given often. give special attention to mental exercises.

Drawing--White's system continued, with models.

Writing--Copy books Nos. 3 and 4.

Physiology--Pathfinder No.2 finish and review.

Rhetoricals--Once a term. Each part prepared and rehearsed one week before recited.

Gymnastics--Daily

Morals and Manners--Prepared lessons once a month.

### GRAMMAR SCHOOLS
### First Year.

Reading--Fifth Reader with supplementary reading twice each term.

Spelling--Ten words written daily four days in the week. Fifth day, oral review of the week's work.

Language-Review of previous year's work.

Numbers-First term: Text book to interest with much supplementary work.

402

Second term: Text book to stocks and investments. Third term: Text Book to partnership and general review of year's work.

Geography--First term: Text book to page 38. second term to page 75. Third term to page 110. Supplementary work throughout the year.

Drawing--White's system continued.

Writing--Copy Books Nos. 4 and 5.

Rhetoricals--Twice a term.

Gymnastics--Daily.

### Second Year.

Reading--Fifth Reader, with supplementary work.

Spelling--Twelve words written daily. Oral Reviews.

Grammar--Well's Grammar to rules of syntax.

Analysis--Composition with special reference to letter writing..

Numbers--First term. Text book to addenda.

Second term--Text book to mensuration.

Third term--Text book completed. Tablet work. Mental exercises.

Geography--Text book completed and reviewed.

Physiology--Hygienic Physiology to health and disease with frequent review. Constant use of chart.

Rhetoricals--Twice a term.

Gymnastics--Daily.

### Third Year

Reading--Fifth Reader completed. Supplementary reading from Dole's American Citizen.

Spelling-Fifteen words written daily four days in a week. Oral exercises the fifth.

Grammar--Text book finished and reviewed.

English Analysis--Criticism on easy words and sentence building. Composition work.

Numbers--Text book finished and reviewed.

History--Barnes' History completed during first two terms.

Book-keeping-Meservy's Book-keeping, single entry during last term.

Drawing--White's system continued.

Writing--Copy Book No. 6.

Rhetoricals--Recitations, declamations and compositions regularly.

Gymnastics--Daily.

Morals and Manners--Prepared lessons every month. Occasional talks.

## HIGH SCHOOL
### First Year

Fall term
Latin lessons.
Arithmetic
Algebra

Winter term
Latin Lessons.
Algebra.
English Analysis.

Spring term
Nepos.
Algebra.
Rhetoric.

### Second Year

Fall Term
Nepos.
Greek Lessons.
Geometry.
Sight Reading.

Winter term
Cicero.
Greek lessons.
General History.
Penmanship.

404

Spring term
Cicero.
Anabasis.
Geometry.
Elocution.

## Third Year

| Fall term | Winter term |
|---|---|
| Vergil. | Vergil. |
| Anabasis. | Anabasis. |
| Geometry. | Cicero. |
| Mythology. | Latin Prose |
| Composition | |

Spring term
Vergil.
Sallust.
Homer's Iliad.
Elocution.

## ENGLISH COURSE
### First Year

| Fall term | Winter term |
|---|---|
| Arithmetic, | Arithmetic, |
| Robinson's, | Eng. Analysis, |
| Geography, Physical, | Physical |
| Geography, | |
| English Grammar, | Algebra. |
| Reading and Spelling. | |

Spring term
Reading,
Book-keeping,
    double entry,
Eng. Composition,
Algebra.

### Second Year

| Fall term | Winter term |
|---|---|
| Algebra, | Geometry, |

Physiology,
Physics,

Civil Government,
Rhetoric.

Spring term
Geometry,
Botany,
Zoology.

### Third Year

Fall term
Chemistry,
Astronomy,
Philosophy,
Geometry.

Winter term
General History,
Mental

Eng. Literature.

Spring term
Geology,
Moral Philosophy,
Eng. Literature.

Exercises in Composition and Declamation occur every two weeks throughout these courses.

St. Albans Schools, C. B. Haskell, Book and Job Printer, 1894

# FIVE CORNERS SCHOOL - 1930

**ROW 1** - Verne McLean, Junior Clifford, --- Killiam, Carroll Patterson, Phyliss Nelson, Mary McLean, --- Killiam, Donald McLean, Philip Nelson, Muriel Crocker **ROW 2** - Doris Clifford, Katherine Nelson, Barbara Weymouth, Ruby Patterson, Thelma Crocker, Doris Downs, --- Killiam, Genny Clifford, Adele Patterson, Beauford Patterson **ROW 3** - Dana Smith, Halver Badger, Durwood Patterson, Willard Killiam, Victor Springer, Lindell Cain, Lynwood Page

SUPREME COURT-SOMERSET COUNTY-1905

ROW 1 - F. S. Parsons - A. C. Goodwin
        G. H. Fairfield - O. S. Hoskell
ROW 2 - C. V. Burns - Fred Finson
        Jos Adams - W. S. Bemis
ROW 3 - Alonso Brown - L. E. Brewster
        J. E. Buker - B. P. Barker
        D. M. Foster

BRYANT FLOAT-ST. ALBANS-1913

\*\*\* PROGRAM \*\*\*

| | |
|---|---|
| Master of Ceremony | Brian Hanson |
| Prayer | Rev. Barbara Chandler Huse |
| Flag Salute | |
| National Anthem | Tom Boatman |
| Sketch of Town History | Ruth Knowles |
| Introductions & Comments | Michael Wiers |
| Keynote Speakers | Sen. Margaret Chase Smith State Senator Jerome Emerson |
| Trumpet Trio | Dean Neal David Bowman Scott Jones |
| Solo | Tom Boatman |
| Benediction | Rev. Gordon Burke |
| Closing Remarks | Brian Hanson |

BALLOON LAUNCH-ST.ALBANS CONSOLIDATED
SCHOOL

ST. ALBANS 175TH ANNIVERSARY PLANNING
COMMITTEE

Left to Right
 Walter Butler - Brian Hanson -
 Ruth Knowles

# ST. ALBANS 175TH CELEBRATION
## (1988)

St. Albans - A parade, dinner theater, and musical program featuring "Yodelin' Slim" Clark highlighted the festivities held June 3-5, 1988, in honor of the town's 175th year.

The celebration opened June 3 with a balloon launch by students at the St. Albans Elementary School. The children also buried a time capsule, which will be unearthed at the town's 200th birthday in the year 2013.

On June 4, a parade headed by honorary grand marshall Sen. Margaret Chase Smith was held, with many businesses and organizations from St. Albans and the surrounding towns participating. Floats included St. Albans' oldest piece of plowing equipment, a Linn tractor, as well as some of the town's newest firefighting apparatus.

Non-commercial float winners included: First Place - St. Albans' Union Church; Second Place - The Chatterbox Club; Third Place - St. Albans' Grange.

Commercial float winners included: First Place - Snowman's Construction; Second Place - Arnie's Rocking Horse; Third Place - T.D.S.

Plaques were awarded to the Bangor, Nokomis, and Central (East Corinth) high school bands, and to the SAD 48 Junior High School Band.

A special St. Albans 175th Birthday cake was baked by Donna Provencher and Jackie Paterson. The cake was cut by Glenice Avery Lord, one of the town's oldest residents, who was born June 4, 1898 on St. Albans Mountain. Other prominent senior citizens included Elizabeth Bishop, who was born in Fort

411

Fairfield in 1889 and moved to St. Albans in 1921; Vera Libby Moor, who was born on the Ballard Road in 1892; Ruth Finson Bubar, born on St. Albans Mountain in 1895, Pearl Varney Merrill, born on Peak's Road in 1897; and Vera Emery Hanson, who was born on St. Albans Mountain in 1897.

Following the parade, a memorial service featuring former Senator Smith and State Senator Jerome Emerson as the keynote speakers was held in the town hall yard. Ruth Knowles presented a sketch of the town's history, followed by a trumpet trio composed of Dean Neal, David Bowman, and Scott Jones. A benediction was offered by Rev. Gordon Burke.

A music program was held in the afternoon, featuring St. Albans resident "Yodelin' Slim" Clark and his wife, Kathy. A musical group from the St. Albans school also performed.

St. Albans 175th anniversary commemorative plates decorated with an aerial view of the town were available for $25 each at the town office.


Source:   Bangor Daily News

Ninety-nine squares make a big quilt, and a special one for St. Albans residents. Members of the St. Albans Matrons Circle were tacking the quilt for the town's 175th anniversary celebration. Each square is made and signed by a woman from the community, in remembrance of all of the women of the community, living and dead. Participating are (from left) Rosalie Bowman, Donna Provencher, Ellen Bowman, Bernice Burdin, and Pearl Merrill.

## General Committee

Ruth Knowles - Chairman
Walter Butler - Assistant Chairman
Everett Graham - Treasurer
James Seekins - Honorary Vice Chairman
Brian Hanson - Assistant Chairman
Marjorie Carlow - Secretary
Fred Cooper - Honorary Chairman

### Historical Committee
Brian Hanson        Darrell Butler
Ruth Knowles        Elaine Mower

### Program Committee
Ethelyn Bowman        Ellen Cooper
          Michael Wiers

### Correspondence Committee
Marian Spalding        Jane Russell
          Libby Wiers
Ruth Springer - Honorary Member

### Advertising Committee
Kevin Bowman        Phillip Bowman
Roberta Mower        Brent Mower
Everett Graham        Marjorie Bubar
Brian Mower

### Printing Committee
Brian Hanson        Ethelyn Bowman
Ellen Cooper

### Souvenir Committee
Walter Butler        Douglas Frati
Everett Graham        Phillis Graham

### Antique Committee
Helen Finson        Crystal Robertson
Walter Butler        Phyllis Graham
Norman Bailey
Pearl Merrill - Honorary Member
Guy Smith - Honorary Member

## Crafts
Donna Provencher

## Church Committee
| | |
|---|---|
| Diane Dunham | Doris Ballard |
| Linda Huff | Ann Smith |
| Laura Smith | Diane Landry |
| Marjorie Bubar | Dennis Smith |
| Jennie Springer | |

## School Committee
Velma Walker
Staff of the St. Albans School

## Art Committee
Douglas Frati     Raymond Clark
Marjorie Martin Chisholm - Honorary Member

## Sports Committee
Boyd McNally     Greydon Turner
Paul Ramsdell

## Decoration Committee
David Crocker     David Gould
Timothy Ballard   St. Albans Fire Dept.

## Traffic and Police Committee
Harry Taylor     David Cotta
Bennie Melanson - Honorary Member
Gordon Woodman - Honorary Member

## Reception Committee
Ruth Powers     Ruth Knowles
Angilee Seekins - Honorary Member

## Photography Committee
Brian Hanson     Douglas Parkhurst

# PROGRAM

Friday, June 3rd, 1988
  11:30 - Public Picnic at St. Albans
      School
  1:00 - Balloon Launch at school
  2:00 - Time Capsule to be sealed at
      school
  6:30 - Dinner Theatre at Town Hall
  7:30 - Play by St. Albans Players

Saturday, June 4th
  9:30 - Parade
  9:30 - 5:00     Art Show at Grange Hall
  9:30 - 5:00     Craft Show - Grange Hall
  11:30 -         Program at Town Hall Yard
                  Prayer -
                      Rev. Barbara Chandler
                  Flag Salute
                  National Anthem -
                          Mr. Tom Boatman
                  Sketch of Town History -
                          Michael Wiers
                  Brief Remarks
                  Keynote Speaker
                  Song by Tom Boatman
                  Trumpet Trio -
                          David Bowman
                          Dean Neal
                          Scott Jones
                  Benediction -
                      Rev. Gordon Burke

416

## OTHER ACTIVITIES

| | |
|---|---|
| 11:00-1:00 & 2:00-4:00 | Open house at Church |
| 12:00-2:00 & 3:00-5:00 | Antique Show at Chatterbox Club |
| 12:00-1:00 | Chicken Barbeque at Fire Hall |
| 1:30- | Musical Program (featuring Slim Clark and St. Albans school children) |
| 3:00 - | Softball |
| 7:30 - | Theatre at Town Hall |

**ST. ALBANS**

**1813 - 1988**

**Town of St. Albans**
175th Anniversary
St. Albans, Maine 04971
Incorporated 1813

Ruth Knowles - Chair
RR 1 Box 3595
St. Albans, ME 04971
Walter Butler - Co-Chair
Brian Hanson - Co-Chair
Marjorie Carlow - Secretary
Everett Graham - Treasurer

SCHEDULE OF EVENTS

FRIDAY - JUNE 3rd.

| | | |
|---|---|---|
| 10:00 a.m. | Public Showing 1963 Film......... | School Gymnasium |
| 11:30 a.m. | Public Picnic.................... | School Playground |
| 1:00 p.m. | Balloon Launch.................. | School Playground |
| 2:00 p.m. | Time Capsule.................... | School Front Yard |
| 6:30 p.m. | Dinner Theater.................. | Grange Hall |
| 7:30 p.m. | St.Albans Players............... | Town Hall |

"George Washington Slept Here" directed by Ellen Cooper

SATURDAY - JUNE 4th.

| | | |
|---|---|---|
| 9:30 - 11:00 | Parade | |
| 9:30 - 5:00 | Craft Exhibit.................... | Grange Hall |
| 9:30 - 5:00 | Art Exhibit..................... | Grange Hall |
| 9:30 - 5:00 | Antique Exhibit................. | Chatterbox Club Rooms |
| 11:00 | 175th Program.................. | Town Hall Grounds |
| 11:00-1:00 & 2:00-4:00 | Open House................. | St. Albans Union Church |
| 12:00 - 1:00 | Barbeque....................... | Fire Hall |
| 12:00 - 1:00 | Open House..................... | St.Albans School |
| 1:30 | Music Program.................. | Town Hall Grounds |
| 3:00 | Old Timers Softball Game......... | Ball Diamond |
| 7:30 | Theater - St. Albans Players...... | Town Hall |

" George Washington Slept Here" directed by Ellen Cooper

SUNDAY - JUNE 5th.

| | | |
|---|---|---|
| 10:30 | Church Service & Special Music.... | St. Albans Union Church |

"Sounds of Praise" conducted by Carolyn Moffett
North Deering Alliance Church, Portland, Maine

**175th Anniversary Celebration**
**June 4, 1988**

# Felicitations

JOHN R. MCKERNAN, JR.
GOVERNOR

STATE OF MAINE
OFFICE OF THE GOVERNOR
AUGUSTA, MAINE
04333

April 22, 1988

Dear Friends:

On behalf of the State of Maine it is my distinct honor and pleasure to offer congratulations to the Town of St. Albans on its 175th Anniversary. While I regret that I am unable to join you personally, I am pleased to have the opportunity to share in this very special occasion.

The strength and character of a town is not measured by the bricks and boards upon which it is built, but rather by the spirit and fortitude of its people. The Founding Fathers of St. Albans would stand proud in 1988 as they did in 1813, for the strength and spirit of their original community endeavors.

I join with you as St. Albans celebrates its 175th year in both the spirit of the past and promise of the future.

With best wishes,

Sincerely,

John R. McKernan, Jr.
Governor

JRM:mas

May 25, 1988

Ms. Ruth Knowles
Chair, 175th Committee
Town of St. Albans
RR1, Box 3595
St. Albans, Maine  04971

Dear Ms. Knowles:

    This is just to follow up my letter to you of
April 19 concerning your kind invitation for me to
attend the 175th Anniversary Celebration scheduled for
Saturday, June 4.

    This is an event I had hoped to be able to attend.
Unfortunately, my schedule for that date has become such
that it will be impossible for me to join you.  However,
I want to thank you again for asking me and I hope you
will accept my very best wishes for what I know will be
a most enjoyable and festive event.

    Again, my thanks for inviting me and for your
patience in awaiting my reply.

    With warm regards, I am,

                    Sincerely,

                    William S. Cohen
                    United States Senator

WSC:cww

**United States Senate**
WASHINGTON, DC 20510

June 4, 1988

Ruth Knowles, Chair
Town of St. Albans
175th Anniversary
St. Albans, Maine   04971

Dear Friends:

I am very sorry I cannot be here today to share in the celebration of St. Alban's 175th birthday.

The changes that Maine has seen in the period since 1813, when St. Albans was first established, are probably as great as any in a comparable period of human history.

But the passage of those many years has not changed the most important thing about St. Albans, which is the sense of community spirit, pride and neighborliness that makes it such a fine place to live.

If the people who settled here in St. Albans in 1813 could join today's festival, watch a modern parade, eat a hot dog -- unheard of in their time -- the modern gadgets might surprise them, but the spirit of the community would not make them feel like strangers.  They would take the same pride in St. Albans as today's citizens.

I know everyone will have a wonderful time at today's celebration and I know, as well, that St. Albans will be celebrating continuing anniversaries like this for many many years into the future.

.   With best regards.

Sincerely,

*George Mitchell*

George J. Mitchell
United States Senator

# Margaret Chase Smith

June 6, 1988

Dear Ruth Knowles:

It was a great privilege for me to be with you
all at your 175th anniversary celebration. As
I tried to say in my few remarks, I was overwhelmed
at the numbers out, the results of what must have
been a tremendous effort on the part of you and all
of those associated with you in preparing for this
great event. As I said, I was overwhelmed to see
how many communities participated, especially the
bands that were there. The floats were unusual with
almost everybody represented and, of course, above
all, the day was perfect. You were fortunate to
have the program such a meaningful and pleasant one
from the prayer to the benediction.

I will treasure my plate and the history and after
enjoying it in the house by myself, I will have
these placed in the Margaret Chase Smith Library
Center where you will see them, hopefully, when you
are over.

I would like to thank many of those who were so kind
in their remarks about me, their presentations, and the
general welcome given me, but I hardly know how to
do this as there were so many. To miss any, would
not be good. If you have any suggestions about
getting word to everybody to the effect as far as
my reactions were concerned, I would be pleased to
have them.

I do hope you will come over one of these days. If
you could let me know, then I would be sure to be
here. June is rather a heavily scheduled month and
I sometimes have to be away, but plan it so that you
can come over during the middle of the day so that
we can have lunch and talk about all that you did to
bring about this wonderful event and the reactions
that you have heard about. None, of course, could
be other than as mine were--absolutely perfect.
Thank you very, very much for including me.

Sincerely,

Neil Hill - Skowhegan, Maine 04976

## In Memory Of

## Gladys M. Bigelow

Born June 20, 1892 in St. Albans
Died December 8, 1986 in St. Albans

*Her life was dedicated to God and was filled with
limitless opportunities for joyous service.
The influence of such a life never dies.*

**St. Albans Historical Society**
**2002**
First Row, l-r: Marjorie Bubar-Treasurer, Shelda Madigan-Secretary,
Phyliss Dami  Second Row: Wendall Bubar, Ronnie Finson-Vice-
President, Ann Smith, Joseph Madigan-President, George Dami
absent-Executive Dir. Ron Russell

# CHAPTER XX
## TOWN NOTES

### ST. ALBANS HISTORICAL SOCIETY

### 2002

President - Joe Madigan
Vice President - Ronnie Finson
Secretary – Shelda Madigan
Treasurer - Marjorie Bubar
Executive Dir. – Ron Russell
Director – George Dami
Director – Wendell Bubar
Director–Richard Weymouth

Members

| | |
|---|---|
| Stacey A. Desrosiers | Arthur Tyler |
| Cindy Mason | Ed & Val Walker |
| Martha Allen | Patricia Weymouth |
| Darrell Butler | Grace Weymouth |
| Ruth Knowles | Peter Duncombe |
| Victor Springer | Ellen Cooper |
| Marie Ann Smith | Walter Walsh |
| Phyllis Dami | Vern & Grace Thomas |
| Curt & Kathy Lombard | Alane Finson |
| Lorraine Post | Lyn Corson |
| Eva Butler | Charles McNichol |

# TOWN OF ST. ALBANS, MAINE
## 2002
### (Population 1836)

**Town Manager**
Larry Post

Administrative Assistant-Lori Lary
Town Clerk – Stacey A. Desrosiers
Bookeeper – Cindy Mason
Road Commissioner – Ronnie Finson
Code Enforcement Officer – William Murphy

**St. Albans Fire Department**
Fred J. Cooper Jr. – Fire Chief
Jason Emery – Assistant Fire Chief
Ronnie Finson – Assistant Fire Chief

**Selectmen – (term) March 2002- March 2003**
James Bullock – Chairman
Curt Lombard
Jimmie Neal

**SAD #48 School Board Directors**
Ronald W. Fowle II- chairman
Perley Martin

**St. Albans Union Church**
Pastor Jamie Cahill

**St. Albans U.S. Post Office**
Postmaster Douglas Spalding

# St. Albans
# Town Officers 2002

**Larry Post-Town Manager with Board of Selectmen
Harry Bridge, Curt Lombard and Jimmie Neal-Chairman**

**Cindy Mason, Bookeeper, Stacy Desrosiers-Town Clerk, and Lori
Lary-Administrative Assistant**

# TOWN OF ST. ALBANS BUSINESSES IN 2002

**Anderson, Nathan & Marti**    **Sebasticook Kart Komplex**
RR2, Box 147A Ellsworth, ME 04605
**Bagley, Timothy**          **C&T Transport**
204 Nokomis Road, St. Albans, ME 04971
**Bailey, Judson**          **Gunsmith**
368 Todds Corner, St. Albans, ME 04971
**Ballard, Bruce**          **Ballard Farm**
517 Palmyra Road, St. Albans, ME 04971
**Ballard, Chris**          **Ballard Sawmill**
156 Ballard Road, St. Albans, ME 04971
**Barden, David**          **Dalou Farms**
90 Mountain Road, St. Albans, ME 04971
**Bennett, Bruce**      **Bennetts Wood Craft & Carpets**
243 Hartland Road, St. Albans, ME 04971
**Bubar Dennis & Dave Whitten    Big Indian Bate Company**
906 Todds Corner Road, St. Albans, ME 04971
**Bubar, David**          **Maple Row Farm**
277 Bubar Road, St. Albans, ME 04971
**Butler, Loren**          **Butler Jacking**
164 Mountain Road, St. Albans, ME 04971
**Cassazza, Ken & Carolyn    St. Albans General Store**
P.O. Box 11, St. Albans, ME 04971
**Chambers, Kenneth**      **Ekco Farms**
23 Hamm Road, St. Albans, ME 04971
**Chapdelaine, Scott**      **Ten Mile River Accessories**
P.O. Box 203, St. Albans, ME 04971
**Delecluse, Michael**      **St. Albans Roofing and Siding**
338 Square Road, St. Albans, ME 04971
**Duncombe, Peter**      **Indian Lake Self Storage**
110 Corinna Road, St. Albans, ME 04971
**Duncombe, Ginnie**      **Bear Essentials**
110 Corinna Road, St. Albans, ME 04971
**Dunham, Kevin**              **Indian Lake Market**
21 Corinna Road, St. Albans, ME 04971
**Emery, Jason**          **St. Albans Sealcoating**
5 Spruce Grove MHP, St. Albans, ME 04971

# TOWN OF ST. ALBANS BUSINESSES IN 2002

**Finson, Ronnie**               **Finson's Excavating**
100 Pinnacle Drive, St. Albans, ME 04971
**Fisher, Allen**               **Northeast Switchgear**
123 Mason Corner Road, St. Albans, ME 04971
**Gee, Newman**               **Natural Knees**
281 Hartland Road, St. Albans, ME 04971
**Hutchins, Harry**               **Lakeview Farm**
108 Nokomis Road, St. Albans, ME 04971
**Hutchinson, Jim**               **Off the Wall Construction**
176 Springer Road, St. Albans, ME 04971
**Johndro, Allen**               **Allen Johndro Carpentry**
767 Todds Corner Road, St. Albans, ME 04971
**Jones, Ed**               **Jones Contractors & Sawmill**
320 Corinna Road, St. Albans, ME 04971
**Lawrence, Amos**               **A P Lawrence & Daughter**
689 Todds Corner Road, St. Albans, ME 04971
**Leavitt, James and Tamara**     **Wavelengths Beauty Shop**
P.O. Box 245, St. Albans, ME 04971
**Lesperance, Christopher**     **Pine Tree Concrete Products**
343 Melody Lane Road, St. Albans, ME 04971
**Lisa, Nichols**               **Designing Minds**
85 Mountain Road, St. Albans, ME 04971
**Lombard, Curt**               **Appleberry Orchard**
234 Dexter Road, St. Albans, ME 04971
**Macchi John**               **Nokomis Road Enterprises**
437 Nokomis Road, St. Albans, ME 04971
**Martin, Jeff**               **Martin Family Farm**
476 Bubar Road, St. Albans, ME 04971
**Martin, Marguerite**               **Wild Wood Camps**
74 Wildwood Lane, St. Albans, ME 04971
**Mcleod, Lewis**               **Mcleods Construction**
26 Water Stree, St. Albans, ME 04971
**Morse, Ricky**               **R & V Auto**
P.O. Box 135, St. Albans, ME 04971
**Mower, Chris**               **Bio-Rem Services**
20 Sandy Point Drive, St. Albans, ME 04971
**Mower, Brent & Brian**               **Sunnydale Farms**
688 Dexter Road, St. Albans, ME 04971

# TOWN OF ST. ALBANS BUSINESSES IN 2002

**Murray, Raymond**          **Rays Chimney Building**
201 Dexter Road, St. Albans, ME 04971
**Nason, Allen**          **Nason Camps**
P.O. Box 197, Hartland, ME 04943
**Norris, Stanley**          **Norris' Garage**
426 Hartland Road, St. Albans, ME 04971
**Parsons, Ann & David**          **Sunrise Café**
122 Hartland Road, St. Albans, ME 04971
**Patten, Edward**          **Patten Farm**
14 Todds Corner Road, St. Albans, ME 04971
**Post, Wesley**          **Harlow Post Farms**
185 Square Road, St. Albans, ME 04971
**Provencher, Donna**          **Donna's Tailoring**
179 Mason Corner Road, St. Albans, ME 04971
**Reynolds, Donald**          **North Road Nursery**
615 Todds Corner Road, St. Albans, ME 04971
**Robertson, Gerald**          **Robertson's Farm**
176 Mason Corner Road, St. Albans, ME 04971
**Shaw, Joyce**          **Glenwood Springs**
26 Springer Road, St. Albans, ME 04971
**Shorey, Keith**          **St. Alban's Mini Mart**
P.O. Box 520, Newport, ME 04953
**Sides, Dean**          **Dean Sides Carpentry**
51 Mah Tah Pass, St. Albans, ME 04971
**Smith, Dennis**          **Indian Stream Hardware**
P.O. Box 38, St. Albans, ME 04971
**Snowman, Michael**          **Snowman's Oil and Soil**
168 Hartland Road, St. Albans, ME 04971
**Springer, Mark**          **Springer's Welding and Sandblasting**
9 Mason Corner Road, St. Albans, ME 04971
**Stanley, Mark**          **MBS Landscaping**
673 Corinna Road, St. Albans, ME 04971
**Stedman, John**          **John A. Stedman & Sons**
74 Ross Hill Road, St. Albans, ME 04971
**Stiffler, Paul**          **Stiffler Construction**
268 Dexter Road, St. Albans, ME 04971
**Taylor, Burton**          **Taylor Dairy Farm**
28 Bubar Road, St. Albans, ME 04971

# TOWN OF ST. ALBANS BUSINESSES IN 2002

**Tozier, David**                    **David Tozier Carpentry**
280 Palmyra Road, St. Albans, ME 04971
**Wallace, Brian**                    **Wallace Gun Shop**
375 Dexter Road, St. Albans, ME 04971

# A Postmistress to be Remembered

It was February 14, 1941, that Hilda Bishop Chadbourne became the new postmistress in the little town of St. Albans, Maine. It was the beginning of a long and eventful life of community service.

Hilda was born in Palmyra, Maine, on September 28, 1915, to Harold and Sylvia (Stanley) Furbush. She had three brothers, Perry, Herbert, and Clarence. Their home was on Warren Hill, in Palmyra, Maine, not far from the original Furbush homestead. That original homestead had been handed down from Hilda's great grandfather, John Furbush, who came to Palmyra. He purchased the Colonial mansion, then considered to be the best farm and home in Palmyra, in 1855.

In the early 1800s Joseph Warren supervised the clearing of land and the building of the Warren homes on the Hill. Joseph was the son of Dr. John Warren of Boston, Massachusetts, who purchased the towns of Hartland, St. Albans, Palmyra, and Corinna.

Hilda grew up on Warren Hill. She attended the Gale School in Palmyra, and then graduated from Hartland Academy in 1929. After that, she attended Farmington Normal School. She then taught in the Egypt School in Palmyra, the Pond school, the Merrill school and the village school of St. Albans. Her first home in town was located on Water Street just left of the St. Albans town hall.

After being hired as postmistress, Hilda's duties began in the Batchelder building. This two story structure, prominently located in the center of the village, housed not only the St. Albans post office, but also five apartments. The post office itself was on the ground floor. Hilda renovated the ground floor office several years after beginning her duties. She had the baggage room of the post office made into a kitchen and half of the lobby converted into a bedroom. She moved with her children as soon as it became available.

In those early days most homes were heated by wood and the Batchelder building was no exception. Hilda's morning fires were started by burning old papers with fine kindling wood. Hilda vowed this kept her chimney clean and prevented chimney fires. But it was fire that destroyed the Batchelder building on January 14, 1957. The bitter temperatures reached −14 degrees, making it impossible to fight the twelve hour blaze, as the water froze in the pipes. Hilda, aided by volunteers, saved all the office equipment and records and deposited them across the street in Glen Hanson's store. The cause of the fire was not determined. Remarkably, however, outgoing mail was dispatched on schedule.

For the next few weeks the St. Albans post office was housed in Hanson's General Store until Verne Merrill and Sherburn Lary constructed a temporary office in the barn that had been salvaged from the fire. Hilda moved in with Verne and Pearl Merrill for a short time. She later rented the Mark Randall home.

In 1959 Fred Campbell purchased the old building that had housed the post office and moved it across the street. Then, on the original site of the post office, Hilda built a home. The post office was again located in her house until the new St. Albans Post Office was built on the Main Street.

Being post mistress, selling stamps, making out money orders were only a part of Hilda's service to the community. She was a devoted mother and teacher. She tutored students with special needs, as she was deeply concerned for children that might fall by the wayside and be left out of the learning process.

There were other testaments to her generosity. Jennie Cooley, resident of the past, received a Civil War pension because Hilda cared enough to help. With the assistance of Senator Margaret Chase Smith, Hilda found Jennie's father's discharge papers from the Civil War and personally took them to Washington. They were approved, and the government began to provide Cooley with his overdue pension.

She was also the bearer of important letters during World War II. She would never allow the letters that came in the afternoon to stay in the post office overnight. She would go out of her way to deliver those letters to parents, wives, and children of servicemen on the same day that they arrived. Laura Smith, whose husband was in the service, still remembers her kindness.

Hilda retired on January 16, 1981. She received a certificate from the Postal Service Center in Auburn in recognition of her forty years of service in the St. Albans post office. Hilda is no longer with us, but her faithful service to St. Albans will not be forgotten.

# CHAPTER XX1
# POETIC NOTES

Time

As time moves toward my journey's end,
I know I'm going where I've never been.
Just one thing I ask, Lord, while on my way:
That I make someone happy every day

**Slim Clark**

# Raymond L. (Yodelin' Slim) Clark

An internationally reknowned cowboy singer and yodeler, Raymond L. (Yodelin' Slim) Clark called St. Albans home. There he resided with his wife of eighteen years, Dr. Kathie, a chiropractor, until his death July 5, 2000.

Born December 11,1917, in Springfield Massachusetts, Slim was performing at grange halls and fairs as early as 1930. His early radio work included WHAI in Greenfield, Massachusetts and WKNE in Keene, New Hampshire. Moving to Maine in the early 1950s for the hunting and fishing he so loved, he broadcast out of Bangor on WABI radio and tv. He is still remembered locally for his noontime radio program, "RFD Dinnerbell".

Primarily known as a single act, Slim's bands included "The Red River Rangers" (of which the late Dick Curless was a member), "The Trailriders" and "The Trailsmen". They played throughout New England, New York, and New Jersey. In 1956, Slim signed with Continental Records in New York City, staying with that company for ten years. This was followed by associations with several independent labels. It was through his recording that Yodelin' Slim Clark gained world-wide popularity.

In his seventy years performing, Slim earned numerous awards and has been named to the Country Music Hall of Fame in Maine, Massachusetts, and Rhode Island. In Oct., 1996, he was inducted into Nashville's Walkway of Stars, which he considered the fulfillment of a lifelong dream. In November, 2000, he was posthumously inducted into the Western Music Hall of Fame in Tucson, Arizona, of which he was most proud, as that nationally acknowledged his lifetime commitment to preserving traditional western music.

Besides his musical career Slim was a locally celebrated artist, known especially for his paintings of deer and country landscapes. He loved to make people happy through his talents.
**Source: Kathie Clark**

## Our Country's Flag

It's our country's flag and it
waves
in the breeze.
Over our land and over the seas,
Red, white, and blue, with stars
clearly seen. Flag of our country
this is the theme.

The years have been many since
first you was made. Many lives
given that you could be saved.
Your colors stand for all that is
just
You have never been trailed in
the dust.

Flag of my country, red, white
and blue
Flag of my country, I salute you.

I'm proud of the patriots, who
fought for the right.
And carried our flag through the
thick
of the fight.
Proud of our soldiers who
marched to
the frays.
Proud of the sailors who sailed
far away.
Some sleep in the East and some
in the West, and some with the
poppies
of France on their breast.
They went to their deaths for our
land good and true.
Flag of my country with your
folds
all unfurled, I pray you'll be
honored by all of the world.

**Vertine E. Ellis**

## Old Church Bell

The echo of the old church bell
In our small, country town
For a hundred years, like leaves adrift,
Has floated softly down.

The echo of the old church bell
Aloft in autumn air
Is a welcome sound we stop to hear
While reaping harvest fare.

The silvery echo of the bell
Sails soft as thistle-down
As it chimes our prayers to heaven
And brings God to our town.

**Stella Craft Tremble**

## Echoes From Hackett Hill
### St. Albans Mountain

When the moon in all its
splendor rises from the Eastern
sky
Its beauty still unfolding, we
watch, till, by and by As the
shades of night grow lighter and
the moonbeams' rays advance
It seems to stir one's fancy, and
the senses to entrance,
And in the evening shadows, so
beautiful and still,
We listen to the echoes coming
over Hackett Hill

I can hear the tuneful ringing of
the early settler's ax,
And the women sweetly singing,
as they spin the wool and flax,
The sound of loom and shuttle
coming through the cabin door,
And the footsteps of the
housewife as she walks the
sanded floor.
The baby in the cradle crooning
soft and low
Completes the scene domestic of
a hundred years ago.

And the echoes tell the story of a
sight both weird and grand –
The burning of the felled trees,
when first they cleared the land;
How each neighbor helped his
neighbor, in those strenuous
early days,
Never talking about wages –
never asking if it pays.
They talked not of shorter hours,
- that grim, determined band,
But united to accomplish the
work they had in hand;

And to labor agitators a plan I
now unfold;
Talk less and labor more, like
these laborers of old.

No more the horseback rider
finds his way by spotted trees;
Instead they now use autos, and
the passer never sees
The gleaming of the candle in
the people's homes at night,
But kerosene or gasoline or the
electric light.
Farmers now live in bungalows
with carpets on the floor –
And many's the change both
new and strange, look at it as
you will
Since Judah Hackett cleared the
land on top of Hackett's Hill.

But in the hundred years to
come, will progress be as fast,
As complex, and as wonderful,
as in those that now are past?
Now, while on imagination I
mostly must rely
We can be quite optimistic, and
now will prophecy;
Looking ahead we see the time
when all the people's homes
Will be fitted up for speaking,
each with wireless telephones;
And the future car electric,
through each hamlet as it glides,
Will get power from the ocean,
and the action of the tides.

There will be no stoves, no
furnaces, no coal, no wood, no
fire;

No dirt to litter up the rooms and
rouse the housewife's ire;
Instead, the natty janitress, when
wishing for more heat,
To warn those new styled
houses, or, perchance, cook
things to eat.
Will simply press the button and
let those calories run
Which will then be held in
storage from the heat of
summer's sun.

I can see the new coming settlers
winding over forest trails;
Hear the old shoemaker's
hammer, - hear the cooper,
making pails;
And the flails of the threshermen
beat out a glad refrain
As in the cool of autumn the
thresh out the golden grain.

The skilled (broad-ax men) of
those days could hew straight to
the line,
Preparing frame for house and
barn, of hemlock, spruce and
pine;
When the framing was
completed, from timber straight
and sound,
Invitations to the raising we sent
for miles around.
With those farmer athletes
working as they raised it bend by
bend,
The body of the barn would soon
into the air extend.

And then two crews would
quickly on the beams now take
their place,
To see which should be first to
put the ridgepole into place,

And he who was the lucky man
to drive in the last pin
Would on the ridgepole, at the
end, stand up, and there would
spin
A piece of talk poetic, - a funny
little yarn, -
And more or less prophetic, -
thus proceed to name the barn;-

*Here is a fine frame, stands on a
fine spot;*
*When boarded and shingled and
kept free from rot,*
*My it always be filled with good
herdsgrass and clover,*
*And be know as the "Smith
barn:, all the world over.*
I would not throw too much
taffy on the great exploits of
those
Husky farmers and their sons of
old, for we can well suppose
That while their work they did
not shirk and kept good hours as
well, -
As reason for their robust health,
historians often tell, -
That there were not the causes
that made things fairly hum;
Twas done by means of pork and
beans, and good old Medford
rum.

In the early days we write about,
the truth is well to own,
St. Albans had two villages, and
Hartland was unknown;
Palmyra was the meeting place,
on Central Muster Ground
Of all Militia Companies, for
many miles around,
In which Lieutenant Goodwin
was an officer I'm told,

And also Captain Bigelow, the
strenuous and the bold,
Of approachable demeanor when
the companies broke the ranks,
With jollity unceasing,
overlooking many pranks;
But in discipline a martinet when
on the field in drill, -
This old-time militia captain
from the heights of Hackett Hill.

On the plains of "Bleeding
Kansas" he made himself a name
Where the friends of right and
freedom made National their
fame
Against the "Boarder Ruffians"
he with others took a stand
With a wisdom most prophetic
and a courage that was grand.
Though called by some, fanatics,
the historians relate
They kept the curse of slavery
from entering that state,
And with this noted company,
striving hard to hold their rights,
Captain Bigelow was present in
the thickest of the fights,
and achievements quite historic
give to memory a thrill,
Those echoes as they come to us
from over Hackett's Hill.

In those future times, the freight
cars will still run on the ground;
But the people's transportation
in the air will then be found.
The "Aerial Luxurious", with
appointments very fine,
Gliding through space swiftly
will be truly an "Air-Line",

And the new Gas, Coronium,
propelling shooting cars,
May penetrate the atmosphere
and reach the planet Mars.

Then one hears the buzzing
wireless, shouting the refrain
As the annunciator gives the
coming of a train;
The San Francisco Limited is
shortly to arrive;
Her flying time's four hours ,
and she's due at half past five.
The cross air currents make her
time to-day a little slow –
She flew over the Rocky
Mountains about two hours ago.

The express which flies from
Boston is somewhat over-due;
She left there at one-thirty, and
now it's almost two!
The Over-Seas Flyer makes up
quite a pretty sight,
Flying from New York to
London, on every other night.

The predictions may not be
correct, but it surely will be
found
That the busy wheel progressive
will keep on spinning round,
And if the future resident give an
attentive ear
At the passing of a century, he
certainly will hear
In the cool delightful evening,
calm, beautiful and still,
Echoes of a Nation's progress,
floating 'round old "Hackett
Hill".

**This poem was written by Stuart Hussey Goodwin, father of John E. Goodwin and the
grandfather of John Stuart Goodwin sometime about 1900 or earlier as estimated by
John E. Goodwin**

# ST. ALBANS

Nestled in a lovely valley
In the very heart of Maine
Is a town that I love dearly,
Tho' it has no call to fame
There's a lake within this valley,
Islands where wild life abide.
Loons and wild duck roam the water
Where brown trout love to hide.
Looking down upon this valley
From the pinnacles above,
I see homes, farms, and a steeple,
Symbol of a Christian's love.
Sometimes in the evening
When I know the bright moon fills,
I love to watch as it comes up
Behind the Dixmont hills
Soon moonbeams play upon the water,
What a lovely display!
They make a golden moon path
I see above the milky way.
Breathing deep I smell the sweet grass,
Feel the breeze like velvet 'till
Time to take myself to slumber,
Then I hear a whip-o-will!
Rising early in the morning,
While others are asleep,
With a nice hot cup of coffee
To the window I would creep,
Just to watch the sunrise
As it peers on Big Indian Lake,
Saying to all God's creatures
"Come, time you were awake!"

**Lydia Emery**

## The Legend of Devils Head

Once Upon a time the Devil roamed the world, laughingly looking
for an honest man. While passing through Maine, he came upon a
truly honest man in what we now call "Old St. Albans" and the
shock turned him into stone. Legend has it that as long as each new
generation develops this line of honest men, the devil will remain
locked within St. Alban's mountain. **Author Unknown**

# CHAPTER XXII
# HISTORICAL NOTES

## Land Grant

It would seem that the land in the northern part of St. Albans and some in the eastern part did not come from that granted to Dr. Warren, as Major Sanborn bought this land from Capt. Boutelle of Waterville.

**Taken from History written by the late Pauline Lombard**
**The above has not be researched**

## Successful Farmers Who Came From the County

**Between the years 1915-1916 many families were leaving Aroostook County to purchase farms in central Maine. Among those that decided to set down roots in St. Albans were the following:**

| | |
|---|---|
| Rueben and Helen McLean | Presque Isle, Me. |
| Oran and Mary Neal | Staceyville, Me. |
| Stephen Bubar | Linneus, Me. |
| Corey and Flora Emma Bubar | Linneus, Me. |
| Merrill and Etta Bubar | Linneus, Me. |
| Wesley and Eva Springer | Glenwood, Me. |
| Freemont Webber | Island Falls, Me. |
| Ernest and Bernice Hughes | Mapleton, Me. |
| Byron and Jannie Wiers | Haynesville, Me. |
| Harry and Abbie Ballard | Washburn, Me. |
| Lionel and Shelia Warner | Fort Fairfield, Me. |
| Jessie and Dora Merrill | Printiss, Me. |
| Mansfield and Georgia Harris | N.B. Canada |
| John and Tereasa Bubar | Fort Fairfield, Me. |

**Source: Wendall Bubar, Barney Wiers**

# Early Doctors of St. Albans

The old family doctor that is remembered so fondly from years past carried a little black bag, smelled faintly of lye soap and possessed a heart of gold. The St. Albans region had several of its own beloved doctors. Up until the year 1846, a part of Hartland Village as we know it today, belonged to St. Albans. Then, it was referred to as the Old Mills and the village of St. Albans as the New Mills.

Dr. Calvin Blake was the first doctor of Old Mills, and Dr. Connor was the first doctor of the New Mills. Later, Dr. Charles A. Parsons, born in Buckfield, Maine, Jan. 24, 1824, became another one of the town's doctors. Parsons, the son of Col. Aaron Parsons, received his medical education in Vermont. After his graduation he settled in St. Albans, Maine but then moved and practiced his profession in Wisconsin. However, he later returned to Maine for a few years and lived on the outskirts of Hartland. He died in Friendship, Maine in 1886.

Another St. Albans doctor mentioned in the Maine Register 1901-1902) was Dr. J. H. Murphy. But perhaps one of the most interesting doctors was Dr. Buker, who traveled to New Hampshire where he sold $175.00 worth of his famous Buker kidney pills. His pills were subsequently purchased and sold by the Parkhursts of Bangor. Mr. Buker built the Buker House in the village and kept a hotel. Another doctor well known for his pills, although they were liver pills in this case, was Dr. Randall, who lived in northern St. Albans. Dr. William Trafton was given the title of doctor only because of his liniment. Finally, Dr. Jordan lived on the old Dillingham place in St. Albans and built an office there. Among the last doctors in St. Albans was Dr. E. A. Bean, who practiced for 45 years until he was succeeded by Dr. Moulton.

Lewiston Journal Magazine, Mar. 19, 1927

# Military History

## Civil War

**Levi Llewellyn Leathers** enlisted at Minneapolis in 1863, a private in the 6th Reg. Minn., and was discharged 19 Aug., 1865 and returned to St. Albans. Nearly a half century after his death, through the efforts of Vertine Ellis, a St. Albans teacher, and Senator Margaret Chase Smith, a Civil War marker was placed on his grave.

## World War I

**Emery W. Post**; He was a Word War I veteran serving in France. The son of William and Adeline (Hall) Post.

## World War II Casualties

Errol Austin

Theordore A. Birkmaier

Clyde Lewis, 31 USA died in a German hospital Jan. 19, 1949

## World War II

**Captain Donald E. Fields** enlisted in the U.S. Army in 1941, made a career of the service and was discharged in 1962. He was the son of Oral and Leah Spencer Fields. Captiain Donald E. Fields received numerous medals and is buried in Alexandra National Cemetery in Virginia.

**CPL. HOWARD M. PARKER**- Obituary, St. Albans, Sept. 30, 1952. Funeral services for Cpl. Howard M. Parker, 22, who died of head injuries received in Japan, in August, will be held Thursday at 2 p.m. at the St. Albans Union church, with the Rev. Frank Moffett of St. Albans officiating.

He was the son of the late Archie Parker and Mrs. Phyllis Parker of Dexter. He was born Jan. 4, 1930, in St. Albans and entered the service in 1949, received his honorable discharge and reenlisted in 1951, serving in Japan for a year.

He attended St. Albans schools and lived there until entering the service. Besides his mother he is survived by five brothers, Archie of Dexter; John of Corinna,; Elbridge of Harmony; Ulysses in the U.S. Army stationed in the Panama Canal Zone and Henry of Hartland; seven sisters, Mrs. Madeline Hollister and Mrs. Freda Wheeler, both of Hartland; Mrs. Sarah Humphrey, Mrs. Kathleen Brooks, both of Pittsfield; Mrs. Pauline Parker, Dexter; Mrs. Iona Knights, Palmyra; and Mrs. Arlene Spaulding, Detroit. Several aunts, uncles, cousins, nephews and nieces.

The American Legion Post of Hartland will conduct military services at the Maloon cemetery in St. Albans. on Oct. 2.

Remains are at the Donald H. Shorey funeral chapel in Pittsfield where friends may call until Thursday.

**Cpl. Howard M. Parker**

# Korean War

**Ivan V. Welch** was born Oct. 12, 1928 in St. Albans, son of Delbert and Gerturde Spencer Welch. He was a graduate of the Univerity of Maine at Farmington and later earned a master's degree in education at the Orono campus. He was an army paratrooper in the Korean conflict. Ivan V. Welch is buried in the Maine Veterans Memorial Cemetery in Augusta.

# The Schoolhouse

**Work Day at the
Pond School, St. Albans- 1925**

Office of Superintendent of Schools
Boothbay Harbor-Boothbay-Southport-Monhegan

**Letter from H.B. Clifford, (former Superintendent of St. Albans and
Hartland)**

**Boothbay Harbor, Maine,
December 12, 1925.**

Dear Boys and Girls of the Pond Road School:

I am very sorry that I have been so busy that I have not answered before
the fine letters which you all sent me early in the fall. I was very glad to
get them and Mrs. Clifford and I read them carefully. I hope that my
answer reaches you before the fall term closes for I want to wish each one
of you a very merry Christmas.

We like down here on the seashore very much. This is a very beautiful
part of the state in summer and even at this time of the year it is nice. Last
summer Mrs. Clifford and Stella and Edwin and I had lots of fun here

because the people and the places were all new to us. We used to go digging clams once or twice every week. Several times we went fishing off the rocks where we could look right out to sea. We went berrying in the woods back of the house. A few times we had our lunch on the beach where we could watch the tide come farther and farther in and then go out again.

My new work here is much like what it was back home. Some of the schools are in villages as at Hartland and St. Albans and some of the schools are rural like yours. They are pretty good boys and girls here but of course I haven't become such friends with them yet as I am with you. None of the schools down here have victrolas or libraries or jacketed stoves as your school has, so I shall have to make the people want to get such nice things for these schools.

One of my schools in on Monhegan Island. You will see it on your map of Maine about twelve miles from land. There are 18 children there from grades one to eight and a hundred or more other people on the island. The schoolhouse is near the shore and faces right across to the mainland. On the highest part of the island is a big lighthouse which can be seen way out to sea.

I visited the school November 5th and Fraday evening they had an entertainment and cake sale. After it was over the children gave me a very nice cake to take home with a picture of the schoolhouse on it, made out of frosting. I bought a lobster and some crabvs to take home to Mrs. Clifford. It was a nice place to go, only if it is stormy you have to wait there until the sea is calm again. One superintendent had to stay a week one time.

Stella is in the first grade this year and likes to go to school very much. She will finish her first book next week. I know that she would like to visit the Pond Road School with me again as we all did last year.

I hope you will all have a fine vacation and that you will all be well and happy when I see you again.
Sincerely yours,

Harold B. Clifford

**Harold Clifford was author of several books including *Canada, My Neighbor, Maine and Her People*, and *History of Boothbay Harbor, Maine***

# The Town Halls

In 1842 the inhabitants of St. Albans voted to raise $675.00 to build a town house, and a committee was chosen to select the site and buy the land. They bought of Thomas Skinner, one half acre less three rods of land for $40.00. The contract to build the town house was let to William H. Goodwin the 2nd and a Hiram Goodwin, and the building was completed and accepted by the town in 1843. This building became known as the Opera House.

The building served faithfully to house the many presentations and town functions that occurred over the years. By the early 1900s however it seems that the Hall was in need of repairs. The Town Report published in 1908 contained an article "To see what sum of money the Town will raise for repair of the Town Hall or act on anything thereon." The building was renovated that same year, approximately $2,000 was spent to restore both the interior and exterior of the Hall. On October 23, 1908 the Town celebrated the renewal of the Town House/Opera House with a formal Dedication Ball. Two years later, on Thursday, Oct 27, 1910 the building burned.

A copy of the program from the Dedication Ball

Our present Town Hall was a gift from the Hon. D. D. Stewart and was built in 1911. He gave $9,000.00 to the town of St. Albans. Inside the building remains the plaque inscribed, "Stewart Hall."

Town Halls depicted on a coin minted
in celebration of the Centennial

# CHAPTER XXIII

# FAMILY NOTES

## EARLY FAMILIES OF ST. ALBANS

Here they located on their respective lots, obtained by purchase from the proprietor, and here they erected their first homes in the State. They generally built one or two-room log cabins which served until lumber could be prepared for the construction of substantial houses which are even now seen in the 21$^{st}$ century.
It is hoped that some future historian or genealogist will restore and record the missing branches of these genealogical trees.

**Daniel A. Goodwin**

**A Minister of the Gospel, Daniel Goodwin**
was born on March 15, 1843 in St. Albans and died November 23, 1908, in Pittsfield, Maine. He married Mary Hatfield, (born March 15, 1848 in Poughkeepsie, New York) and they raised two children, Othello and Edyth. Daniel Goodwin performed marriages in St. Albans from 1881-1886. The Goodwin family Bible had its origin c. 1800 when the Bible was presented to Daniel L. Goodwin,

(grandfather of Daniel A. and one of St. Alban's early settlers, arriving from Litchfield, Maine about 1830.

**Martin Bradford** and his wife Tiley (Hayden) came to St. Albans from Readfield. The children were: Mary, b. 1814, married Smiley; Charles, b. 1816; Peter A., b. 1818; Andrew, b. 1820; Abbie, b. 1822, married Foss; Jane, b. 1824, married Smith; Anne, b. 1826, married Stinchfield; James, b. 1828; Emily, b. 1832, married Foss; George, b. 1834.

**Nicholas F. Bragg** and his wife, Mary Hilton, came from Sidney and settled on the Cross Roads Place. The children were: Herbert L., b. 1844; Volney H., b. 1847; Ella C., b. 1849, married Grant; Anthony C., b. 1852; Stephen H., b. 1856; Martha, b. 1858.

**Nehemiah Devereaux** and his wife Sarah Marsh came in 1818 from Castine. Their children were: James, married Sally Marsh; Dennis, married Rhoda Parker; Elisha, married Eleanor York; Jackson; Albridge; Daniel; Nathaniel; and Bertha.
   James, the oldest of these children, married Sally Marsh soon after coming to St. Albans. The children born to them were: Nancy, b. 1820; Daniel, b. 1822; Deantha, b. 1824; Cynthia; Samuel L.; Dorothy A.; Sarah; Milton; James; Althea; Hannah D.

**Charles Dow** and his wife Sarah came to St. Albans in the 1800's. Their children were: Elizabeth, b. Aug. 16, 1839; Harriet, b. Aug. 20, 1840; Cynthia, b. June 22, 1842; Aceneth, b. Nov. 4, 1843; Leander H., b. May 4, 1845; Percival, b. Sept. 9, 1850.

**Israel Douglas** and his wife Patience Sylvester came from Pownal and cleared a farm near Five Corners. He burned charcoal and hauled it to market in Bangor. They brought up a family of thirteen children: Dulcey, married Libby; Eben; Irene, married Nutter; Bethany, married Sanborn; Susan; Angeline, married Martin Charles; Leonard; Mary, married Hall-Duland; Emily, married Mouton; Albert; Naomi, married Henderson Fernald; Olive, married Booker Frost.

**Stephen Emerson** and his wife Hannah Davis came from New Hampshire. Their children were: Charles, b. 1822; Elisha P., b. 1835, married Maria Tripp.

**Simon and Joseph Farnham** moved to St. Albans from Sidney.

**John Fields** and his wife came to St. Albans in 1840 living on the Parkhurst place. Mr. Fields was a contractor and a builder of highways. He did extensive business here and in adjoining counties. They raised a large family of stalwart sons and daughters; one of whom, John I. Fields, served as selectman and tax collector for many years. Of his three sons, L.C. Fields was on the police force in Lynn, MA; G.W. Field practiced law on Oakland, Maine; and Elmer E. Fields was widely known as an expert in estimating the value of timberlands, and had charge of extensive lumber operations.

**John Grant** came soon after 1830 from Freeport. He married Elsie Maloon.

**John Glidden** came from New Hampshire and married Mary Jewett. Their children were: Seldon C; Clarissa, married Simpson; Emily, married Crommett; John; Samuel; Joseph; Mary; Anna, married Cilley.

**Daniel Goodwin** and his wife Sally, came about 1830. Their children were: William; John; Samuel; Matilda, married Clark; Sarah, married Nevens; Margaret, married Foster; Pheobe, married Wardsworth; Betsey, married Johnson.

**Ephraim Goodwin** and his wife Olive came to St. Albans early. Their children were: Sarah, married Johnson; Josephine; Olive; Elizabeth, married Eddy; William; Elmira, married Eddy; Summer, Gilman, Caroline, married Chandler; Hiram.

One of the earliest settlers was **Daniel Hopkins** of Unity, (b. 1792 in Standish). He and his wife Sally Robinson cleared their farm from wild land. Their children were: Chandler, b. 1816; Martha, b. 1818; Sarah, b. 1820; George, b. 1822; Lavinia, b. 1822; Otis, b. 1825; Amanda, b. 1826; Kendall, b. 1833.

**Asa Holway** moved from Cape Cod in 1800 to Fairfield where he married Rebecca Fuller. In 1817, he settled at the head of Indian Pond in St. Albans. Their children were: Xenophen, b. 1801, married Adaline Meloon; Daniel, b. 1803, married Hariett Meloon; Thomas, b. 1805; J. Sullivan, b. 1809, married ? Osborn; Otis, b. 1815, married Prudence Smith.

**Benjamin Ireland**, whose father was Capt., Joseph Ireland, was one of the early settlers of Hartland. He settled in St Albans about 1835, building a log cabin. After arriving, he bought the lumber mill from Mr. Eli Jones.

**Sullivan Lothrop** kept a store on the Hartland Road. He was one of the most influential men that the town ever had because he was very prominent in town affairs and in business. He ran a tannery for some time. His store burned and some town records were destroyed.

**Joseph Nichols** and his wife Elizabeth White Nichols came to St. Albans from West Ossippee, N. H. and settled in the east part of town. Their children were: Charles E.; George F.; Theodore L.; Seavey; Joshua N.; Sylvanus.

**James Nutter** came to St. Albans from New York. The children were: Mary, married Robinson; Samuel, married Orilla Barrett; James, married Raymond; Joel, married Irene Douglass.

**Phineas Parker** came to St. Albans as early as 1820 from the town of Fairfield and settled on Rand Hall. The names of his children, with the exception of two girls follows: Joshua; Phineas; Seth; William; Moses, married Varney; Phoebe, married Parkman; Hannah.

**Isaac O. Robertson** came from Brunswick and cleared from the woods a farm about tow and one half miles from the village, on the road toward Moose Pond. His wife was Hannah P. Bradley. They had a family of four children; Osgood; Sarah, married Foster; Rufus; Hannah.

**Andrew Russell** and his wife Betsey Ward came to St. Albans from Skowhegan and cleared a farm from wild land. The children were: Charles, Asa; Calvin; Caleb; Filene; Hannah; Harriet.

**Thomas Skinner** the son of Christopher Skinner and Hulda Skinner of Wakefield, New Hampshire was born 1793 and died Oct. 22, 1876. He married Hulda Kimball. They were the parents of the following children: Christopher, b. 4 June, 1830, d. June, 1830; Mary Francis, b. 20 July, 1831, married George Whitney; Sarah Olive, b. 8 Jan., 1833, married Frank Webber; John Milton, b. 9 June, 1836, married Ann Leathers; Alvah Herbert, b. 10 Sept., 1841, d. 28 May 1842; Ellen, married Dr. Frank Lyford; Thomas, b. 9 Nov., 1834; Charles Skinner, b. 3 June 1838, married Emma Webber.

Thomas Skinner gave his attention to farming until a few years after his arrival, when he erected the store in the village that was later owned by Stephen Prescott.

One day at the store he had a call from two families for flour. Wheat was then $2.00 a barrel. All outside commodities were shipped to Hallowell or Bangor, and toted over rough roads for fifty miles or more. A barrel of flour was almost unknown in the village. The store team on its next trip bought a barrel of flour which was divided and half delivered to each family.

**Thomas Smith** was another St. Albans pioneer. He lived on Dearborn Hill.

**Patrick Sheane** and his wife Betsey came early to St. Albans. their children were: Woodman, b. 24 Sept, 1818, married Anstrap Dudley; Benjamin Dennis, b. 4 April, 1822; Rebecca, b. July, 1824; Sarah, b. 3 July, 1824; Daniel, b. 17 March, 1826.

One of the most noteworthy of the early-comers to St. Albans was **M. Todd**, the father of Dr. Todd. He built a log house at Todd's Corner and like some of the other pioneers of the region, substituted oiled paper for glass in the windows. The children in the family were: John; Samuel; Plummer; Susan, married Downing; Eliza, married Hoyt.

**Joseph Watson** came from New Hampshire in the year 1804 and settled on Hacketts Hill. His children were: John; Dearborn; Jonathan.

**John Wood** came to St. Albans from England and settled on a farm between Hanson's and Lyford's Corner. He married Jane Gordon of St. Albans. Their children were: Henry P.; Bessie, married Chandler; Anna, married Knight; John; Mary, married Wilkinson; Cyrus.

Information gathered from:

**The East Somerset County Register 1911-1912**
        **By Chatto & Turner**

**Hartland & St. Albans Register of 1904**
        **Compiled by Mitchell, Ramick, & Bean**

**Old Families of St. Albans**
        **By Vertine Ellis**
**Lewiston Journal March 19, 1927**

## Ebenezer Smith and Charity Miller

Ebenezer D. Smith
born            March 1801, Searsmont, Maine
married         about February 24, 1830, Lincolnville, intentions
                published January 1, 1830, Lincolnville, Maine
died            August 8, 1863, St. Albans, Maine
parents         unknown

Charity Miller
born            September 1807, Lincolnville, Maine
married         (2) November 3, 1865, St. Albans, Maine, to Isaiah
                B. Leach (b. October 25, 1803, St. Albans, Maine)

Children of Ebenezer and Charity:

1. *Nancy L. Smith
born            June 20, 1830, St. Albans, Maine
married         intentions published November 23, 1851, St.
                Albans, Maine, to Josiah Nutting Laughton (b. July
                17,1822,Brighton, Maine, d. August 6, 1901,
                Minneapolis, Minnesota)
died            October 15, 1876, Clearwater, MN
eleven children

2. Sarah W. Smith
born            December 9, 1832, Maine
married         December 28, 1856, St. Albans, Maine, to Alonzo
                Chandler (b.April 25, 1828, Maine, d. November
                17, 1900, St. Albans, Maine)
died            May 26, 1903, St. Albans, Maine
children: (1)Alvin Chandler, b. December 15, 1857, d. April 23,
1859; (2) Alson W. Chandler, b. December 18, 1859; (3) George H.
Chandler, b. May 22, 1861, d. March 7, 1863; (4) Annie M.
Chandler, b. July 5, 1864; (5) Oscar M. Chandler, b. December 8,
1865; (6) Lucy A. Chandler, b. June 23, 1872.

3. Mary Smith, born around 1835, Maine

4. Lizzy A. Smith, born around 1837, Maine

5. Eliza Smith
born          around 1838, Maine
married       November 1, 1857, St. Albans, Maine, to David M.
              Rowe (b. 1818,d. April 7,1874, St. Albans, Maine,
              m. (2) Mary Burrill (b. 1836, d. May 8, 1917)
died          May 6, 1859, St. Albans, Maine

6. Olive P. Smith, born around 1840, Maine

7.Saviair or Loise C. Smith, born around 1842, Maine

8. Charity Jane Smith
born          May 24, 1844, St. Albans, Maine
married       Read H. Leach (b. October 17, 1846, Levant,
Maine)
died          June 20, 1914, Levant, Maine
children: (1) Bula C. Leach (b. October 17, 1846, Levant, Maine;
(2) Alice G. Leach, b. October 2, 1872, Levant, Maine, d. May 8,
1882

9. George F. Smith, born June 1849, Maine, died September 25,
1865, St. Albans, Maine
m. (1) January 12, 1830, St. Albans, Maine, to Elizabeth Webber
November 23, 1890, Levant, Maine
St. Albans, Maine

# ST. ALBANS MARRIAGES

## 1921

April 20- Joel T. Neal and Doris Martin

May 28- Herbert Seekins and Harriet Small

June 11- William Carr and Thelma Tracey

June 12- Leland Randall and Catheline S. Bubar

June 24- Lewis Spencer and Eva Brooks

Aug. 2- Charles Thompson and Bernice Leadbetter

Aug. 13- Orin Parkman and Mary Hanson

Aug. 29- Myron E. Martin and Izetta M. Skinner

Sept. 17- Earl Patten and Nellie F. May

Sept. 25- Robie E. Linnell and Neila L. McCarthy

Oct. 2- Wallace E. Nichols and Josephine A. Clay

Oct. 6- Lawrence Schillinger and Julia M. McLuer

Oct. 15- Rosco Hodsdon and Cara M. Frost

Oct. 29- Fred Leroy Chase and Clara E. Wilkins

Nov. 4- Henry E. Osgood and Fay M. Johnson

Nov. 14- Jesse S. Boston and Della A. Dodge

Nov. 23- Harry A. Austin and Doris Whitney

## 1922

Feb 4- Lionel Parker and Bernice G. Ross

Feb. 18- Everett L. Smith and Lois Stubbs

Feb. 18- Earl A. Perry and Grace H. Linnell

Feb. 24- Zenas H. Foss and Addie R. Johnson

May 21- Evan L. Martin and Marjorie E. Green

May 31- Clair E. Perry and Shellie Chase

June 1- George McLaughlin and Florence Pratt

June 10- Corey M. Bubar and Flora E. Fletcher

June 24- Thomas S. O'Connor and Mary E. Ray

June 29- Carroll McPheters and Gertrude M. Field

Aug. 12- Newell Philbrick and Edna M. Hilton

Sept. 2- Roger Williams and F. Nathalie Lewis

Sept. 30- Walter P. Currier and Jane P. Sears

Oct. 21- Fred B. Woodman and Sadie M. Haley

Nov. 4- Mandell H. Foss and Ina B. Emery

## 1923

Jan. 13- Artimus Birkmaier and Augusta A. Neal

Mar. 17- Charles Moore and
May Willard
Mar. 24- Gordon W. Seekins
and Almeda M. Neal
Apr. 29- Bert H. Lovely and
Lena M. Emery
May 22- Alvah K. Nichols
and Ella Varney
June 2- Warren F. White and
Gladys Clark
June 14- Alonzo S. Bragg and
Lizzie Chambers
Oct. 20- Orman A. Bragg and
Doris Getchell
Jan. 26- Fred Whitney and
Helen M. Jepson

### 1924
Mar. 22- Oneil D. Plummer
and Ena M. Emery
June 28- Fred Jones and
Gladys M. Weeks
July 5- Carroll J. Patten and
Mildred Brown
July 12- Ernest E. Newcombe
and Virginia Braley
Aug. 9- Homer F. Ray and
Helen Libby
Oct. 5- Ruel F. Neal and
Lillian McLellan
Nov. 5- Donald L. Bartlett
and Mary E. Cain
Dec. 17- Charles L. Cook and
Eva Spencer
Dec. 21- Winn Bowman and
Oneita Osborne

### 1925
April 19-Albert S. Spaulding
and Clara B. Lewis

Apr. 19- Leland N. Welch
and Labella K. Dewey
June 20- Cecil R. Peasley and
Blanche Elderkin
June 29- Wilfred W. Nadeau
and Stella Martin
Aug. 27- Clifford S. Sawyer
and Ruby H. Dodge
Oct. 30- Dana L. Martin and
Marjorie E. Martin
Nov. 6- Wilber F. Philbrick
and Ferol M. Ricker
Nov. 16- Beecher H.
Woodside and Edith Grant
Dec. 8- Albert Ward and
Mary Thompson

### 1926
Jan. 26- Glen Nickerson and
Marion Crocker
Feb. 10- Harold P. Whitney
and Hildreth Libby
Feb. 22- Dana L. Brown and
Elizabeth Libby
Apr. 20- Minot Lucus and
Leona Carson
June 21- Guy L. Wood and
Edna B. Wood
July 5- Evan L. French and
Francis B. Baine
July 31- Howard R. Weaner
and Mary Potter
Sept. 13- Ernest Powers and
Myrtle E. Philbrick
Dec. 7- Harold M. Brewer
and Dorothy Downes
Dec. 24-Sheldon W. Bubar
and Nellie Fitzsimmons

## 1927

Jan. 28- Sidney R. Mower and Crystal M. Philbrick

Apr. 2- Thomas D. Mills and Ruth M. Mower

May 7- Olen Rowe and Augusta Birchmaier

July 9- Henry M. Johnson and Dorothier Hall

July 16- Joseph F. Seekins and Erma B. Sinclair

July 27- William Braley and Lena S. Ross

Aug. 10- Rollins Chapman and Laura B. Bryant

Sept. 14-Edward D. Farrell and Laura N. Lucus

Oct. 9- Casimer E. Wing and Eleanor M. Springer

Oct 15- William C. Tibbetts and Gertrude O. Copeland

Nov. 6- Harry Nelson and Bernice Snell

Nov. 16- Edward R. Brown and Ina Fields

Nov. 17- Eugene Harris and Pearl Pratt

Nov. 20- Thomas Peakes and Phillys E. Harris

## 1928

Apr. 14- Evan P. Russell and Pearl McPheters

May 29- Vernon M. Snowman and Francis E. Kimball

June 20- Amasa S. Varney and Erma Johnson

June 24- Henry Winchester and Florence L. Merrill

July 3- Gordon W. Seekins and Marion Libby

Sept. 15- Elmer Fisher and Meridith Mower

Oct. 9- Sherman Welch and Marjorie Elderkin

Oct. 10- Rudolph Snow and Isabella Baine

Oct. 14- Milton Bubar and Edith F. Emerson

Oct. 20-Harold Frost and Harriet R. Lowell

Nov. 28- Chester Carson and Maud C. Gallagher

Dec. 27- Clarence Croply and Dillis M. Ellingwood

Dec. 30- Alvin C. Randall and Wynona F. Wood

## 1929

Feb. 23- Leo Schillinger and Dorothy Newcombe

Mar. 9- Clayton Braley and Louise Vicnaire

Mar. 20- Clyde P. Martin and Corinne Duncan

Mar. 24- George F. Bowman and Arlene Osbourne

Mar. 30- John Page and Zetta L. Breed

Apr. 8- Joseph J. Vicnaire and Lucille Burrill

Apr. 28- Charles F. Moore and Charlotte Moore

June 8- Charles H. Allen and Arlene Wellman

June 15- Alexander Curtis Hayward and Edna W. Tracy

June 26- Fred Libby and
Edith Philbrick
June 29- Harold Seekins and
Angilee L. Fuller
July 9- Roland J. Brown and
Sylvia M. Abbott
Aug. 8- Leo Tibbetts and
Florabelle Burrill
Aug. 10- Alfred Brady and
Alice Bryant
Aug. 17- Richard M. Pecken
and Gladys P. Johnson
Sept. 21- Kenneth Hughes
and Dorothea E. Giles

### 1930
Feb. 1- Preston G. Lewis and
Enzer M. Varney
Feb. 15- Harold E. Peasley
and Myrtle B. Simpson
Mar. 4-Norman A. Brown
and Leona Seavey
Mar. 10-Leon E. Bryant and
Maude M. Raymond
June 28- Clinton S. Bailey
and Ruth Ellis
June 28-Robert E. Nichols
and Lois M. Frost
July 14-Herman W. Cates and
Edna L. Patterson
Aug. 2-Sewell L. Frost and
Hattie Leavitt
Sept.20-Edward P. Huff and
Addie R. Allen
Sept. 30-Newell W. Tibbetts
and Clara B. Curtis
Oct 13-William D. Snowman
and Effie M. Corey
Nov. 1-Clarence E. Killiam
and Vivian V. Martin

Nov. 7-Robert M. Gordon
and Annie E. Merrick
Dec. 27-Nathaniel Vining and
Elsie Baird

### 1931
Mar. 8- Charles I. Estes and
Althea R. Merrow
Apr. 17- Harold Bishop and
Hilda M. Furbush
June 7- Harold Weymouth
and Grace L. Griffin
June 20- Halver J. Libby and
Doris E. Bragg
July 3-Clifford H. Wilkins
and Gladys Avery
July 18- Peter P. Vicnaire and
Helen Nichols
Sept. 12-Cyril F. Richards
and June G. Ricard
Oct. 3-Jarvis Bubar and
Phyllis E. Long
Oct. 13-Jerone E. Dodge and
Jennie M. Frost
Oct. 31-Frank W. Elderkin
and Virginia A. Small
Nov. 21-Reginald S. Clark
and Dorothy E. Ballard
Nov.25-Delmont W. Springer
and Jennie A. Seekins
Nov. 29-Harry A. Finson and
Helen M. Baird
Dec.12-Earl R. Patten and
Arlene Wingate
Dec. 24-Bernard L. Avery
and Etta M. Woodman
Dec. 30-Hollis E. Hughes and
Ruth Wingate

## 1932

Jan. 17- Clarence Curtis and Mildred H. Ham

Apr. 9- Arthur P. Vicnaire and Alice Vicnaire

Apr. 16- Fred B. Woodman and Myrtle A. Hunt

June 11- Howard L. Manson and Natalie Pease

July 2- Maynard Austin and Grace Elkins

Sept. 3- Robert D. Moody and Mary E. Hart

Oct. 1- Ralph Philbrick and Gweldlyn Webber

Nov. 1- Norman E. Hart and Louise D. Walker

Dec. 24- James Hart and Evelyn Hart

Dec. 28- George N. Linnell and Madeline M. Moore

## 1933

Jan. 7- Bryon B. Ballard and Meridith M. Welch

Mar. 23- Laurence Dodge and Lena Frost

Mar. 28- Donald E. Brooks and Almira Nutter

May 15- Floyd N. Nichols and Ada McLean

July 15- Glenn C. Martin and Helen M. Parker

Sept. 23- George Bubar and Helen E. Gould

Sept. 30- Maurice Emery and Evelyn Bishop

Oct. 21- Levere F. Hart and Marion C. Snowman

Nov 11- Donald A. Snowman and Jennie M. Southards

Nov. 18- Floyd H. Emery and Doris L.Pelkie

Nov. 19- Alonzo T. Williams and Myrtle Powers

Dec. 23- Clair H. Lewis and Louise M. Frisbie

## 1934

Feb. 3- Daniel F. Southard and Katherine B. Nutting

May 26- Herbert A. Davis and Florice A. Greene

June 9- Howard N. Prescott and Evelyn W. Seekins

July 28- Winfred H. Allen and Mertie T. Parkman

Oct. 13- Arthur Bowman and Rosilie M. Folsom

Nov. 14- Albion E. Libby and Janet Fowke

Dec. 12- Jonathan Knowles and Evelyn Crocker

Dec. 23- Donald Fields and Blanche E. Marsh

Dec. 25- Cecil E. Nason and Arlene E. Lowell

## 1935

Feb. 12- George Bowman and Helen Nichols

Feb. 28- Robert E. Martin and Clara F. Tobie

Apr. 20- Edward C. Hubbard and Ina F. Brown

May 17- Nathan W. Richards and Lena E. Mcbane

June 28- Varland L. Greene and Bertha Gray

June 30- Ramond Swan and Thelma B. Bryant

July 27- William C. Dewolf
and Hope M. Hart
Aug. 3- Alfred C. Seekins
and Charlotte Waldron
Aug. 4- Harry R. Sally and
Francis Jipson
Aug. 10- Fremont E. Emery
and Charlotte Burgess
Sept. 13- Robie E. Linnell
and Hazel G. Turner
Oct. 10- Casimer E. Wing
and Arlene Bowman
Nov. 16- John E. Weeks and
Geneviene P. Clifford
Nov. 28- Calvin Seavey and
Phyliss Brooks
Dec. 21- Darrell E. Badger
and Evelyn N. Lovejoy

## 1936
Jan. 4- Clyde C. Knowles and
Gladys M. Hart
Feb. 4- Peter P. Vicnaire and
Sophie Hamilton
Mar. 3- Frank W. Brooks and
Georgie C. Duncan
Apr. 22- Lyndon Pratt and
Gertrude Gallagher
May 20- Joseph G. Ouellette
and Margaret Randcourt
June 27- Ernes E. Wood and
Meredith Parkman
Aug. 27- Shirley B. Small
and Dorothy Schaefer
Oct. 8-George Elderkin and
Ellen Daggett
Oct. 10- Cleo A. Ross and
Cordilla Dickey
Oct. 17- Phillip Rice and
Eleanor Parker

Oct. 31- Henry F. Brown and
Madeline Dewey
Dec. 19- Ellsworth J.
Tompson and Ora V.
Carmichael

## 1937
Jan. 27-Walter E. Gowin and
Ada B. Nichols
Feb. 6- Clyde M. Lewis and
Erma Lord
Feb. 20- Francis M. Thomas
and Ruth A. Ham
Apr. 18- Ralph E. Knowles
and Althea Harding
Apr. 21- Durwood V.
Patterson and Thelma E.
Crocker
May 29- John Johnson and
Hilda Tibbets
June 26- Howard W. Bates
and Althea Robertson
June 26- Ernest E. Newcomb
and Denise S. Laney
Aug. 1- Perry Furbush and
Marion Thorne
Aug. 28- Joseph Connell and
Barbara M. Richards
Sept. 18- James D. Seekins
and Francis R. Waldron
Sept. 22- Edson P. Buker and
Mildred M. Dyer
Oct. 2- Joseph Pease and
Mary E. Libby
Oct. 9- Floyd Nichols and
Natalie Pease
Oct. 16- Leon W. Elliott and
Doris P. Gifford
Oct. 23- Rodney Parsons and
Madeline M. Field

Nov. 14- Archie M. McMullen and Juliet J. Forteene

Nov. 27- John W. Williams and Ruby S. Patterson

Dec. 8- Herbert Patterson and Goldie Field

# ST. ALBANS DEATHS

**1897-1898**

E.C. Buker
Caroline Huff
E.T. Burbank
Francis Hall
Betsey Goodridge
Olive Weeks
S.L. Kincaid
Dennis Coston
Gertrude Palmer
Winnifred L. Leavitt
Mary J. Seavey
Granville Rogers
Susan Snell
James Bayantur
Deborah A. Denning
Clarity G. Holway
Charles Whitten
Ellen Hopkins
Mary E. Berry
Rose Frost
Ruth E. Sampson
Armenda D. Holmes
Infant of Fred Finson

**1898-1899**

Sarah Taylor
Stephen Mayo
Emma Soule
Sarah Mason
Gertie Parker
Maud Raymond
Lizzie Stevens
Melvin McClure
Mary J. Currier
Daniel Wood

George H. Hurd
L.L. Lucas
Emma Goodwin
John Robinson
Lettie B. Kneeland
Augusta Estes
Melser Estes

**1899-1900**

Nancy Parkhurst
Fremont Baker
James Weeks
Judah Cook
Laura Osborne
Sarah Gray
Clarence Emery
Peter Bradford
James Winslow
W.P. Varney
Elizabeth Carson
H.A. Hurd
Oliver Welch
Mae E. Shaw
N.H. Vining
Clarence Baker
Irene A. Nutter
J.O. Matthews
Infant Emery
Ann M. LaBree
John Parker
Mrs. Warren Willey
Octava Moore
Edward Wood
Julia Boston
Mary Benney
Lois Badger
Effie M. Merrill

## 1900-1901

William Goodale
Ira J. Atwood
Josephine E. Turner
Emery Nutt
Rebecca Vining
Charles C. Russell
Eva Plummer
Charles Welch
Abby Elliott
Ann Mae Hilton
Alonzo Chandler
R.W. Webb

## 1902-1903

Lucretia F. Taylor-65
Samuel Withee-82
Lula Hatch-19
Anne Cole-28
Ira Wheeler-82
George Abbot-41
Elmyra A. Ryerson-71
Carrie Emery-8
Lydia Ross-59
Horace Farnham-60
Alton Bragg-23
Glenn Nutter-3 da.
Angenetta Emery-70
Joel Nutter-78
B.P. Burton-56
Fred Parker-4
Daniel Weeks-61
Aaron Eastman-63
Zilpha Frost-21

## 1903-1904

Amos Wells
Jane Probest

John Wellman
Julietta F. Robertson
Infant Baird
Mary Scott
Susan Cook
N.B. Turner
Minnie Nichols
Almena Martin
Levi Leathers
George Nye
Hildah Frost
Benj. Parkhurst

## 1904-1905

John Boynton
Sarah Frost
Sarah Wing
Wilson Bigelow
Alson S. Whittier
James B. Atwood
Marion Ina Webb
Lydia Bigelow
Elizabeth Martin
Louise D. Buker
David D. Brown
Emery Getchell
Louis Rollins
Timothy Hopkins
A.F. Denning
Charles H. Ross
Betsey Foss
Fred L. Brown
Harriet Fernald
Hattie Dorr
William H. Snell
Charles A. Wing
George Scott
Francis Field
Eunice Osborn
A.S. Varney

Jennie R. Martin

**1905-1906**

Cora S. Frost
Lucy Ray
Reda Deveraux
Philander Parkman
Alma Wilkins
Laranzo D. Davis
Audrey E. Tarr
Sylvia Russell
J.B. Dow
Lena Blanche Avery
Annie B. Johnson
Maria Parker
Fannie Jenkins
Infant Jackson
Harold Nutter
Earle S. Parker
Earnest Field
Alice Field

**1906-1907**

Phineas Merrill
Hiram Martin
John L. Field
Daniel Field
Chalmer R. Avery
Foster Carson
Mabel Libby
Alice Reynolds
Daniel Foss

**1907-1908**

Lewis T. Heath-84
Mary A. Robinson-80
Marreus O. Smart-68
Lydia R. Cooley-87

James Patten-80
Lizzie Merrill-60
Mary A. Robinson-80
Caroline C. Russell-62
William Frost-79
Stephen Prescott-52

**1908-1909**

Gustavis Page
Harold Libby
George Forsythe
Fred Thompson
Mrs. Ellen Clark
Edwin S. Packard
Hannah Stone
Mary Grant
Melvin Bigelow
Sarah Field
Kenneth Porter
B.G. Fairbrother
Jessie C. Moore
Ann Reynolds
Hannah S. Varney
Orrin Frost
John S. Sanborn

**1909-1910**

Franklin Wright-53
Mary C. Turner-84
John Osborn-82
John Leathers-71
Helen Hurd-70
Seth B. Randall-72
John Finson-83
Lucy Braley-68
Clarissa Hurd-65
Narcissa Libby-68
Gustavus D. Berry-62
Charles D. Bemis-62

Carrie Christie-59
Samuel Pingree-53
Joseph Sanborn-26
John H. Bowman-72
Elizabeth Emery-89

## 1910-1911

Grace Frost
Allie Withee
E.L. Eastman
C.A. Eastman
C.A. Merrow
Daniel Huff
Carnelia Palmer
Rebecca Porter
Pomelia Bigelow
Moses V. Richards
Elisha D. Emerson
Daniel Clark
Edwin Parker
Clara Johnson
Jessie W. Dodge
Marcina Foss
Sewell Brown
Annie Bowerman

## 1911-1912

Lewis Fish
Araminta D. Stewart
Joseph H. Pheland
Winifred Leadbetter
Doratha Nichols
Luella B. Rowell
Esther Fairbrother
Darius Emery
Hiram Hawes
Jane Phinney
Betsey Goodwin
Susan Fairbrother

Melissa S. Brooks
Guy C. Merrill
William P. Winslow
H.E. Philbrick
Mary A. Marryman

## 1912-1913

Edward Libby
Nina B. Smith
Unice E. Kilbreth
Mark Anery
Harriet R. Green
Samuel L. Devereaux
Laura G. Luce
Mary Labree
Charlie Magoon
Matilda H. Ireland
Bertha Magoon
James F. Clark
Lawrence Bragg
Isaac Fairbrother
Charles A. Southard
Maria A. Parker
William Thurston
James F. Clark

## 1913-1914

Clara Parkman
Mary E. Nye
Nettie M. Field
Alton Nichols
J.F. Hilton
Wyna B. Seekins
David Devereaux
Doris Nichols
Aurora Pingree
Harlan Gower
Joseph W. Welch
Franklin Luce

A.W. Peakes
Lorana Ward
Joseph W. Marsh
Christina Crocker

## 1914

3-12-Ervin M. Martin-43
3-22-Parenthal Philbrick-64
3-24-Sylvanus Lowell-67
4-6-Caroline Weeks-73
4-19-Addie A. Emery-56
5-30-Marie Emerson
6-1-Ruth M. Mower-75
6-7-Abbey Bigelow-73
6-20-Geo. W. Martin-71
9-1-Charles Mason-69
9-5-Everett W. Seekins-3 mos
9-14-Hattie R. Emery-61
9-14-Martha Sinclair-72
11-7-S.H. Goodwin-65
12-2-Seldon J. Martin-40

## 1915

1-16-Ralph E. Ireland-34
2-6-Mary Daggett-84
2-17-James R. Munn-68
2-25-Francis M. Wilkins-42
2-26-Lorin L. Frost-9 mos
3-6-Lizzie E. Stone-65
3-11- Martin W. Palmer-69
3-14-Francis A. Blaisdell-65
3-17-Clyde Parker-5 mos
4-7-Bert York-44
5-25-Sabra Tracey-54
5-29-James L. Fisher-75
6-6-Charles G. Goodwin-53
6-14-Emily M. Gray-84
6-28-William Forsythe-79
9-1-Betsey Bradford-89

11-28-Sylvanus Nichols-56
12-15-Simon S. Parker-76

## 1916

1-27-Frank Hollis-49
1-27-Isaac Osborn-96
1-30-Jacob Wing-76
2-7-Charles Douglas-89
3-13-Carrie A. Page
3-19-Cullin S. Ireland
3-20-Helen Hanson
4-7-Relief Philbrick
5-25-Bell Leach
5-30-Anson Holway
6-6-Frank Austin
6-15-Sullivan Johnson
6-27-Ida Mills
6-28-Sewell Frost
6-28-Howard Mills
7-14-Infant Wing
9-20-Willard Nichols
10-15-Infant Rose
11-14-Dovina H. Smith
12-2-Mark F. Detson

## 1917

1-9-Lewis B. Johnson
1-17-Jennie Woodbury
1-25-Freman Moody
2-4-Mary Webb
3-16-Ruth M. Warren
5-31-Anthony Bragg
6-22-Infant Ellingwood
6-22-Sarah E. Grant
7-21-Harrison O. Turner
11-10-G.M. Foss
11-26-Alonzo Burrill
12-31-David D. Stewart

## 1918

1-13-Henrietta Frost
1-29-Eunice Carson
2-14-Clifford Bragg
3-22-Lizzie Bonney-61
4-10-E.F. Tracey-71
4-22-Francis Martin-16
5-21-Elizabeth Bragg-62
6-13-Joseph Palmer-70
7-1- Ernest Emery-24
7-19-Martha E. Holway-76
8-8-Stella Johnson-50
8-29-Charles G. Mower-85
9-8-Burnett Pomary-48
9-13-Calvin B. Southard-69
9-25-Karl L. Martin-25
10-24-Francis M.Chandler-83
10-26-Benjamin Lampher-38
10-28-Abbe Southard-76
11-2-William H. Goodwin-82
11-21-Charles G. Martin
12-8-George W. Clark-82

## 1919

1-10-Mary C. Wilkins-64
3-4-Leon F. Libby-32
3-10-Andrew J. Stanhope-81
4-22-John S. Parker-83
5-26-Frank Vining-47
5-30-Catherine Sanborn-91
5-21-Alfred E. Parker-46
6-4-Hugh C. Chrisholm50
7-5-Clyde Buker-33
9-1-Wilda A. Smith-75
9-5-Alzeda Robertson-32
9-18-Daniel L. Frost-79
9-24-A.W. Corcker-69
10-1-Inez Goss-31
11-1-L.P. Southard-68

12-19-Susan Fuller-79
12-23-Delia M. Cooley-69

## 1920

1-2-Chandler Porter-79
1-3-Ellen Getchell-80
1-11-Lovina Porter-85
2-2-Amos Lawrence-65
2-11-Clara A. Weld-57
4-3-Melvin Cooley-78
4-16-Alton W. Tracy-28
4-20-Lindley H. Magoon-75
4-24-Drusella Butler-77
6-6-Mabel Clark-64
6-15-Beldon Southards-76
6-17-Melissa Southards-73
6-28-Lynwood Wyman-2mos
8-19-Ansel S. Burdick-76
10-3-Annie L. Jipson-72
12-8-Virginia Nichols-12

## 1921

1-2-Harrison Braley-81
1-7-Daniel Hanson-76
1-29-Charles H. Bonney-68
2-21-Doris Welch-12
3-23-Annie S. Knights-80
3-31-Sarah Moore-67
4-2-Clara Nickerson-33
5-10-Myra B. Cyphers-58
5-24-Lydia Bowman-72
8-18-Will G. Batchelder-55
8-26-Hannah A. Atwood-63
9-3-Nioma Lucus-95
10-18-Ellen J. Parkman-72
12-20-Viola D. Osborn-1 mo

## 1922

1-29-Edgar H. Martin-62

3-30-Lena M. Corson-5 mos.
4-23-Mary A. Richards-77
4-25-Luella Felker-59
5-18-George Barker-77
5-26-Eliza A. Southards-71
8-18-John E. Hatch-75
9-9-Ella I. Wing-61
9-17-Horace Dunlap-79
9-26-Ruth A. Neal-16
10-12-Lewis Spencer-4 mos.
11-10-Edgar Knights-59
11-17-Zenas P. Emery-72

## 1923

1-21-Mildred Osgood-9 mos.
1-24-Carrie Ward-47
2-20-Lydia E. Ireland-87
2-19-Mary E. Lincoln-93
3-7-Gertrude Hazelton-26
5-18-David N. Grant-83
6-30-Susan Hatch-75
8-9-William A. Bigelow-67
8-11-Edward J. Emery- 3mos.
9-12-Samuel W. Green-53
9-25-Walter Butler-69
10-6-Bertha Hilton-54
4-1-Samuel Lowell-73
4-9-Phoebe J. Orr-80
5-29-W. Scott Osborn-62
6-10-Edna Emery- 3 mos.
10-10-Clanie Vicnaire-2 mos.
10-31-Estella Bragg-61
11-1-Lilla S. Merrick-58
11-6-Edward Gilmore-63

## 1924

1-14-Bernice B. Steeves-26
1-27-Elmer A. Cooley-47
1-30-Joseph Patten-93

2-1-Lewis Spencer-25
2-3-Rebecca Martin-71
2-28-Abiatha Tyler-80
4-2-David Longley-88
5-23-Joseph Johnson-85
5-29-Mary A. Gilmore-84
6-8-Eunice Getchell-77
6-14-Andrew J. Parker-65
7-31-John C. Merrill-78
9-16-Osgood Robertson-68
11-11-Stephen Lucus-73
12-2-Adelade C. Avery-71
12-17-Laura Lombard-69
12-23-Bessie Hunt-3

## 1925

1-8-Sarah Crocker-87
1-9-Elden E. Wilkins-34
1-20-Maxine Richards-9
1-21-Edith Crocker-43
2-9-Emma Nichols
2-23-Joseph O'Brian-19
3-8-Iva French-27
3-19-Wilbur J. Tracey-63
3-28-Charles H. Hawes-78
3-31-Hazel F. Jones-3 mos.
4-21-Edith Osbourne-46
5-13-Thomas Peakes Jr-1day
5-14-Francis Peakes-27
6-20-Myra G. Frost-58
6-28-Annie Cramhette-16
7-7-Lucy Farham-54
9-4-Joseph Libby-79
9-5-Fred A. Brown-84
9-12-Frank Hanson-81
9-29-Mellissa Cole-91
10-11-Adeline Sewell-85
11-8-Margaret Nichols-1 yr
11-8-James A. Frost-71

11-8-Thankful Hart
11-11-Oscar Smart-2 mos.
12-7-Susie Seekins-71

## 1926

2-5-Leah Field-32
2-19-Charleen Harding-2days
3-9-Herbert L. Cole-60
4-16-Sarah Patten-93
4-19-Stephen Bragg-69
4-25-Pamelia P. Dearborn
5-4-Dorothy Patten-5 days
5-11-Monria Taylor-80
6-1-Francis Lovell-71
6-7-Jean B. Sawyer-11 days
6-24-Oral Field-41
7-11-Harold Brooks-15
7-11-Earl Brooks-13
8-18-Flora L. Wellman-78
10-2-Orin A. Parkman-90
10-18-Elden H. Chapman-62
12-15-Charles Cooley-83

## 1927

1-4-Henry H. Worthen-77
1-14-Abbie Tracy-79
1-28-George F. Nichols-74
2-15-Ruby Field-3 mos.
3-23-Ethel Luce-45
5-22-Milton L. Merrill-81
5-23-Jesse S. Boston-80
5-29-Ella Chambers-81
6-11-Morris Smart-11 days
6-22-Georgie Snowman-51
7-15-Wendall Mower-1 day
8-18-Damaris Palmer-80
8-20-Steven Seavey-67
8-23-William Philbrick-52
8-27-Alfred P. Brown-77

9-8-Hannah Weymouth-86
9-18-Harold Brewer, Jr.-1mo
11-8-Frank Whiting-77
11-24-Jane L. Page-87
12-12-Lillian Richards-57
12-18-Alfred Baird-68

## 1928

1-1-Luella E. Martin-66
2-2-Beatrice Frost-16
2-24-Margurite Welch-4 days
3-15-Baxter Woodbury-68
3-26-Nellie Frost-70
4-4-Mae Moore-60
5-15-Coar Huff-54
6-4-Alfreda E. Trafton-75
6-25-Eleanor M. Wing-18
7-4-Freeman Butler-91
7-30-Frank Bryant-52
8-17-M. Annie Clary-84
8-27-Cora Southards-36
9-2-Almeda M. Philbrick-66
9-10-Edward Crooker-67
9-27-Emily Wilkins-83
10-15-Ellen Moore-85
10-26-Coriden Black-60
12-1-Bernice Frost-38
12-9-Elizabeth Magoon-79
12-14-Henry C. Prescott-71

## 1929

1-17-Elizabeth Doyen-79
1-26-Joan Ramsdell-96
2-6-James Emery-76
2-16-Daniel Hanson- 1day
3-3-Donald Hart-16 days
3-31-Joseph O. Sturtevant-93
5-4-Henry Warren-73
7-8-Arvilla Weymouth-86

8-4-Wilbur Nichols-32
8-4-Hiram B. Weymouth-86
8-8-Guy Wellman-51
9-10-John Gardiner-87
9-17-John H. Jipson-78
10-15-Doris Kinney-30
10-22-Malinda Thompson-67
12-3-Ann A. Hilton-88
12-16-Harold W. Frost- 3 mo.
12-24-Harland Neal- 1 yr

## 1930

1-2-Nellie Patten-27
1-4-Ida Cookson-79
1-26-Nancy Dearborn-69
2-1-Calvin Braly-57
2-12-Maria Brown-55
3-3-Flora A. Parkman-81
3-28-John H. Libby-68
5-12-Bertha Batchelder-57
5-17-Dana R. Worthan-29
5-23-John Honning- 2yrs
6-4-John P. Parker-70
7-18-U.S. Parker-62
8-2-Foster Brooks-62
8-27-Lydia Pearl-72
8-30-Benjamin Elliott-87
9-22-Ansel E. Tilton-75
10-16-Etta H. Hanson-84
10-19-Hannah Sturtevant-78
11-8-Walter Wilkins-77
11-8-Jane Louise Field-43
12-2-Cora G. Robbins-73
12-17-Jack A. Foster-1 yr

## 1931

1-27-Preston W. Libby-74
2-11-John Foster-36
2-16-Charles H. Bigelow-77

3-13-Dorice V. Vicnaire-20
3-24-Lucinda Gray-91
3-31-Sylvia Crocker-92
3-31-Abner P. Powers-69
4-5-Lois Bigelow
4-9-Edward Brown-26
5-8-Geneva R.Nutter-2days
5-30-Emma Nelson-71
5-31-Frank Goodale-74
6-1-Oline Farnham-88
7-22-Jessie M. Stone-87
9-17-George Clay-62
9-25-Anna Abbott-72
10-1-Maude Wellman-51
10-22-Walter Hilton-69
10-29-Clara A. Parker-41
11-2-Elsie Vicnaire-1 mo
12-1-Medora F. Finson-63
12-10-Elmer E. Johnson-62

## 1932

1-3-Nathaniel Field-74
1-9-Cora B. Chapman-67
1-17-Hattie Smith-69
1-28-Florence Smith-60
2-12-Fred Lucus-77
3-2-Earnest Hopkins-58
3-3-Ella M. Raymond-58
3-3-Sadie Woodman-25
3-21-Peter O. Vickneire-43
3-25-Almon L. Avery-81
4-4-Emma Bradford-71
4-6-David H. Grant-79
5-1-Gloria Frost-13 days
5-27-Arlene Patten-25
5-29-James Martin-81
6-3-Andrew Welch-72
6-4-Lillian Johnson-62
6-6-Mary Brooks-79
6-10-0Freeman Mills-64
6-14-Eva Turner-75

8-3-Willis Gordon-66
8-22-Ester L. Bigelow-93
11-11-Clark Ellis-75
11-13-Wesley Frost-67
11-19-Evie W. Fellows-69
11-28-Herbert B.Fisher-65
12-10-Clara Chase-35

## 1933

1-3-Horace G. Atwood-79
1-9-Ida A. Brown-71
1-16-Alice H. Seekins-71
2-26-Wynona Randall-29
4-4-James A. Elderkin-76
5-9-Volney H. Bragg-85
5-10-Eliz. A. Longley-87
5-30-Millie Parker-65
6-14-Augusta L. Cole-87
6-22-Thomas L. Martin-ll mo
7-17-Charles F. Mower-71
8-2-Jennie Elliott-26
10-27-Bernice Colburn-39
11-15-Carrie B. Stanhope-53
12-29-Wallace Parker-9 days

## 1934

1-2-Scott Hanford-55
1-20-Frank Lucas-80
2-3-George W. Linnell-68
2-8-Cecil A. Nichols-8 yrs
2-16-Clara Frost-
4-22-Earl G. Field- 2 mos
5-4-Charles F. Tibbetts-63
5-15-Eunice M. Smith- 1 yr
6-5-Ella T. Tilton-74
6-16-George A. Welch-50
6-28-Martha A. Frost-85
6-29-Albion L. Kilbreth-77
7-6-Ethel L. Parkman-53

7-9-Chester Field-53
7-21-Angelia Martin-74
7-28-Walter Tobie-49
8-24-Myrtle G. Blake-58
9-13-Lincoln Merrick-74
11-6-Harriett E. Baird-72
12-1-Thane Clifford-38

## 1935

1-13-Mary E. Leavitt-74
1-21-Elwin Grant-63
1-31-Florence Welch- 1 mo
2-3-Celia A. Russell-71
2-11-George W. Parker-66
2-12-Mary R. Mitchell-89
2-15-Thomas C. Hartwell-79
3-3-Francis Sargent-85
3-17-Julia M. Robinson-90
4-12-Addie S. Carr-79
4-15-Nettie Whiting-86
4-17-John G. Berry-70
4-19-Mary E. Goodwin-75
4-20-Myra E. Parker-73
5-19-Carlton C. Harvey-73
6-7-George R. Wing-70
6-29-Norman Hart-21
8-10-Clossom C. Hanson-67
8-25-Carrie Goodwin-73
9-20-Richard Libby-2 mos
10-16-Joseph F. Fritz-62
12-22-Blanche Lovejoy-64
12-28-Stella M Nadeau-28
12-31-George W. Goodale-71

## 1936

1-12-Susie J. Lucas-70
1-14-Eva Wing-68
3-8-Mable Pratt-57
3-11-Arthur W. Pettigrove-65

3-20-Susie Stickney-79
3-21-Elizabeth H. Burrill-91
3-21-Marchell M. Rediker-84
4-4-William H. Watson-69
4-22-Carol O. Watson-67
4-28-Stephen Seeking-58
4-28-Annie A. Grant-78
5-8-Lucy E. Nutter-80
5-20-William W. Hartwell-80
6-11-Annie G. Hersey-66
6-18-Eleazer G. Crocker-76
11-9-William J. Frost-76
12-14-Lizzie M. Cole-63

**1937**

1-8-Minnie E. Gray-70
1-12-Loren Tracey-76
1-19-Maude Bryant-27
1-31-William Nutter-86
2-1-Will E. Richards-56

3-3-Florence V. Chisholm-60
3-14-Minot Lucas-49
3-16-Flora A. Leadbetter-83
3-28-Florence L.
McLaughlin-49
3-28-John Burton-76
3-30-Sherman Welch-53
6-10-Thurza E. Foss-76
6-24-Laforest Libby-56
7-6-George Taylor-66
7-30-Phyllis E. Peakes-31
9-1-Albert F. Hurd-75
9-16-Jesse E. Ray-82
9-20-John L. Russell-62
11-2-Ellen A. Butler-79
12-19-Hiram S. Raymond-45

**Source: St. Albans Town
Reports 1897-1937**

# CHAPTER XXIV

# END NOTES

### Each Year People Return...

*Paul E. Proctor came back to St. Albans in the summer of 2002 tracing his lineage. The following concerns the late Senator Margaret Chase Smith. Seemingly insignificant things that Margaret Chase Smith did reached out and impacted a great many people.*

During her tenure as Representative and Senator of the state of Maine, Margaret Chase Smith was required to travel frequently. In order to meet scheduled requirements, the United States Air Force at Andrews Air Force Base in Virginia was used quite extensively. Because of its speed, endurance, and reliability a unit of T-39 Sabre twin engine jet aircraft was utilized to accomplish this task. One of the servicemen who flew on these aircraft was S/Msgt Paul E. Proctor from Newport, Maine.

Sgt. Proctor related that to show her gratitude to these Air Force personnel who supported these missions, Senator Smith would as she left the aircraft leave a "rose" in the seat she occupied or on the table of the aircraft. This token of gratitude was discussed by the aircrews of the T-39 Aircraft and greatly appreciated.

Sgt. Proctor also related that Senator Smith was instrumental in helping locate the body of his wife's brother who was missing in action (MIA) later confirmed killed in action (KIA), during the Second World War. Initially reported wounded in action, the army, because of wartime conditions, could not locate Tsgt Doncet in any of its field hospitals. After many months and due to her untiring effort, his body was located in a cemetery in France and returned home to Pittsfield, Maine to his parents for burial.

One should never underestimate the effect your personal history, and even local history, could have on future generations. Remember Job in the Old Testament of the Bible lamented the fact that his word were not written down when he said, "Oh that my words were now written," but subsequently they were written and now present a beautiful testimony of the Redeemer.

There is a great deal of information concerning St. Albans and its people out there just waiting to be discovered. My sincere thanks to the citizens of St. Albans for their support, and may God bless each and every one.

Ruth M. Knowles

CPSIA information can be obtained at www.ICGtesting.com

228537LV00006B/55/P

9 780788 424625